OFFICIAL

PREPARATION MATERIAL

Cambridge English

MINDSET

FOR IELTS

An Official Cambridge IELTS Course

STUDENT'S
BOOK

3

MAP OF THE BOOK

UNIT 5 – p93
HISTORY

Exam skills: p93
- Yes / No / Not Given
- Matching features

Learning strategies:
- Identifying a writer's claims or views
- Understanding paraphrase

Language focus:
- Vocabulary related to monarchy and rulers
- Second, Third and Mixed conditionals

Exam skills: p100
- Tables and bar charts (Part 1)

Learning strategies:
- Describing information in tables and bar charts
- Achieving a high score for Coherence and Cohesion

Language focus:
- Discourse markers for Part 1 essays

Exam skills: p105
- Multiple choice (two or more answers)
- Multiple matching

Learning strategies:
- Attitude and opinion
- Understanding paraphrase

Language focus:
- Vocabulary related to attitude and opinion
- Past time expressions

Exam skills: p110
- History (Parts 2 and 3)

Learning strategies:
- Grammatical Range and Accuracy
- Agreeing / disagreeing with the proposition in the question

Language focus:
- Past time expressions
- Expressions for agreeing / disagreeing

UNIT 6 – p114
SCIENCE AND TECHNOLOGY

Exam skills: p114
- Diagram completion
- Summary completion (with and without options)

Learning strategies:
- Skimming and scanning
- Understanding paraphrase

Language focus:
- Word families (Parts of speech)
- Future tenses

Exam skills: p122
- Problem and solutions (two-in-one) essay (Part 2)

Learning strategies:
- Grammatical Range and Accuracy

Language focus:
- Verb patterns
- Discourse markers of concession
- Participle clauses for complex sentences

Exam skills: p127
- Multiple choice (two or more answers)
- Flow-chart completion

Learning strategies:
- Explaining cause and effect

Language focus:
- Discourse markers for cause and effect

Exam skills: p133
- Science and technology (Parts 1, 2 and 3)

Learning strategies:
- Grammatical Range and Accuracy
- Buying time to answer

Language focus:
- Verb patterns

UNIT 7 – p139
TELEVISION, NEWS AND CURRENT AFFAIRS

Exam skills: p139
- Matching information
- Short answer questions
- Matching sentence endings

Learning strategies:
- Locating information in a text
- Understanding paraphrase

Language focus:
- Vocabulary related to journalism
- Passive

Exam skills: p146
- Pie charts (Part 1)

Learning strategies:
- Describing percentages and fractions
- Describing a pie chart
- Grammatical Range and Accuracy

Language focus:
- Expressing approximation
- Passive

Exam skills: p150
- Sentence completion
- Flow-chart completion

Learning strategies:
- Using signposting language to follow a talk
- Understanding paraphrase

Language focus:
- Vocabulary related to journalism

Exam skills: p155
- Television (Parts 1, 2 and 3)

Learning strategies:
- Correcting yourself / clarifying

Language focus:
- Vocabulary for describing TV
- Pronunciation: corrective stress
- Passive expressions with impersonal *it*

UNIT 8 – p160
CULTURE

Exam Skills: p160
- Review of task types

Learning strategies:
- Reviewing reading skills

Language focus:
- Relative clauses

Exam skills: p167
- Describing a process (Part 1)
- Opinion based essay (Part 2)

Learning strategies:
- Writing a complete essay

Language focus:
- Vocabulary related to handicrafts
- Passive
- Sequence discourse markers

Exam skills: p173
- Note completion
- Sentence completion

Learning strategies:
- Using notes to follow a talk
- Checking your answers

Language focus:
- Word formation
- Prepositions in relative clauses

Exam skills: p178
- Culture (review of all 3 parts of the test)

Learning strategies:
- Review of speaking skills

Language focus:
- Review of discourse markers for speaking
- Clauses with indefinite pronouns

MINDSET LEVEL 3 AUTHORS

With a thorough understanding of the essential skills required to succeed in the IELTS test, let our team of experts guide you on your IELTS journey.

Greg Archer

Greg Archer is an experienced, Delta-qualified teacher and teacher trainer who, after working in a number of countries, put down his teaching roots in his home city of London. He trained, qualified and began working as an IELTS Examiner in both Writing and Speaking at International House in 2012, and continued doing so after his move to Cambridge in 2013. Since then, he has been teaching at an international college, at various times managing the English department, developing appropriate courses to run alongside A Level and GCSE study, and primarily teaching IELTS and English for Academic Purposes classes to students whose ambition is to enter a UK university or use English as a medium of instruction. He has a particular interest in Intercultural Rhetoric, and the way in which it impacts on writing skills.

Greg would like to thank Simon Williamson for his stimulating editorial counsel, Neil Holloway as the *Mindset* all-seeing eye, and Alice and Billy for being so understanding when deadlines loomed.

Claire Wijayatilake

Claire Wijayatilake is originally from Brighton, UK, and has been teaching English since 1988. After obtaining a Spanish degree at King's College London and a CELTA qualification, her first teaching job was in Spain. She moved to Colombo, Sri Lanka after meeting her Sri Lankan husband, and worked for British Council, Colombo for 16 years as a teacher, CELTA trainer, IELTS examiner and examiner trainer. She was a founder member of SLELTA (Sri Lanka English Language Teachers' Association) in the 1990s and has presented at conferences around the world. After completing her MA TESOL at the Institute of Education, London, she moved into international education as a teacher trainer and, later, a Principal. She completed her PhD in Applied Linguistics and English Language Teaching at Warwick University in 2012, after which she worked in a number of UK universities, teaching English for Academic Purposes. Claire is currently Director of English at IH London.

OTHER MINDSET AUTHORS FOR THIS SERIES

 Lucy Passmore

 Jishan Uddin

 Peter Crosthwaite

 Susan Hutchison

 Natasha De Souza

 Marc Loewenthal

The *Mindset for IELTS* authors have extensive experience teaching in the UK and globally. They have helped prepare students for the *IELTS* test from all over the world, including:

China, UK, Pakistan, Middle East, Republic of Korea, Italy, Indonesia, Sri Lanka, Kazakhstan, Greece, Russia, Spain

HOW DOES MINDSET FOR IELTS WORK?

AVAILABLE AT FOUR LEVELS

FOUNDATION LEVEL	LEVEL 1 Target Band 5.5	LEVEL 2 Target Band 6.5	LEVEL 3 Target Band 7.5

CORE MATERIAL

- Student's Book (print and digital).
- Online skills modules for Reading, Writing, Listening, Speaking plus Grammar and Vocabulary.

ADDITIONAL MATERIAL

- Customised online modules for specific L1 groups that focus on areas where help is most needed, informed by the Cambridge English Learner Corpus.
- Academic Study Skills online module that prepares students for the challenges of studying a university-level course taught in English.

TAILORED TO SUIT YOUR NEEDS

Mindset for IELTS gives teachers the ultimate flexibility to tailor courses to suit their context and the needs of their students.

GIVES TEACHERS CHOICE

- Course design means teachers can focus on either the skills or the topics that their students need the most help with.

CUSTOMISATION

- Online modules can be used in the classroom as extension work or as extra practice at home, allowing the teacher to customise the length and focus of the course.

- Additional online modules designed for specific L1 learners can be incorporated into the course.

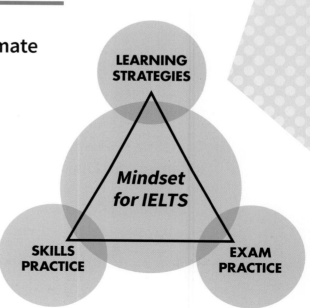

COURSE CONFIGURATIONS

The *Mindset for IELTS* course comprises 5 key components:

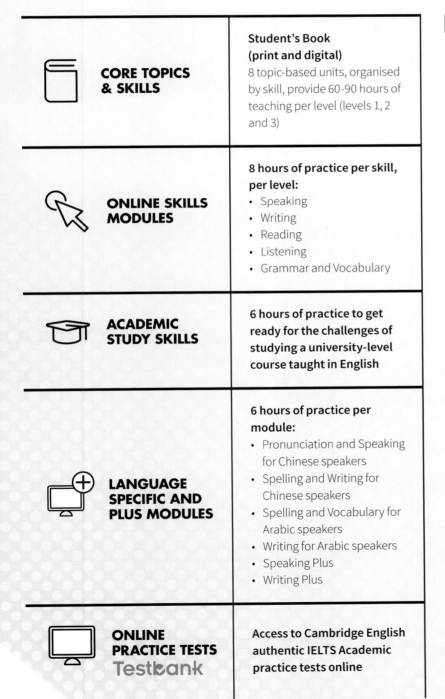

CORE TOPICS & SKILLS	**Student's Book (print and digital)** 8 topic-based units, organised by skill, provide 60-90 hours of teaching per level (levels 1, 2 and 3)
ONLINE SKILLS MODULES	8 hours of practice per skill, per level: • Speaking • Writing • Reading • Listening • Grammar and Vocabulary
ACADEMIC STUDY SKILLS	6 hours of practice to get ready for the challenges of studying a university-level course taught in English
LANGUAGE SPECIFIC AND PLUS MODULES	6 hours of practice per module: • Pronunciation and Speaking for Chinese speakers • Spelling and Writing for Chinese speakers • Spelling and Vocabulary for Arabic speakers • Writing for Arabic speakers • Speaking Plus • Writing Plus
ONLINE PRACTICE TESTS Testbank	Access to Cambridge English authentic IELTS Academic practice tests online

01▶ SKILLS MODULES

8 hours of practice per skill, including Reading, Writing, Listening, Speaking plus Grammar and Vocabulary.

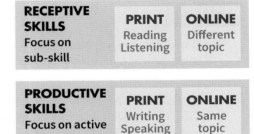

RECEPTIVE SKILLS Focus on sub-skill	**PRINT** Reading Listening	**ONLINE** Different topic
PRODUCTIVE SKILLS Focus on active production	**PRINT** Writing Speaking	**ONLINE** Same topic

02▶ LANGUAGE SPECIFIC MODULES

Extra practice for areas that need the most work, informed by the Cambridge Learner Corpus.*

ARABIC

• Spelling and Vocabulary
• Writing

CHINESE

• Pronunciation and Speaking
• Spelling and Writing

Plus modules focus on common areas of weakness and are suitable for all first languages.

PLUS

• Speaking
• Writing

*Currently the same module is used for Level 1 and Level 2.

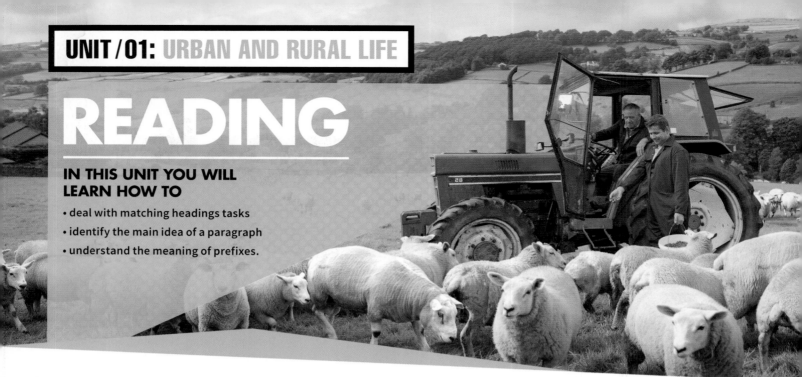

READING

IN THIS UNIT YOU WILL LEARN HOW TO

- deal with matching headings tasks
- identify the main idea of a paragraph
- understand the meaning of prefixes.

LEAD-IN

01▷ Read the paragraph below about the island of Mallorca. With a partner, discuss why some of the underlined nouns are preceded by *the*, and others have no article. Do you know any other article rules for geographical features?

Mallorca, the biggest of the Balearic Islands, is situated in the Mediterranean Sea, some 300km from the Valencian coast of Spain, and is an exciting mix of urban energy, rural adventure and coastal calm. Although it isn't popular with the Spanish as a tourist destination, it annually welcomes people from all over Europe (particularly from the United Kingdom, France and Germany), who may head for Alcudia Beach, or go hiking in the Tramuntanas, a mountain range that runs from the northeast to the southwest of the island. The busy capital city, Palma de Mallorca, contrasts entirely with the traditional rural towns and villages in the heart of the island, such as Algaida or Binissalem.

02▷ Think of a geographical area in your country and write a short paragraph like the one above, paying special attention to the correct use of articles. Swap your paragraph with a partner and correct each other's work where necessary.

MATCHING HEADINGS

03▷ Look at this title and discuss with a partner what you might expect to read in the passage.

The World's Most Unusual Towns and Cities

 This type of task requires you to choose a heading which correctly summarises the whole paragraph. Often, it is possible to find one sentence in a paragraph which conveys the main idea – this is known as the *topic sentence*.

The topic sentence can frequently be found at the start of the paragraph, but can appear in the middle, or even at the end. Sometimes a paragraph may not have one single, clear topic sentence at all, and the main idea can only be understood by reading the paragraph in full.

04 ▷ Read the first sentence of a paragraph about the city of Auroville, India. It is the topic sentence. Which of the three options seems to be the most likely heading? Why?

In today's world of conflict, greed and constant struggles for power, Auroville – aka 'the City of Dawn' – claims on its website that it was planned and built to create the ultimate model of unity, peace and harmony that can be projected across all humanity.

A The reason why attempts to create the perfect city always fail

B An urban ideal designed for an imperfect world

C A conflict between reality and imitation

05 ▷ Read the full paragraph and check your answer.

In today's world of conflict, greed and constant struggles for power, Auroville – aka 'the City of Dawn' – claims on its website that it was planned and built to create the ultimate model of unity, peace and harmony that can be projected across all humanity. It has no government, no one owns any property, and money rarely, if ever, changes hands. There is no leader and rules do not exist. While most experiments at creating the perfect city do not meet with success, the majority of Auroville's residents believe their city to be an exception. Although its critics point to the fact that levels of crime have been creeping up for some years now, its citizens choose to remain there, still believing in its utopian dream, still following its path towards a better world.

TIP 05

The heading you want will probably not use the same words as those which appear in the paragraph, but will paraphrase the ideas.

06 ▷ Read this opening sentence about Longyearbyen. Which heading seems to fit this sentence best?

Longyearbyen, Norway, holds the record for being the furthest north city in the world, boasting the world's most northerly school, airport and university.

A An unwelcoming place to die

B A city at the top of the world

C An unusual approach to regulation

TIP 06

Be careful: sometimes the first sentence of a paragraph seems to fit entirely with one particular heading. However, don't be caught out – you still need to check by reading the whole paragraph.

0 7 ▶ Now read the full paragraph and think about the overall message of the paragraph. Which heading now best fits the paragraph?

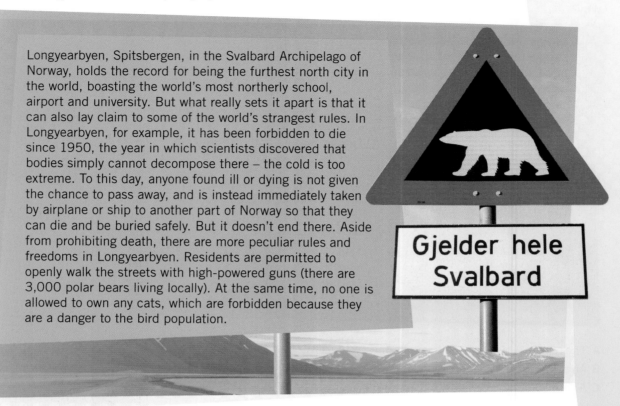

Longyearbyen, Spitsbergen, in the Svalbard Archipelago of Norway, holds the record for being the furthest north city in the world, boasting the world's most northerly school, airport and university. But what really sets it apart is that it can also lay claim to some of the world's strangest rules. In Longyearbyen, for example, it has been forbidden to die since 1950, the year in which scientists discovered that bodies simply cannot decompose there – the cold is too extreme. To this day, anyone found ill or dying is not given the chance to pass away, and is instead immediately taken by airplane or ship to another part of Norway so that they can die and be buried safely. But it doesn't end there. Aside from prohibiting death, there are more peculiar rules and freedoms in Longyearbyen. Residents are permitted to openly walk the streets with high-powered guns (there are 3,000 polar bears living locally). At the same time, no one is allowed to own any cats, which are forbidden because they are a danger to the bird population.

Gjelder hele Svalbard

0 8 ▶ Underline the main topic sentence in the paragraph.

0 9 ▶ Read the first sentence of the next paragraph about Marloth Park in South Africa. Find words or phrases that correspond to the underlined words in the headings A–C below.

Despite the fact the town of Marloth Park is close to the Kruger National Park, one of the largest game reserves in Africa, and despite the constant threat of visits from wild animals such as lions and hippopotamuses, its anxious residents are not allowed to build fences around their houses to keep out their neighbours.

A An unusual approach to <u>regulation</u>
B Dealing with the occasional <u>dangers of the wild</u>
C Where <u>humans and animals</u> cautiously <u>co-exist</u>

1 0 ▶ Now focus on the adverbs and adjectives in the headings. Which heading is no longer a possible answer?

A An <u>unusual</u> approach to regulation
B Dealing with the <u>occasional</u> dangers of the wild
C Where humans and animals <u>cautiously</u> co-exist

TIP 10

Pay particular attention to adjectives and adverbs in headings and texts, as they may help you to eliminate an incorrect heading immediately.

1 1 ▷ Read the rest of the paragraph and decide on your answer.

In fact the only fence permitted in the town was built by the local authority, interestingly, with the aim of keeping humans out of the park, rather than containing the animals inside. Consequently, it is not unusual to see giraffes or elephants causing traffic jams, for example, and even predator attacks on humans are unnervingly common – a lion was recently said to have mauled and eaten an escaping burglar. Yet even after this, while some residents then called for all lions to be rounded up and shot, others suggested that they be allowed to walk the thoroughfares as a type of crime control, after an increase in the number of burglaries. Everywhere in Marloth Park, a wary understanding exists between man and beast.

1 2 ▷ Identify the main topic sentence in the paragraph.

1 3 ▷ Some paragraphs have no clear topic sentence. Read this paragraph and make notes about its main idea.

The real Hallstat is in Austria and is proud to be a traditional UNESCO* World Heritage Site. The Chinese Hallstat is a carbon copy, built in Guangdong province, China, by a millionaire who sponsored the construction of the imitation town. It cost approximately $940 million to build, and looks exactly like the real Hallstat, all the way down to its wooden houses, its narrow streets, and its funicular railway. When the residents of Austria's Hallstat (including the mayor) were invited to visit it, they expressed pride that their town was considered so improbably beautiful that it had been reproduced in its entirety, but they still had cause for complaint. Originally, the Chinese company had promised to meet with the Austrian residents to confirm that they were happy for their homes to be copied; instead, they simply sent their employees to Austria to take photos, and they returned home to China without speaking to a single resident of the original Hallstat.

* *United Nations Educational, Scientific and Cultural Organization*

1 4 ▷ Use your notes to help you choose the correct heading.

A A conflict between reality and imitation

B The importance of official recognition

C The result of encouraging wider investment

PREFIXES

1 5 ▷ Identify the prefixes in the underlined words. Then work out a general meaning for each.

A An <u>unusual</u> approach to regulation

B An urban ideal designed for an <u>imperfect</u> world

C Where humans and animals cautiously <u>co-exist</u>

16▸ With a partner, think of some words that begin with the prefixes in the box. Then discuss what the general meaning of each prefix is.

| post- | for-/fore- | sub- | multi- | anti- | mis- | non- | pre- | over- | under- |

17▸ Using the correct prefixes from the box above, change the words in CAPITALS into the correct forms.

A The tourist brochure for Marloth Park ensures that visitors are WARN about the wild animals they may encounter walking the streets.

B One thing you can always be sure of in Longyearbyen – the cemeteries will never be POPULATE.

C The residents of Hallstat believed that they would be consulted by the company building a copy of their town – but it turns out they were INFORM.

D Auroville was founded according to a(n) GOVERN system of rules and beliefs.

[EXAM SKILLS]

18▸ Read the passage and answer questions 1–6.

The Reading passage has six paragraphs, A–F. Choose the correct heading for each paragraph from the list of headings below. Write the correct number, i–viii.

1 Paragraph **A** _____
2 Paragraph **B** _____
3 Paragraph **C** _____
4 Paragraph **D** _____
5 Paragraph **E** _____
6 Paragraph **F** _____

List of headings

  i The benefits of collaboration
 ii A forerunner of the modern metropolis
iii A period of intense activity and plans completed
 iv A clear contrast between then and now
  v The rise and mysterious decline of Cahokia
 vi An archaeological theory to explain Cahokia's development
vii The light and dark of archaeological finds
viii A city completely unlike any of its contemporaries

CAHOKIA – ANCESTOR OF TODAY'S CAPITAL CITIES

A A thousand years ago the Mississippians, a diverse group of Native Americans who lived in the area which is today known as the south-eastern United States, took a small village on the Mississippi River and turned it into one of the world's first great urban centres. Cahokia, as it has been called by archaeologists, became as large as London was in the 11th century, and some would argue that it was just as forward-looking and prosperous as its European equivalents. Sophisticated, cosmopolitan and ahead of its time, Cahokia was at the heart of ancient society in North America; an ancestor of today's capital cities.

B In one respect in particular, Cahokia was quite unusual compared to other cities around at the same time. Archaeologists working on the site have found enough evidence over the past fifty years to conclude that, at a certain time, around 35% of the population were not from Cahokia at all; it seems that many of the tribes that lived all along the Mississippi River at some point began to relocate to Cahokia. These researchers have been unable to find more than a handful of other examples of such relocation of tribes, but they do know that something about Cahokia attracted thousands of people to this regional centre. And that, they postulated, appears to have been thanks to a small group of planners who one day decided to redesign the entire village.

C After the redesigns of the village were put in place, the Native Americans at Cahokia worked with tireless determination to carry them out. Over the course of a few decades, they transported huge volumes of soil from the nearby countryside to create 120 huge mounds of earth, the biggest of which rose to one hundred feet. On top of these, they built a vast urban environment, complete with a vibrant town centre, municipal buildings, and a fifty-acre plaza at the foot of the biggest mound. What makes it even more impressive to our modern imaginations is that, with no machinery then, they used their bare hands and woven baskets to dig up and carry the soil from the surrounding regions back to their city-in-waiting. Eventually, after these efforts, the vision of the city planners was fulfilled, but even they could not have predicted how popular Cahokia would become.

D From this period on, Cahokia was alive with intense activity, and grew in size every year, partly because of the co-operation between the residents. While the men busied themselves with manual work, like constructing new buildings, or hunting and fishing in the forests and rivers within a day's walk of the city, the women made sure that the fields stayed healthy and grew crops, and the homes were kept clean. In many ways, it seems to have been the ideal place to live, and one with an exciting and prosperous future ahead of it. And yet, having become a major population centre around AD 1050, by 1350 it had been almost completely abandoned. Somewhere in the course of 300 years, something happened to Cahokia to cause this, but it is an enigma that even archaeologists or historians themselves struggle to resolve.

E This rather curious state of affairs exists today because researchers have never found a single piece of evidence that can conclusively explain why the residents left. Academics who have studied other Native American sites have always found weapons of war buried deep underground. And yet, the bows, arrows and swords that littered the ground at these other sites were nowhere to be seen at Cahokia. Other factors, such as disease or colonisation from European invasion, do not seem to be possible in this case, as common as they were elsewhere at that time. The absence of definitive theories as to Cahokia's decline is highly unusual, but then again, Cahokia was no ordinary city and perhaps comparisons with other urban centres of the time cannot be made.

F While academics remain bemused as to why the residents fled the city, we can still marvel at the individual artefacts that archaeologists have discovered: the jewellery worn, the pots used to cook in, the small workshop at the base of one of the mounds. That said, there is also a more unpleasant side to their investigations. Human sacrifice, it seems, was a common fact of life in Cahokia; even if we cannot be sure whether this was for religious or for other reasons, we can have no doubt that it happened frequently. The bodies of hundreds of people, mostly young women, have been found buried in mass graves, and the way in which they died was often horrific. A sombre reminder that even 'advanced' city states had their shadowy sides.

GO FURTHER ONLINE

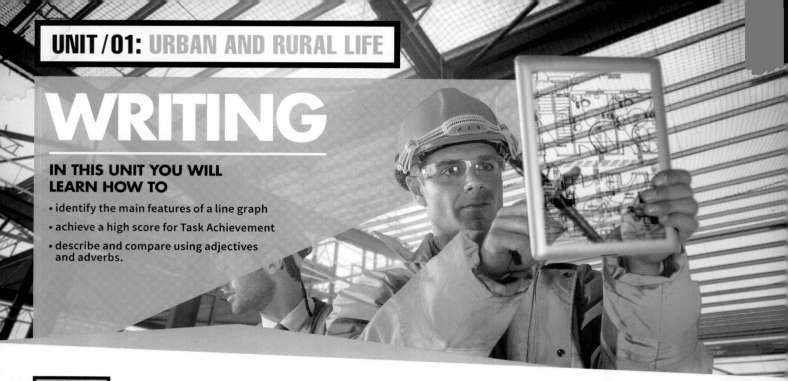

WRITING

IN THIS UNIT YOU WILL LEARN HOW TO

- identify the main features of a line graph
- achieve a high score for Task Achievement
- describe and compare using adjectives and adverbs.

LEAD-IN

01 ▷ Using the verb *to grow* and the adverb *rapidly*, complete the sentences to describe the information in the graphs. Focus on the correct verb tense in each case, bearing in mind the time phrases you are given and the dates in the graph.

1 Since five years ago, _____*sales have grown rapidly*_____ to 90,000.
2 Between _____ to 90,000.
3 From 2020 to 2030 _____ to 90,000.
4 By the year 2000, _____ to 90,000.
5 By the year 2025, _____ to 90,000.

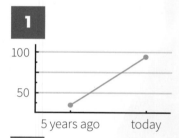
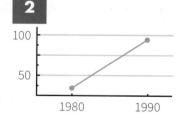
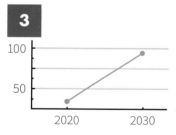
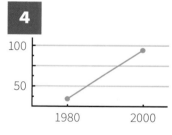
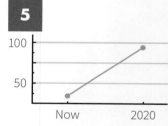

02 ▷ With a partner, make correct sentences using a verb from column 1, an adverb from column 2 and a time phrase.

Example:

Student A: *increase, slowly, by the year 2000*
Student B: *By the year 2000, it had increased slowly to 90%.*

Verb	Adverb	Time phrase
increase	dramatically	by the year 2000
decrease	slowly	from 1995 to 2000
fall	sharply	for the next ten years
rise	consistently	between 2010 and now
climb	gradually	by the year 2030
drop	steadily	since 2016

TASK 1 – TASK ACHIEVEMENT

Task Achievement (TA) is the mark you get for how well you answer the question. There are a number of common mistakes that prevent candidates from getting a high score in TA. These are:

- not including an overview statement
- misreporting data
- not highlighting key information or trends
- not including enough or any data
- speculating or giving an opinion about why changes have occurred
- using an inappropriate tone
- writing fewer than 150 words
- not including a final summary or concluding paragraph, or producing one which doesn't summarise the main features.

03 **With a partner, make notes on the main features in this Task 1 line graph.**

The line graph below shows the main reasons people gave for moving away from a particular capital city to the countryside.

Summarise the information by selecting and reporting the main features, and make comparisons where relevant.

TIP **03**

As you look at a graph/table/chart for the first time, ask yourself:
- Are there any common trends in the graphical information?
- Does any of the information differ from the rest in an obvious and significant way? If so, how?
- Is there anything that two or more categories have in common?
- Is there anything that only happens once?

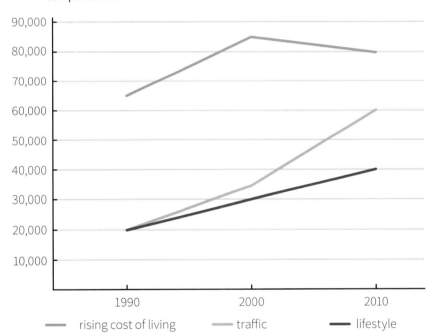

— rising cost of living   — traffic   — lifestyle

04 **Look at this description of the line graph above. It would not get a good score for Task Achievement. Why not?**

Answer 1

The line graph illustrates the main reasons people gave for moving away from a capital city to the countryside.

The main reason was traffic. In 1990, 66,000 people left the city because of this, followed by 85,000 in 2000. 70,000 left in 2010, so it actually went down in those last ten years.

It was different for the other two reasons, which both started a lot lower than rising cost of living and both kept going up between 1990 and 2010. Subsequently, both categories saw large increases, with traffic first going up a lot between 1990 and 2000 and then even more clearly after that. Lifestyle went up to 30,000 initially, then up again until 2010.

The description from exercise 4 has been rewritten, but there is still room for improvement. Read it and think about how it could be improved. Then match the teacher's comments (A–D) to the numbered sections (1–4).

Answer 2

> The line graph sets out the main motivations people expressed for relocating to the countryside from the city in the years 1990, 2000 and 2010. The overall trend for the period is of an increase in the numbers moving away from the city.
>
> According to the graph, the main reason for relocation was the rising cost of living. In 1990, 65,000 people left the city because of this, then 85,000 left in 2000, then 80,000 people moved away in 2010, so it actually increased by 20,000 initially (between 1990 and 2000), before going down by 5,000 in those last ten years between 2000 and 2010 (**1**). This drop of 5,000 could have been because people generally had less money in 2010 than they did in 2000, so they couldn't afford to move. (**2**)
>
> It was a different story for traffic and lifestyle. Both had the same number of city leavers at the start of the period. Subsequently, both categories saw increases, with traffic first going up by a large number between 1990 and 2000 and then even more steeply after that. Lifestyle leavers rose consistently over the whole period, going up to 30,000 initially, then up again to 2010. (**3**)
>
> So, what does it all mean? For me, the answer is crystal clear. Overall, the graph shows that a huge number of people moved away from the city to the countryside in a twenty-year period. (**4**)

A Don't speculate – you shouldn't suggest reasons for any change. All you need to do is report what you can see on the graph.

B This section is too mechanical – avoid simply listing the changes to a single category like this. Focus more on highlighting the key figures and trends.

C Better – you have included a conclusion this time, but it doesn't really summarise the key features. Your tone here is inappropriate – it sounds like you're writing a magazine article. Remember to keep the tone more formal and scientific.

D This section makes its points more clearly but fails to include key data to demonstrate the points.

06 ▷ **With a partner, discuss which option works best as a summary/conclusion for this task. Give reasons.**

A To sum up, people left the city for three main reasons, all of which rose significantly between 1990 and 2000. Traffic changed the most rapidly, lifestyle changed the least, and rising cost of living was the only reason that went down.

B Overall, the graph suggests the number of people relocating to the countryside rose across the period. Cost of living was the main reason for relocation by some distance, despite a fall in numbers in the second half of the period. Traffic saw the greatest overall increase, with lifestyle seeing a relatively slow but steady rise.

C All in all, the rising cost of living rose from 65,000 to 85,000 and then 80,000, and was the highest of all three reasons. Traffic had the biggest increase from 20,000 up to 60,000, while lifestyle changed the least (20,000 / 30,000 / 40,000).

TIP 06

Don't include data in your conclusion – it is a summary of the trends shown in the whole graph, and you do not need to repeat specific information.

DESCRIBING CHANGES WITH ADJECTIVES AND ADVERBS

07▸ Look at these notes that another candidate made for this line graph, which helped them to write a more effective description. Complete the sentences with the adjectives in the box.

consistent	highest	joint-lowest	lowest	notable	overall	stable

Rising cost of living: the (1) _highest_ point of any reason in any year (85,000 in 2000); the only one to decrease (to 80,000 in 2010)

Traffic: greatest (2) _overall_ rise (40,000); most (3) _notable_ rise between 2000 and 2010 (25,000)

Lifestyle: Most (4) _consistent_ and (5) _stable_ increase (only 20,000); remained the (6) _lowest_ of all three reasons-

Traffic and Lifestyle: (7) _joint-lowest_ in the first year presented (20,000 in 1990)

08▸ Look at the following adverbs which describe the manner of change. With a partner, decide which ones would be inappropriate for a Task 1 answer.

abruptly	~~amazingly~~	gradually	inconsistently
markedly	noticeably	~~predictably~~	progressively
sharply	~~shockingly~~	significantly	~~surprisingly~~
steadily			

TIP 08

This kind of task requires you to report the data objectively. Avoid using adverbs which give your subjective interpretation or opinion of the data, e.g. *worryingly*.

09▸ For the adverbs in exercise 8 that are appropriate for a Task 1 answer, discuss how you would expect the line to appear on the graph.

Example: steadily = *the line went up or down at a constant rate without many fluctuations*

10▸ Change the underlined words in the sentences into the form given in brackets and then rewrite the sentences. The first one has been done for you.

1 The category of 'Lifestyle' <u>increased the most consistently and stably</u>. (adjective + noun)
The most consistent and stable increase was seen in the category of 'Lifestyle'.

2 Traffic <u>rose steadily</u> as a reason for moving to the countryside between 1990 and 2000 … (adjective + noun)

3 … but then <u>there was a marked increase</u> between 2000 and 2010. (verb + adverb)

4 The number of people moving to the countryside for lifestyle reasons <u>grew consistently</u> across the whole period shown in the graph. (adjective + noun)

TIP 10

If your answer includes a range of structures, you can improve your score in another category, Grammatical Range and Accuracy (GRA), so vary your combinations (verb + adverb, adjective + noun). When using an adjective + noun combination, we can use the structure *There is/ are* or verbs like *see* or *experience*. For example: *The figures saw a sudden fall in 2010.*

2- the steady rise of traffic was a reason for moving to the countryside

3- But then it increased markedly between ..

4- there was a consistent growth in the number of people moving

GO FURTHER ONLINE

11 Use the information and language from this lesson to answer this Writing Task 1.

You should spend about 20 minutes on this task.

The line chart below shows the results of a survey giving the reasons why people moved to the capital city of a particular country.

Summarise the information by selecting and reporting the main features, and make comparisons where relevant.

Write at least 150 words.

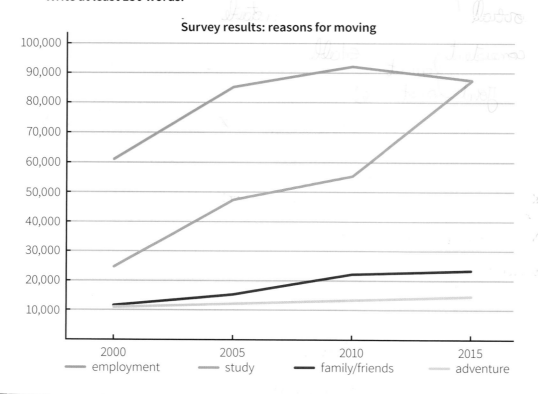

Survey results: reasons for moving

— employment — study — family/friends — adventure

UNIT / 01: URBAN AND RURAL LIFE

LISTENING

IN THIS UNIT YOU WILL LEARN HOW TO

- successfully deal with Section 1 form completion tasks
- correctly understand names and numbers
- develop your paraphrasing skills for multiple-choice questions
- understand and use future time conditionals.

LEAD-IN

01▷ Think of a city you would like to spend some time in. Discuss with a partner which options you would prefer and why.

- A visit to a museum OR a stroll through the park?
- A city tour OR a sports event?
- An evening at a restaurant OR at the theatre?
- A day wandering around the shops OR exploring the backstreets?
- Seeing the city by day OR at night?

02▷ Read these sentences that you might hear when deciding to go on a city tour. Look at each group of words in bold type. Decide which is NOT a synonym of the others and explain how it differs. In one sentence there are no synonyms.

'As long as you (**1**) book / select / reserve your tickets online at least 24 hours in advance, you can get a special (**2**) discount / reduction / bargain of 10%.'

'Hi, my name is Lucy and I'm going to be your (**3**) curator / presenter / guide for today's visit of the Trumpington Tower Museum. Can I remind you that all (**4**) visitors / explorers / guests will need to show their tickets at the (**5**) guard room / front desk / main entrance as soon as they come in.'

'When the tour finishes, you will have some free time to (**6**) explore / navigate / wander around the town centre for 30 minutes. The tour bus will (**7**) pick us up / collect us / let us on at 15:45 in the town square, next to the monument, and it will leave on time, provided everyone is on board.'

Many tasks in the IELTS Listening test test your ability to recognise *paraphrases* or *synonyms*. You need to be able to understand the key ideas in a question and listen for these ideas expressed in different words in the recording. However, the answers you write will *always* need to be exactly as you hear them – and must also be spelt correctly.

03 ▶ Here is a section from the Museum of London Life website. What words might you expect to read in the gaps? Think of as many possibilities as you can. Are any of them paraphrases/synonyms of each other?

LONDON – FROM COUNTRYSIDE VILLAGE TO URBAN METROPOLIS

HOME   **ABOUT**   PHOTOS   CONTACT

The Museum of London Life takes you on a thrilling journey from **1** _Ancient_ times in the city to modern-day life and beyond. Your trip through history begins with a look at how **2** _prehistorical History_ humans used to live when London was just open countryside. This is followed by a 'walk through the ages'. In every room you are surrounded by fascinating exhibits – images, photos, maps and all kinds of **3** _objects_ from years gone by. After you leave the here-and-now, when you have finished the **4** '_Contemporary_ London' section, you will be transported into the final era – the **5** _2nd_ century, to be precise – as you look at how the city might continue to evolve in the future.

04 Listen to a guide talking to a group of visitors to the Museum of London Life and fill the gaps in exercise 3. Write **ONE WORD AND/OR A NUMBER** in each gap.

05 Listen again to the guide and read the script on page 206. Underline the words he uses to paraphrase the brochure.

1 'thrilling journey from ancient times in the city to modern-day life and beyond'
2 'how prehistoric humans used to live'
3 'when London was just open countryside'
4 'surrounded by fascinating exhibits – images, photos, maps and all kinds of objects from years gone by'
5 'you will be transported into the final era – the 22nd century, to be precise'

FORM COMPLETION

Section 1 is the least difficult of the four parts of the Listening test and is often a form completion task. If you are aiming for a high score, it is important that you listen carefully from the first moment you hear somebody speak and try to get all ten marks for Section 1. After all, each question carries one mark, which is exactly the same as the later, more difficult sections.

06 Look at the booking form. With a partner, consider what kind of information you expect to hear for each question.

You will hear an employee at the Museum of London Life taking a booking.
*Complete the form. Write **NO MORE THAN TWO WORDS AND/OR A NUMBER** for each answer.*

MUSEUM OF LONDON LIFE   Booking Form

See how Londoners lived from Prehistoric times through to the 22nd century.

Name:	1	James ~~Gerret~~ Graeme
Address:	2	96 Mounts Hill Road, London, 3 E15 2TP
Telephone:	4	0 · 770 464
Discounts:		4+ people: 10%
	5	10+ people: _____ 15 _____ %
	6	Students: _____ 15 _____ %
	7	Students: 20% for groups of at least _____ 4 _____ people
Price for entry:	8	£ 4.25
Special exhibition:	9	Underground _____ London
Date of visit:	10	12th _____ July

07 Listen and complete the form.

08 ▶ For each piece of information in the questions, which of the options would you NOT hear?

1 410266 (part of a telephone number)
A four, one, oh [*pause*] two, double six
B four, one, zero, two [*pause*] two sixes ↺
C four, one, zero, [*pause*] two, six, six

2 18th century (period)
A eighteen century ↺
B the eighteenth century
C century eighteen ↺

3 2012 (year)
A two zero twelve ↺
B two thousand and twelve
C twenty twelve

4 20/7/76 (date)
A July the twentieth, nineteen seventy-six
B twenty, seven, seventy-six ✗
C twentieth of seven of seventy-six

5 Baker-Jones (name)
A B-A-K-E-R, hyphen, J-O-N-E-S
B B-A-K-E-R, line, J-O-N-E-S ✗
C B-A-K-E-R, dash, J-O-N-E-S ✗

6 £5.40 (price)
A five pounds forty pence
B five forty
C five forty pence ↺

7 museuminfo@history.org
A museuminfo (one word) at history point org ↺
B museuminfo (one word) at history full stop org
C museuminfo (one word) at history dot org

8 09.00
A nine A-M
B oh-nine A-M ↺
C nine in the morning

TIP 08

If you know the conventions for expressing information in English, you will avoid making a mistake with your answer. Make sure you practise:
- numbers (money, dates, years, telephone numbers)
- spelling of names (people, places, addresses, including email addresses), paying special attention to letters which represent problem sounds for your language

[MULTIPLE CHOICE]

For multiple-choice tasks, you will normally hear all three options mentioned in the recording in some way, but only one will answer the question.

The correct answer is often a paraphrase, so when you read the question stem and the possible answers, think about what can and can't be paraphrased. For example, if you have a question where all three options are proper nouns, you only need to focus on the key words in the stem, and how these might be re-phrased.

09 ▶ Look at the questions and the options. Discuss with a partner whether the underlined words and phrases could be paraphrased in the recording, and how they might be said.

Example: produce a document showing his booking
show his booking reference, provide a reservation print out

Choose the correct letter, A, B or C.

1 If James can't produce a document showing his booking, what does he have to show to collect his ticket?
A his passport
B his debit card ↺
C his smartphone

2 The museum employee most appreciates the way the museum
A is designed.
B talks about the city's inhabitants.
C is involved in fundraising for the local community. ✗

10▶ Listen to the recording and answer the questions in exercise 9.

04

11▶ Listen again and read the script on page 206. Make notes on the following.

04
1 The order in which the three multiple-choice options are mentioned
2 The words in the audio that correspond to each option

Listen again and read the script on page 206.

GRAMMAR FOCUS: FUTURE TIME CONDITIONALS

12▶ Look at the sentences. With a partner, divide each sentence into two clauses and decide which part needs to happen first for the second to be the result (i.e. which part is the condition, which is the result).

1 I'll book tickets for that as well today, provided there is something special that I'm particularly interested in.
2 You'll get your tickets fine, as long as you can produce the payment card you bought the tickets with.
3 Once we leave the part of the exhibition called 'Contemporary London', we will move into the 22nd century.
4 Unless something dramatic happens, I should be working here for a long time.

13▶ Underline each future time word or phrase in exercise 12 that indicates the condition. Which of those words or phrases could be replaced by 'if' with no change to the meaning of the sentence?

14▶ Choose the correct answers from each pair of options to complete the rule.

Future time conditionals follow the same structure as the **first** / **second** conditional:
If + **present** / **past** simple, ... / ... *will* / *would* + 'to' infinitive / bare infinitive

15▶ Imagine you are a tour guide taking tourists to a museum. Complete the statements to make sentences you might say to your tourists.

1 You can get a discounted ticket as long as .. you are a student
2 Once everybody has bought their ticket, .. then you can go in
3 You won't get lost provided .. if you are with company
4 Now everybody is free to explore the museum. You can go wherever you like as long as .. you come back in 15 min.
5 Your bus back to the hotel will depart as soon as .. everybody is there
6 Do not touch or take photos of the exhibits unless .. I say it is ok. here

TIP 10

Don't write down the first piece of information that seems to fit the gap. Sometimes in the Listening test, the speaker will talk for longer than you might expect before the correct answer becomes clear. For example, a speaker may seem to confirm an answer and then change their mind.

1 6 ▶ Listen and answer questions 1–9.

05

Questions 1–6

Complete the notes below.

Write **NO MORE THAN TWO WORDS AND/OR A NUMBER** *for each answer.*

Name:	Mr 1 David Cottienham *(Cottenham)*
Current address:	4 West Cottages, Humblington, Devon, 2 DV 12 8HA
Destination address:	8b Greenend Road, E19 4RR
Date of move:	30 August
Time booked:	3 7:30 evening
Value of insurance cover:	4 £ 60 thousand pounds
Total cost for service:	around £2,000
Telephone number:	(07238) 5 244810
Website:	www. 6 We-move-U .co.uk

Questions 7–9

*Choose the correct letter, **A, B** or **C**.*

7 The removals package that the man chooses is

   A Premium.

   B Silver.

   C Economy.

8 The woman believes that the best thing about We-Move-U is that they

   A cost less than people expect.

   B are very efficient.

   C provide excellent service to their clients.

9 After the man makes a booking, there will be

   A no more charges.

   B a 10% charge when the move is completed.

   C a charge if the man changes the day of his move.

GO FURTHER ONLINE

UNIT / 01: URBAN AND RURAL LIFE

SPEAKING

IN THIS UNIT YOU WILL LEARN HOW TO

- review all three parts of the Speaking test
- analyse good and bad answers to parts of the test
- correctly use future time conditionals in the Speaking test.

01▶ Complete this IELTS Speaking test quiz. Then compare your answers with a partner.

1 How long does the full Speaking test last?

   A 8–10 minutes   B 11–14 minutes   C 17–20 minutes

2 Which part of the test is a two-way discussion with the examiner about abstract issues and ideas?

   A Part 1   B Part 2   C Part 3

3 The assessment criteria Fluency and Coherence relates to

   A the range of vocabulary you use.

   B grammatical structures and accuracy.

   C the flow of your speech and how you connect your ideas.

4 Which part of the test is known as the 'Long Turn'?

   A Part 1   B Part 2   C Part 3

5 Which parts of the test are linked by topic/theme?

   A Part 1 and Part 3   B Part 1 and Part 2   C Part 2 and Part 3

6 In the assessment criteria, what is indicated by **GRA?**

   A Grammar Rules and Application

   B Grammatical Rules and Accuracy

   C Grammatical Range and Accuracy

7 Describe the focus of the questions in Part 1.

   A Simple general questions, familiar topics, personal focus

   B More complex questions based on one topic only, personal focus

   C More complex questions based on one topic only, impersonal focus

8 How long do you get to prepare your answer in Speaking Part 2?

   A 1 minute   B 30 seconds   C 45 seconds

02▶ Discuss with a partner what you find easy/difficult about each part of the Speaking test and why.

SPEAKING TEST – PART 1]

03▶ **Read the questions. Which ones would probably NOT be asked in Part 1 of the Speaking test?**

1 Do you live in a house or an apartment?
2 If you could choose any country to visit, where would you go?
3 What are the main issues affecting life in your town?
4 What do you like about the area where you live?
5 How might overpopulation affect city life in the future?
6 How often do you use public transport in your town/city?
7 Why is it important to look after places of natural beauty?
8 Do you often visit parks in your town/city?

⊙ Part 1 questions focus on general familiar topics that reflect your everyday life, rather than complex or abstract questions.

04▶

06

Listen to three candidates answering three of the questions in exercise 3. For each question, what does the candidate do wrong?

SPEAKING TEST – PART 2]

TIP 04

- Never memorise complete answers to questions before the exam. It is normally obvious to examiners when a candidate does this and it may affect your score.
- Aim to show a variety of verb forms and grammar structures – but they must be correct if you want a high score.
- Vary your vocabulary. Use synonyms and paraphrase to express your ideas using different words.

05▶ **Which Part 2 task card is an accurate example of what you would be given in the IELTS test?**

A

Describe a rural town that you plan to visit in the future.

You should say:

close to the border Scotland

- where the town is
- when you would like to go *AS SOON AS Francho for 2 semesters*
- who you would go with

and explain what you would like to do there.

B

Describe this town in a rural area.

State whether you would like to go there and why.

C

Describe a town in a rural area that you plan to visit in the future.

You should say:

- how far it is from your home
- when you plan to go
- why it is important for people to spend time in places like this

and explain what is being done to maintain it as an area of outstanding natural beauty.

TIP 06

When answering the Part 2 question, you do not need to try and give equal time to each of the four prompts. Some prompts will be easier to expand on than others.

06▶
07

Listen to an answer to the task card in exercise 5. Does the candidate cover all the prompts in equal detail? What effect would this have on his score?

SPEAKING TEST – PART 3]

0 7 ▶ Listen to a candidate giving good answers to Part 3 questions. For each answer (1–5), choose the corresponding question (A–E), and write the letter.

1 **D**   2 **E**   3 **A**   4 **C**   5 **B**

A If private cars were completely banned from the most overcrowded cities, what might happen?

B How was family life different before transport links connected most towns and cities?

C Which is preferable, living on the top floor of a studio apartment block in a city, or in a beautiful house in the middle of the countryside?

D Why do people decide to move from the city to the countryside?

E How might overpopulation affect city life in the future?

0 8 ▶ Read questions A–E again and read the script on page 208. What was each question asking the candidate to do? Discuss with a partner and choose from the list of 'functions' below.

(i) Make a prediction

(ii) Compare and contrast

(iii) Consider a hypothetical situation

(iv) Suggest cause and effect

(v) Analyse past and present

TIP 08

Thinking about the *function* of the question being asked will help you to develop your answer and decide what language and structures to use.

0 9 ▶ Read these comments on the candidate's performance. Write the correct marking criteria they correspond to: Fluency and Coherence (FC); Lexical Resource (LR); Grammatical Range and Accuracy (GRA); Pronunciation (P).

1 Uses stress and intonation appropriately, e.g *NOT just NAtionally, but INternationally.*

2 Uses a good range of more advanced structures naturally, e.g. *... if you were just visiting the city, it probably wouldn't bother you ... | That might sound ridiculous now, but cities are likely to keep expanding at the rate they are currently ...*

3 Speaks fluently with very rare hesitation or repetition.

4 Avoids making grammatical mistakes.

5 Uses varied vocabulary that is relevant to the topics discussed.

6 Develops the topics fully and appropriately; supplies answers of an appropriate length.

7 Every answer can be understood very easily.

8 Uses less common vocabulary, including collocation and idiomatic phrases, e.g. *the bright lights of the big city | traditional family unit | it's too over the top for some.*

9 Uses appropriate phrases to introduce and connect ideas, e.g. *Generally speaking, though ... | Having said that ...*

1 0 ▶ Listen again to the candidate and notice how she does these things.

GRAMMAR FOCUS: FUTURE TIME CONDITIONALS

11▶ In the Part 1 section earlier, the candidate gave a weak answer which would not score highly for GRA. It included the sentence below. Why is this incorrect?

As soon as we will finish class, we will go.

12▶ In the Part 3 section you listened to in exercise 7, the candidate gave strong answers which would score well for GRA, and included the sentences below. Complete the sentences with the correct *future time phrases* from the box. Then listen and check.

| As long as | As soon as | By the time | Providing that | Unless |

A _As Long As_ people are happy to use buses and bikes instead of their cars, life will continue as normal.

B _By the time_ I'm a grandparent, I think it will be even more different.

C _Providing that_ I make enough money, I'll definitely be on a top floor myself one day.

D _As soon As_ you get older and have a family, you start thinking it's time to move.

E _Unless_ this changes, we're going to need more and more homes for everyone.

13▶ Look at exercise 12 again and answer the questions.

1 What happens to the meaning of sentence **E** if you use *Once*?
2 What happens to the meaning of the sentences **A** and **C** if you use *When*?
3 In which sentence is the grammar different from the others? Why does the speaker decide to use this structure here?

PRONUNCIATION

14▶ Listen again and put a circle around the stressed syllables in each sentence A–E in exercise 12.

Example: As long as people are happy to use buses and bikes instead of their cars, life will continue as normal.

15▶ Listen again and practise saying each sentence with the correct pronunciation.

[EXAM SKILLS]

1 6 ▶ Think about how you would answer these Part 1 questions. Then ask and answer them with a partner.

- In your city, what do you usually do at the weekend?
- When you were last in the countryside, who did you go with? Why?
- In the town or city you live in now, what are your favourite pastimes?

1 7 ▶ Read the Task 2 card. Then practise making notes for one minute, and deliver your long turn to a partner.

Describe a city where you have lived in the past.

You should say:

- where the city was
- why you were living there
- how long you lived there for

and explain what you liked and disliked about living there.

GO FURTHER ONLINE

1 8 ▶ Ask and answer the Part 3 questions with a partner.

1 Do you think that within the next 100 years we will be trying to build new cities on other planets?

2 What would happen if the government put limits on how many people were allowed to live in big cities?

3 Today, many young people move away from smaller towns to big cities. What effect does this have on these small towns?

UNIT / 02: HEALTH

READING

IN THIS UNIT YOU WILL LEARN HOW TO

- review skimming and scanning skills
- correctly answer flow-chart and table completion questions
- understand and correctly use quantifiers
- use paraphrase to help you answer sentence completion questions.

LEAD-IN

01▷ Look at the pairs of words related to health. Use a dictionary to check what part of speech they are and write the underlined suffixes in the table.

1 metabol<u>ism</u> / metabol<u>ic</u>
2 harm<u>ful</u> / harm<u>less</u>
3 nutrition<u>al</u> / nutrit<u>ious</u>
4 preven<u>tion</u> / prevent<u>ative</u>
5 diet<u>ary</u> / dietic<u>ian</u> / diet<u>er</u>
6 treat<u>ment</u> / treat<u>able</u>

TIP 01

Learning suffixes can help you decode unknown words in a text. Most suffixes are specific to one part of speech and some have very specific meanings.

Noun	Adjective
-ism	

02▷ Answer the questions.

1 What is the difference in meaning between the suffixes *-ful* and *-less*? → *opposite*
2 What does the suffix *-able* mean? — *Possible*
3 To what part of speech do we add *-able* in order to form the adjective? → *verb*
4 What do the suffixes *-er, -or* and *-ian* have in common apart from being noun suffixes? — *People suffixes*
5 Which part of speech uses all the following suffixes: *-ify, -ise/-ize, -ate, -en*? → *Verb*

Skim reading a text before you look at the questions not only helps you with tasks that require you to identify the general idea of paragraphs, but also with more detailed reading tasks. This is because your skim read can help you to form a 'mental map' of the text, which will help you to identify the correct areas to look for answers in.

0 3 ▷ **Look at two versions of a sentence. In each, different words have been blanked out. Which version shows the kinds of words you should be focusing on when you skim read? Give reasons.**

Version 1

It is ▭ to ▭ how ▭ has ▭ , given that the ▭ ▭ in the ▭ its ▭ a mere ▭ .

Version 2

▭ astonishing ▭ contemplate ▭ popular junk food ▭ become, ▭ ▭ first fast food restaurant ▭ US only opened ▭ doors ▭ century ago.

0 4 ▷ **Without reading a full sentence in any of the paragraphs, skim read the text below. Try to notice the key meaning-carrying words in each one. Then match the main ideas/functions (1–6) with each paragraph.**

1 Provides an explanation for the way people act

2 Makes a prediction

3 Outlines a growing phenomenon

4 Describes a process

5 Contrasts opposing viewpoints

6 Relates a problem to a specific group of people

0 5 ▷ **Discuss with a partner which words or phrases gave you the answers to exercise 4.**

THE UNSTOPPABLE RISE OF BURGERS AND FRIES

A It is astonishing to contemplate how popular junk food has become, given that the first fast food restaurant in the US only opened its doors a mere century ago. Since then, high-calorie processed meals have taken over the world, with multinational restaurant chains aggressively chasing levels of growth that show no signs of slowing down. Much of this expansion is currently taking place in less developed parts of the world, where potential for customer loyalty is seen as easier to develop, but it is not just in these areas where such growth is visible. Indeed, a recent study from the University of Cambridge found that the number of takeaways in the United Kingdom rose by 45 per cent between 1997 and 2015. This explosion in the takeaway trade is not an inevitable outcome of what we call 'progress'. On the contrary, it comes in the face of an increasing body of evidence that we are heading for dietary disaster.

B Yet, despite nutrition experts' best efforts to educate people about the dangers of a diet filled with processed food, it appears that the world doesn't want to listen. Medical specialists point out that, although eating too much unhealthy food is likely to be as dangerous in the long-term as smoking, regular consumption of high-calorie food has somehow become more socially acceptable than ever. While local authorities in some towns and cities have taken measures to combat the rise in this trend by limiting the number of fast food outlets permitted to be open simultaneously, critics argue that people have every right to make their own decisions about what they eat and how they choose to live. However, the way in which we have come to binge on takeaways isn't only a personal issue of weight gain, or of buying larger clothes. The consequences of mass overconsumption should strike fear into the hearts of everyone.

C Research suggests that there is an evolutionary reason as to why people compulsively overeat – it is simply part of our innate behaviour. When humans evolved, we did not have the abundant supply of food that we enjoy today, and so eating was more about survival than pleasure. We became more likely to opt for high-calorie foods, with high fat content, that could sustain us through cold winters when the supply of nourishment became sparse. This explains why a 600-calorie burger seems so attractive: it awakens our primal side, makes us feel well fed, inspires contentment. Processed food stimulates the reward response in our brains, so we feel compelled to overeat, and not necessarily in a healthy way. Junk food acts as a trigger for chemicals such as the 'feel-good' dopamine to flood through the brain and induce a sensation of happiness. Meanwhile, high amounts of sugar and sodium (one of the chemicals in salt and other ingredients of fast food) cause a huge surge in blood sugar, pushing it to unnatural levels.

D This occurs within the first few moments of eating a high-calorie meal. From there, routinely processing such high levels of sodium is impossible, and the body's organs are pushed beyond their natural working capacity in trying to do so. The kidneys cannot remove all the excess salt from the blood, and thus an overdose of sodium causes the heart to pump faster while transporting blood through the veins. There are multiple dangers of high blood pressure, especially for the elderly and in the long-term. Sodium taken on in such quantities can lead to dehydration, a condition whose symptoms are extremely similar to hunger, and this leads to a painful truth: as soon you have finished your junk food meal, you immediately start to crave another. Thereafter, the body starts to digest the food. Usually, this takes between four and 12 hours, but with fast food, where the fat content is so much higher, the same process lasts at least three days.

E A number of studies have shown how young people can become even more addicted to junk food than adults. When a child eats a burger, the same neurological processes occur as in their parents: their brain's reward system is awoken, dopamine is released, a spontaneous feeling of excitement results, their blood sugar rockets, and so on. An adult can apply their maturity to understand that this thrill is not entirely without drawbacks, and that they need to control their urge to eat more. However, a child cannot necessarily see any negative consequences to this urge and the potential effects of their lack of self-control, so they find it far more difficult to exercise restraint and moderate their food consumption.

F It is common to read or to hear criticism of the junk food industry that does so much to promote the overconsumption of its products. But it does not appear that any of this criticism is changing widespread dietary habits in any substantial way. What is more, the humble burger has been elevated to such a point that many people no longer see it as simple, *on-the-go* food. It has arguably become a stylish and aspirational part of one's daily diet. Consider, for example, how some television companies recently made several series of programmes encouraging unnecessary overeating, in which the host devours dish after dish of unhealthy, fatty meals until they are full – and then far, far beyond. While such glamorisation exists, it is difficult to see how our collective march towards a global obesity crisis can ever be halted.

◎ You will need to use different scanning skills in the Reading test. Sometimes, you will be looking for a name, number or title, for example. This is the least difficult task to do successfully, as you will be able to use capital letters, numbers, and *italicised* words. Long, technical words such as 'cardiovascular' are also easier to find.

Candidates aiming at a higher score should be able to scan a passage for synonyms or full paraphrases of the key words or ideas in a question. It could be that you need to find a single word, but the more difficult questions require you to search for a phrase, or a sentence, that corresponds with those key words or ideas. This requires a greater range of vocabulary and understanding of meaning and suggestion.

0 6 ▷ **Discuss with a partner which of the following techniques will help you to find specific information when you scan a passage.**

a Moving your eyes from left to right along each line

b Moving from the bottom of the page to the top, quickly moving your eyes left and right

c Breaking a paragraph into four sections (top right, top left, bottom right, bottom left) and moving your eyes around each one

d Moving your eyes in a 'zig-zag' pattern from top to bottom, or bottom to top, of the passage

0 7 ▷ **Scan the passage on pages 31–32 for the following information.**

1 the names of two chemicals

2 a proportional increase

3 a unit of measurement

4 five parts of the human body

COMPLETING FLOW-CHARTS / TABLES / NOTES

0 8 ▷ **Use the words of the flow-chart to help you decide in which part or parts of the text the answers can be found.**

 These exam tasks require you to complete the gaps in a flow-chart, table or set of notes using a specified number of words. Usually the answers will be located in one part of the text only but sometimes you will need to look at the text as a whole. Answers are usually – but not always – in the same order as in the text, and are usually fairly close together. The words you need will be in the text in the same form.

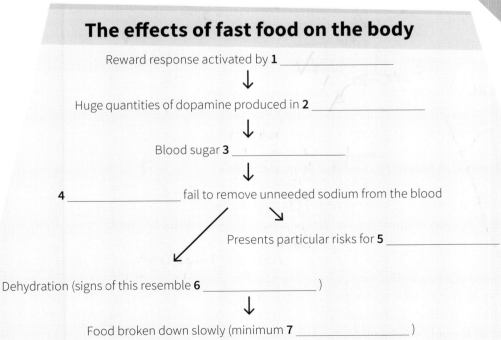

The effects of fast food on the body

Reward response activated by **1** _____

↓

Huge quantities of dopamine produced in **2** _____

↓

Blood sugar **3** _____

↓

4 _____ fail to remove unneeded sodium from the blood

↘

Presents particular risks for **5** _____

↙

Dehydration (signs of this resemble **6** _____)

↓

Food broken down slowly (minimum **7** _____)

09▷ For each question, choose NO MORE THAN TWO WORDS from the text to complete the flow-chart in exercise 8.

10▷ Look at the title of the table completion question. In which section of the text will you find the answers to enable you to complete the table?

TIP 09

Once you have identified the parts of the text where the answers will be found, predict what kind of information is missing in each gap (name, numerical information, adjective, etc.). Then read in detail to find it.

Differences in adult and child reactions to eating processed food

Adult	Child
Eats – dopamine released Reward system activated	Eats – dopamine released Reward system activated
Can understand negative consequences Rationalises excitement by relying on 8 _____	Cannot understand negative consequences Unable to resist the 9 _____ to consume more food
Can hold back cravings Stops eating	Does not show 10 _____ Continues to eat

11▷ For each question, choose ONE WORD ONLY from the text to complete the table.

[SENTENCE COMPLETION]

These tasks use many of the skills you need for completing a flow-chart, notes or table. However, the questions will be in the order in which they appear in the text and it is more likely that you will need to find the answers from two or three sections of the text or even the text as a whole.

12▷ Look again at paragraph A of *The unstoppable rise of burgers and fries*. Find and underline paraphrases for:

1 pursuing
2 a large part of the growth in the fast food industry
3 huge success of the fast food industry
4 growing proof

TIP 12

Find paraphrases of the key ideas in the sentence stems you are given to help you locate the answers.

13▷ Complete the sentences. Choose NO MORE THAN TWO WORDS from the text for each answer.

1 Global food corporations are fiercely pursuing ways in which to increase their _____ .

2 The fast food industry is particularly building its presence in areas that are _____ .

3 Despite more and more proof of its negative effects, the huge success of the fast food industry is leading us into _____ .

14▷ Find and underline paraphrases for these phrases.

1 the public seems unconvinced (paragraph B)
2 developed initiatives to change fast food consumption habits (paragraph B)
3 an instinctive characteristic people share (paragraph C)
4 transforming the way most of the public view and consume food (paragraph F)
5 glamorous (paragraph F)

15 ▶ Complete the sentences. Choose NO MORE THAN TWO WORDS from the text for each answer.

1 Much of the public seems unconvinced that if they eat an excess of _____ , they will become ill.

2 Many urban councils have developed initiatives to change fast food consumption habits by issuing restrictions on how many _____ can sell fast food.

3 A number of scientists believe that an instinctive characteristic people share causes them to _____ .

4 One problem is that a fast food diet has become glamorous and _____ .

GRAMMAR FOCUS: QUANTIFIERS

16 ▶ Compare these sentences with underlined quantifiers to the correct versions of these sentences in exercise 15. Then match them with the common error explanations A–C.

1 <u>Much of</u> public seems unconvinced that … they will become ill.

2 <u>Many of the</u> urban councils have developed initiatives …

3 <u>A number of</u> scientists believes that an instinctive characteristic …

3 **A** The subject is actually plural and therefore the verb does not agree.

1 **B** The noun which follows the determiner is uncountable and must be preceded by 'of the'.

2 **C** When we talk about a noun in general terms, we use *most*, *much* or *many*. Including 'of the' means we are referring to one of a specific group, which is not the case here.

EXAM SKILLS

17 ▶ Read the passage and answer questions 1–14.

THE GROWING GLOBAL THREAT OF ANTIBIOTIC RESISTANCE

Antibiotics have been one of humanity's success stories for hundreds of years, being responsible both for saving the lives of millions of patients and for helping scientists to take enormous steps in the fields of medical and surgical treatment. But this success has come at a price. The growing resistance of many bacterial strains to the curative effects of antibiotics is such a concern that it has been referred to, in some quarters, as the greatest threat to our continued existence on earth. We have become careless, it is argued, not only in our reliance on the quick fix of medicine if we feel even slightly under the weather, but also in taking the availability of antibiotics for granted, using them incorrectly, not following the prescribed dosage. This has given rise to a new form of superbacteria, a type which is able to fight off antibiotic treatment with ease.

Although their resistance to antibiotics has been built up over a long period of time, bacteria actually replicate extraordinarily quickly, and any resistance developed is also duplicated as they divide. In addition, those bacteria carrying resistance genes happen to spread those genes further via 'horizontal gene transfer', a process whereby one bacterium passes on the resistance gene from another without even needing to be its parent. What makes the spread of these strains more difficult to control is that it occurs in a cyclical process. In the case of humans, when a person becomes infected and the resistant bacteria set up home in the gut, the sufferer has two choices: look for help or stay at home. In seeking medical assistance, whether through an appointment to visit their local doctor, or taking themselves to hospital, they contaminate other patients, later to be discharged and sent home. The resistant bacteria then spread out into the local community. This is also the end result if the infected person decides not to seek any medical assistance at all: they keep the bacteria at home and allow them to breed without treatment.

Livestock also play their part in dispersing these newly evolved, bullet-proof microorganisms into the food chain. These resilient bacteria do not discriminate between man and beast, and so animals play host to the very same bacteria as are found in humans, with the end result that our farms and abattoirs have become breeding grounds for inter-species infection. In fact, even after slaughter, these bacteria can easily survive on animal carcasses, remaining alive and reproducing until the point of purchase and beyond, eventually invading our systems when we ingest the flesh as infected meat. So is the answer simply to become a vegetarian? Sadly not. The very same resistant bacteria will leave a host animal's gut in the form of faeces, which are employed in agriculture as manure to support food crops. From there, the wheat, maize and corn that are grown for human consumption transport the bacteria into our bodies. There really is no escape.

That said, there is always something that can be done to try and minimise any risk, however much of a lost cause it might seem. In 2014, after accumulating data from 114 countries, the World Health Organization (WHO), issued a set of guidelines intended to tackle the increasing problem of resistance. Doctors and pharmacists were advised to avoid prescribing and dispensing antibiotics as much and as often as possible. Only when treatment is utterly necessary should they resort to doing so, while the greatest of care should be taken to ensure that the antibiotics they provide are the correct ones to treat the illness. In turn, the general public must play their part by only taking antibiotics as prescribed by a doctor, as well as making sure they see out the full course, even if they feel better before the antibiotics are finished. Additionally, they should never share their medication with others or – astonishing as it may seem that this would need to be stated – buy drugs online.

Away from the individual and onto organisations, the WHO has urged policymakers to invest in laboratory capacity and research to track increasing drug resistance as it happens, over time. Our leaders and governors were also advised to ensure that use of antibiotics is strictly regulated, something that can only be achieved through cooperation between themselves and the pharmaceutical industry. If innovation in research were encouraged, and new tools developed, the WHO argued, the threat might yet be contained. But herein lies the biggest challenge of all. Antibiotic development has slowed down considerably over recent decades as the pharmaceutical industry becomes ever more governed by profit margins. Since they are used for a relatively short time, and are often effective in curing the patient, antibiotics are nowhere near as lucrative as the drugs that treat long-term disorders, such as diabetes or asthma. Because medicines for chronic conditions are so much more profitable, this is where pharmaceutical companies invest their time and money. A further stumbling block is the relatively low cost of antibiotics, newer examples of which tend to cost a maximum of £1,000 to £3,000 per course. When compared with cancer chemotherapy, for example, a process of treatment that costs tens of thousands of pounds, the discrepancy becomes impossible to mend.

As a race, humans have seen remarkable health benefits over the years as a huge number of illnesses have been treated by antibiotics, but we now face a global emergency as antibiotic-resistant bacteria are beginning to emerge more rapidly and frequently than ever before. Not only has this created a potential health crisis, since we are increasingly unable to provide the sick with treatment as a result of worldwide overuse of these drugs, but it is also unlikely to be tackled any time soon, as the powerful pharmaceutical companies are primarily driven by profit and see little benefit in researching and creating new antibiotics. It simply does not work on the balance sheet, and so it falls to governments and individuals around the world to find ways to manage the crisis. Coordinating such efforts will not be easy.

Questions 1–7

Complete the flow-chart below.

*Choose **NO MORE THAN TWO WORDS** from the passage for each answer.*

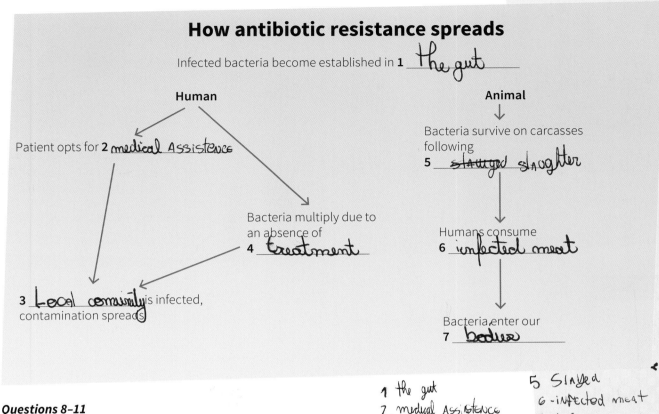

How antibiotic resistance spreads

Infected bacteria become established in **1** _the gut_

Human

Patient opts for **2** _medical Assistance_

Bacteria multiply due to an absence of **4** _treatment_

3 _Local community_ is infected, contamination spreads

Animal

Bacteria survive on carcasses following **5** ~~staurged~~ _slaughter_

Humans consume **6** _infected meat_

Bacteria enter our **7** _bodies_

(handwritten notes)
1 the gut
2 medical Assistance
3 Local comunity
4 treatment
5 Slayed
6 -infected meat
7 - bodies

Questions 8–11

Complete the table below.

*Choose **NO MORE THAN TWO WORDS** from the passage for each answer.*

Recommendations from World Health Organization

Medical professionals	General public
• Only prescribe antibiotics when there is no alternative. • Prescribe or dispense correct treatment on a case-by-case basis.	• Only take antibiotics prescribed by a doctor. • Take the complete **8** _course_ . • Avoid **9** _online_ purchase of medication.
Governments/Policymakers	**Pharmaceutical industry**
• Give money towards increasing **10** ~~data~~ _laboratory_ with which to monitor the continuing development of resistance to antibiotics. _capacity_	• Co-operate with policymakers to fund new kinds of research in order to find **11** _New tools_ with which to fight the threat of antibiotic resistance.

Questions 12–14

Complete the sentences below.

*Choose **NO MORE THAN TWO WORDS** from the passage for each answer.*

12 The rapid emergence of antibiotic-resistant bacteria could put a stop to the _health benefits_ that have been enjoyed by humanity.

13 Owing to its _worldwide overuse_, antibiotic treatment of people with illnesses is becoming dangerously less effective.

14 With pharmaceutical companies preoccupied with profit, responsible governments and individuals must take steps to tackle the _crises_ themselves.

GO FURTHER ONLINE

UNIT / 02: HEALTH

WRITING

IN THIS UNIT YOU WILL LEARN HOW TO

- effectively answer 'advantages and disadvantages' questions
- write topic and supporting sentences, developing your ideas in each paragraph
- achieve a high score in Coherence and Cohesion
- correctly use less common discourse markers.

LEAD-IN

0 1 ▷ Complete the table with words and phrases from the box. Use a dictionary if necessary.

| benefits | pros | on the downside | positives | drawbacks | issues |
| negatives | cons | on the plus side | problems | on the upside | |

Advantages (synonyms / paraphrases)	Disadvantages (synonyms / paraphrases)
- Pros - benefits - on the plus side on the upside	Negatives - drawbacks issues Cons - problems on the downside on the upside

0 2 ▷ Look at the list of ideas. In pairs or groups, brainstorm and make notes on advantages and disadvantages for each, based on the subject of health.

Example: Doing contact sports

  Advantages: *excellent form of physical exercise; improves reactions and reflexes; fighting sports teach you to defend yourself, often require strong focus, so good for mental health*

  Disadvantages: *easy to get injured; some contact sports actually intend to harm opponents; people can be killed*

1 Living in a busy city

2 Increased life expectancy in many societies

TIP 0 2

It's a good idea to start the planning of any Task 2 writing by brainstorming ideas. Make a list of the things you can talk about and then prioritise them in order of importance. Decide which to include and which not, and then decide what would be a logical sequence for presenting these ideas.

MAIN AND SUPPORTING IDEAS

0 3 ▶ Use the phrases below to write topic sentences for your ideas from exercise 2.

1 One problem with … is …
   One problem with increased life expectancy is an ageing population that puts a strain on health care services.

2 The main advantage of … is …

3 The principle issue with … is …

4 One obvious negative effect of … is …

5 Another disadvantage of … is …

6 Overall, the benefits of … outweigh the drawbacks because …

0 4 ▶ Read the topic sentence and the possible supporting ideas for it below. Which two are not effective at developing the topic sentence idea further?

One obvious benefit of participating in a contact sport is the improvement in one's physical health and well-being.

1 Regularly taking part in a demanding and potentially dangerous activity leads to enhanced physical conditioning, as well as improved speed of thought and reaction time. — B

2 Any physical exercise, however minimal, is bound to improve fitness in some way, but studies show that boxing, in particular, produces the fittest and sharpest athletes of any sport there is. — A

3 On the other hand, it is arguable that the potential dangers involved in doing so – and injuries are inevitable, after all – outweigh any benefits that may be felt or gained.

4 Despite the fact that there have been many accidents, and even occasional fatalities, the vast majority of people who take part gain a high level of fitness and rarely, if ever, suffer injury. — C

5 The healthier you are, the less likely you are to visit a doctor, and this can only be a good thing as it is often difficult to get an appointment to see a medical specialist. — D

6 Not only that, but the sometimes risky nature of sports such as rugby or ice hockey also demand intense levels of concentration that positively affect mental awareness. — D

D IMPORTANT

0 5 ▶ Match the four possible supporting ideas you identified in exercise 4 with their function (a–d) in relation to the topic sentence.

a It gives a specific supporting **example**. — 2

b It uses a **cause and effect** argument to clarify the idea. — 1

c It supports the topic sentence but shows a **contrasting** view that looks at another side of the argument. — 4

d It adds an **additional** point to strengthen the idea in the topic sentence. — 6

0 6 ▶ Write two supporting sentences for this topic sentence. Use two different functions.

One significant drawback is the fact that participating in contact sports can cause injury and, in some extreme cases, death.

◎ Good paragraphs in essays usually begin with a *topic sentence* (expressing the main idea of the paragraph) which is then followed by *supporting ideas* – explanations, examples, etc. which 'support' or 'clarify' the idea of the topic sentence. Topic sentences should introduce and establish the main idea of each paragraph clearly and simply. Avoid trying to write anything too complex or long. You can go into more detail with your supporting ideas.

TIP 04

Think carefully about the kind of supporting ideas you want to follow your main idea and what their functions are.

COHERENCE AND COHESION

07 ▶ For this Task 2 'advantages and disadvantages' question, discuss with a partner in which order you could put the notes so that they form a logical paragraph.

In terms of personal health and fitness, what are the advantages and disadvantages of living in a busy city?

- e.g. 250 gyms in my capital city
- In cities – many gyms
- Traditional idea – rural life is healthier; not true
- Gyms part of larger chains, people can use any in city

08 ▶ The discourse markers in this paragraph are missing. Think about the function of the supporting ideas and then choose the discourse markers from the box that would fit in each gap. There are three possibilities for each gap.

What is more	By way of example	For instance
Consequently	Because of this	As a result
For example	In addition to this	Moreover

One positive aspect of city life is that there are generally a large number of fitness complexes available for members of the public to join, and most cater for the requirements of all their customers, whether those be for running machines, for weight training and so on. **1** _____ , in my city alone there are somewhere in the region of 200 individual facilities, allowing residents the opportunity to stay healthy wherever they live or work. **2** _____ , these gyms are often part of larger chains, and it is convenient for their members to be able to visit a range of locations if they wish to do so. **3** _____ , although living in rural areas is traditionally assumed to be better for one's health, the sheer quantity of available facilities in modern cities means that this stereotype is changing.

09 ▶ Read a candidate's paragraph and answer the questions.

One of the advantages of living in a city is that there are many gym facilities. <u>For example</u>, in my capital city there are more than 250 gyms. <u>What this means is that</u> there is a lot of choice available to the public. <u>Furthermore</u>, these gyms are often part of larger chains <u>because</u> people can visit any gym, in any location, in any city, meaning that there are options for everybody regardless of their lifestyle. <u>Despite this</u>, people usually believe that rural life is better for your health. <u>This is because</u> the traditional belief is that living in the countryside means that you do more exercise. <u>However</u>, the increasing number of gym memberships in cities does mean that this attitude is slowly changing.

1. Does the paragraph have a clear topic sentence? If so, what is it?
2. Do the ideas follow logically from one another?
3. What function (example, cause and effect, addition or contrast) does each have of the underlined discourse markers have?
4. Which discourse marker is incorrectly used? Can you suggest an alternative?
5. Which discourse marker(s) could be omitted without impeding the logical flow of ideas?

The examiner will pay attention to how well you can produce an essay that is *coherent* (easy to follow and to understand) and *cohesive* (the essay flows naturally and logically from one idea to the next). It is therefore important that your main and supporting ideas are connected to form paragraphs that are easy to read and convey your ideas or arguments clearly.

TIP 08

Discourse markers are words and phrases used to communicate certain language functions. For example, *On the other hand* is a discourse marker to introduce a contrasting point or idea. Using a variety of them in writing is particularly important for constructing solid arguments and paragraphs, and improves your Coherence and Cohesion score.

TIP 09

You can also lose marks for misusing or overusing discourse markers. Not every sentence needs one. Consider whether the meaning of your sentence/paragraph is affected without them. If your meaning is clear, perhaps it is not necessary to use one.

10 ▷ Look at the essay question and the three introductions below. What are the strengths and weaknesses of each one?

Many countries offer a free health care system to their citizens rather than relying on private health care.

Discuss the advantages and disadvantages of having a free system, and give your opinion.

A In many countries, basic health care provision for the population is funded and maintained by the state, yet for many others only private care is available. This raises the question of why some countries choose one system over the other. What are the pros and cons of offering free healthcare?

B Basic health care is a basic human right, but having a free system has both upsides and downsides. In this essay I will discuss them, including the ideas of how such a system is essential for poorer elements of society and the problems of paying for and maintaining a system like this. Overall, I think the advantages outweigh the disadvantages.

C Some countries offer a free health care system and others rely on private health care. What are the advantages and disadvantages of free health care and what is my opinion on it?

TIP 10

Your introductory paragraph for this kind of essay should:
- clearly state the situation/context and question that you will discuss in the body of the essay in a way that sounds engaging to the reader
- *not* simply repeat the words in the question, but paraphrase the ideas into your own words
- give your position clearly at the beginning of the essay because this is a key part of the question.

11 ▷ Read these conclusions for the essay question in exercise 10 and, in pairs, discuss the questions below.

A In conclusion, there are many advantages and disadvantages to having a free health care system.

B Overall, the advantages of offering free health care outweigh the disadvantages. Whilst there clearly is a financial cost to governments and taxpayers, the fact that everybody has access to health care regardless of their financial situation easily justifies this cost.

C In summary, weighing up both sides of the argument, I would say that although providing free health care does have some downsides, particularly financial ones for the country in question, the fact that no one in that society has to worry about medical bills more than justifies having it.

1 Which conclusion(s) do you prefer? Give reasons.
2 Are there any discourse markers or other phrases in them that you could use in your own conclusions? Underline them.

TIP 11

Your concluding paragraph should briefly summarise what you have said in the body of your essay and state your own position on the question.

EXAM SKILLS

12 ▷ Answer the Writing Task 2 below.

You should spend about 40 minutes on this task.

In many countries around the world, life expectancy is increasing.

Discuss the advantages and disadvantages of this situation and give your own opinion.

Write at least 250 words.

GO FURTHER ONLINE

LISTENING

IN THIS UNIT YOU WILL LEARN HOW TO

- correctly answer table completion and note completion tasks
- use headings and completed cells in tables to help you predict correct answers
- correctly use a variety of determiners and quantifiers.

LEAD-IN

01 ▶ Complete the table by choosing the correct options for each part of the IELTS Listening test.

Section	Situation	Number of Speakers
1	everyday, social / educational or training	1 / 2 / 2 or more
2	everyday, social / educational or training	1 / 2 / 2 or more
3	everyday, social / educational or training	1 / 2 / 2 or more
4	everyday, social / educational or training	1 / 2 / 2 or more

02 ▶ With a partner, tick the situations you might hear in the Listening test.

1 Two people discussing what they like to eat to stay healthy
2 A university lecturer talking about the history of a medical procedure
3 A guide instructing people how to find a gym and a swimming pool in a town
4 A university tutor discussing the contents of a fitness magazine with her students
5 A call to a customer services centre for information on an exercise class
6 Three students discussing a research project on life expectancy in Japan
7 The organiser of a sports day describing what happened in a football match
8 A student telling her parents about her sports team at university

03 ▶ Of the correct answers to exercise 2, in which sections of the test (1–4) would you expect to hear each one?

[TABLE COMPLETION]

 For this task, the correct answers are specific words from the recording in the same form as you hear them, and in the same order as the questions. Make sure you check your answers for errors like the following, which can lose marks:

- incorrect spelling
- exceeding the given word limit
- repeating words that are already in the table
- omitting key details such as measurements (km, grams).

04▶ Using the information you are given in each table, discuss with a partner what you think are the situational contexts for each one. Then use the words in the box to complete the titles for tables A, B and C.

TIP 04

Read the table before you listen to help you decide what kind of context or situation is being described. This can help you determine what kind of information you are going to hear.

| Records | History | Centre | Classes | in |
| Exhibition | Discoveries | Sports | Medical | Olympic |

A _____ _____ _____

Event	World record	Year	Room
Men's 100m sprint	9.58 seconds	2009	1 _____
2 _____	29 min 17.45 sec	2005	Parker Room
Javelin		1990	Main Auditorium
…	…	…	…

B _____ _____ _____

Discovery	Scientist	Nationality	Modern benefits
3 _____	Alexander Fleming	Scottish	a) combat bacteria b) development of antibiotics
Germ theory	Girolamo Fracastoro	Italian	a) smallpox vaccination b) combat viruses
DNA	Friedrich Miescher	4 _____	a) combat diseases b) 5 _____
…	…	…	…

C _____ _____ _____

Class	Days and Times	Instructor
Aerobics	Mondays at 7 pm Wednesdays at 6 _____	Susan
Futsal	Saturdays at 12 pm and 3 pm	7 _____
8 _____	Sundays at 4 pm	Ting
…	…	…

05 ▶ Look at exercise 4 again. For which questions (1–5) might these be possible answers?

Example: *question 1 – d (The Archer Suite)*

a Women's 10K
b Marco and Victor
c Swiss
d The Archer Suite
e gene therapy
f table tennis
g penicillin
h 6.30 pm

TIP 05

Use the time before the recording starts to predict what information is missing. Predicting can help you decide what you are listening for, e.g. what part of speech (noun, verb, adjective, adverb) and what kind of information. You will also know from the instructions in the question how many words are required for the correct answer.

06 ▶ In which section (1–4) of the test would you expect to see each table? Listen to the start of these recordings and confirm your answers.

10

Recording 1: Table A: Section _____
Recording 2: Table B: Section _____
Recording 3: Table C: Section _____

TIP 06

Table completion tasks usually occur in Section 1 but can appear in other sections of the Listening test, with the complexity of the table and the recordings becoming more challenging in the later sections of the test.

07 ▶ You are going to hear someone asking for information at a Societies' Fair – an exhibition where university clubs display information about their activities and hope to attract new members. With a partner, discuss what sort of information you might hear for each gap.

TIP 07

Use the table heading to help you focus on what information you need to complete.

University Societies' Fair

Societies	Location	Contact
1 _____	Room A12	Paul
Vegan	2 _____	Peter
Healthy Eating	3 _____	Catherine
4 _____	Gym	Sarah
Road Running	Car Park	5 _____

08 ▶ Listen and complete the table. Write NO MORE THAN TWO WORDS AND/OR A NUMBER for each answer.

11

09 The sentences are taken from the recording. For each sentence, choose which of the three options are grammatically possible (there can be more than one correct answer for each question).

1 Oh, there are **a number of the** / **numbers of** / **a number of** socs that might suit you.
2 Peter and Paul are actually brothers. **Both they** / **Both of them** / **Both** are really nice.
3 I don't think **either of those** / **either of** / **either** socs are for me.
4 **All of the** / **All of** / **All** main types of exercise are covered here.
5 **None of those** / **Not of those** / **None of** are really my kind of thing – I'm more of a runner.
6 **The whole** / **The whole of the** / **The whole of** university turns out to support them.

10 Correct the mistakes in bold in this leaflet. One of the words/phrases in bold is correct.

Healthy Eating Society

(**1**) **Some of people** assume that the Healthy Eating Society (HES) is simply about salad and seeds, and that our members are (**2**) **all of them** humourless and over-serious. The truth is completely different. The HES encourages you to enjoy food – (**3**) **any of the** food – and there are (**4**) **none** meals that are 'forbidden'. We just emphasise moderation.

Twice a week, (**5**) **every of us** go out for dinner together. (**6**) **Some of** restaurants we have visited serve food that is high in fat, but that is the whole point of eating healthily – treat yourself, but not too often.

And every week a group of us get together to cook a meal to share, which can have some interesting results!

(**7**) **Many of the** people believe that you can't both be healthy *and* eat high-calorie meals. We believe that you don't have to choose (**8**) **either** one above the other: it is possible to do (**9**) **each**.

And this is an idea that (**10**) **whole** of our members would agree with. Come along to our stall at the Societies' Fair and see for yourself.

NOTE COMPLETION

> In note completion tasks you can apply similar strategies to those you use for table completion.

11 ▶ Look at the note completion task. What type of information do you expect to hear for questions 1–6? Choose from a–f. Do not answer the questions yet.

Questions 1–6
Complete the notes below.
*Write **NO MORE THAN TWO WORDS AND/OR A NUMBER** for each answer.*

University Road Running Society

President of Society: 1 _____
Members run on average 20K each 2 _____
Last race took place over 3 _____ in 4 _____
Team vest for this year: white with a 5 _____ stripe.
Annual membership fee: 6 £_____

a price
b period of time
c distance
d name
e design or colour
f place

12 ▶ For questions 1–6 in exercise 11, with a partner, discuss which is the least likely answer from the three options given in each case. Give reasons.

1 Claire Enwark / Claire / Clare Ennark
2 week / fortnight / year
3 100km / 10km / 100m
4 Oxford / a sports centre / Manchester
5 blue dark / dark blue / pale blue
6 150 / 5000 / 50

13 ▶ Listen and answer the questions in exercise 11.

12

EXAM SKILLS

14 ▶ Listen and answer questions 1–10.

13

Questions 1–5
Complete the table below.
*Write **NO MORE THAN TWO WORDS AND/OR A NUMBER** for each answer.*

Healthy Eating Society Weekly Plan

Day	Activity	Time	Location of meal
Wednesday	Restaurant: 1 _____ food	7.30	High Street
Thursday	Prepare a meal together	8.00	2 _____
Friday	Restaurant: European food	3 _____	4 _____ in town
Saturday	5 _____	12.00	canteen

Questions 6–10
Complete the notes below.
*Write **NO MORE THAN TWO WORDS AND/OR A NUMBER** for each answer.*

Extra information for Healthy Eating Society members

Cost of membership: 6 _____
Average length of restaurant dinner: 7 _____
Leave the waiters an extra: 8 _____
To book a place, best to send Catherine: 9 _____
Rule – never talk about: 10 _____

GO FURTHER ONLINE

UNIT / 02: HEALTH

SPEAKING

IN THIS UNIT YOU WILL LEARN HOW TO

- improve your score for Fluency and Coherence (FC)
- extend your Part 1 and Part 3 answers
- correctly use and pronounce a range of discourse markers.

LEAD-IN

01▶ The following idioms describe problems you should try to avoid if you want to express yourself fluently. What do they mean in the context of the Speaking test? Use a dictionary if you need to.

1 going round in circles
2 losing your thread
3 stumbling over your words
4 labouring the point
5 beating about the bush
6 talking at a mile a minute

02▶ Complete the sentences using the idioms from exercise 1 in the correct form.

1 I got too nervous in the Speaking test and kept _____ .
2 I was really nervous at the start of the Speaking test and realised I was _____ , so I took a deep breath and slowed down.
3 I'm not going to _____ – unless you start working harder in class, you won't get more than a 6.0 in your IELTS test.
4 This Reading question is impossible. I keep thinking I've got the answer, but then realise I haven't. I'm just _____ .
5 My teacher gave me a lower score in my Writing Task 2 essay. She said my second paragraph was far too long and I ended up _____ . She said I should have moved on to discuss some other aspects of the question.
6 In Speaking Part 2, the candidate began OK, but then she _____ and started talking about things unrelated to the task card.

TIP 01

Including idiomatic language is a very good way to improve your Speaking score. However, you should only use the idioms and phrases you are comfortable with, and that you know how to use correctly and appropriately.

In the Speaking test, 25% of the marks are given for Fluency and Coherence (FC). You can lose marks for the following:

- repetition (of language or ideas)
- having to correct yourself too often (because you are not being understood)
- talking too quickly or slowly
- long pauses before answering or between sentences
- overusing / not using / incorrectly using discourse markers or linking phrases
- giving answers that are too short.

03 ▷ Listen to two candidates answering a Part 3 question. Discuss with a partner which of the two would get more credit for Fluency and Coherence (FC). Give reasons.

14

TIP 03

Don't worry if you are not producing entirely accurate sentences when you are talking. There is a big difference in the accuracy of *spoken* and *written* language. For example, saying 'um' and 'uh' is a normal part of natural speech – it will not affect your score if they occasionally appear in your answers. Equally, beginning a sentence with *and* or *but*, which you should not do when you write, is perfectly natural in spoken English.

[ANSWERING PART 1 QUESTIONS]

 Part 1 questions ask you to talk about personally focused, familiar topics, and to respond with your personal experiences and opinions. You are not expected to speak at length, but make sure you answer the question and try to give complete answers, supported with examples, reasons, etc. Unlike in Part 3 questions, you are not expected to bring in other opinions or views or a balanced argument.

04 ▷ Listen to and read the answers to this Part 1 question. Decide which candidate gives an appropriate answer. Give reasons for your choice.

15

Examiner	How often do you eat healthy meals?
Candidate 1	I'm very much a sociable type of person, so whether I'm eating at a restaurant or at home, as long as there's company around me – could be with friends, could be with family, could be both – personally, I tend not to notice too much where I am and I'll eat pretty much anything.
Candidate 2	Well, there's a lot of pressure these days on people to eat the right sort of things. However, it seems like every day there are new pieces of conflicting advice from the government, or from doctors, about what we should and shouldn't be eating, so who actually knows? For example, one week there's a study telling us chocolate is bad for us and then the next week, there's another which says it's good for us. I try to eat healthy food when I can, but think it depends on what you mean by 'healthy'.
Candidate 3	It depends what you mean by 'healthy', but I try to keep my intake of junk food down to a minimum. And most days I make sure that I have at least some fruit and vegetables, even if it isn't as much as I should. Also because I'm young and in relatively good shape, I don't worry about my diet too much at the moment to be honest.

Discourse markers are words and phrases that link ideas together and make what you say more coherent. They cover a variety of functions: giving reasons, examples, introducing contrasts, etc. Try to use a variety of them to connect your ideas. For example, for adding information, you can use simple everyday markers like *and, as well, too*, but also more lexically complex ones like *In addition, I would also add*, etc.

0 5 ▶ Look back at the candidates' answers in exercise 4. They use common everyday discourse markers. Find examples for each of the categories below.

Adding detail to the previous point: _____

Introducing a contrasting idea: _____

Giving a reason or explanation: _____

Giving an example or clarification: _____

Introducing an opinion: _____

0 6 ▶ Look at the first part of this answer to a Part 1 question. Then listen to four different ways to continue the answer and complete the table with words from the box.

16

Examiner How do you like to relax?

Candidate If I had to choose, I'd say that I most like to sink into the sofa, put my feet up and lose myself in a good movie.

Discourse markers
On top of that   That said   In particular   The thing is

Functions
A Giving a reason for the previous point
B Giving an example related to the previous point
C Adding detail to the previous point
D Introducing an idea that contrasts with the previous point

Candidate	Discourse marker used to extend answer	Function of the discourse marker
1		
2		
3		
4		

0 7 ▶ Look at the first part of an answer to the examiner's question and think of how you could develop it with a) a reason, b) an example, c) an additional detail and d) a contrast. Use the discourse marker given.

Examiner How important is it for you to eat healthily?

Candidate It's something I really want to do more of, as I really value my health, and I'm pretty sure I don't do it often enough.

a (*reason*) The thing is, …

b (*example*) For instance, …

c (*additional detail*) I would add that …

d (*contrast*) Having said that, …

DEVELOPING PART 3 ANSWERS

While you should keep your answers on a personal level in Part 1, you will lose marks in Part 3 if you do the same thing again. For example, the question 'Which is more important in sport, winning or taking part?' may sound like it is asking what is more important *to you*; however, in Part 3, you should aim to widen your answers and relate them to other people, different societies and hypothetical situations.

08▷ **Listen to an answer to the Part 3 question and answer the questions below.**

17

Examiner What reasons do people have for becoming vegetarian?

1 Does the candidate only answer on a personal level or does he 'widen' his answer?

2 How many different points does the candidate make?

3 Match the discourse markers he uses (i–iv) with their functions (a–d).

i	On the grounds that	a	adding detail to an idea
ii	To build upon my point a little more	b	giving a reason or justification
iii	Looking at it from another point of view	c	concluding an argument with a final point
iv	Ultimately	d	contrasting by giving a different perspective/opinion

09▷ **Read the Part 3 question and answer and choose the discourse markers that fit best and that you think would receive a higher score from an examiner. There may be more than one answer.**

Examiner Do you think governments should have more influence on people's health?

Candidate Absolutely. I strongly believe governments should introduce laws to help society reduce the amount of unhealthy foods we consume. Some countries have proposed a tax on fizzy drinks (**1**) **so that / on the grounds that / essentially** it will discourage people from drinking so much. (**2**) **Such as my country / In particular, this is true of my country / Take my country by way of example**, where consumption of soft drinks is incredibly high. (**3**) **That said / But / On the other hand**, we must take responsibility for our own health (**4**) **as well / also / too**. We cannot expect politicians to do everything. (**5**) **Ultimately / Overall / At the end of the day**, we are the only ones who can improve our health.

TIP 09

Make sure with discourse markers that you learn the differences in function and usage between them. Don't assume that because they have a common function you can use them interchangeably. For example, not all discourse markers appear at the beginning of a sentence. Some are used as a subordinate clause within a sentence, e.g. 'Playing tennis, *to name one example*, is a fantastic way to keep in shape.' You should be able to find all the discourse markers in this unit in a good dictionary and see examples of how they are used.

1 0 ▶ Look back at all the discourse markers in this section. In pairs, discuss the following questions.

1 Which ones can you use confidently?

2 Which ones are you less confident about using?

3 Can you think of any discourse markers for the following functions that we have not mentioned in this section?

- Adding detail to the previous point
- Introducing a contrasting idea
- Giving a reason or explanation
- Giving an example or clarification
- Introducing an opinion
- Concluding with a final point or summarising an argument

[EXAM SKILLS]

1 1 ▶ Make notes about how you would answer these Part 1 questions. Then ask and answer them with a partner.

1 Do you prefer eating healthy food or fast food?

2 Which sport do you play or do regularly?

3 Do you think you have enough free time to relax?

GO FURTHER ONLINE

1 2 ▶ Make notes about how you would answer these Part 3 questions. Then ask and answer them with a partner.

1 Why has convenience food become so popular over the past few years?

2 In the future, what sort of relaxation activities will be popular?

3 What benefits do competitive sports have for the people taking part?

4 Should physical education be compulsory for all school children?

READING

IN THIS UNIT YOU WILL LEARN HOW TO

- answer True / False / Not Given and multiple-choice questions
- identify main and supporting ideas
- use past tenses correctly.

LEAD-IN

0 1 ▷ **Ask and answer these questions in pairs.**

1 What form(s) of art do you like?
2 Are you good at any forms of art?
3 Can you name any famous works of art that you like?
4 What forms of art or artists are popular in your country?

0 2 ▷ **Match a word from box A with a synonym or near-synonym from box B.**

A		
installations	materials	concepts
groundbreaking	abstract	sculpture
experiment	techniques	cast

B		
ideas	innovate	conceptual
media	innovative	methods
mould	exhibitions	figure

[TRUE, FALSE, NOT GIVEN]

◎ This task type asks you to look at statements and decide if they agree with the information in the text or not. TRUE means the information matches what the text says, FALSE that the information is contradicted by the text, and NOT GIVEN means that the statement is neither confirmed nor contradicted. NOT GIVEN statements often refer to ideas that are mentioned but not enough information is given for you to say if it is TRUE or FALSE.

TIP 0 3

Skim read the text quickly before looking at the questions. This will give you a general idea of the structure of the text which will help you locate information quickly and avoid wasting time looking in the wrong part of the text.

0 3 ▷ **Read the text on pages 53–54 in one minute. (Ignore the underlining in the text.) Which statement matches the structure of the text?**

A A history of Modern Art
B A look at the similarities and differences between two Modern artists
C A look at the strengths and weaknesses of two Modern artists

04 ▶ **Which paragraph contains the following information?**

1 The materials Rauschenberg worked with
2 Why Warhol is more famous than Rauschenberg
3 A definition of Modern Art
4 The artists' early lives
5 Warhol's main work
6 Both artists' performance art

05 ▶ **Read Paragraph B carefully. Match each statement 1–3 with its answer. One is True, one is False and one is Not Given.**

1 Rauschenberg was often unwell as a child.
2 Both artists had a positive relationship with their mothers.
3 Warhol began to develop his ability as an artist when he went to New York.

06 ▶ **Highlight the parts of the text where you found the information for exercise 5. Why might some candidates think the Not Given statement was True or False?**

07 ▶ **Statements 1–3 are Not Given in the text. Match them with the reasons some candidates might think they *are* given (a–c).**

1 Conventional materials are not used in Modern Art.
2 Rauschenberg and Warhol influenced each other's work.
3 Warhol grew up in a working class part of his home town.

a This information is given but about a different person.
b Some of the words are used in the text.
c We might expect this to be true, given the focus on these two artists in the text.

08 ▶ **Read paragraphs A, B and C. Are the following True, False or Not Given?**

1 Neither artist is known by their birth name.
2 Rauschenberg first achieved artistic fame in his home town.
3 Paris was the best place for Modern artists in the 1950s.
4 Neither artist believed in distinguishing between high and low art.
5 Art critics were shocked by Rauschenberg's use of everyday objects in his work.

TIP 06

Not Given statements are often based on information you might expect to be in the text but isn't, and often use words that do appear in the text itself. Read each statement and the relevant part of the text very carefully before deciding whether the ideas are given or not. Make sure you are clear who is being referred to in the text.

20TH CENTURY MODERN ART CHAMPIONS: RAUSCHENBERG AND WARHOL

A The term 'Modern Art' refers to art from the period 1860s to 1970s and encompasses the work of such well-known names as Vincent Van Gogh, Paul Cézanne and Pablo Picasso. Modern Art represents the discarding of the artistic traditions of the past in favour of a spirit of experimentation. It conceptualised the functions of art in new ways and introduced different ideas about the nature of materials. Two artists who had a huge impact on modern art in the twentieth century were Robert Rauschenberg and Andy Warhol. Arguably, they both had an important influence on art as we know it today, but whereas Warhol became a household name, Rauschenberg is remembered only by those in the artistic community.

B Milton Ernest Rauschenberg, who later became known as Robert Rauschenberg, was born in Port Arthur, Texas in 1925, while [1]<u>Andrew Warhola – Andy Warhol – was born in 1928 in Pittsburgh, Pennsylvania</u>. Both were of European heritage, born to working class families. In Rauschenberg's case, his childhood environment was hardly inspiring – a blue-collar town that has been described as a 'cultural wasteland with no art'. His father had no understanding of art and gave him no encouragement. His mother, on the other hand, supported her son as much as she could. For much of his life, [2]<u>Rauschenberg had been waiting for the opportunity to leave his hot, sticky, industrial home town</u> and he did so in 1944, moving to California. Like Rauschenberg, Warhol was close to his mother. A sickly child, he spent a lot of time at home with her. Though he was missing a lot of school, [3]<u>he was developing his artistic skills and tastes</u>, so it was actually an important period of his life. He eventually enrolled in the Carnegie Institute in Pittsburgh, where he took his first steps into the art world. Eventually, both artists gravitated towards New York, [4]<u>which, by the early 1950s, had taken over from Paris as the centre of the Avant Garde*</u>.

C Artistically, what the two have in common is the willingness to innovate, take chances and be different from everything that had gone before. Both were a new type of artist who embraced and drew inspiration from popular culture. Both rejected the orthodoxical views of 'high' and 'low' art. To their minds, anything could be art. Rauschenberg produced paintings and sculptures and even combined them to produce mixed media, working with a variety of less conventional materials including silk, metal and glass. [5]<u>It has been said that</u> 'the whole world was his canvas'. He was the ultimate scavenger, prepared to use anything he could find in his artworks, even going so far as to incorporate such disparate objects as socks, bedspreads and car parts into his work. His 1953 piece entitled *Automobile Tire Print* was conceptual art as never seen before and would ensure him a place in the art history books.

D Warhol's work was equally innovative, drawing from the world around him, but somewhat different in approach. He rose to fame with his iconic *Campbell's Soup Can* series, which even today is seen as one of the most definitive images of the Pop Art movement. [6]<u>The simple red and white depictions of an everyday item have been hanging in kitchens and cafés around the world since the 1960s.</u> It's a similar story for his iconic series of movie star portraits – including such popular culture figures as Marilyn Monroe, Elvis Presley and Elizabeth Taylor. Like Rauschenberg, he didn't limit himself to just one medium. In 1964 he produced his first exhibition of sculpture, which consisted of hundreds of imitation supermarket product boxes, most famously Brillo and Heinz. It was an exhibition which confounded critics and helped cement his credentials as an artist challenging the status quo.

E Not content with subverting the conventional art forms of painting and sculpture, both Rauschenberg and Warhol experimented beyond them. Rauschenberg collaborated with musicians, costume designers, dancers and even scientists, never ceasing to expand the possibilities of what art could be. He has been described as 'the wind blowing through the art world, pollinating everything'. Warhol, too, dabbled in other fields, including rock music and film, and engaged in Performance Art, with his multimedia show *The Exploding Plastic Inevitable* becoming one of the works he is best remembered for. This show pioneered many lighting innovations which rock musicians have been using in their shows since the 1960s.

F Both Rauschenberg and Warhol were extremely prolific, the former's career spanning six decades, whilst the latter is a household name whose work has been adopted by several generations. What differentiates them is that Warhol courted publicity. He wrote books and co-founded a magazine, *Interview*, which reported on film, fashion and popular culture. He socialised with celebrities and had several TV shows, which helped spread his fame. In contrast, Rauschenberg didn't seek the limelight. His name is not widely known outside the art world, but that does not diminish his influence upon it. Given that Warhol's work is immensely reproducible and commercial, brightly coloured and attractive to buyers, it is easy to see why Rauschenberg's productions with salvaged garbage and street signs would lack the same popular appeal. However, this great innovator still deserves to be remembered for his unique contribution to Modern Art.

* Avant Garde – *new and modern ideas in art*

MULTIPLE-CHOICE QUESTIONS

 The multiple-choice task type consists of a mix of questions and sentences to complete. In both cases, there are four options to choose from. Some sets of questions will focus on one paragraph or part of the text. Others will focus on the text as a whole. The questions follow the order of the text.

09 ▸ Read the question below but cover the options. Write your own answer. Then compare it to the options.

1 What is the main similarity between Warhol and Rauschenberg in terms of their work?
A They always used unusual materials.
B They both became very famous.
C They were both risk takers.
D Their work always combined painting and sculpture.

TIP 09
A useful strategy is to use the key words in the question stem – or synonyms of them – to help you identify the correct part of the text. Read the sentence or sentences carefully. Think of your own answer to the question and see which of the options matches it the closest.

10 ▸ Read the parts of the text (A–D) that correspond to each option in exercise 9. Match them with the explanations (1–4) that follow.

A 'He [Rauschenberg] was the ultimate scavenger, prepared to use anything he could find in his artworks, even going so far as to incorporate such disparate objects as socks, bedspreads and car parts into his work.'

B '… whereas Warhol became a household name, Rauschenberg is remembered only by those in the artistic community.'

C 'Artistically, what the two have in common is the willingness to innovate, take chances and be different from everything that had gone before.'

D 'Rauschenberg produced paintings and sculptures and even combined them to produce mixed media, working with a variety of less conventional materials including silk, metal and glass.'
'Like Rauschenberg, he [Warhol] didn't limit himself to just one medium. In 1964 he produced his first exhibition of sculpture, which consisted of hundreds of imitation supermarket product boxes, most famously Brillo and Heinz.'

1 This cannot be the answer because the artists produced paintings and sculpture, not always a combination of the two.
2 This is the correct answer.
3 This cannot be the answer because it only refers to Rauschenberg.
4 This cannot be the answer because it tells us that only Warhol gained fame.

TIP 10
Remember that all the options will be mentioned in the text in some way but only one will completely answer the question.

11 ▸ Now answer this question by finding the relevant section of the text. Explain to your partner why the other options are incorrect.

In what way are the artists' backgrounds similar?
A Their mothers were the most important influence on them.
B They were born in America to families with ancestry in Europe.
C Their families pushed them to go to Art School.
D Their families moved to New York.

IDENTIFYING MAIN AND SUPPORTING IDEAS

 Some multiple-choice questions test your ability to identify the main idea of a paragraph as opposed to the supporting ideas. The main idea is the message the writer wants to communicate with the paragraph, and the supporting ideas are facts, examples, etc. which back up the main idea.

12▶ Answer the two questions. Explain how you decided on your answers.

1 The purpose of Paragraph D is …
   A to illustrate Warhol's love of fame.
   B to highlight the differences between Warhol and Rauschenberg.
   C to suggest Warhol's work was better than Rauschenberg's.
   D to give an overview of Warhol's early ground-breaking work.

2 What is the main idea of paragragh E?
   A Both artists worked outside of traditional artistic genres.
   B Warhol's work influenced rock music.
   C Both artists engaged in performance art.
   D The Exploding Plastic Inevitable is a well-known piece of work.

TIP 12

Typically the main idea is at the start of a paragraph in the opening sentences, but this is not always the case, so skim read the whole paragraph to form an opinion of the general message it is trying to communicate, and then look at the options to see which one paraphrases your opinion. The incorrect options are often mentioned in the paragraph as supporting ideas.

GRAMMAR FOCUS: PAST TENSES

13▶ Match the underlined parts (1–6) of the reading text on page 54 with a tense.

present perfect continuous	_____
present perfect simple	_____
past perfect simple	_____
past perfect continuous	_____
past simple	_____
past continuous	_____

14▶ Match each tense in exercise 13 with its use.

a To describe completed actions in the past
b To describe an action happening around a given time in the past
c To describe a continuous action that started in the past and is still happening now
d To describe an action completed before a given time or other action in the past
e To describe an action that happened in the past but has a connection to or important effect on the present
f To describe an action or repeated actions up to a given time in the past

15▶ Choose the correct form of the verb.

1 Warhol's celebrity portraits **had been / have been / were** popular since the 1960s.
2 Rauschenberg **was marrying / married / has married** Susan Weil in 1950 but their marriage only **had lasted / lasted / had been lasting** until 1953.
3 Artists **have now been developing / had now been developing / had now developed** Rauschenberg's ideas for more than half a century.
4 The advent of digital technology **had / has had / has been having** a big impact on the art world.
5 When Rauschenberg arrived in New York, Warhol **had been living and working / has been living and working / lived and worked** there for several years.

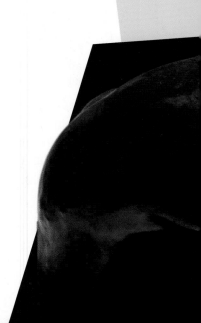

1 6 ▶ Read the passage and answer questions 1–9.

MODERN AND POST-MODERN SCULPTURE

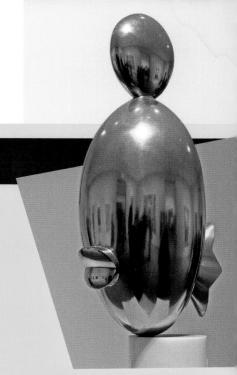

A Modern sculpture has its origins in the work of Frenchman Auguste Rodin. Born into a modest family in 1840, Rodin began his creative journey in the 1860s, a journey that would lead to him being remembered as the 'bridge' between traditional and modern sculpture. Before Rodin, sculpture told stories about the past: religion, history, myth and literature. Sculptures typically left little to the imagination. Figures tended to be idealised in some way to avoid any imperfections of the model. Rodin can be considered a realist in that he refused to improve on what he saw in front of him. He considered all of nature beautiful and if a model was old and wrinkled, he would be portrayed as such. Moreover, like much of the art that he helped inspire for later generations, his work spoke to the emotions and imagination: both his and his viewers'. The stories he told were internal and conceptual and there was no right or wrong way to interpret them.

B Rodin was inspired by the fragments of Greek and Roman sculpture that were being discovered by archaeologists during his time. He was one of the first sculptors to treat fragments or parts of figures as complete works of art. One of his most famous works is *Large hand of a pianist*. In this piece he demonstrated one of the characteristics of Modern Art – to make visible things that are not, such as energy, sound and rhythm. He sculpted elongated fingers to make visible music being played effortlessly. Groundbreaking for its time, this concept has been taken forward by sculptors right up to the present day.

C Rodin worked mainly in bronze and was fascinated by the effect of light on irregular surfaces. In particular, he realised that light bouncing off textured bronze surfaces could create the illusion of movement. He pioneered two new techniques: *marcottage* and *assemblage*. *Marcottage* means creating a new work by putting together pieces from different existing works. *Assemblage*, which was further developed later by artists like Picasso, began with Rodin's technique of repeatedly casting the same figure and using multiple casts to create a new piece.

D The Late Modern Period (1900 to 1945), which saw the rise of extreme distortion* – and then abstraction** – in sculpture can be seen as a natural development from the pioneering work of Rodin. Romanian French sculptor Constantin Brancusi was one of the leading exponents of this style. He attempted to reduce the physical world to three basic forms: egg, pebble and grass blade. The development of Rodin's assemblage also continued and came to represent the *building* of sculptures rather than carving or moulding them. Picasso's sculptures were called 'Constructions' and used a range of different objects and materials. The rise of minimalism, a movement that reduces sculpture to its most essential features, comes very much from this tradition.

E Thanks to the work of these 'forefathers', Modern sculpture embraces many forms and styles. It is increasingly common to see it created outdoors, often in view of the spectators. One form of outdoor sculpture is known as Earth Art, which is based on nature and makes use of rocks, branches, leaves, dirt, soil, water and other naturally occurring materials. Another offshoot is kinetic sculpture – sculpture that involves moving parts. Mobiles are one such example. Early examples had moving parts powered by wind or touch and later some were even powered by machines. Other pioneering forms of Modern sculpture include ice sculptures used in culinary art and sound sculptures – such as Aeolian harps 'played' by the wind.

F Art installations are another example of how sculpture has developed in the Modern and Post-modern eras. They can be defined as a work of art consisting of multiple components, often though not necessarily in mixed media, usually exhibited in an indoor gallery space in an arrangement specified by the artist. Installations are multi-sensory experiences built for a specific time and space. They are often highly imaginative and bring different materials together to create something original and unexpected. The audience is drawn to them because they are immersive, often allowing audience participation. One such installation was *Cloud City*, a huge construction created by Argentinian sculptor Tomás Saraceno. It consisted of 16 interconnected modules, 16.5 by 8.5 metres, displayed on the roof of the Metropolitan Museum of Art in New York. Visitors were able to walk up and inside the modules.

*distortion – *twisting out of shape*
**abstraction – *depicting ideas, not actual objects*

G In fact, these days sculpture increasingly involves the public. The use of digital technology has further increased the possibilities of creating art that reaches everyone. Digital installations allow artists to 'play' with the boundary between the real world and virtual reality and give new opportunities for active participation in the artwork by the spectator. Touch, physical participation and social interaction are now common features of the experience of going to see art. Modern sculpture has come a long way since Rodin got the ball rolling in the 1860s, and the future promises limitless possibilities.

Questions 1–6

Do the following statements agree with the information given in the reading passage above?

Write

TRUE if the statement agrees with the information

FALSE if the statement contradicts the information

NOT GIVEN if there is no information on this

1 Before Rodin, sculpture was very realistic.
2 Rodin expected people to interpret his sculptures in their own way.
3 Rodin studied the sculpture techniques of the Greeks and Romans.
4 Rodin felt that incomplete figures were still artistic works.
5 His *Large Hand of a Pianist* tries to convey music being played.
6 Rodin believed the surfaces of sculptures should be smooth.

Questions 7–9

*Choose the correct letter, **A, B, C** or **D**.*

7 Assemblage
   A was first used by Pablo Picasso.
   B uses only three basic forms.
   C involves several artists working on the same theme.
   D creates a single composition from a number of versions of an individual.

8 What is the purpose of paragraph E?
   A to explain the meaning of Earth Art
   B to explain how kinetic sculpture has evolved
   C to introduce the idea of outdoor sculpture
   D to show examples of innovative forms of Modern sculpture

9 Art installations
   A always use mixed media.
   B are always outdoors.
   C usually allow viewers to interact with them.
   D typically last a long time.

GO FURTHER ONLINE

WRITING

IN THIS UNIT YOU WILL LEARN HOW TO

- describe changes on a map, including which tenses to use
- summarise information with appropriate discourse markers
- ensure good Coherence and Cohesion in your answer.

LEAD-IN

0 1 ▷ Put the verbs into the correct category.

demolish	extend	knock down	enlarge	put up	alter
modernise	replace	tear down	develop	flatten	erect
relocate	expand	renovate	convert	construct	

Build	Change	Remove
		demolish

0 2 ▷ For each of the verbs in exercise 1, what are the nouns? Use a dictionary if necessary.

Example: demolish (v) – *demolition* (n)   extend (v) – *extension* (n)

0 3 ▷ Ask and answer the questions in pairs. Include as many words from exercises 1 and 2 as possible.

1 Describe where you live. What kind of housing / facilities / features does your area have?
2 How has your home town changed since you were little? What are the key changes?
3 If you could change anything about the architecture and design of your home town, what would you change and why?

0 4 ▷ Look at the exam task. Match the introductions (1–4) with the comments on them (A–D).

The maps show part of the town of Poulton in 1900 and 1935.
Summarise the information by selecting and reporting the main features and make comparisons where relevant.

Poulton In 1900

This task requires you to summarise the main changes to a plan or map between two time periods. There are three important elements to this kind of text:

- a good introductory sentence which explains what information will follow
- middle paragraphs that focus on the key changes in a concise form, supported by examples
- a summary of the main points presented.

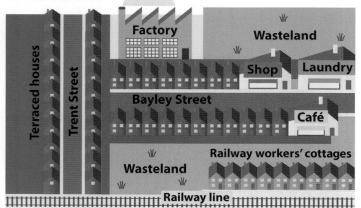

Poulton In 1935

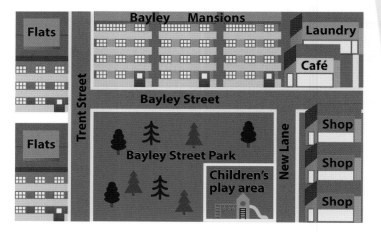

1 The maps show that in 1900 there were many terraced houses, some railway workers' cottages, a factory, café, small shop, a railway line and some wasteland. In 1935, this situation had changed and had become a residential area with shops and a park.

2 The maps show part of the town of Poulton in 1900 and 1935.

3 The maps show how the residential area around Bayley Street and Trent Street in Poulton was modernised between the years 1900 and 1935.

4 Bayley Street and Trent Street have changed a lot in the time period.

TIP 0 4

Introductions should set the scene for what comes next in the text. Avoid simply repeating the words in the question and write one or two concise sentences which clarify for the reader what you are going to talk about.

A This introduction is taken directly from the question.

B This is a good introduction to the maps as it is clear what the writer is going to talk about.

C This gives very little information about the maps, so is not a full introduction.

D This includes too many details to be an introduction and includes examples that should be in the main body of the answer.

05 ▸ Look again at the two maps. Categorise the following features as either *industrial*, *residential*, *commercial* or *recreational*.

Example: blocks of flats – *residential*

children's play area

Bayley Mansions

café

terraced houses

railway line

laundry

Bayley Street Park

shops

wasteland

TIP 05

In the main body of your answer, you will get more marks if you *summarise* the information in the map rather than listing all the changes. Try to group details together under main headings; for example, a swimming pool, cinema and bowling alley are all 'recreational facilities'.

06 ▸ Look at the two maps and make notes on how the area changed:

- residentially
- commercially
- industrially
- recreationally

07 ▸ Read a sample answer for the question. Choose the best discourse markers.

TIP 07

Use a wide range of discourse markers to illustrate for the reader the points you are making; for example, adding a similar point, contrasting or summarising.

SAMPLE ANSWER

The maps depict an area of the town of Poulton in the years 1900 and 1935 and the urban developments that took place. (1) **Overall / In summary**, there were a number of notable changes to the buildings and amenities of this area.

In 1900, this area had a combination of residential and industrial features, but by 1935 the industrial features had largely disappeared. (2) **When / Whereas** in 1900 a railway line ran through the neighbourhood, by 1935 this had been removed. (3) **Furthermore / Nevertheless**, the terraced houses which used to dominate the 1900 map had been replaced by blocks of flats by 1935, and the areas of wasteland had gone.

(4) **Another major change to the area / One thing they did** in 1935 was the development of more commercial and recreational features. The demolition of a second row of houses on Bayley Street and the removal of the railway line made room for a spacious park and children´s play area. (5) **On the commercial side / Thinking commercially**, to the right of the park some new shops were built on the aptly named New Lane, replacing the small shop of 1900, and the café and laundry were relocated and expanded.

(6) **To sum up / At last**, the area was renovated extensively, seeing fundamental changes to its residential accommodation, and its commercial and recreational facilities were developed.

0 8 ▷ Match the functions (a–e) with the correct discourse markers in exercise 7. Some may fit into more than one category.

   a to introduce a summary of all the main ideas previously mentioned

   b to introduce a similar point

   c to introduce a contrast

   d to change from one point to another

   e to make a general statement that sums up the ideas you want to mention in your answer

0 9 ▷ Think of alternative discourse markers for each of those used in the sample answer. In some cases, you will need to change the structure of the sentence.

   Example: Overall – *In general, Generally speaking*

COHERENCE AND COHESION

Coherence means making the text flow and includes ordering information and paragraphing. *Cohesion* is joining individual elements such as clauses, sentences and paragraphs together. This includes discourse markers, but also other aspects such as avoiding repetition through the use of pronouns and synonyms.

1 0 ▷ Match these examples of cohesion (1–5) from the text with their type (a–e). Use the underlined words and phrases to help you decide.

   1 … in 1900 <u>a railway line</u> ran through the neighbourhood, by 1935 <u>this</u> had been removed, …

   2 … amenities of this <u>area</u>. […] Whereas in 1900 a railway line ran through <u>the neighbourhood</u> …

   3 … the <u>industrial features</u> had largely disappeared. Whereas in 1900 a <u>railway line</u> ran through the neighbourhood …

   4 … for <u>a spacious park</u>. […] to the right of <u>the park</u>, …

   5 … a number of notable <u>changes</u> to the buildings and amenities of this area. […] <u>Another major change</u> …

   a repetition of the same noun a few sentences later to show continuation of an idea

   b using a demonstrative pronoun to avoid repetition

   c using the definite article because the noun has been used before

   d giving a second more specific noun as an example of the first more general noun

   e using synonyms to avoid repetition

1 1 ▷ Look at this list of features which might be found in a cohesive text. Then look back at the sample answer in exercise 7. Which features were *not* included in it? Why not?

   1 an opening sentence or paragraph explaining what the maps show, with an overview of what the writer is going to talk about

   2 a general statement of a change the writer feels is important

   3 supporting statements which give more specific details about a general statement

   4 speculation as to why the changes took place

   5 a recap/summary of the main points covered

   6 your opinion of the changes

1 2 ▶ Look at the two maps of a beach hotel at different times. Make notes on the key changes in the following areas:

- accommodation
- facilities
- recreation

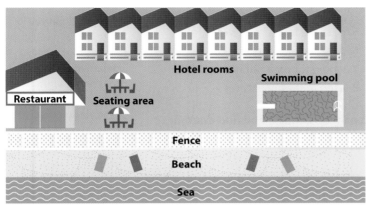

Beach hotel 2003

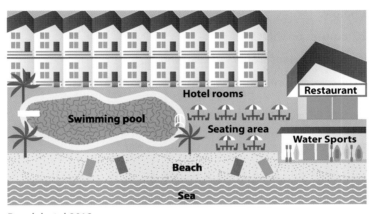

Beach hotel 2013

1 3 ▶ With a partner, read this candidate's answer. Discuss and find examples of the following coherence and cohesion features.

1 a statement to introduce a change the writer feels is important

2 the use of discourse markers to give cohesion

3 the use of synonyms and paraphrase to avoid repetition

4 the use of pronouns, possessive adjectives, articles

SAMPLE ANSWER

The maps show changes to a beach hotel between 2003 and 2013. Generally speaking, the changes illustrate the extension and improvement of its facilities during the ten-year period.

The most striking alteration is to the hotel's capacity, with an increase in the number of rooms, and in particular the construction of an extra storey above the initial row of rooms. Another significant change is the relocation of various facilities. By 2013, the swimming pool and restaurant had been moved and its seating area had been enlarged.

Recreation had more prominence by 2013. This can be seen in the fact that the 2013 pool is considerably larger than ten years previously and a water sports centre had been built on the beach in front of the hotel. On top of this, the fence which divided the hotel from the beach had been removed by 2013, allowing free access to the beach.

To summarise, the hotel underwent an expansion of its accommodation and recreational amenities in the ten years between 2003 and 2013.

1 4 ▶ Look at the list of tenses. Which ones would you expect to use for a 'describing changes on a map' task like the ones in this section? Why?

1 past simple

2 past continuous

3 present perfect simple

4 present perfect continuous

5 past perfect

6 past perfect continuous

7 *would* for past habits

8 *used to* for past states

1 5 ▶ Look back through the two sample answers on pages 61 and 63 and find examples of the tenses you chose in exercise 14.

TIP 1 4

Make sure that you focus on the dates/times given in this kind of task as they will help you determine which tenses are most appropriate. For example, if the second map says 'Now' then you are likely to be using past simple and present perfect to describe the changes.

EXAM SKILLS

1 6 ▶ Answer the Writing Task 1 below.

You should spend about 20 minutes on this task.

The maps show the outskirts of the town of Fosbury in 1980 and 2015.

Summarise the information by selecting and reporting the main features and make comparisons where relevant.

Write at least 150 words.

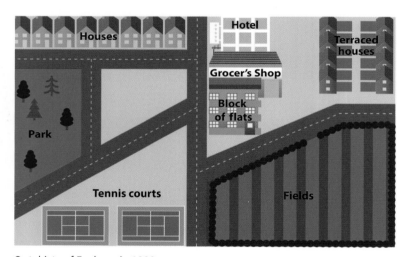

Outskirts of Fosbury in 1980

GO FURTHER ONLINE

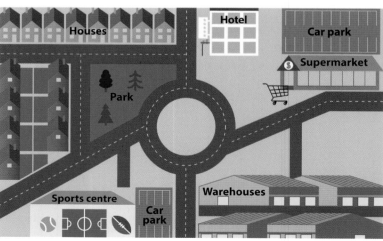

Outskirts of Fosbury in 2015

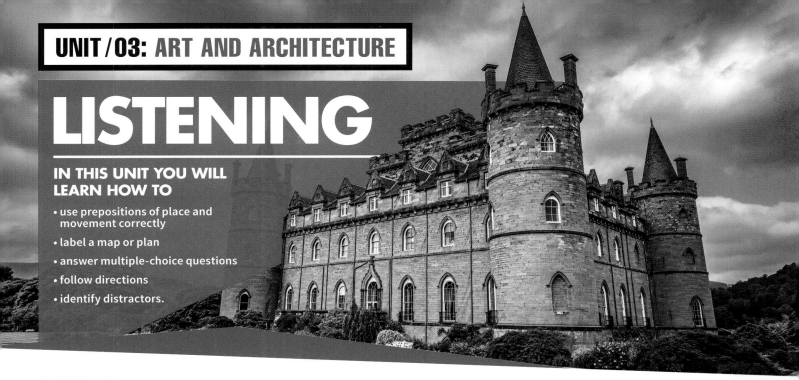

UNIT /03: ART AND ARCHITECTURE

LISTENING

IN THIS UNIT YOU WILL LEARN HOW TO

- use prepositions of place and movement correctly
- label a map or plan
- answer multiple-choice questions
- follow directions
- identify distractors.

01▶ Look at the floor plan of the ground floor of a stately home and complete the directions with the correct preposition from the box. There may be more than one possible answer and you can use each preposition more than once. Which two prepositions can you not use here?

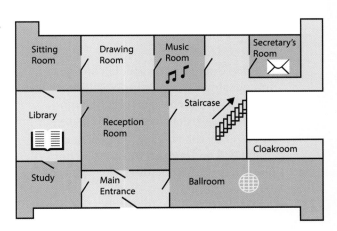

above	between	across from
at	into	of
across	close to	opposite
in	below	on
behind	from	to
via	through	up

1 To get to the staircase from the main entrance, go _____ the reception room and take the door _____ your right.

2 The sitting room is _____ the top left-hand corner _____ the map.

3 The library is _____ the sitting room and the study and you can enter it _____ either room or _____ the reception room.

4 The cloakroom is adjacent _____ the ballroom.

5 The secretary's room is _____ the music room.

6 Standing _____ the foot of staircase, facing the stairs, you can see the secretary's room diagonally _____ you _____ the left-hand side.

7 The staircase will take you _____ to the first floor.

8 _____ the back of the house and just _____ the reception room, you can find the drawing room.

02 ▶ Look at these places that might be mentioned in a tour of a building like the one in exercise 1. Discuss with a partner what you know about the function of each room.

1 the landing   *the level area at the top of some stairs or between staircases*
2 the lobby
3 the drawing room
4 the cloakroom
5 the pantry
6 the cellar
7 the attic
8 the ballroom
9 the servants' quarters
10 the conservatory

[LABELLING A MAP]

03 ▶ Look at a map of the ground floor of a castle museum. Match the directions (1–3) with places A–C on the map.

1 From the main entrance, go past the library on your right, enter the Exhibition Room and turn right.
2 Pass the Grand Hall on your left and go straight ahead. Go into the Exhibition Room and turn left. You have to walk through another small room to get to this place.
3 As you enter the building, you will find the Grand Hall on your left. You will find this place in the corner of the Hall.

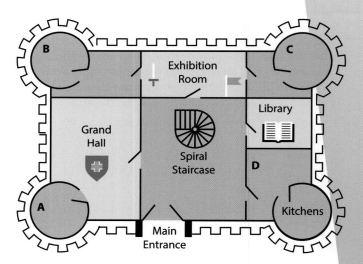

04 ▶ Write similar directions for the location of place D. Then compare in groups.

05 ▶ Listen and answer the question.

18

Room A is
A Lord Westchester's bedroom.
B the gift shop.
C the aviary.

06 ▶ Listen and label room B.

19

Room B is _____ .

07 ▶ Listen again. Look at the places that were mentioned that are NOT the correct answer. Make notes on why they are incorrect.

19

Spiral Staircase   Exhibition Room   Anteroom

08 ▶ Listen and label rooms C and D using words from the box.

20

| anteroom | dining room | kitchen | sewing room | sitting room |

TIP 06

It is important to stay focused on what you are listening for. You will hear a lot of irrelevant information and also some that seems relevant, but may not be. For example, if you are listening for a location, you may also hear information about dates and people, which you need to ignore. You will also hear other locations mentioned which are not the correct answer. These are called distractors.

MULTIPLE-CHOICE QUESTIONS

 This task gives you a series of questions and you choose from three options. Usually all the options will be mentioned in some way in the recording, but only one answers the question. Make sure you are clear on what the question is asking you. It is important to keep listening and not settle for the first option mentioned, as it may well be a distractor.

09▷
21

Listen and match the century with the information about the castle.

1 11th century   a The Westchester family became the owners.

2 12th century   b The castle had its origins at this time.

3 13th century   c The living quarters were added.

10▷
21

Listen again and answer the question.

In which century did Westchester Castle become a residence?

A 11th   B 12th   C 13th

11▷
22

Listen to how the following three words are explained. Make notes on what words the speaker uses to describe them.

1 drawbridge   2 turrets   3 moat

TIP 11

Don't worry if you don't understand some of the words in the question stem or options. Often less common vocabulary will be explained in the recording. Even if it is not, you can usually work out if the answer is correct by listening carefully to the words around the words you don't know.

12▷
22

Listen again. Which part of the castle is still in good condition?

A the drawbridge   B the moat   C the turrets

13▷
23

Listen and write the missing words.

The castle would have had **1** _____ in the basement to store enough food for many months in case of a siege. Unfortunately, we are no longer able to enter the basement area as it's not safe, but we know that there are underground **2** _____ used for escape and for making sorties, or attacking raids, against the enemy. This castle is unusual in that there has been no evidence found of **3** _____ – underground prison cells. Perhaps they never took any prisoners!

14▷

Answer the question based on the recording you have just heard.

Which were NOT located underground at Westchester?

A dungeons   B storerooms   C tunnels

TIP 14

Make sure you read every question carefully as sometimes you might be asked to choose which option is NOT … .

EXAM SKILLS

1 5 ▶ **Listen and answer questions 1–10.**

Questions 1–6

Label the map opposite.

*Write the correct letter, **A–I**, next to questions 1–6.*

1 gift shop
2 beehives
3 holiday cottages
4 dairy
5 museum
6 estate office

Questions 7–10

*Choose the correct letter, **A, B** or **C**.*

7 How many unpaid helpers does the National Trust have?

   A about 62,000
   B about 5,899
   C about 4.24 million

8 The main aim of the National Trust is

   A to make money from its properties.
   B to preserve historical properties.
   C to donate money to property owners in financial difficulties.

9 A couple can join the National Trust for a year for

   A £64.
   B £108.
   C £114.

10 Paying membership fees by direct debit also gets you

   A a pair of binoculars.
   B a National Trust handbook.
   C three copies of the National Trust magazine per year.

Holloway Estate

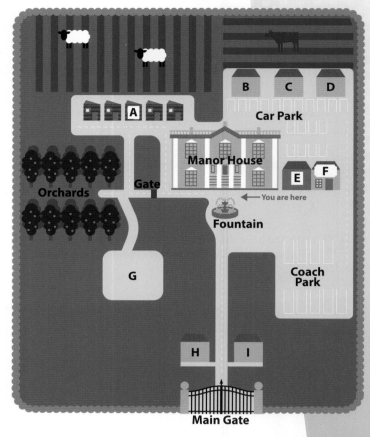

 GO FURTHER ONLINE

UNIT / 03: ART AND ARCHITECTURE

SPEAKING

IN THIS UNIT YOU WILL LEARN HOW TO

- make notes for your long turn in Part 2
- structure your long turn
- use a range of spoken discourse markers.

LEAD-IN

01 ▶ Read these reactions to works of art. Do you think the person liked the art he/she was reacting to? Write *Yes*, *No*, *Not Sure* next to each one.

1 I'm not sure what to make of this one.
2 I can really relate to this.
3 This is very powerful.
4 I'm not sure what the artist is trying to convey.
5 I like the simplicity of this.
6 There's a bit too much going on.
7 I don't quite get the point of it.
8 It evokes strong feelings of nostalgia/empathy/sadness.
9 I wouldn't hang it on my wall. To be honest, it leaves me cold.
10 It's too abstract for my taste.

02 ▶ Look at the examples of art on the page. What is your reaction to them? You could use some of the expressions from exercise 1.

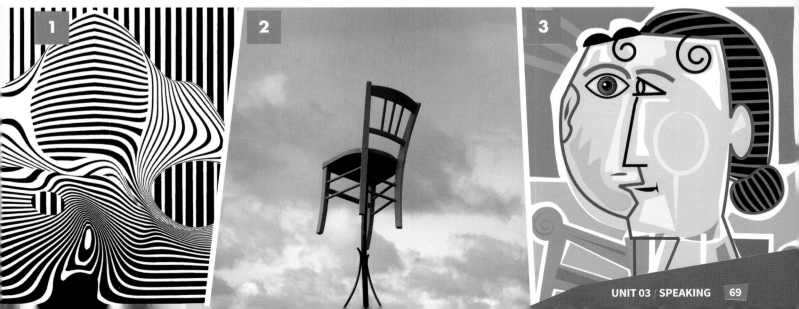

SPEAKING PART 2 – LONG TURN

MAKING NOTES

03▶ Look at the Part 2 task card and the notes a candidate called Claudia made in preparation for her talk. How could they be improved?

Describe someone whose creative or artistic work you like.

You should say:

- what you know about the life of this person
- what kind of creative work this person does/did
- why you like his/her work

and describe the way his/her work makes you feel.

> The artist I like is Salvador Dalí.
> Born – around 1904? Catalunya, Spain.
> Died – late 1980s?
>
> He was famous as a surrealist painter.
> Famous painting – Persistence of Memory
> Why I like his work – symbolism, he is interested in Maths and Science

04▶ Listen to the candidate doing the task. Take notes on the content. Rewrite the notes above.

25

05▶ Swap notes with a partner.

1 Did your partner use 'key word notes' (without articles, prepositions, etc.)?
2 Did he or she use short forms?
3 Do his or her notes cover all the points on the task card?

06▶ Work together to improve both sets of notes.

07▶ Make your own notes for the task in exercise 3.

08▶ Show your notes to your partner. Can he or she understand what you are planning to say?

09▶ Look at the notes another candidate, Yaz, made for his talk on his favourite artist. Discuss the advantages or disadvantages of using this style of notetaking.

10▶ Rewrite your notes as a mind map.

For Part 2 of the Speaking test you talk for 1–2 minutes, based on instructions on a task card. You have one minute to make notes for your talk. Make sure you cover all four points on the card.

TIP 04

Don't waste time writing unnecessary words like articles (*a, the*) or prepositions (*in, to, at*). Just write the key words. Use initials or shortened forms of words to save time.

TIP 07

Part 2 tasks do not require any specialist knowledge, so here you don't have to talk about an artist in the sense of the fine arts (painting, sculpture, drawing, etc). You could talk about someone from other creative fields such as music and film making.

TIP 11

The bullet points act as a structure for your talk. Use a range of spoken discourse markers to help make your structure clear to the examiner.

11 ▶ Look at the script of Claudia's talk about Dalí. Divide it up into the four points on the card. Has she talked about the four points in order?

The creative person I have chosen is Salvador Dalí. I visited the Dalí Foundation in Figueres last year, and it made a great impression on me. He was born in Catalunya in Spain. ¹I'm not sure of the exact year but I think maybe around 1904 and he died in about the late 1980s, when he was in his 80s. He was a surrealist painter, so he used symbolism a lot. ²What that means is in his paintings things don't look like what they are. One of his most famous paintings is called *The Persistence of Memory* and it shows watches or clocks that are very soft, ³which is supposed to show that time is not as most people understand it. He was fascinated by Maths and Science, and so am I, so ⁴that is one reason why I like him. ⁵Another reason is that he was quite unconventional – and even eccentric in his behaviour, so that makes him an interesting character, who was not like other people. The same is true of his art. And what's more, he didn't just stick with painting. ⁶Later in his life he did sculpture and worked on film sets. ⁷So, to put it in a nutshell, I like the fact that he was innovative and totally different from others. ⁸Oh, and one more thing, the colours in his work are amazing, so they're good to hang on your walls – not the originals of course! His work makes me feel proud because he's from my country – from my region, ⁹actually, and he brought fame to Catalunya.

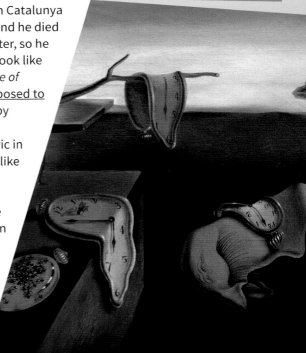

12 ▶ Match the underlined phrases and discourse markers (1–9) in the script above with their functions (a–i).

a to emphasise that this is surprising information
b to introduce a clarification
c to show a shift in time
d to show uncertainty
e to add something the speaker had forgotten to say
f to add a further reason
g to introduce the first reason
h to talk about intention
i to summarise what has been said

13 ▶ Listen to Yaz's talk. Follow it using his notes in exercise 9. Write down any discourse markers Yaz uses.

26

Listen again and fill in the gaps. Use up to THREE words.

26

For my creative person I'm going to talk about the British artist David Hockney. So, **1** _____
saying that he was born somewhere in the North of England, possibly Yorkshire, but I'm not 100% sure about
that. I'd say he was born in about the 1930s as he's still alive today but he's getting on a bit.

OK, **2** _____ to talk about his art. He's a modern artist and he was part of the Pop Art
movement. **3** _____ a painter, he's a photographer and printmaker, so he's pretty versatile.
He paints country scenes and for some reason he used to love painting swimming pools.

So why do I like him? **4** _____ , it's because of the colours he uses. His paintings are so bright
and cheerful. They show real things you can recognise; **5** _____ they have a modern feel. Lots
of modern art is so abstract, you have no idea what it's supposed to be, but Hockney is different.
6 _____ , when I see Hockney's paintings, I feel happy and relaxed. I feel as if it's warm and
sunny. I suppose it's that feel-good factor that makes me like him so much. So, **7** _____ .

 In pairs, work together to practise the Part 2 task in exercise 3. Use the following points to guide you.

1 Choose a set of notes to use either from exercise 7 or exercise 10.
2 Plan what you will say and make a note of useful phrases and discourse markers you might use.
3 Take turns to give your talks. If possible record them.
4 When your partner is speaking, check that they:
   • cover all the points on the task card
   • structure their talk well using discourse markers.
5 Give each other feedback using the recorded talks and the notes you made.

 Repeat your talks and see if you can improve them.

 **GO FURTHER ONLINE**

[EXAM SKILLS]

17 **Do this sample test with a partner. Take turns to ask and answer.**

Part 1

1 Do you enjoy drawing and painting? (Why? / Why not?)
2 Did you enjoy drawing and painting when you were a child? (Why? / Why not?)
3 What kind of things did you do in Art lessons at school?
4 Do you have any art in your home?

TIP 17

Remember that Part 1 questions in the actual IELTS test are on a different topic from that covered in Parts 2 and 3. However, for Exam Skills sections in this book, each part will be on the same topic.

Part 2

Describe a visit to an art gallery or museum where you saw
artworks or interesting objects.

You should say:

   • where this place was
   • what kind of art you saw
   • how you felt about the visit

and say whether you would recommend the place to a friend.

Part 3

What can you learn about different cultures from their art work?
Should governments fund art galleries and public art projects?
How do you think art might develop in the future?

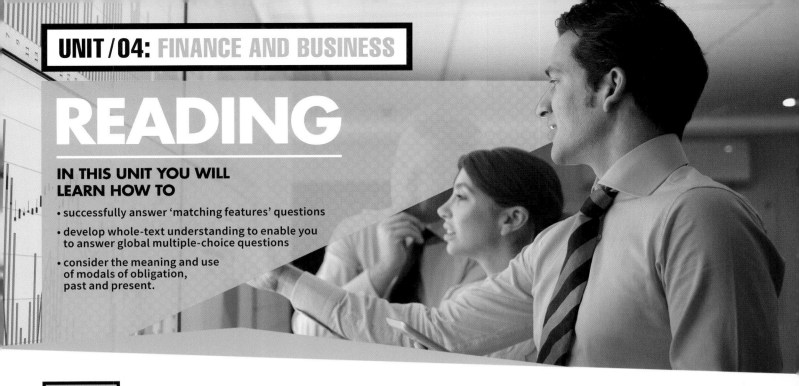

READING

IN THIS UNIT YOU WILL LEARN HOW TO

- successfully answer 'matching features' questions
- develop whole-text understanding to enable you to answer global multiple-choice questions
- consider the meaning and use of modals of obligation, past and present.

LEAD-IN

0 1 In pairs, discuss the similarities and differences between the pairs of words and phrases.

1 financial crash / recession

A financial crash is when a financial system stops working. A recession is a period of economic decline.

2 loan / mortgage

3 regulations / laws

4 go bankrupt / go bust

5 borrower / lender

6 savings / investments

0 2 What do you know about the global financial crash in 2008? In pairs, talk about the causes and effects.

MATCHING FEATURES

In this type of task you are given a list of options, or 'features' – for example, the names of people, publications, years – and you need to match them with the questions. To do this, you need to search the text to establish which part of the text correctly corresponds with the statements given in the questions. In this task type the questions will *not* appear in the same order as the answers are given in the text.

0 3 Look at the reading passage on page 75. How can you identify which is:

1 the name of a writer the first time they are mentioned?

2 the name of the writer when they are next mentioned?

3 the title of a book / article / academic paper?

4 the exact words written in a book / article / academic paper?

04 ▶ Look at the exam task and focus on the options below. Scan the passage and put a box around the names where they are mentioned in the text. Do not try to match the statements yet.

Look at the following statements and the list of people below. Match each statement with the correct person, A–C.

1 The plan to make a greater number of people wealthy from mortgage repayments was foolish.

2 The credit ratings agencies did not fulfil their essential reason for existing.

3 The investment banks are not solely responsible for the problems that caused the crash.

4 The bankers' careless way of working was essentially a form of exploitation from which they got more wealthy.

5 Accepting the false assurance of AAA credit ratings without question badly damaged the global economy.

6 Government failure to bring the problem to an end led to another profit-driven industry becoming involved.

> **List of people**
> A Alicia Pillory
> B Dr Alfred Moran
> C Charles Vane

05 ▶ Read paragraphs 1–3. The opinions below come from either Alicia Pillory or Charles Vane. Discuss with a partner who is responsible for each argument, and explain where in the text you found the answer.

1 The plan to make a greater number of people wealthy from mortgage repayments was foolish.

2 The credit ratings agencies did not fulfil their essential reason for existing.

3 Investment banks are not solely responsible for the problems that caused the crash.

06 ▶ Referring to paragraphs 4 and 5, decide whose opinion is being paraphrased here.

4 The bankers' careless way of working was essentially a form of exploitation from which they got more wealthy.

5 Accepting the false assurance of AAA credit ratings without question badly damaged the global economy.

6 Government failure to bring the problem to an end led to a new profit-driven industry becoming involved.

07 ▶ Look again at this sentence from paragraph 6. Whose view is being given: the writer of the passage, Alicia Pillory, Charles Vane or Dr Alfred Moran?

'… those people who borrowed money to buy a house, knowing that they could never afford to pay that money back in their entire lifetimes, must take the major share of the blame.'

TIP 04

Scan the text before you read the questions, putting boxes around the options (names, etc.) given in the list. Do not simply <u>underline</u> them – they might later get lost as you continue to underline more and more key phrases in the passage in your search for correct answers.

TIP 05

By skim reading the text first, you can also form an idea of the tone of what each person says. Normally they will take one side of an argument (e.g. in favour of or against something), so thinking about which side they take can often help you decide where to look first for the answers.

TIP 07

Be careful. The writer of a passage does not always use 'quotation marks' to report the opinions or arguments of another person. Sometimes, reporting these views will be introduced with a phrase such as 'as writer x explains,' but it can also be less explicit than this.

1 There was once a widely held belief that people who were in debt, but who could not afford to pay back that debt, should be punished severely. At the end of the 19th century, those unable to repay what they owed were arrested, taken to court, and ultimately sent to 'debtors' prisons', locked away until they had worked off what they owed. To be in debt, in the eyes of society, was unacceptable. And yet, by the time we reached the first years of the 21st century, the idea that owning debt was something positive, even productive, had become commonplace in many parts of the world. So much so, that the global financial crash of 2008, in the eyes of many observers, was entirely inevitable.

2 At the end of the 20th century, the general financial climate was stable and healthy. Commercial banks and investment banks for a number of years had mostly functioned separately from one another. When people put their income or savings into an investment, it was often done without a great deal of risk, and they tended not to make an astonishing amount of money. But this was soon to change in a disastrous way, writes Alicia Pillory in *The Great Deception*. In the early 2000s, 'investment bankers devised an opportunity to make huge profits by buying mortgage loans from commercial banks and mortgage lenders'. She explains how the investment banks then created 'packages' of these loans and sold them to individual investors. 'The grand, misguided theory was that any repayments would have to be made to the companies or people who now owned the mortgages, and everyone would get rich.'

3 Huge numbers of investors brought their money to the table. They were given confidence by the fact that the packages being offered to them had apparently been assessed and passed by the credit rating agencies. The main purpose of these organisations is to evaluate in a neutral way the amount of risk an individual or company might face in a potential investment. The fundamental problem, as Charles Vane sets out in *The End of Innocence*, was that these credit rating agencies were actually paid by the investment banks themselves, and the agencies were happy to provide the first-class 'AAA' ratings which did so much to convince potential investors to part with their money: 'which is actually very far from being neutral'. It seems unthinkable now that this was the case, but it was not uncommon at the time. 'We have to take that into consideration before isolating and criticising the investment banks too harshly.'

4 The investment banks, now free to offer home loans to anyone, regardless of how much that person earned or was even likely to earn, began offering mortgages to new borrowers: people who were in low-paid employment, and who had no savings at all. Huge levels of debt were provided to those who, within two or three years, would have no way of meeting the monthly repayments. 'So many people were taken advantage of,' writes Pillory, and 'this irresponsible lending behaviour was never made to stop, with no ultimate consequences for the bankers, who simply became very, very rich'. She maintains that the authorities could, and should, have put a stop to it earlier. Instead, 'at this point, another industry saw the potential for profit and greedily stepped in'.

5 Insurance companies commonly offer protection against personal debt (for example, when somebody takes out a mortgage but wants to make sure that, if they suffer an unexpected accident and cannot work, the debt will be paid not by themselves, but by that company). However, in the early part of the 21st century, people suddenly became able to buy insurance for properties they did not even own. In other words, when a family could no longer afford the repayments on their home and had to leave, another person – who they had never met, maybe even living on the other side of the country – could claim a huge amount of money from the insurance company, simply because they had bought a policy for that particular property. In *The Crash: Reasons and Repercussions*, Dr Alfred Moran writes, 'The AAA ratings gave everyone a dishonest guarantee that the system could not collapse. Unfortunately for the world's economy, the insurance companies followed those ratings blindly.' Eventually, in 2008, the system did indeed collapse, on a devastating scale.

6 Despite this, he emphasises, it should not be overlooked that it was actually the investment banks who paid the ratings agencies in the first place, and so the AAA rating was essentially funded by those who would exploit it – it is they who are most to blame. Pillory contends, however, that we should vent our strongest anger towards the dangerously 'hands-off' approach of western governments at the time, while Vane avoids placing the entire blame at the feet of either the banks, or their governments and regulators. He maintains that, in the western world, the attitude towards debt is careless. 'Chinese people, for example, often put 30% of their income into saving; this sensible attitude to money is commonly seen in Asian countries. In comparison, in Europe and the US, you rarely see anyone putting aside more than 5% of their earnings. This is extremely unwise.' By extension, those people who borrowed money to buy a house, knowing that they could never afford to pay that money back in their entire lifetimes, must take the major share of the blame.

7 As Alicia Pillory laments, 'We are living through the worst recession for 80 years, all because a comparatively small number of people working in the financial sector could not control their greed.' Whatever the root causes of this highly devastating period in our history, the one thing that experts seem to agree on is that our shared financial wellbeing is unlikely to return to full health at any point soon. Perhaps it is even time to reconsider some 19th-century notions of how we are supposed to feel about debt.

*mortage – *a loan given by a bank that enables someone to buy somewhere to live (e.g. house, flat)

GLOBAL MULTIPLE-CHOICE QUESTIONS

 This task asks you to reflect on or summarise the text as a whole. Typically, this task will ask you to identify the **main idea** of the passage (a sentence which summarises the writer's position), its **purpose** (why the author wrote it) or the **most suitable title** (a simple statement that summarises the content of the text for the reader).

08▷ Use the hints given below the options to help you answer this question.

Choose the correct letter, A, B, C or D.

What is the writer's main idea in the Reading passage?

A The global financial crisis would not have happened if people were still imprisoned for being in debt.

B Certain nationalities should follow the lead of others in order to become financially stable.

C The global financial crisis was created by a number of groups and has had only negative effects.

D Worldwide attitudes to financial responsibility are to blame for the global crisis.

> **Hints**
>
> A Which parts of the text mention debtors' prisons? Why are they mentioned?
>
> B Who exactly is suggesting that certain nationalities are failing to take care of their finances adequately?
>
> C How many different groups of people are said to have been involved in the financial crisis? Does the writer put forward any positive effects of the crisis?
>
> D Which 'attitudes to financial responsibility' are described in a negative way? Are there any people in today's societies whose approach to financial responsibility is mentioned in a positive light?

09▷ Look at options A–D and answer the global multiple-choice question. Check that the information in both parts of the sentence (green and orange) is correct to help you decide.

Choose the correct letter, A, B, C or D.

What is the writer's purpose in the Reading passage?

A To compare approaches to savings and investment in the 19th and the 21st centuries

B To summarise different interpretations of the main causes of the global financial crisis

C To criticise investment banks' unhealthy concept of debt

D To detail which processes caused the global financial crisis to happen

TIP 09

For 'purpose' questions, make sure that both parts of the option are correct.

10▷ Answer the question using the underlined key words to help you.

Choose the correct letter, A, B, C or D.

What is the best title for this Reading passage?

A The <u>History of Debt</u> in the <u>Modern Era</u>

B <u>How</u> the <u>Banks created</u> a <u>Global Recession</u>

C <u>Disasters</u> in <u>Finance</u> and <u>Investment</u>

D <u>The Crash</u>: is there <u>anyone</u> to <u>blame</u>?

TIP 10

For 'Choose a title' questions, ask yourself:
- If I saw this title, what would I expect to read in the passage? What arguments or evidence might be given? How much does the passage differ from these predictions?
- Does the option give the main idea of the whole passage, or just a section/paragraph from it?
- Is the option too general or abstract to be correct?

1 1 ▶ Do the words *in italics* refer to a present or past situation? Scan the text to locate the sentences in context and check.

1 We *have to take* that into consideration.

2 the authorities *could and should have* put a stop to it

3 when a family could no longer afford the repayments on their home and *had to leave*

4 it *should not be overlooked*

5 those people who borrowed money to buy a house […] *must take* the major share of the blame

6 Perhaps it is even time to reconsider some 19th-century notions of how we *are supposed to feel* about debt.

1 2 ▶ Correct the modal verb mistakes in bold in these sentences.

1 I realise that the meeting is due to finish now, but I **had to** say something before we leave.

2 It is sad that his company has just gone bust, but he really **should have** taken out such a big loan.

3 A vital element of a successful business is communication: there absolutely **must to be** honesty and openness between the management and the rest of the staff.

4 I had to give a presentation at work first thing this morning, but I was too tired to do a good job. I really **ought to get** more sleep last night.

5 When you arrive at work, you **are supposed to have signed** in at reception. I forgot to do that this morning.

EXAM SKILLS

1 3 ▶ Read the passage and answer questions 1–7.

Questions 1–7

Look at the following statements and the list of studies below. Match each statement with the correct study, A–C.

1 Unlike in previous years, a willingness to experiment with a wide range of possible roles is visible in all groups of job-seekers.

2 Younger people are being denied the chance to develop the social skills necessary for the modern office environment.

3 Many modern positions can be more easily terminated than ever before.

4 Claims of economic expansion are demonstrably incorrect.

5 An unforeseen problem has led to an increase in the number of people available to work.

6 Much of today's workforce do not feel constrained by a lack of familiarity with a new position.

7 Refusal to conform to traditional behaviour models at work is a positive step.

> **List of studies**
> A *Employment as a Myth*
> B *Unfair Returns*
> C *How the Market Adjusts to Opportunity*

 GO FURTHER ONLINE

Question 8

What is the best title for this passage?

A The Conflict between Young and Old in the Workplace

B Modern Employment: the Need for Adaptability

C The Changing Face of Working Life

D What Today's Workforce Really Wants

The accepted concept of a career path followed a similar pattern for decades. After completing their education, people would enter the adult world of work, settling down to a job in which they would likely remain from that point onward. Not only would this occupation provide their income for their entire working life, it would also allow them a healthy pension when they retired and moved into old age. Over the past twenty years, however, the relationship between a wage earner and their chosen profession has changed enormously. Today, the idea of a 'job-for-life' has all but disappeared, to be replaced by an unforgiving world of unstable employment. Some observers even argue that current society appears to pit old against young in a constant battle to find work of some description, all against a backdrop of increasing debt and economic difficulties.

At the same time, the government regularly releases figures that suggest that the economy is prospering, evidencing this claim with the fact that the unemployment rate continues to fall annually. Given this claim, logic would seem to dictate that, since there are fewer people out of work, an increasing number of people are enjoying a regular income. To dispute this, Frank Thomas's 2016 study on the nature of work, *Employment as a Myth*, revealed an interesting and contradictory interpretation. There are indeed more jobs available. However, a huge number of these are casual, temporary or short-term positions, all of which are low-paid and create little in the way of tax income for the government. This has a number of debilitating long-term effects, not least because this assurance of a growing economy is based more in myth than fact. Thomas explains, 'Without tax income, the economy cannot grow; if the economy stays weak, new jobs will not be created.'

He also illustrates how, around the world, increases in life expectancy have created a problem for a huge number of retired workers, who are starting to find that the sum of money they have saved for their retirement does not stretch far enough to provide the financial security that they had expected. As a result, there has been a widespread return of these workers to the job market, very often in search of the type of casual employment that was once the preserve of people in their late teens and early 20s. Lois Lawrence expands on this view in *Unfair Returns*: 'Older people are taking opportunities away from their grandchildren. Post-education, those new to the world of work are not able to earn any sort of living wage, nor are they getting the opportunity to develop the 'soft skills', e.g. social intelligence, that will enable them to flourish in the job market.'

For Lawrence, the days of the salaried worker – comfortable, assured, financially secure – are coming to an end, and are being replaced by a new model: the exploited worker. Instead, these are the days of the 'zero-hours' contract, where an employee is told by an employer to be *available* for work, but is not necessarily given any, and so earns nothing for their time simply spent waiting. She argues that this is causing even more inequality in the employment market, as business leaders realise that they have no obligation to provide their staff with a full- or part-time contract, and can therefore avoid additional expenditure. The 'zero-hours' worker receives no holiday or sick pay, and is considered to be self-employed, so has to pay their own taxes. They also have no hope of stability, and can be instantly dismissed without any hope of recourse. Employment laws, written decades ago at a time when the vast majority of the country's workforce benefitted from permanent positions, do not protect the new breed of worker from being unfairly dismissed at a moment's notice by their manager.

Less pessimistic interpretations of today's employment market do exist elsewhere. A 2015 study by William Haroldson, *How the Market Adjusts to Opportunity*, advocated a definition of a new type of multi-skilled worker: the model employee who not only refuses to age, but also does not want to work in the same office every day, or even to be an employee in the first place. In such a progressive, forward-looking environment, young and old are supposed to collaborate extensively, sharing the benefits of each other's talents and prior knowledge. Furthermore, although younger people are traditionally thought to be more willing to try any number of routes into work before deciding on an industry in which they want to develop, such an approach to employment no longer excludes workers of a more advanced age. Thomas agrees: 'Most of today's self-starters believe that the job market offers a vast array of potential opportunities from which they can learn and gain experience. Whether they have a wide range of existing experience, or none at all, is irrelevant to them.'

Moving from job to job is no longer seen in a negative way, he goes on to argue. In the past, anyone with a series of short-term positions on their CV was seen as unreliable or disloyal. Most of today's self-starters, however, approach the job market as a vast source of possibilities, while employers themselves are more likely to be entrepreneurs who are willing to accept job mobility without question, and less likely to punish potential staff for doing so. One positive result of this development is that 'soft skills' such as social intelligence can therefore be learnt in a new way, and through a greater number of person-to-person encounters than used to be available. This has been made possible through the fact that so much of human contact today now takes place in one enormous meeting room – the internet. Even if it means that the people in contact are not actually present together in the same room, the encounter still happens.

UNIT /04: FINANCE AND BUSINESS

WRITING

IN THIS UNIT YOU WILL LEARN HOW TO

- produce a balanced 'agree/disagree' essay
- write an introduction and conclusion for this type of essay
- use a range of discourse markers to help sequence your ideas logically
- understand exactly what the essay question is asking you to write.

LEAD-IN

01 With a partner, discuss what you understand by the term 'financial responsibility'.

02 Discuss the following statements with a partner. Make a list of points that support or oppose the ideas given. Think about the following: examples, reasons/explanations, causes/effects.

1 People today are more concerned with owning material possessions than with developing friendships and family relationships.

2 Levels of consumer debt are increasing across the world. To address this, a new subject should be introduced in secondary schools: how to manage personal finances.

AGREE/DISAGREE ESSAYS

03 With a partner, discuss how the *italicised* words in each B statement might change your approach to the question when compared to the A statement.

1 A People today are more concerned with owning material possessions than with developing friendships and family relationships.

B People today are *only* concerned with material possessions, *even if it has negative effects on* friendships and family relationships.

2 A Levels of consumer debt are increasing across the world. To address this, a new subject should be introduced in secondary schools: how to manage personal finances.

B Levels of consumer debt are increasing *dramatically* across the world. To address this, a new *compulsory* subject *must* be introduced in *all* secondary schools: how to manage personal finances.

 This task asks you to say to what extent you agree or disagree with a statement on a certain topic. You can do this in different ways. For example:

- present objectively both sides of the argument to give a balanced view, before explaining in your conclusion which side of the argument you favour
- agree/disagree entirely with the statement given, and produce an essay that clearly argues in favour of one side.

It is recommended that even if you entirely favour one side of the argument, you mention any opposing arguments to show the examiner you have considered your position.

TIP 03

Make sure you consider every word in the rubric; try to analyse closely what the question is asking you to do – it may be different to the idea you initially think is being presented.

WRITING AN INTRODUCTION

04 ▶ Read the exam task and the introductions (1–4). Match each one with the teacher's comments about them (a–d).

People today are more concerned with owning material possessions than with developing friendships and family relationships.
To what extent do you agree with this statement?

1 It has been argued that in today's world, everybody spends more of their time preoccupied with what they buy and less concerned with maintaining close ties with the people around them.

2 It is said that people today are more concerned with owning material possessions than with developing friendships and family relationships. In this essay I will explain the extent to which I agree with this idea.

3 I agree with the statement and in this essay I will explain why.

4 It has been suggested that these days we tend to prioritise the accumulation of possessions over the development of relationships with those closest to us. Whilst there is some truth in the assertion that the world has become more materialistic, it is not necessarily true that this is at the cost of our loved ones.

A *You have explained your position on the statement but have failed to include any information relating to the statement in your introduction.*

B *Your introduction is clear, but you should paraphrase the question statement in your own words.*

C *This is a good introduction that paraphrases the question and clearly explains the line of argument you will take in the body of your essay.*

D *You have paraphrased the question statement well, but have failed to explain how you will answer it.*

◎ There are a number of ways to write an introduction for an essay like this. However, all introductions should clarify what the question is asking you to discuss, and should explain how you plan to answer it. As with all IELTS Writing introductions, you will score higher if you paraphrase the question in your own words.

TIP 04

It is good practice to make your position (to what extent you agree) clear in the introduction in case you run out of time in the exam and don't finish your essay. This will prevent you losing too many marks on Task Response.

05 ▶ Look at the following plans for three essays for the task in exercise 4 (main body only, introduction and conclusion missing). Discuss with a partner how each essay differs in its overall approach to answering the question.

Essay Type 1	Essay Type 2	Essay Type 3
Paragraph 1: ' Agree' – Sales of gadgets / luxury items at highest point ever – Gadgets allow you to create social media profiles = encourage people to create false image of material success	Paragraph 1: 'Agree' – Today's world = more materialistic than ever; economy relies on debt and consumer spending – Popularity of luxury goods is increasing, friends competitive about owning the most exclusive brands	Paragraph 1: 'Disagree' – Most people understand that material possessions are less important than human relationships – Owning material possessions does not = greed; today's world is run on expensive technology – people need this to function in society
Paragraph 2: 'Disagree' – People have always needed human contact and always will – Material possessions actually allow more contact with friends and family around the world (e.g. smartphones = social media)	Paragraph 2: 'Agree' – Methods of communication less personal as a result of expensive technology (e.g. people speak less on the phone, use instant messaging apps instead) Paragraph 3: 'Disagree' – Not everyone is materialistic, depends on personality, upbringing, friendship groups – Some cultures still maintain family unit as strongly as ever	Paragraph 2: 'Agree/Disagree' – Some people point to popularity of TV shows about being rich = materialistic society – Other people argue that greed/ selfishness is rewarded with money/ status – BUT there have always been materialistic people obsessed with status – Not necessarily 'people today' – it is just more visible with modern media

06 ▶ For this next Agree/Disagree question, read the arguments that a candidate has written for their essay. For each argument, put a tick (✓) if the argument is in favour of the statement, and a cross (✗) if the argument is against it. Ignore the numbered gaps for now.

TIP 06

One strategy for this kind of essay is to write the body of the essay first (the main arguments for and against) and then write the introduction when you can clearly see what your arguments are. That way your introduction will relate better to what follows it.

Levels of consumer debt are increasing across the world. To address this, a new compulsory subject should be introduced in secondary schools: how to manage personal finances. To what extent do you agree or disagree?

1 _____ , given the growing amount of individual debt around the world, there is no better time to learn about the negative effects of personal debt than at school. Students would be less likely to borrow what they could not afford, and more likely to stay in credit when they reach adulthood. ☐

2 _____ , I believe that teaching teenagers how to manage their money within the school curriculum would be vital in allowing them to become financially independent, even before the age of 18. They would feel more confident in being able to control their daily or monthly expenditure, and less reliant entirely on their parents for support or 'top-up' money. ☐

3 _____ , some would argue that teenagers are often too immature to become truly financially responsible, and so the classes would be a waste of teaching time. ☐

4 Others point out that teaching the concept of financial responsibility as a new subject would unfairly favour those students who are good at maths, and even that it would be just another way for them to get the best grades. ☐

5 _____ , in my experience, neither of these last two points are particularly valid. Most teenagers are keen to become financially independent as soon as they possibly can, while even the best mathematicians can experience difficulties with money at some point. ☐

07 ▶ Read the arguments in exercise 6 again and discuss the questions. Note that there is no introduction or conclusion for this essay yet.

1 How many arguments agree with the essay question and how many disagree?
2 Are the arguments in a logical order or would you reorder them?
3 How would you group the arguments in paragraphs?
4 Look again at the three essay plans in exercise 5. Which essay type is this: 1, 2 or 3?
5 How do you think the candidate will summarise their position in their conclusion?
  a They will strongly agree with the statement in the question.
  b They will strongly disagree with the statement.
  c There are arguments on both sides but overall they will agree.
  d There are arguments on both sides but overall they will disagree.

SEQUENCING IDEAS

For this kind of essay, think carefully about the discourse markers you will use to form a logical essay structure and to present arguments within your paragraphs:

• sequence markers (*Firstly, Secondly,* etc.) to present different arguments in order
• addition markers (*In addition, Furthermore, Moreover,* etc.) to extend or develop the ideas in your arguments
• contrast markers (*However, Despite this, On the other hand,* etc.) to introduce points on the other side of an argument.

0 8 ▶ Look at the arguments in exercise 6 and the numbered gaps. Which of the discourse markers in each group of three does NOT work in the corresponding gaps? Why?

1 First / Primarily / To begin with
2 Secondly / Following / Next
3 That said / On the other hand / Alternatively
4 Despite of this / In spite of this / Despite this

TIP 0 9

Make sure that you are clear and explicit in your ideas and arguments as you develop them. The examiner will not try to 'read between the lines' to establish what you are trying to say if it is not apparent.

0 9 ▶ Both paragraphs A and B would lose credit in the way they answer the Task 2 question here. Why?

It is unacceptable that people who work in certain professions, e.g. finance, media, entertainment and sport, are paid such high salaries while others, who do more important jobs in society, are underpaid.
To what extent do you agree or disagree?

A While the financial rewards in some professions are considerable, this does not always cancel out the difficulties that people working in these areas encounter, such as a loss of privacy. Furthermore, they often need to be away from home and their families for long periods. That said, there are so many people around the world who would love to be famous or rich, and it requires a huge amount of hard work and dedication.

B Undoubtedly, those working in high-profile professions can earn astonishing amounts of money. However, this often comes at a price, whether that involves the loss of privacy for celebrities, or long working days in the case of financiers. Other people may believe the opposite, but in my eyes they are mistaken.

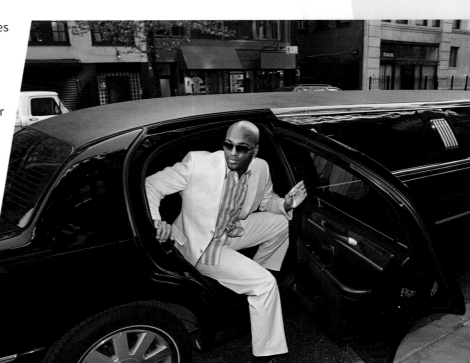

1 0 ▶ Rewrite the end of paragraph A from the previous exercise starting at the point shown, so that it finishes with a logical counter-argument.

While the financial rewards in some professions are considerable, this does not always cancel out the difficulties that people working in these areas encounter, such as a loss of privacy. Furthermore, they often need to be away from home and their families for long periods.

That said, there is an argument …

WRITING A CONCLUSION

1 1 ▶ Look at these notes from a candidate's answer (this is an example of an Essay Type 1 approach). Then decide which of the sentences (1–4) below correspond to the gaps (a–c) to create a logical conclusion. There is one sentence that you do not need.

> DISAGREE
> — Worth the money – create entertainment, role models
> — High-profile people lose privacy / family suffers
> AGREE
> — Often excessive earnings, even though talented
> — More people want to be celebrities, not interested in becoming teachers, doctors, etc.

In conclusion, (a) _____.

Granted, (b) _____ .

(c) _____ .

1 these high-earners create happiness and act as role models for younger people, often while their own privacy and well-being suffers

2 I can see no reason why people in high profile positions should not be paid as well as they usually are

3 it is important to consider that a lot of doctors and surgeons also get paid a huge amount of money

4 others in society often earn too little for the important work they do, but it shouldn't mean that these talented individuals are paid less

1 2 ▶ Which of the discourse markers in the box are appropriate for beginning the conclusion to a Task 2 Agree/Disagree essay?

| To conclude | To sum up | On the whole | Basically |
| Summarising | The point is | In summary | CONCLUSION: |

1 3 ▶ Following on from the main body of the essay you worked with in exercise 6, and using the conclusion template from exercise 11, write a suitable conclusion for the full essay.

EXAM SKILLS

1 4 ▶ Answer the Writing Task 2 below.

You should spend about 40 minutes on this task.

The most important consideration when choosing any career or job is having a high income.

To what extent do you agree or disagree?

Write at least 250 words.

GO FURTHER ONLINE

UNIT / 04: FINANCE AND BUSINESS

LISTENING

IN THIS UNIT YOU WILL LEARN HOW TO

- use the questions to help you follow a talk
- successfully complete short-answer questions
- correctly answer diagram-labelling tasks.

 Discuss these questions with a partner.

1 What was the last thing you bought that you could describe as good value for money?
2 Describe something expensive that you had to save up to buy.
3 Why do some people prefer physical money to debit or credit cards?
4 Do you think that in the future we will live without physical money?
5 What is the safest way to protect your money?

[SHORT-ANSWER QUESTIONS]

USING THE QUESTIONS TO HELP YOU FOLLOW A TALK

 Look at the 'short-answer questions'. What do the questions tell you about the content and organisation of the lecturer's talk?

1 What were used as an ancient type of currency for trade?
2 What were the first coins made in Greece a natural mixture of?
3 Which material did the Chinese use in the seventh century BC to make coins?
4 What did most early Chinese coins resemble?
5 What distinguished the coins of the first emperor of China, Shi Huangdi, apart from being circular?
6 According to historians, what was the purpose of the round jade discs that Shi Huangdi's coins were based on?
7 Which aspect of previous Chinese coins was not kept for Shi Huangdi's coins?
8 Which industrial process can Shi Huangdi's coin-making be seen as a primitive example of?

 This task asks you to answer *Wh-* questions using a given word limit. The questions will be in the order in which they are referred to in the recording and must be answered using the exact words from the recording.

TIP 02

As the questions follow the order of the information in the recording, read them through before you begin, as this will help you understand the structure of the recording.

03▶ Look at the first four questions from the exam task. What do the underlined words tell you about the answer you will need to listen for?

1 What <u>were</u> used as an ancient type of currency for trade?
2 What were the first coins made in Greece a <u>natural</u> mixture of?
3 Which <u>material</u> did the Chinese use in the seventh century BC to make coins?
4 What did <u>most</u> early Chinese coins resemble?

04▶ With a partner, think of possible answers you might hear in the recording for these questions.

1 What were used as an ancient type of currency for trade?
feathers, cows or sheep, crops, beads, etc.
2 What were the first coins made in Greece a natural mixture of?
3 Which material did the Chinese use in the seventh century BC to make coins?
4 What did most early Chinese coins resemble?

TIP 04
It can be helpful to try to predict what the answers will be, but remember that your answer must use the same words that you hear on the recording.

05▶ Using your ideas for 1–4 above, for each question write a possible sentence that you might hear in the recording that gives the answer and paraphrases the words in the question. The first one has been done for you.

1 What were used as an ancient type of currency for trade?
Thousands of years ago, feathers were used as a means of payment.
2 What were the first coins made in Greece a natural mixture of?
3 Which material did the Chinese use in the seventh century BC to make coins?
4 What did most early Chinese coins resemble?

TIP 05
The questions use words that paraphrase what is said in the recording, so it can help if you think of other ways the questions could be worded.

06▶ Listen to the first part of the lecture and answer questions 1–4 above. Use NO MORE THAN THREE WORDS for each answer.
27

07▶ Look at the rest of the short-answer questions for this section. With a partner, discuss ways of expressing the underlined words.

5 What <u>distinguished</u> the coins of first Chinese emperor, Shi Huangdi, apart from being <u>round</u> in form?
6 According to historians, what was the purpose of the round jade discs that Shi Huangdi's coins were <u>based on</u>?
7 Which <u>aspect</u> of previous Chinese coins was not <u>kept</u> for Shi Huangdi's coins?
8 Which industrial process can Shi Huangdi's coin-making be seen as a <u>primitive</u> <u>example</u> of?

08▶ Listen to the second part of the lecture and answer questions 5–8 above. Use NO MORE THAN TWO WORDS for each answer.
28

[DIAGRAM LABELLING]

◎ This task requires you to listen and complete the labels on a diagram, either by choosing from a list or, as in sentence completion tasks, by keeping to a word limit, normally a maximum of two words. In this section we will practise the latter. Use similar strategies to those for short-answer questions.

TIP 09

You will only be expected to complete and correctly spell a label with a technical term if the word(s) is/are similar to a recognisable homograph, i.e. a word with the same spelling but a different meaning.

09▶ Look at the diagram and try to predict what kind of word is missing from each gap.

Label the diagram below. Write **NO MORE THAN TWO WORDS AND/OR A NUMBER** *for each answer.*

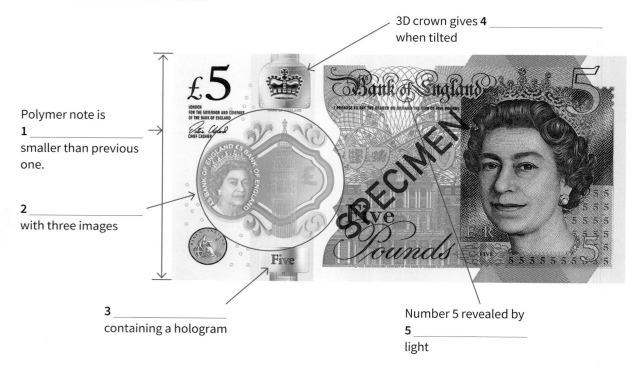

3D crown gives **4** _____ when tilted

Polymer note is
1 _____
smaller than previous one.

2 _____
with three images

3 _____
containing a hologram

Number 5 revealed by
5 _____
light

10▶ Listen to this new part of the lecture on the same topic and answer questions 1–5.

🎵 29

11▶ Look at a candidate's answers to questions 1–5. Why would each one be marked incorrect?

1 15
2 see through window
3 sliver patch
4 effect
5 UV ultra-violet light

TIP 10

Make sure you are clear on how to express numbers in all forms as they can come up in this task. Also remember that words connected by a hyphen (-) count as one word and that you will lose the mark if you make a spelling mistake.

[EXAM SKILLS]

1 2 ▶ **Listen and answer questions 1–10.**

30

Questions 1–5

Answer the questions below.

Write **NO MORE THAN TWO WORDS AND/OR A NUMBER** *for each answer.*

1 Which type of people are particularly attracted to wealth that can be easily transported?
2 What did the ancient Egyptians invent in order to protect their wealth?
3 After which year was the dead bolt lock created?
4 What did the Romans add to Egyptian lock designs?
5 What made Roman locks more difficult to break open than Egyptian locks?

Questions 6–10

Label the diagram below.

Write **NO MORE THAN TWO WORDS AND/OR A NUMBER** *for each answer.*

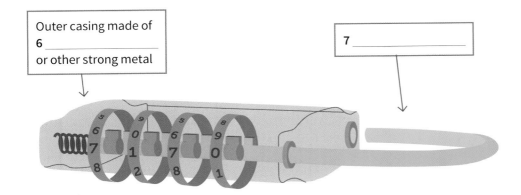

Outer casing made of
6 _____
or other strong metal

7 _____

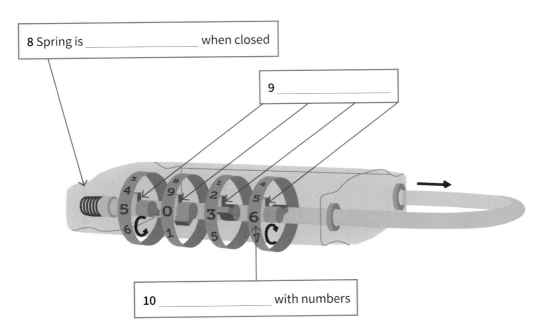

8 Spring is _____ when closed

9 _____

10 _____ with numbers

**GO FURTHER
ONLINE**

UNIT /04: FINANCE AND BUSINESS

SPEAKING

IN THIS UNIT YOU WILL LEARN HOW TO

• improve your score for Lexical Resource
• use a range of expressions for introducing opinions
• correctly use discourse markers to help justify your arguments
• review correct grammar and pronunciation of modals of obligation.

LEAD-IN

01▶ With a partner, decide which word in each pair is the correct collocation on the topic of business.

1 market **research** / **investigation**
2 product **development** / **progression**
3 **launch** / **trigger** a new product
4 business **chance** / **opportunity**
5 **have** / **make** a profit
6 **objective** / **target** market
7 customer **happiness** / **satisfaction**
8 time **management** / **organisation**
9 sales **amounts** / **figures**
10 **shut** / **close** the deal
11 **apply** / **claim** for a loan
12 **ask for** / **file for** bankruptcy

02▶ Listen to a candidate answering a Part 3 question. As you listen, check your answers to exercise 1.

31

03▶ Write a definition for each collocation in exercise 1. Use the listening script on page 213 to help you if necessary.

Example

market research *when you speak to your customers and/or look at similar products to help you design a new product*

TIP 01

Using collocations correctly will help you to achieve a higher score in the Speaking test, particularly if they are less common. For example, for the underlined phrase in the sentence '*before you go into business with a new product, you always need to do a plan*', the correct collocation is *make a plan*. Less common collocations like *come up with a plan* or *devise a plan* would gain you even more credit.

To get a high score in the Speaking test, look for ways to show that you have a wide and varied vocabulary, so try to avoid using the same phrases again and again. For example, instead of saying 'I think shopping is boring,' you could use a less common, more complex phrase, such as 'I find shopping can get quite tedious', or an idiom such as 'Shopping bores me stupid / to tears / to death'.

04▶

32

Read this transcript of a candidate's answer to a Part 3 question. Match the underlined phrases (1–8) to their more complex alternatives (a–h). Then listen and check.

Examiner Why has online shopping become so popular with so many people?

Candidate To be honest, I understand why people like it, but I'm not sure why (**1**) <u>people like it so much</u>. I suppose the main reason must be that it's so easy and convenient. You can just relax at home, at work, (**2**) <u>anywhere</u>, and do your shopping. Plus, (**3**) <u>there is so much you can buy</u> on the internet and, (**4**) <u>most importantly</u>, once you've paid, it quickly gets delivered to your door (**5**) <u>without having the problem of</u> going to a busy high street. So there are plenty of (**6**) <u>advantages</u> to online shopping. But, for me, (**7**) <u>the best way to shop is always by going to</u> the store itself and having a look at whatever it is you're thinking of buying. Also, you have the sales assistants to talk to, and they can (**8**) <u>help and give you good advice</u>.

a point you in the right direction
b there's very little you can't buy
c real plus points
d above all else
e it holds so much appeal
f there's no substitute for heading to
g wherever you are
h without having to deal with the hassle of

05▶

Look at an examiner's question and its answer. With a partner, discuss how you could change the phrases in italics to improve the candidate's score for Lexical Resource. Use the expressions in exercise 4 to help you.

Examiner Why do some people have problems managing their personal finances?

Candidate I suspect it might be because it has become so easy to get credit from banks: credit cards, overdrafts, *anything you think you need*. Of course, there are a number of *advantages* to this – you can buy whatever you want more quickly, and you don't have to pay the loan off until later, so I do see why *people like it so much*. And online banking has actually made it easier to do this *without having the problem of going into the branch* and standing in a queue for ever. *There's so much you can do* through your online account. For example, you can apply for a loan *anywhere you are*, and most of the time you'll be given the money. But, for me, there's no substitute for speaking face-to-face, where a bank advisor can *help and give you good advice*, as far as savings or debt is concerned. *Most of all*, they won't allow you to get into debt that you can't pay back.

06▶

33

Listen and compare the recording with your suggestions. Use the listening script if necessary.

TIP **05**

You don't need the same level of formality in the Speaking test as you would in the Writing test. For example, *real plus points* may feel a little informal, but would be likely to gain more credit from the examiner than *advantages*, which is a much more common word.

EXPRESSING AND JUSTIFYING OPINIONS

07▶ Look at the following phrases and decide if they mean *I think it's (very) important* (write I) or *I don't think it's (very) important* (write N).

1 It's not a matter of life or death.
2 It's pretty inconsequential.
3 It's an absolute necessity.
4 It's neither here nor there.
5 It's a must.
6 It's far from being essential.
7 It is absolutely crucial/vital.

TIP 07

Some questions in Part 3 ask you to evaluate how important something is, so make sure you can express your opinions in a variety of ways. Questions that do this often contain phrases like:
  • How important is it …?
  • Which is more important to people …?
  • Why is … seen as important?

08▶ Complete the answers to the Part 3 style questions using your own ideas, reasons and/or examples to expand your answer.

1 How important is it to stay out of debt?
   For me, it's a must. …
   For an increasing number of people these days, it's not a matter of life or death. …

2 Why are so many people today concerned with owning the newest versions or updates of technology?
   I'm not sure. It's pretty inconsequential to my life, but …
   Perhaps they just think that it's an absolute necessity, and …

3 Why do you think that many people place so much value on money and wealth?
   It's hard to say. Personally, I don't really think it matters, but …
   For some people, it's absolutely essential because …

09▶ Match sentences 1–5 with the discourse markers in the box. Use all the discourse markers.

clearly	apparently	by and large	arguably
conceivably	for the most part	undoubtedly	feasibly
supposedly	from where I stand	as far as I'm concerned	

TIP 09

Particularly in some Part 3 questions, you might need to explain why you believe something to be true, or to express to what extent you feel your words to be true.

1 This may be true, I read/heard it somewhere.
2 I am sure this is true (objectively).
3 I can't say for definite, but in some way it may be true.
4 As a general rule it is true.
5 This is my personal opinion.

10 ▶ **Read the statements and make notes on how you would respond to them, using words and phrases from exercise 9. Then, with a partner, take turns to respond.**

1 Some people believe that it is far better to be self-employed, as anyone who works for a company is doing nothing more than earning money for somebody else.

   A *Arguably that is true, but at the same time, not everybody wants to be self-employed. I think that, by and large, people are happy to work for companies.*

   B *Undoubtedly the part of the statement about earning money for somebody else is true, but an employee is also earning a salary and often has job security from working with a company, so I'm not sure I agree with the statement.*

2 Banks should not be allowed to issue credit cards to anyone under the age of 21.

3 Technology has made it easier to pay for everything. However, without paper money, people don't realise how much they are spending and this is creating more debt.

4 If you want to become a successful businessperson, you absolutely have to take Business Studies at university.

5 The world would be a better place if it was run by business people rather than politicians.

6 In life, it is more important to save than to spend.

GRAMMAR FOCUS: MODALS OF OBLIGATION

11 ▶ **Which of the options here are correct? Why? / Why not? Sometimes more than one is correct.**

According to some people, in order to become a success in business you (**1**) **had to / have to / have got to** concentrate on your studies in school. Well, my father would certainly disagree. When he left school, he knew that you (**2**) **mustn't / don't have to / didn't have to** be ultra-qualified to succeed. He certainly didn't get the best grades in his class when he was there. When he left school, he felt that he could eventually become more of a success than his classmates, but knew that he (**3**) **had to / would have to / needed to** use his natural business acumen to get ahead.

He (**4**) **must work / should have worked / had to work** long hours during the whole time he was setting up his business. Although, not everything he did was perfect. He had failures as well as successes. Once, he lost everything! I remember my mother being upset and saying to him, 'If you didn't want to lose all of our family savings, you (**5**) **didn't have to / shouldn't have / needn't have** made such a risky investment!' But my father is such a good businessman that she (**6**) **didn't have to / mustn't have to / hadn't to** wait long before we were pretty wealthy again, and going to the best restaurants once more.

PRONUNCIATION OF *HAVE*

 The word *have* can be spoken either as a 'strong' *have* (/hæv/), or a 'weak' *have* (/əv/), depending on how it is used in a sentence. The strong form tends to be used when *have* is a main verb, and the weaker pronunciation comes when *have* has a more grammatical function.

12▶ Read this Part 3 question and answer. For each underlined *have*, decide if it is a strong /hæv/ or a weak /əv/. Then listen and check.

34

Examiner   Should school children (**1**) <u>have</u> lessons on financial responsibility?

Candidate   Yes, for me, it is absolutely essential. I didn't (**2**) <u>have</u> lessons like these at school, but I think they would (**3**) <u>have</u> benefitted me a great deal. For example, when I got my first credit card, I now know I should (**4**) <u>have</u> paid more attention to the implications of using it. I found I was spending too much, and often forgot to make the repayments, so I got into debt very quickly. Perhaps if I'd understood them better, I might (**5**) <u>have</u> avoided this.

[EXAM SKILLS]

13▶ Do this Part 2 task with a partner. Try to talk for two minutes.

Describe something expensive you have bought for yourself.

You should say:

- where you bought it
- why you bought it
- how often you use it

and explain how you felt when you bought it.

14▶ With a partner, ask and answer these Part 3 questions.

1 In what way are people's attitudes to money different to previous generations'?
2 Now that paper money is hardly ever used, how has this changed our relationship with money in general?
3 Some people believe that online shopping has brought only benefits to our lives. Would you agree?
4 What are the risks involved in starting your own business, as opposed to being employed in a full-time, salaried position?
5 How important is it that people learn to manage their finances better?

 GO FURTHER ONLINE

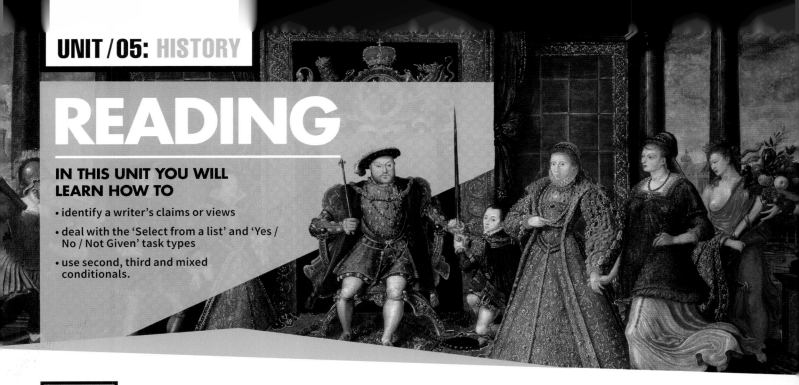

UNIT /05: HISTORY

READING

IN THIS UNIT YOU WILL LEARN HOW TO

- identify a writer's claims or views
- deal with the 'Select from a list' and 'Yes / No / Not Given' task types
- use second, third and mixed conditionals.

LEAD-IN

01 ▷ Which countries still have a monarchy today? Can you name any current or past kings or queens?

02 ▷ Which five of the following words are not specifically associated with royalty?

monarchy	sovereign	rule	abdicate	era	regent
dynasty	emperor	reign	leader	heir	coronation

03 ▷ Look at the groups of words. For each group, choose one odd-word-out. Why is it different? There may be more than one correct answer.

Example: queen   empress   monarch   princess

Monarch is the odd-one-out because the others are all female royalty and a monarch can be either male or female. / Princess is the odd-one-out because the others are rulers.

1 kingdom	empire	realm	dynasty
2 sovereign	regent	emperor	king
3 abdicate	reign	rule	govern
4 coronation	crown	investiture	ceremony

IDENTIFYING A WRITER'S CLAIMS OR VIEWS

04 ▷ Skim the text on page 94 quickly and answer the questions. Give reasons for your answers.

1 What is the purpose of the text?
  A to inform and entertain
  B to argue and persuade
  C to criticise monarchies and rulers

2 Which of the following do you think summarises the author's view on royalty?
  A pro-royalty
  B anti-royalty
  C neither pro- nor anti-royalty

 Some exam tasks require you to be able to identify a writer's claims (what they are presenting as a fact) or the writer's views (personal opinions expressed by the writer). Skim reading a text first can give you a feeling for the overall tone of it and help you understand what the writer is trying to communicate.

ECCENTRIC LEADERS

A When we think of kings, queens, emperors or any kind of royal leader, what usually comes to everyone's mind is dignity, power, ornate dress or majestic figures sitting elegantly on their thrones dispensing favours or wisdom to their subjects. Although many monarchs have done justice to this vision, throughout the world and throughout history there have also been a number of bizarre, frankly eccentric, rulers.

B The French have had their fair share of idiosyncratic kings. Charles VI, who reigned from 1368 to 1422, was not always aware that he was king and often forgot that he had a wife and children. There were times when he believed that he was made of glass and had his manservants put rods into his clothing so that he would not shatter! Charles the Mad, as he was known, would run around the palace grounds howling like a wolf until, eventually, his son-in-law had to take over as regent.

C Turning now to Russia, one of their more eccentric tsars, or leaders, was Fyodor 1 (1557–1598). He is said to have been simple-minded, and earned the nickname Fyodor the Bellringer for the almost childlike pleasure he took in ringing church bells. Not only did he allegedly lack the intelligence to rule, he also had no interest in doing so, leaving the running of the state to his wife's brother, Boris Godunov. Happily for him, rather than it being seen as a disadvantage, his subjects saw his childlike simplicity as being divinely inspired. However, as he died childless, his death marked the end of the Rurik dynasty and the beginning of a tumultuous period in Russian history known as the 'Time of Troubles'. Had he left an heir, Russian history might well have gone in a different direction.

D England too can boast of at least one peculiar monarch, George III, who reigned from 1760 to 1820. One of his most evident quirks was his speech and famously he once produced a sentence containing 400 words with only 8 of them being verbs! He once purportedly shook hands with a tree, believing it to be the King of Prussia! However, history often ignores the successes of his reign. He was the first English king to study the sciences, of which he became a patron, with the construction of the King's Observatory in Richmond amongst his achievements. But his supposed episodes of madness, particularly towards the end of his life, remained a concern, and according to the standards of the day, George was subjected to some bizarre and inhumane treatments in an attempt to cure them. Interestingly, there is some speculation from historians that had it not been for these treatments, he would not have been quite so unstable.

E Roman emperors are also said to have had some bizarre characters among their number, and Caligula, who ruled from 37–41 AD, probably has the worst reputation. Amongst other things, he was reported to have been an insomniac, roaming his palace all night and engaging in lengthy conversations with the Moon and Jupiter. He allegedly even appointed his horse as a senator, building it a stable out of marble and inviting it to dinner with his guests. However, it should be pointed out that many of these 'reports' about Caligula were written more than 80 years after his death, so their accuracy is open to question. What's more, if we compared his supposed behaviour to that of many of the other Roman emperors, quite a few of them would almost certainly be regarded as even more eccentric.

F One queen who was actually 'accused' of madness was Joanna (Juana) of Castile, who reigned from 1504 to 1516. However, again, whether this was the case or not is subject to debate. Certainly some of her behaviour could be regarded as unconventional, especially for the time. She was said to have been very jealous and on one occasion attacked and cut off the hair of a rival for her husband's affections. On the other hand, by many accounts she was a gifted and intelligent woman with a talent for diplomacy. The fact that both her father and her own son declared her mad and unfit to rule so that they could reign in her stead raises the question of whether the accusations were actually motivated by political ambition. Whatever the case, historians have dubbed her Joanna the Mad and, sadly for her reputation, this is unlikely to change.

G As we know from modern-day news reporting, just because something appears in print, it doesn't necessarily mean it is true, and it is all too easy to ruin someone's reputation with gossip and hearsay. Perhaps we should keep this in mind when we read about these colourful historical characters and remember that some of them may have been unfairly judged. After all, we all have our own strange habits and quirks. I for one think we should celebrate royal eccentricity. It certainly makes reading history much more interesting.

0 5 ▶ Find these sentences in the text. For each, decide if the author is making a claim or expressing a view.

1 Although many monarchs have done justice to this vision, throughout the world and throughout history there have also been a number of bizarre, frankly eccentric rulers.

2 Happily for him, […] his subjects saw his childlike simplicity as being divinely inspired.

3 He was the first English king to study the sciences …

4 I for one think we should celebrate royal eccentricity. It certainly makes reading history much more interesting.

TIP 0 5
'Claims' are the author's interpretation of the facts of a situation; in this case, this is what happened in the lives of these rulers. Views are subjective, expressions of the author's personal opinion on the situation.

SELECT FROM A LIST

 This task tests your ability to match statements with something from the text, often a person. You don't need to focus on the whole text to do this task – just find the sections that mention the options in the list. Some of the options may be mentioned in various places in the text. The instructions will tell you if each option may be used more than once.

0 6 ▶ Look at the exam task. Focus on the four options A–D. Scan the text and say in which paragraphs they are mentioned in the text. Do not try to answer the questions yet.

Look at the following statements and the list of people below.
*Match each statement with the correct person, **A–D**.*
*Write the correct letter **A, B, C** or **D** next to each statement.*

1 He believed himself to be very fragile.
2 He didn't really want to be the ruler.
3 It is claimed he talked to celestial bodies.
4 He supported the advancement of scientific research.

List of people
A Caligula
B George III
C Charles VI
D Fyodor I

0 7 ▶ Read the section of the text on Caligula again and then read the statements a–d about him. Which one of them is a paraphrase of one of the statements (1–4) in exercise 6?

a He ruled from 37 to 41 AD.
b He was a poor sleeper.
c He had conversations with the Moon and Jupiter.
d He made his horse a senator.

0 8 ▶ Complete the missing information about Charles VI. Then decide which statement in exercise 6 relates to Charles VI.

He reigned from 1368 to 1422.
He forgot _____
He believed _____
His son-in-law _____
He ran around the palace grounds, howling _____
Statement _____

TIP 0 7
The questions in this task type may relate to the views/claims of people mentioned in the text. Remember that the statements will be paraphrases of the words in the text.

0 9 ▶ Now read the sections about Fyodor I and George III. Then decide which of the remaining statements in exercise 6 corresponds to each of them.

Fyodor I: statement _____
George III: statement _____

YES, NO, NOT GIVEN

 This task is similar to True / False / Not Given. However, the focus is not based on factual information but rather on interpreting the writer's views or claims. This task type is often used with more complex argumentative texts in the exam.

10 ▷ These views and claims (1–4) are made in the text (*Yes* statements). Match them with the words from the text (a–d) which state the view.

1 Most people probably have a favourable view of royalty.
2 George III's condition was made worse by the therapies he was given.
3 Caligula was probably not the most bizarre ruler that his empire had.
4 Joanna of Castile may have been the victim of political intrigue.

a … if we compared his supposed behaviour to that of many of the other Roman emperors, quite a few of them would almost certainly be regarded as even more eccentric.

b … what usually comes to everyone's mind is dignity, power, ornate dress or majestic figures sitting elegantly on their thrones dispensing favours or wisdom to their subjects.

c The fact that both her father and her own son declared her mad and unfit to rule so that they could reign in her stead raises the question of whether the accusations were actually motivated by political ambition.

d … had it not been for these treatments, he would not have been quite so unstable.

11 ▷ These statements contradict the views and claims of the writer. Locate the part of the text where they are found. Which words or phrases help you to realise the statements contradict the views of the writer?

1 Fyodor I was disliked by his people.
2 Joanna of Castile showed no capacity as a ruler.
3 The stories about Caligula's behaviour are completely trustworthy.

12 ▷ Read the statement and then re-read paragraphs A and G. Why is this answer *Not Given*?

History shows that the majority of rulers are eccentric.

13 ▷ Are the following claims made by the writer? Write *Yes*, *No* or *Not Given*.

1 Countries should be ashamed of their eccentric monarchs.
2 All of the rulers were replaced by close relatives.
3 Russian history might have been different if Fyodor had had children.

TIP 12

'Not Given' answers often partially relate to ideas mentioned in the text, but which are neither confirmed nor contradicted, or they relate to information you would expect to see in the text but which isn't actually there.

GRAMMAR FOCUS: SECOND, THIRD AND MIXED CONDITIONALS

Second and third conditionals are sentences that describe present or past hypothetical situations (the *if* clause) and their hypothetical results (the result clause).

Second conditionals deal with a hypothetical present situation and its hypothetical present or future result. For example, *If I were king, I would reduce taxes*.

Third conditionals present a hypothetical past situation and its hypothetical past result. For example, *If I had been king, I would have reduced taxes*.

It is also possible to mix these two conditionals to give, for example, a hypothetical past situation and its hypothetical present result.

1 4 ▶ Complete the table with the correct structures, A–D.

A *would* + verb
B *would have* + past participle
C *If* + past simple / past continuous
D *If* + past perfect / past perfect continuous

Conditional type	*If* clause (situation)	Result clause
Second (hypothetical present situation with hypothetical present or future result)	If + past simple / past continuous	*would* + verb
Third (hypothetical past situation with hypothetical past result)	*If* + past perfect / past perfect continuous	*would have* + past participle
Mixed 1 (hypothetical past situation with present result)	1 _____	2 _____
Mixed 2 (hypothetical present situation with past result)	3 _____	4 _____

1 5 ▶ Look at these conditionals from the text. Which type is each one?

1 … if we compared his supposed behaviour to that of many of the other Roman emperors, quite a few of them would almost certainly be regarded as even more eccentric.
2 … had it not been for these treatments, he would not have been quite so unstable.
3 Had he left an heir, Russian history might well have gone in a different direction.
4 Without them, history would be a lot less interesting.

TIP 1 5

Note that there are variations in these structures. We can use other modals like *could* and *might* instead of *would* and sometimes the '*if* clause' does not use the word *if*. For example, we might use an inversion (*If he had known* → *Had he known*) or express the *if* clause with a paraphrase (*Without his rule* = *If he had not ruled*).

16 ▶ Read the passage and answer questions 1–10.

● ● ● ◁ ▷

THE PHARAOHS OF ANCIENT EGYPT

HOME **ABOUT** PHOTOS CONTACT

A pharaoh was a political and religious leader of Ancient Egypt. He – or, less often, she – enjoyed two titles: 'Lord of the Two Lands' and 'High Priest of Every Temple'. 'Two Lands' referred to the unification of Upper and Lower Egypt, which occurred during the First Dynasty in about 3150 BCE. King Menes (now believed to be King Narmer) was the first to be depicted wearing the two crowns of Egypt. The word pharaoh is the Greek form of 'pero' or 'per-a-a', which literally means 'great house', a reference to the royal residence. The honorific title first appeared in what is now known as the New Kingdom period of 1570–1069 BCE. Prior to that, the pharaohs were known as kings and addressed as 'Your Majesty' by both members of the court and foreign dignitaries. A tradition which started during this period and was maintained into the Pharaonic period was that foreign rulers addressed the king or pharaoh as 'Brother'.

As time passed, the pharaoh came to be considered a god on earth, a kind of intermediary between gods and humans. It was believed that after death, a pharaoh became Osiris, god of the dead. As such, probably their key role in Ancient Egyptian society was a religious one. In particular, each pharaoh oversaw the building of great monuments and temples to pay homage to the gods, as well as statues commemorating their own achievements. It was the pharaoh who chose the site of temples and officiated at religious ceremonies.

In addition to the religious duties, the pharaoh had civil duties such as making laws, collecting taxes and deciding on the work to be done, and he owned all the land in the country. According to Joshua J. Mark (www.ancient.eu), the pharaoh's chief responsibility was to maintain Ma'at or Universal Harmony, and warfare was an essential part of this. As well as defending the borders, it may have been considered necessary for the sake of harmony to attack neighbouring lands to gain natural resources.

Most of the pharaohs were male. In *Exploring Ancient Egypt*, Ian Shaw notes that there were only two or three women who were pharaohs, though many women held considerable power as the 'great wife', the first wife of the reigning pharaoh. Hatshepsut, the first female pharaoh, who ruled from 1473 to 1458 BCE made her mark on history. Owen Jarus points out that statues depicted Hatshepsut, whose name means 'foremost of noblewomen', as a male king complete with beard. She is remembered for her building projects, which were more ambitious than those of her ancestors. These included several obelisks and a Palace of Ma'at. She is buried in the Valley of the Kings in a huge funerary complex. However, her memory was not honoured. Egyptologist Joyce Tyldesley claims her tomb was defaced by her nephew and successor, Thutmose III, who wanted to take credit for her achievements. Hatshepsut's mummy was discovered in 2007. She had died aged 50, balding and suffering from diabetes. In spite of the desecration of her tomb, history remembers her as a great leader.

In Ancient Egypt kingship usually passed from father to son. However, changes of leadership were not always peaceful, nor did they always happen according to tradition. Some, like Hatshepsut, seized power illegally, and when they did so they typically claimed divine right. Sometimes crown princes were prepared for their future role in advance by being appointed co-regent, which would help them become accustomed to the importance of their role. Enthronements were major events, which celebrated a new beginning. The new reign, it was hoped, would signify an end to evil and injustice. The pharaoh had great, but not absolute, power. To achieve his aims, it was usual for the pharaoh to lavish gifts of power and possessions on those who could help him, such as military leaders, members of the priesthood and the scribal elite.

New information about the pharaohs is still coming to light. A new burial site, potentially as important as the Valley of the Kings, was discovered in 2014 by archaeologists from the University of Pennsylvania in the United States. Danish archaeologist Kim Ryholt first speculated about the existence of a lost dynasty of Ancient Egypt, while legendary Egyptologist Flinders Petrie discovered the site in 1902 but never excavated it, believing the tomb to be of too modest a size to be of significance. The discovery of the mummy of King Senebkay at this site in Abydos, about 100 km north-west of the Valley of the Kings, is the first definitive proof of another pharaonic dynasty.

According to the archaeologist on the project, Forster Mueller, there were more kings and therefore certainly more tombs nearby. Although the tomb had been vandalised by ancient looters, the team from Pennsylvania managed to piece together most of King Senebkay's skeleton. Another project member, Josef Wegner, admits that what they are hoping for is an intact tomb that somehow escaped the looters, though realistically it is fragments they are looking for. They deciphered Senebkay's name from hieroglyphics found inside the tomb. The 3,600-year-old King had been tall for his time at 1.75m and had died in his late 40s. This evidence of a third dynasty of pharaohs is an exciting discovery for all those interested in the history of Ancient Egypt. Even in the twenty-first century, the great pharaohs may still have more secrets to reveal.

Questions 1–6

Do the following statements agree with the claims of the writer? Write

   YES   if the statement agrees with the claims of the writer

   NO   if the statement contradicts the claims of the writer

   NOT GIVEN   if it is impossible to say what the writer thinks about this

1 Conflict with other countries was seen as compatible with maintaining peace in Egypt.
2 Pharaohs' wives often exerted great influence.
3 The first female pharaoh was particularly influential.
4 Hatshepsut came to power in the traditional way.
5 Military leaders, priests and scribes would attend enthronement ceremonies.
6 King Senebkay's skeleton was stolen by grave robbers.

Questions 7–10

Look at the following statements and the list of people below.

Match each statement with the correct person, **A–E.**

7 He believed a specific burial site was unimportant.
8 He acknowledges the prospect of finding an undamaged grave is unlikely.
9 He believed that there were probably more pharaohs buried close to Abydos.
10 He claimed there had been a pharaonic dynasty that no one knew about.

List of people
A Kim Ryholt
B Flinders Petrie
C Forster Mueller
D Josef Wegner
E Ian Shaw

GO FURTHER ONLINE

UNIT / 05: HISTORY

WRITING

IN THIS UNIT YOU WILL LEARN HOW TO

- describe information in a table or bar chart
- use linkers and cohesive language to improve your Coherence and Cohesion score for Task 1
- avoid repetition of language to improve your Coherence and Cohesion score for Task 1.

LEAD-IN

0 1 ▷ Discuss these questions in groups.

    1 What goods are manufactured in your country?

    2 Do you think manufacturing is increasing or decreasing?

    3 What goods are imported and exported?

    4 How does this compare with imports and exports in the past?

0 2 ▷ Match the terms (1–4) with their definitions (a–d).

1 heavy industry	**a**	small business carried out at home
2 cottage industry	**b**	extracting raw materials, such as forestry, fishing or mining
3 service industry	**c**	manufacturing large articles or materials, such as ships or steel
4 primary industry	**d**	tourism, catering, plumbing, etc; also known as the tertiary sector

03 ▷ Look at the Task 1 practice question and the table. With a partner, discuss the questions below.

The table gives information about the number of deep mines producing coal in the UK between 1913 and 2015.
Summarise the information by selecting and reporting the main features and make comparisons where relevant.

◎ Most table and bar chart-based Task 1 questions will ask you either to describe changes over time OR compare two or more sets of information. Sometimes you might have to do both. The language you need will vary depending on the type of task.

Year	Number of mines
1913	3024
1923	2607
1943	1690
1963	943
1983	170
2003	20
2015	5

1 What is the general trend in these figures?
2 Which years or time periods would you focus on as the most salient?

 04 ▷ Look at the marking criteria for IELTS Writing and read a candidate's answer to Task 1. What do you think are its strengths and weaknesses?

Marking criteria

Task Achievement: How well the question is answered, including identifying the key features

Coherence and Cohesion: How the text is organised, and how ideas are sequenced and connected together logically to make it easy to follow

Lexical Resource: The range and precision of vocabulary used

Grammatical Range and Accuracy: The range and precision of the grammatical structures used

SAMPLE ANSWER

The table shows the number of deep coal mines in the UK between 1913 and 2015. Obviously, there is a decline over the period. We can say that coal mines almost disappeared and there were only 5 left in 2015.

In 1913, there were 3024 deep coal mines but this number began to decrease. The number of mines fell sharply and consistently over the subsequent years. Nevertheless, in 1943 there were 1690 mines left. This means that in a period of thirty years, the number of mines had almost halved. By 1963, this figure had virtually halved again.

Surprisingly, in the 1980s we see another huge reduction, with the number falling to around 20% of 1963 levels. By the time the current century began, there had been another decrease. In 2003, the number of deep mines producing coal dropped to 20. At last, we see that there are only 5 mines left.

In conclusion, there was a decreasing trend in mining in Britain for the duration of the period shown in the chart.

This marking criterion covers how the answer is organised, how well the information is linked together and whether it makes sense to the reader. Key aspects of this include:

- paragraphing
- the correct and varied use of linkers (words or phrases) to introduce points in a clear way and to connect ideas logically, allowing the reader to follow it easily
- use of referencing words and phrases, such as pronouns, to avoid repetition.

0 5 ▶ **Read this feedback from a teacher on coherence and cohesion in the candidate's answer in exercise 4. Choose linkers from the box to replace the inappropriate highlighted linkers (1–4). Can you think of any other alternatives for these linkers?**

The order of information is appropriate and you have divided it into paragraphs. However there is some inappropriate use of linkers. For example, in the first paragraph, is 'obviously' the best choice here? It could imply that everyone should know this information.

In the second paragraph, what do you mean with the word 'nevertheless'? Do you want to show a contrast?

In the third paragraph, why is it 'surprising' that the 1980s saw a 'huge reduction'? This implies knowledge from outside the data set, which shouldn't be included in Task 1 answers. Are you saying that you are surprised? What do you mean by 'At last' here in the same paragraph? This implies that you are relieved by this figure.

1 Obviously
2 Nevertheless
3 Surprisingly
4 At last

For example
By the end of the period shown, in 2015,
The clear trend in the figures is that
It is striking that

TIP 0 6

You can improve your Coherence and Cohesion score if you can use a variety of discourse markers correctly. For Task 1 questions like these, try making your own lists of discourse markers that you can use, and classify them by their function. Practise using them when you do exam practice questions so that you learn to choose appropriate ones depending on the question.

0 6 ▶ **Look at this answer by another candidate about the same table. The coherence and cohesion is much better in this one. Find discourse markers that perform the functions listed on the next page. There may be more than one answer for each function.**

SAMPLE ANSWER

The data shows how many deep coal mines were in operation in the UK at various points in the 100-year period between 1913 and 2015. The overall trend is clearly one of decline. In fact, by the end of the given time frame, deep mines had almost ceased to operate in the UK.

In the early decades of the twentieth century, there were still thousands of coal mines in Britain: to give a specific example, there were 3024 of them still operational in 1913. However, the process of closing down the UK's deep mines had clearly begun: by 1923, the number had fallen to 2607. By the middle of the century, it was apparent that the days of British coal mining were numbered. In 1963, the figure fell below 1,000 for the first time.

One of the most striking features of this table is that the deterioration of Britain's coal mining industry accelerated even further in the 1980s and was almost complete by the turn of the twenty-first century.

1 To emphasise or exemplify an idea or point that you are making

_____ In fact; to give a specific example; One of the most striking features of this table is _____

2 To provide an overview of the evident tendencies in the data

_____

3 To show a contrast with previous information

_____

4 To introduce key time periods in the data

_____

0 7 ▷ Look at this bar chart which shows data on the manufacture of passenger cars in 2015. With a partner, discuss the following questions.

1 What is the most important information in this chart?
2 Which regions of the data would you focus on to make comparisons?
3 How would you organise your answer based on this data?

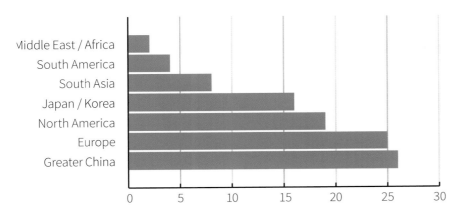

World passenger car production by area (%)

0 8 ▷ Now look at a sample answer which summarises and reports the data in exercise 7. Some of the discourse markers have been removed. Fill the gaps with words or phrases from the box.

although	in terms of	Turning next to	respectively	By contrast
Whereas	moving on to	What stands out is	For the purposes of this data set	

The bar chart gives the percentage of passenger cars manufactured by different regions of the world. **1** _____ , the world is divided into seven regions, with the total adding up to 100%.

2 _____ that the regions of Greater China and Europe lead the way **3** _____ the manufacture of passenger cars, with 26% and 25% **4** _____ . **5** _____ , very few cars are produced in the Middle East and Africa: just 2% originate from that area.

6 _____ the Americas, a sharp contrast can be seen between the Northern and Southern parts of the continent. **7** _____ North America can boast 19% of the world's passenger car production, South America manufactures just 4% of this type of vehicle.

Finally, **8** _____ Japan and Korea, **9** _____ they are just two countries rather than a whole region, they account for a sizeable proportion of the total, at 16%.

0 9 ▶ Find words and phrases from the box in exercise 8 which match these functions.

1 Showing contrast: _____ , _____ , _____

2 Introducing a new point/idea/section: _____ , _____ ,

_____

3 To emphasise or exemplify an idea or point that you are making:

_____

4 To introduce a statement which clarifies the data: _____

5 To indicate that some information is in the same order as connected information
mentioned in a previous statement: _____

1 0 ▶ These are extracts from the sample answers in exercises 6 and 8. What information does each underlined word or phrase allow the writer to avoid repeating?

1 The overall trend is clearly <u>one</u> of decline. *a trend*

2 the 100-year period between 1913 and 2015 … by the end of <u>the given time frame</u>

3 … there were still thousands of coal mines in Britain: to give a specific example, there were 3024 <u>of them</u>.

4 the process of closing down the UK's deep mines had clearly begun: by 1923, <u>the number</u> had fallen to 2607.

5 North America can boast 19% of the world's passenger car production, South America manufactures just 4% of <u>this type of vehicle</u>.

**GO FURTHER
ONLINE**

EXAM SKILLS

1 1 ▶ Answer the Writing Task 1 below.

You should spend about 20 minutes on this task.

The bar chart shows the percentages of the UK workforce in five major industries in 1841 and 2011.

Summarise the information by selecting and reporting the main features, and make comparisons where relevant.

Write at least 150 words.

Percentage of UK workforce in each industry

Manufacuring: 36% (1841), 9% (2011)
Services: 33% (1841), 81% (2011)
Agriculture / Fishing: 22% (1841), 1% (2011)
Construction: 5% (1841), 8% (2011)
Energy / water: 3% (1841), 1% (2011)

■ 1841   ■ 2011

UNIT / 05: HISTORY

LISTENING

IN THIS UNIT YOU WILL LEARN HOW TO

- describe trends and periods in history
- answer 'Select from a list' and matching tasks
- identify attitude and opinion
- use prepositions of time correctly.

01 Look at the following time phrases. For each, decide which option(s) are NOT correct.

a **in** / **during** / **on** the 1070s

b in the **end** / **early** / **mid** twentieth century

c during the Victorian **period** / **season** / **era**

d **from** / **between** / **in** 1642 and 1649

e **in** / **after** / **before** the restoration of the monarchy

f **between** / **from** / **in** 1914 to 1918

g **since** / **during** / **on** the 9th century AD

h in the first **half** / **era** / **decade** of the twenty-first century

i in the **past** / **recent** / **last** 200 years

02 Try to match the events (1–9) with the time periods (a–i) in exercise 1. Then listen and check your ideas.

35

1 The monarchy has existed in England …

2 Elizabeth II became Queen of England …

3 There was a Civil War in England …

4 The Tower of London has had many functions …

5 The Tower of London was built by William the Conqueror …

6 The First World War lasted …

7 King Charles II gained control of the Tower of London …

8 The Tower of London became a tourist destination …

9 The number of visitors to the Tower of London rose to 2 million per year …

[SELECT FROM A LIST]

In this task type you have to choose two correct answers from a list of five options. Make sure you read the question and options carefully before you listen. Try to identify the key words and phrases in the options – the ones which carry the main meaning. Think of different ways to express these ideas as the recording will most likely use different words.

03▶ Read the 'Select from a list' question. The key words are in bold. Choose a synonym for each bold word from the box below. Do not answer the question yet.

*Which **ONE** of these is **NOT** mentioned as a previous use of the Tower of London?*

A a **home** for a **king or queen**
B a place where **arms** are kept
C a **place of worship**
D a **destination** for **sightseers**
E a place where **currency** is **manufactured**

| church | money | attraction | residence | royalty | weapons | made | tourists |

04▶ Listen to the first part of a talk about the Tower of London and answer the question in exercise 3.

36

05▶ Read the question and the list of statements. For each of the key words and phrases in bold, think of different ways of expressing them, including using different parts of speech.

*Which **TWO** of these statements about the history of the Tower are true according to the speaker?*

A Henry the Eighth **ordered the construction of** the Tower of London.
   It was built by, commissioned the building of, had the Tower of London built
B King Charles the First **controlled** the Tower throughout the English Civil War.
C **Enemies** of Henry the Eighth **lost their lives** in the Tower.
D There was a **zoo** in the Tower for **six centuries**.
E Charles the Second **got back** the Crown Jewels from his enemies.

TIP 05

Be careful. The words you hear on the recording may be synonyms for the whole statement or you may hear the ideas expressed using different parts of speech or grammatical structures. For example, in the statement the key word might be a noun but in the recording the speaker might express the same idea using a verb phrase.

06▶ Listen and answer the question in exercise 5 by choosing TWO statements from the list A–E.

37

TIP 06

Be careful. The options in this type of task will not be in the same order as the recording.

07▶ Look at the exam task. Before you listen, use the strategies from exercises 3 and 5 to pick out the key words and think of different ways of expressing them. Then listen and answer the question.

38

*Which **TWO** statements are **NOT** true about the Tower of London today?*

A The birds called ravens have left the Tower.
B There is a special person to look after the ravens.
C The ravens can be dangerous.
D The guards called Beefeaters also act as tourist guides.
E Anyone can become a Beefeater.

ATTITUDE AND OPINION

 Some exam tasks require you to identify the attitudes or opinions of a speaker on a certain subject. Listen for opinion verbs, adjectives, adverbs and expressions. Also focus on the speaker's reactions and responses to a situation, as how someone reacts can reveal a lot about how they feel.

08▸ Match a word or expression from the box with each group of words which express a similar attitude or opinion.

challenging	sub-standard	famous	My favourite part was
phenomenal	frightening	dazzling	apprehensive

1 It didn't live up to my expectations   disappointing   inadequate   _____
2 gorgeous   stunning   exquisite   _____
3 out of this world   impressive   It took my breath away   _____
4 I really like how   I love the way that   What pleased me the most was   _____
5 horrifying   terrifying   gruesome   _____
6 anxious   on edge   I had butterflies in my stomach   _____
7 iconic   legendary   renowned   _____
8 heavy going   I really struggled with it   tough   _____

09▸ Now read these comments from speakers. For each, what do you think the speaker's opinion or attitude to the situation is?

1 To be honest, I was glad when the tour ended. I was beginning to think it never would.
   A interested   B bored   C angry

2 I usually hate museums, but in this one the hours just flew by and sadly, before I knew it, it was time to leave.
   A frustrated   B angry   C fascinated

3 Pete said that the Science Museum was out of this world. Well, there's no accounting for taste. I certainly won't be recommending it to anyone.
   A disappointed   B delighted   C impressed

4 To be frank, that exhibit had an incredible effect on me. I cried my eyes out afterwards.
   A surprised   B moved   C frightened

5 When I heard that there was an exhibition on space travel, I was over the moon. And it more than lived up to my expectations.
   A pleased   B indifferent   C surprised

10▸
39

Listen to two students discussing their ideas for a presentation on The Tower of London and do the task.

Which TWO opinions are NOT agreed on by both of the speakers?

A It is not realistic to talk about the entire history of the Tower.
B There is not enough to say about the Beefeaters and ravens.
C The Fusilier Museum topic would appeal to most students.
D Including a competition would be a good idea.
E The Crown Jewels would be the best topic to present.

MULTIPLE MATCHING

 In this task type you match one set of information (numbered) with another (lettered). For example, you match people or places in the recording with comments they make or comments made about them. There are two versions of this task – one with more lettered options than questions, so some of the letters are distractors, and one with more questions than options, so the letters can be used more than once.

11▶ You are going to listen to two students discussing other tourist attractions in London. First, look at the exam task. Think of different ways of paraphrasing the comments.

What comments do the speakers make about the tourist attractions?
*Choose **FIVE** answers from the box and write the correct letter, **A–G**, next to questions 1–5.*

Tourist attractions

1 Madame Tussauds _____
2 Buckingham Palace _____
3 Westminster Abbey _____
4 The Tower of London _____
5 The London Bridge Experience _____

> **Comments**
> **A** It had previously had a display of real royal clothes.
> **B** Many famous artists are buried there.
> **C** It updates its exhibits from time to time.
> **D** It lived up to its reputation.
> **E** The queues were too long to get in.
> **F** It always has beautiful flower displays.
> **G** It has hosted many royal weddings.

12▶ Listen and answer questions 1–5 in exercise 11. Were any of your suggested paraphrases used in the recording?

40

[EXAM SKILLS]

13▶ Listen and answer questions 1–7.

41

Questions 1–5

What problem is associated with each of the topics Adrian is considering?

*Choose **FIVE** answers from the box and write the correct letter, **A–G**, next to questions 1–5.*

1 History _____
2 Trade routes _____
3 Conflicts _____
4 Architecture _____
5 Modern life _____

Problems

A Most people are not aware of this aspect.

B It would involve too much investigative work.

C It is too large a topic.

D It could be too technical.

E It might take the focus off Petra.

F Most people would not be interested in this aspect.

G Academically, it is an inappropriate topic.

Questions 6 and 7

*Which **TWO** points about water management are NOT made by the speakers?*

A Petra's water management was more advanced than that in other comparable areas.

B The topic of water management systems is very complex to understand.

C In Petra the people knew how to get the most out of all the sources of water available to them.

D The advantages of water management were enjoyed by all levels of society equally.

E Watering crops was a top priority.

GO FURTHER
ONLINE

SPEAKING

IN THIS UNIT YOU WILL LEARN HOW TO

- use a range of past time phrases
- improve your score for Grammatical Range and Accuracy
- use expressions for agreeing and disagreeing
- develop your answers in Part 3.

LEAD-IN

01 ▶ Explain these historical periods to your partner using different words.

1 in the second half of the twentieth century   *about 1950 to 1999*
2 during the Middle Ages
3 during the Renaissance
4 at the turn of this century
5 in the early decades of the twentieth century
6 at the start of this millennium
7 in prehistoric times
8 in 3100 BC

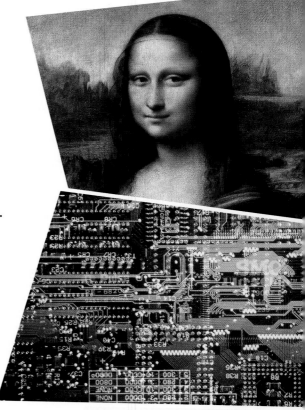

02 ▶ Match these historical events/trends with the time periods in exercise 1.

a cave paintings
b the First World War
c the medieval period
d rapid growth of technology
e the start of the Egyptian Pharaoh dynasties
f Y2K (2 answers)
g developments in art, literature, science and intellectual inquiry

03 ▶ Think about major historical events that have occurred in your country. Tell your partner about them using expressions in exercise 1 or in the box.

about _____ years ago	when my parents/grandparents were young
in the _____ th century	in the recent/distant past
in around 1923	during the _____ war

In the Speaking test, a quarter of the marks are awarded for Grammatical Range and Accuracy. This means it is not enough to avoid mistakes: you have to use a range of complex grammatical structures accurately to achieve the higher score bands.

0 4 ▷ Read the Part 2 task card. Then listen to Daniel and answer the questions.

42

Describe an important historical event in your country.

You should say:

- when it happened
- who was involved
- what caused the event

and explain what people think about the event nowadays.

1 Which of the points on the card does Daniel mention?
2 In which order does he mention them?
3 Do you think Daniel would get a good score for his answer? Why?

0 5 ▷ Look at the script of Daniel's Part 2 task. Match the underlined phrases (1–10) with the grammatical structures (a–j).

Actually, I can talk about a historical event that I witnessed in person in my country. It happened in November 1989, when I was just a young boy, about 10 years old. All my life (**1**) there had been a wall (**2**) dividing our city – and our country – into East and West. I often saw the wall when I went around town with my family or friends. It was a fact of life. I never (**3**) expected it to come down in my lifetime, but I often wondered what (**4**) it would have been like to live on the other side. As I lived on the Western side, I had been on the other side several times, but I knew that my aunt and my cousins, (**5**) who lived in the East, (**6**) were not allowed to come over to our side. But that winter's night it all changed. We could hear people running through the streets shouting 'Tor auf' – 'Open the gate!' Even though it was past midnight, my parents took my sisters and I to the wall. It was like a huge street party. People (**7**) were dancing and shouting, everyone was excited. At midnight they opened the checkpoints and people from the East flooded through. We bought a huge bunch of flowers from a stand. My sisters and I handed them out to people coming across from the East to welcome them. At the time I didn't know what caused the event, but later I found out it was the end of the Cold War. People still think of this event as a symbol of peace. I was very (**8**) fortunate to be present to see history being made. Those of us (**9**) who live in Berlin often think what life (**10**) would be like today if the wall hadn't come down on that fateful night in 1989.

a verb + object + infinitive
b adjective + infinitive
c mixed conditional (past action, present result)
d defining relative clause
e non-defining relative clause

f past continuous tense
g passive voice
h participle clause
i modal perfect
j past perfect tense

06 ▶ Now read the script of another candidate doing the task. Find 10 grammatical errors and match them with the error types (1–10) below.

One event I remember well is my parents taking me to the Beijing to see Opening Ceremony of Olympics. It was held in 2008, when I was 12 years old. My father explained me that it was a very important event in our country. I never went to the Beijing before. It was the exciting day of my life. I remember 2008 drummers were all doing the same thing. If one made a mistake, the whole show will be ruined. But no one made a mistake. It was perfect! There were people dressed in colourful costumes fly across the stage. Small children was dressed in national clothes. A small girl was singing beautifully. When our national anthem played, we all stood up and sang. I felt so proud. I never forget that day!

1 past perfect tense needed	6 subject/verb agreement in passive
2 present participle needed	7 future simple needed
3 third conditional error	8 superlative error
4 unnecessary article	9 verb pattern error
5 article missing x2	10 past continuous used instead of past simple

07 ▶ At the end of his task, Daniel from exercise 5 was asked the additional question 'Do children learn about this event at school?' Listen to three possible answers to this question. Which is the best? Give reasons.

TIP 07

At the end of your talk, the examiner may ask one or two follow-up questions. The aim of the follow-up question(s) is to round off Part 2, so don't introduce new ideas. Answer the question in a full sentence or two, taking about 15 seconds at most.

AGREEING OR DISAGREEING

08 ▶ Look at these Part 3 questions on the subject of history. Listen to a candidate called Minji answering the questions. Match the questions (1–4) with the words Minji uses to begin each answer (a–d).

1 Do you think it's important for children to learn history at school?
2 You said children should learn the history of their own country. What about world history?
3 Do you think most children are interested in learning history these days?
4 Can technology help us learn about history?

a I'm not so sure about that.
b Absolutely!
c Yes, definitely.
d To be honest, I'd say probably not.

In Part 3 the examiner may ask you questions which require you to agree or disagree. Try to use a variety of responses to show your agreement or disagreement to impress the examiner with your range of language. Remember that Part 3 questions require more extended answers, so make sure you provide reasons, explanations, examples, etc. to support what you say.

09 ▶ Listen again. Make notes to summarise what Minji says to expand her answer.

10 ▶ Look at the expressions for agreeing and disagreeing and put them into three columns: Agree / Neither agree nor disagree / Disagree.

Well, there are two ways to look at this.	Certainly.	It's hard to say.	Not really.
Definitely not!	Possibly.	To some extent	Sure.
To be frank, it's not very …	Of course.	Without a doubt	No, not at all.

11 Read the script of Minji's Part 3 answers on page 216. Identify the following grammatical structures from the underlined phrases.

1 verb *-ing* as the subject or object of a sentence x2
2 *without* + verb *-ing*
3 passive x3
4 superlative
5 modal verbs x2
6 defining relative clause with *where*

12 Match the Part 3 questions (1–4) with their functions (a–d).

1 Why has attendance at museums declined so much in recent years?
2 Can you think of any jobs or careers for which the study of history is very important?
3 Is the way history is taught in schools different from how other subjects are taught?
4 What important events do you think might take place in the future?

a Compare two things
b Speculate about something
c Make predictions about the future
d Explain the causes of something

TIP 12

In Part 3 you will not be asked questions about your own experience or about very familiar topics. You will be asked to give reasons for something or to explain the results of events, or to imagine what might happen in the future. These questions require more advanced structures and vocabulary.

13 In pairs, look at all the Part 3 questions in exercises 8 and 12. Write answers for each question. Focus on the following:

• Think about the function of the question, and answer appropriately.
• Use a word or expression of agreement or disagreement if appropriate.
• Give an extended answer.
• Use more advanced grammar structures and vocabulary.

EXAM SKILLS]

 GO FURTHER ONLINE

14 Do these sample exam tasks with a partner. Take turns to ask and answer.

Part 2

Describe an interesting person from history.

You should say

• who the person was
• what historical event(s) they were involved in
• where or how you learned about this person

and say why you found this person so interesting.

Part 3

What lessons can we learn from studying the past?

What events have happened recently that you think will be remembered as important in history?

Do you think museums are the best way to get children and young people interested in history?

Do you think it is important for literature and films about past events to be historically accurate?

UNIT / 06: SCIENCE AND TECHNOLOGY

READING

IN THIS UNIT YOU WILL LEARN HOW TO

- do summary completion tasks with and without boxes of options
- label a diagram
- check your understanding of future tenses.

LEAD-IN

01▶ Find the ten words in this paragraph where the writer has made a mistake with the part of speech.

Technology has greatly improved the life of many people around the world, according to a considerable amount of researches that has been conducted over the past century. The use of the internet in particularly has become so widespread in so many countries that our daily existence would now be imaginable without it. This is not necessarily a positive developed. As the work of Guillerme Vínculos concludes, when social media first started to become popularly, it was an innocence extension of the standard types of interaction between friends and new acquaintances. These days, however, there are two noticeably extremes, both negative. One is where the platform is used as a substituted for human-to-human contact. The second is where it is employment as a way to bully or aggressively intimidate other people.

02▶ Compare your answers with a partner. Then make a list of the incorrect and correct forms of the words you have identified, noting the part of speech in each case. The first one has been done for you.

	Incorrect	Correct
1	*life (noun, singular)*	*lives (noun, plural)*
2		
3		
4		
5		
6		
7		
8		
9		
10		

SUMMARY COMPLETION WITH OPTIONS

◎ There are two types of summary completion tasks in the Reading test: *with* options to choose from and *without*. Both test your reading skills, especially skimming and scanning to locate specific information. The information you need to complete the summary can come from a single section or various sections of the text, so read the task through first to help you find which part(s) you need to focus on.

0 3 ▶ **Read the summary completion task, which is based on the text *The Future of Virtual Reality* on pages 116–117, and answer the questions below. Do not try to complete the summary yet.**

Complete the summary using the list of words, A–J, below.
Write the correct letter, A–J.

VR: How popular can it become?

There is some debate as to whether VR will ever become something used in a
1 _____ way, rather than predominantly in niche areas of technology. On the one hand, experts say it is **2** _____ that by 2030, HMDs will have become part of our everyday lives. On the other, it is also possible that they will go the same way as other **3** _____ technologies, such as CDs or PDAs. This is because most home consoles and computers are **4** _____ of coping with the VR software. Thus, even enthusiastic users are likely to be **5** _____ to endure the resultant physical side-effects.

A mainstream	B interactive	C unable	D reluctant	E outmoded
F operational	G incapable	H essential	I conceivable	J functioning

1 What do you notice about the options in the box you have to choose from?
2 Use these questions to help you locate which parts of the reading text you need to focus on to complete the gaps.
  a What does the title of the summary tell you?
  b Which parts of the summary can you use to scan the passage and locate the information quickly?
  c In which paragraph of the reading text does it talk about HMDs as part of our lives?
  d In which paragraph of the reading text are CDs and PDAs mentioned in connection with HMDs?

0 4 ▶ **Complete the task in exercise 3.**

TIP 0 4
This type of summary question requires you to write the *letter* that corresponds to each option, so DO NOT write the words you are given as options onto your answer sheet or you will not gain the marks, even if you are correct.

THE FUTURE OF
VIRTUALREALITY

A For the next ten years, various aspects of society could be going through enormous change as Virtual Reality (VR) technology moves towards fully operational and interactive implementation of its potential. To what extent VR establishes itself as an integral part of our lives, and how quickly it is likely to move from niche technology to common usage throughout society, is currently under discussion. However, many experts are of the opinion that VR may well have become sufficiently developed for it to form an essential part of life by 2030 (if not sooner). Over 40 million people currently own VR headsets, and this figure is expected to double over the next three years. By 2025, we may well have reached the point at which almost 200 million users own a VR viewing device, the Head Mounted Display (HMD), more commonly known as a VR headset.

B The ultimate aim of these headsets is to generate a 360-degree, 3D virtual world, enabling the viewer to enjoy what they are watching without the physical limits of a TV, computer or cinema screen. There are two LCD displays, one for each eye, which display images being sent by the computer or some such device (via an HDMI cable) or on the screen of a smartphone inserted into the front of the headset. Lenses, set inside the HMD between the user's eyes and the LCD displays, are necessary to counteract the natural differences between what one human eye and the other simultaneously see.

C These lenses enable two 2D images of the display to be viewed, thus creating a tailored picture for each eye. These combine to create the illusion of 'real life' in 3D. The HMD also uses 'head tracking', a system that follows the principle of aircraft flight, tracking three measurements known as pitch, yaw and roll (or movement along the x, y and z axes). It means that when the user tilts their head up, down, or to the side, VR follows these motions and allows them to 'see' all around them.

D With such technology in place, one of the most notable sectors in which VR is likely to have far-reaching effects will be the games industry. In this field, traditional games are in development even now with far greater scope for creativity than ever before. Role Playing Games (RPGs), in which a gamer plays the part of a character from a first-person viewpoint, moving through an entirely imagined, graphically rendered world, are nothing new. However, VR games designers will be able to add to this existing appeal by enabling the user to look all around themselves at a fully immersive world, one in which the flow of the narrative can more easily be controlled by the gamer, rather than the creator.

E Despite this, games designers currently appear to be more attracted to the untapped potential of new approaches to their end product. For example, games may become less about employing motor skills, such as swift reflexes or hand–eye coordination. Instead, the aim may be to enjoy the experience of a VR world in a more unhurried way, with traditional game mechanics (e.g. accumulating points, moving through a series of levels) running alongside as a secondary concern.

F   Other fields are similarly going to find their landscapes greatly altered. Educators, for one, will be presented with a vast array of new opportunities through which to pass on knowledge. Within the next five to ten years, teachers may become able to move completely away from the course book or flat screen – even the classroom itself – and into an immersive world of instruction and learning. By way of example, history students could be taken into the epicentre of the world's greatest battles and conflicts, experiencing and understanding the machinations of victory first-hand. Medical students may be provided with the opportunity to travel through the human body as if they were themselves the size of a blood cell, building their comprehension of how veins and arteries, or nerve systems, are interconnected. Music students will be able to watch a VR orchestra perform their new composition in a venue of their choice, whether that be the local concert hall or even the Sydney Opera House.

G   Current HMDs do not allow for any dialogue to take place between the user and the simulated people they encounter in the VR world. However, this is unlikely to be the case forever; a student of Mandarin should one day be able to 'walk' the streets of Beijing, conversing with the local native-speakers, and practising the regional pronunciation. Similarly, by the year 2021, the concept of travel may have undergone a profound transformation. Parts of the world currently inaccessible to most people, whether because the expense of flying is too great or because those places are too remote to be easily reached, will become open to visitors in the form of exact VR replicas of the original cities, rainforests, beaches and so on. Not only is this bound to please avid travellers, it could also appease the concerned environmentalist; the number of commercial flights operating each day might well decrease as people opt for VR vacations.

H   Despite its potential to change life as we know it today, it is also possible that VR will ultimately fail to catch on, and HMDs will be consigned to history in the same way as were CDs, MiniDisc players and Personal Digital Assistants (PDAs). After all, even the technology that today seems improbable will at some point become outdated. If this does indeed occur, the most likely cause of its failure will be that the vast majority of computers and consoles available for the home market lack the required processing power. One potentially disastrous side effect of underpowered hardware is that latency issues – when what the viewer sees on the display fails to catch up with the movement of their head – can cause motion sickness in the HMD wearer. Even the most devoted VR enthusiast may be unwilling to accept this as the consequence of their interest in new technologies.

SUMMARY COMPLETION WITHOUT OPTIONS

 For this version of the task, you need to use exact words from the text to fill the gaps. The gaps can require more than one word and must fit grammatically, and, as with the other summary task, they can come from anywhere in the passage and will not necessarily be found in the same order as they appear in the text.

06 ▷ Read the summary completion task, which is based on the text on pages 116–117, and answer the questions below. Do not try to complete the task yet.

Complete the summary below.
*Choose **NO MORE THAN TWO WORDS** from the passage for each answer.*

APPLICATIONS OF VR

The influence and effects of VR technology will be **1** _____ . This will be most noticeable in one particular **2** _____ – Video Games. Since games designers and developers are increasingly able to use their **3** _____ in new ways, the conventional mechanics and concerns of game playing may become **4** _____ . Further changes are likely to happen away from this field as well: teachers will be able to enter an **5** _____ that enables learning to take place away from the typical classroom setting; Music students could theoretically listen to their latest **6** _____ being played in the Sydney Opera House, while students of Medicine will be able to understand how so many parts of the human body are **7** _____ . Furthermore, differing approaches to travel may mean that fewer flights are taken, as people 'virtually' visit the destinations of their choice. This development is likely to please environmentalists as well as **8** _____ .

1 Which parts of the text contain the information you need?
2 Are the answers you need all individual words?

07 ▷ Look at a candidate's answers for questions 1 and 2 of this summary. Why are they grammatically incorrect?

1 extensively
2 sectors

08 ▷ With a partner, discuss what part of speech you will probably need to look for to complete each of the remaining gaps.

09 ▷ Complete the summary in exercise 6.

DIAGRAM LABELLING

10 Scan the passage quickly and decide in which paragraph(s) you are most likely to read about the diagram below.

Label the diagram below.
*Choose **NO MORE THAN TWO WORDS** from the passage for each answer.*

How a VR headset works

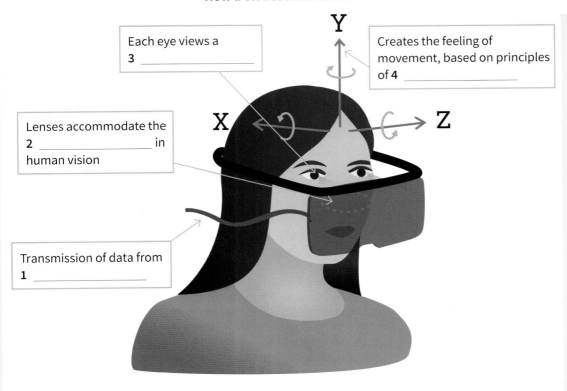

Each eye views a
3 _____

Creates the feeling of movement, based on principles of 4 _____

Lenses accommodate the
2 _____ in human vision

Transmission of data from
1 _____

Diagram-labelling tasks normally require single- or multiple-word answers from the text. They usually relate only to a specific part of the text.

11 Label the diagram in exercise 10.

GRAMMAR FOCUS: FUTURE TENSES

12 With a partner, discuss how the meaning of the sentences changes when options A, B and C are used in the gaps.

1 Expert opinion suggests that, in 2030, an entirely new form of non-physical communication _____ that will make today's social media appear positively prehistoric.

   A will be developed   **B** will have been developed   **C** will develop

2 Many inventors look at what they have created and think to themselves, 'I'm going to be rich soon because I know this _____.'

   A works   **B** will work   **C** could work

3 Educators seem to be in broad agreement that Coding _____ the most important and popular subject in schools, colleges and universities around the world.

   A might become   **B** may well become   **C** is about to become

13▶ Read the passage and answer questions 1–9.

HOLOGRAPHICS AND ANIMATION IN MUSIC AND PERFORMANCE

A For hundreds of years, the more forward-thinking elements of science and technology have stoked imaginations in the world of entertainment. For example, a huge number of science fiction movies were produced over the 20th century, a period during which space exploration became first a possibility, then a reality. Many such films depict situations in which one character (in full bodily form) interacts with a 3D, holographic image of another. Despite the optimism in some quarters, genuine interaction with holograms in the real world is still as far from becoming a reality as ever. Additionally, there is some doubt as to whether the existing, limited holographic technology is even worth exploring any further. However, what is currently available has begun to be used for entertainment purposes in a wide range of industries.

B The music industry is one. It has sought to take advantage of this technology since its infancy. There have been numerous examples – concerts and events – during which audiences have been able to watch modern vocalists sharing the stage with holographic images of performers who departed this world some time ago. In fact, the technology has been developed to such an advanced stage that it is almost possible to stage an entire concert 'performed' by dead rock stars. Critics have argued that this is exploitative of both audience and musician, pointing out the questionable morality of putting on stage an artist who has no way of refusing to be there.

C On the other hand, it might be argued that, to modern audiences so accustomed to a daily intake of entertainment viewed almost entirely on 2D screens, on-stage animation allows people once again to embrace the excitement of the 3D, live arena. Such shows, its advocates argue, are likely to become commonplace as the world of entertainment expands its horizons. (Great actors could also be resurrected to take their place on the theatre stage, for example.) This is due in no small part to the fact that the on-stage technology making this possible is actually less complex than one might expect, certainly if, rather than a true holographic performance, reflective technology is used instead.

D To achieve this, a laser projector shoots down an image beam that is set up to be exactly perpendicular to the floor. If the angle of projection is greater or less than 90 degrees, even by the tiniest amount, the projection will fail. As the song is being played, the animated image is projected onto a mirrored surface which has been set into the stage floor. This set up means that a 'suspension of disbelief' can be created within the onlooking audience, as it collectively sees the moving image while, at the same time, the transparent foil used to make the screen is invisible, stretched back as it is at an angle of 45 degrees. There is no maximum or minimum height at which projection fails to work, and, after a series of relatively simple calculations, the laser projector can be simply fixed to a lighting rig set up high above the stage.

E The future of holographic performance does appear rather limited, however, particularly in the context of bringing musicians back to life in this way. For one thing, it is impossible to create a new performance from old videotape, and there is a limited amount of original footage of these icons that was shot while they were alive. It is unlikely that a great deal more will be found. Following on from this, the only way to generate an entirely new show would be through Computer-Generated Imagery (CGI) and this, for most fans, would defeat the object of the exercise entirely. Finally, most of this past footage was shot on acetate film, which cannot come close to the modern ultra HD technology that is the bare minimum required for a truly lifelike reanimation. Consumers would soon grow tired of these limitations, however much of a novelty the experience might once have been.

F Away from the revival of past performers, it is now possible to film and project ultra HD holographic visuals in real time, in just the same way as they might appear on a 2D screen. In this way, the individual musicians in a group could 'perform' together on the same stage, even though they may be in completely different locations at that moment in time. This has led some people inside the music industry to predict a future of bands touring without needing to leave the rehearsal studio, but any investment of either time or money into this area does seem risky. It would be highly unlikely for any fan to buy a ticket to watch their favourite artists, knowing that the performance they have paid to see is not technically a live show, and the musicians they admire do not wish to be present in the same room as they are.

G Essentially, then, stage projection of deceased stars of entertainment is a straightforward endeavour, but one limited both in visual appeal and available source material. Real-time, 3D representations of artists are becoming ever more accurate, but have less appeal for audiences than authentic performances do. As is often the case, the will to create something new and exciting for consumers of entertainment is hindered by the technology currently available to it.

Questions 1–5

Complete the summary using the list of words, *A–J*, below.

Write the correct letter, *A–J*.

While the music industry has begun to explore potential uses for holographic technology in the context of live performance, critics argue that the staging of a **1** _____ to include a fake performance from a deceased artist is both exploitative and morally questionable. Despite a belief elsewhere that 3D **2** _____ in live shows will inevitably become commonplace, it is more likely that the lack of original **3** _____ will limit how much can be achieved. Additionally, real-time holographic concerts and tours could potentially be staged that allow the artists to remain in a practice **4** _____ while performing, but it is thought that this is unlikely to hold much **5** _____ for audiences.

A appeal	**B** event	**C** rehearsal	**D** animation	**E** screens
F footage	**G** concert	**H** artists	**I** innovation	**J** studio

Questions 6–9

Label the diagram below.

Choose **NO MORE THAN TWO WORDS** from the passage for each answer.

GO FURTHER ONLINE

The projection of on-stage 3D animation

Laser projector attached to a **6** _____

Image is sent in a **7** _____ from projector

Animation of artist hits a **8** _____

45°

Audience sees image as reflected onto a **9** _____ screen

WRITING

IN THIS UNIT YOU WILL LEARN HOW TO

- write a 'two questions in one' essay
- increase your chances of a high score in Grammatical Range and Accuracy (GRA)
- write complex sentences with *despite/although* concession clauses and participle clauses.

LEAD-IN

01▷ **Discuss the questions with a partner.**

1 How many different social media accounts do you have?
2 What effect does social media have on your relationships with your friends and family?
3 Do you think people use social media too often?

02▷ **Decide which options are grammatically correct. Sometimes more than one option is correct.**

1 The IT security team has **advised** / **recommended** / **suggested** that we don't give out personal information to strangers on social media.
2 I don't **advise** / **recommend** / **suggest** spending more than two hours on social media every day – it is better to speak to people face-to-face.
3 I **advise** / **recommend** / **suggest** against using the same password for all your social media platforms.
4 He was looking for a new gaming laptop so I **advised** / **recommended** / **suggested** to him that he look at comparison reviews on YouTube.
5 As I love photos, my sister **advised** / **recommended** / **suggested** Instagram to me.

TIP 02

Make sure you are clear how common verbs in writing are used grammatically in a sentence. Many require specific grammar or structures and it is easy to confuse them.

03▷ **Make a note of the verb patterns that can be correctly used for the verbs *advise* and *suggest*, and write an example sentence to help you remember how to use them. Here is an example with *recommend*.**

(i) *recommend + (that)* + clause*
I recommend (that) you limit the time you spend playing online games.

(ii) *recommend + -ing*
I recommend limiting the time you spend playing online games.

(iii) *recommend + something + to + someone*
I recommended a new study app to my brother.

* optional

TWO QUESTIONS IN ONE ESSAY

 Generally with this type of Task 2 essay, you will need to consider your response to a statement in two ways: one objective, one subjective. The first question might ask you to set out causes, problems or reasons behind a particular situation, and the second might ask you to give your opinion, or to say how much you agree with the statement. A good structure would be:

- Introduction
- Answer the first question
- Answer the second question
- Conclusion

04 Look at the essay question and a candidate's essay. Then discuss questions 1–4 below with a partner.

Social media has completely changed the way family and friends communicate with each other.
What are the reasons for this?
Is this a positive or negative development?

Social media was introduced to the internet around twenty years ago. It has since gone from strength to strength. Many people initially dismissed social media as a passing fashion. They believed that it would never replace face-to-face communication. There are many downsides to this development, but I believe that overall it has had a positive effect on our lives.

One of the main reasons why social media websites are so popular is that they are a very convenient way of contacting friends and family. At the touch of a button, it is possible to communicate with somebody you are close to on the other side of the world. In the past, people were able to speak to each other on telephones but they had to make sure that they were both at home to make or answer the call at an agreed time. Furthermore, if someone is a fan of a certain actor or singer, they can easily message that person and tell them so. In return, the fans can get updates on the films or songs the actors or singers are planning to release next, so this is a huge change from the way this communication happened in the past.

In my opinion, the increasing popularity of social media is a positive development. It allows everyone to stay in touch constantly, even though it is not in person. For example, if a young person decides to stay out late, they can just phone their parents and let them know. In the past, they would have needed to find a telephone box, and to have the correct change to be able to make a call, and this may have caused their parents to worry.

In conclusion, social media has a number of negative sides, but overall it is a positive development. I would recommend that everyone has at least one account that they use every day.

1 Does the candidate make their position on the statement clear?
2 Did the candidate answer the first question correctly?
3 Did the candidate answer the second question correctly?
4 Does the conclusion summarise the essay correctly?

If you only write short, simple sentences in an IELTS essay you will not achieve a high score in GRA, even if there are no mistakes at all. To score well, you will need to show that you can correctly write more complex sentences. Complex sentences are typically ones that combine two or more sentences or clauses into one, often using grammatical or discourse markers. In Unit 8 you will see how relative clauses can create more complex sentences, but here we will look at the correct use of contrast discourse markers and participle clauses.

GRAMMAR FOCUS: COMPLEX SENTENCES – EXPRESSING CONTRAST / CONCESSION WITH *DESPITE* AND *ALTHOUGH*

05 ▶ Read the first half of another candidate's essay based on the question in exercise 4. Find the two sentences in the second paragraph that use discourse markers of contrast/concession.

> First introduced to the internet around twenty years ago, social media has since gone from strength to strength. Many critics have suggested that it is affecting the closeness of family relationships, arguing that people spend too much time staring at screens rather than actually talking to each other. I believe that it brings more advantages than disadvantages to our lives.
>
> One of the main reasons why social media has had such an effect is that it does not require a great deal of effort or planning to connect with friends and family. In the past, people were able to talk to each other on the phone, but they had to make sure that they were both at home to make or answer the call at an agreed time. Another reason is that it fulfils our basic need for human contact, even between people who are on the other side of the world to each other. Despite the fact that people need to communicate regularly with their loved ones in order to be happy, it appears that physical contact is not as vital as once thought. Evidence suggests that contentment in relationships can actually be achieved through social media.

06 ▶ Which of the phrases below are grammatically correct paraphrases of the underlined part of this sentence from paragraph 2?

Despite the fact that people need to communicate regularly with their loved ones in order to be happy, it appears that physical contact is not as vital as once thought.

1 Despite people needing to communicate regularly with their loved ones ...
2 Despite people need to communicate regularly with their loved ones ...
3 Despite people's need to communicate regularly with their loved ones ...

07 ▷ In which of the options (1–3) in exercise 6 can the word *Despite* be replaced with *Although* to form a grammatically correct sentence?

08 ▷ Read the sentence, which is taken from the essay in exercise 5. Then look at sentences 1–4 below, which are paraphrases of it. Decide if they are grammatically correct and, if not, make any changes so that they are.

In the past, people were able to talk to each other on the phone, but they had to make sure that they were both at home to make or answer the call at an agreed time.

1 In the past, although people were able to talk to each other on the phone, but they had to make sure that they were both at home to make or answer the call at an agreed time.

2 In the past, although the ability to talk to each other on the phone, people had to make sure that they were both at home to make or answer the call at an agreed time.

3 In the past, despite able to talk to each other on the phone, people had to make sure that they were both at home to make or answer the call at an agreed time.

4 In the past, although able to talk to each other on the phone, people had to make sure that they were both at home to make or answer the call at an agreed time.

09 ▷ Write complete sentences using *despite* or *although*.

1 wi-fi technology is cheaper than ever / certain parts of the world still have no internet access

2 Virtual Reality headsets are now available to buy / most home computers lack the processing power to make them worthwhile

3 it is extremely important to learn science at school / some students are better suited to studying arts subjects

4 space exploration receives a limited amount of government funding worldwide / it has uncovered a huge amount of information about the way the universe works

COMPLEX SENTENCES – PARTICIPLE CLAUSES

 Participle clauses combine two sentences or clauses, both of which share the same subject, and make a single sentence. They use:

- the *present* participle of a main verb for active sentences
- the *past* participle / 3rd form for passive sentences.

They can perform a number of different functions, such as giving background information, reasons, results or conditions. Correct use of participle clauses will help to improve your GRA score.

10 ▷ Look at these examples of complex sentences produced from simple sentences. In pairs, discuss how this has been done, using the underlined words to help you.

1 *Original sentences:* Social media <u>was first introduced</u> to the internet around twenty years ago. It has since gone from strength to strength.
   Participle clause sentence: <u>First introduced</u> to the internet around twenty years ago, social media has since gone from strength to strength.

2 *Original sentences:* Many critics have suggested that it is affecting the closeness of family relationships. <u>They argue</u> that people spend too much time staring at screens rather than actually talking to each other.
   Participle clause sentence: Many critics have suggested that it is affecting the closeness of family relationships, arguing that people spend too much time staring at screens rather than actually talking to each other.

11 ▶ Using the examples from exercise 10, transform sentences 1 and 2 to make each one a single participle clause sentence. There may be more than one possible answer.

1 Young people are greatly excited by social media. They believe that it is a necessary way to keep in contact with their friends.

2 Some people argue that social media is the perfect tool for modern communication. They draw attention to the fact that family members and friends often find it impossible to spend time with each other.

12 ▶ Look at ideas A and B (each expressed in two sentences) and then at a rewritten version of the third paragraph of the essay from exercise 4. For each set of ideas, underline where the writer has paraphrased them in complex sentences in the essay.

A It is possible to argue that social media has created a society in which people spend less face-to-face time with friends and family. However, it has revolutionised the way in which we relate to one another.

B Most people would not welcome a return to an old-fashioned style of communication. They are more accustomed now to this convenient new form of interaction.

> With this in mind, it seems logical to suggest that the positive sides of social media are more significant than the negative. Although it is possible to argue that it has created a society in which people spend less face-to-face time with friends and family, social media has revolutionised the way in which we relate to one another. It is easier than ever to keep in touch with old friends, to post pictures of exciting moments in our lives, or to send a quick message to parents. Most people would not welcome a return to an old-fashioned style of communication, being more accustomed now to this convenient new form of interaction.

13 ▶ Read through the model essay paragraphs in exercises 5 and 12. Then decide which option, A, B or C, is the best conclusion for this essay.

A In conclusion, social media has proved to be a success because people greatly enjoy the benefits it brings, adapting their approach to friendships and family relationships in order to maintain and improve these bonds in new ways. This is clearly more of a positive than a negative development.

B In conclusion, I would argue that there are more positive than negative aspects to the effects of social media on our friendships and family relationships.

C In conclusion, there are too many reasons to outline in a short essay, both in favour and against social media, so perhaps it is better simply to stay neutral: both positives and negatives are roughly equal.

GO FURTHER ONLINE

EXAM SKILLS

14 ▶ Answer the Writing Task 2 below.

You should spend about 40 minutes on this task.

We are becoming increasingly dependent on computer-based technology.

How do you think it will change in the future?

Is it good for us to rely so much on computers?

Write at least 250 words.

LISTENING

IN THIS UNIT YOU WILL LEARN HOW TO

- complete multiple-choice questions with multiple answers and with single answers
- answer flow-chart completion tasks
- use less common phrases to explain *cause* and *effect*.

LEAD-IN

01 Look at these subjects for talks at a Science and Technology Festival. Which ones would you be interested in?

Technology for Medicine

Computer Game Design

Houses and Apartments of the Future

Driverless Cars – Benefits and Drawbacks

How to Get the Best Grades In Science

02 Now look at the schedule. With a partner, have a conversation about what lectures you would be able to see. Try to use a range of future tenses.

6.00 pm	6.30 pm	7.00 pm	7.30 pm	8.00 pm
	Houses and Apartments of the Future			
Technology for Medicine				Computer Game Design
			Driverless Cars – Benefits and Drawbacks	
		How to Get the Best Grades in Science		

Example:

A 'Technology for Medicine' will have finished by 6.45, so we should be able to see 'How to Get the Best Grades in Science'.

B I <u>won't be able</u> to see 'Driverless Cars', as <u>I'll be watching</u> the lecture on 'Houses and Apartments of the Future'.

[MULTIPLE-CHOICE QUESTIONS]

 There are two types of this task: questions with one correct answer from three possible answers, or questions with more than one possible answer. In Section 3 of the Listening test, these tasks become more difficult because they often test your ability to understand the *opinions* or *arguments* that the speakers put forward, rather than facts or pieces of information (as in Sections 1 and 2).

03▷ Read the exam question and options (A–E). Decide which phrase(s) (1–10) mostly closely relate to each option.

Which TWO concerns do Dylan and Tanya agree are the most important about the Science and Technology Festival?

A cost of entry

B distance between venues

C choosing between talks

D scheduled times of the talks

E relevance to their course

1 pick which ones to go to

2 a waste of time for our courses

3 ticket prices

4 run from one talk to another

5 the schedule must be really tricky to plan

6 pay a lot on the door

7 it's almost impossible to decide who to see

8 the lecture rooms around campus are pretty spread out

9 not going to be related to my studies

10 timings in the programme

TIP 03

Remember that the words in the recording will usually paraphrase the options.

Listen carefully in the test because you usually hear all options referred to in some way.

Remember that here you must listen for what both speakers agree on.

04▷ Listen and do the exam task in exercise 3.

45

05▷ Listen to part of the recording again and complete the conversation. Then answer the questions below.

46

Tanya If we do have to pay a lot on the door, I'll only be able to see one or two. **1** _____ that there won't be anything related to my studies.

Dylan **2** _____ , but it's not so much that I'm worried about it being a waste of time for our course, and with a student discount we definitely shouldn't have any concerns about ticket prices. **3** _____ is how to pick which ones to go to.

Tanya **4** _____ – there are so many interesting speakers, it's almost impossible to decide who to see. Plus, the lecture rooms around campus are pretty spread out, so **5** _____ we'll be able to make it to each venue in time.

Dylan **6** _____ , neither am I.

a Which of the gaps contain phrases that relate to the most important concerns, and which to agreement?

b Read the agreement phrases carefully in context. Which one seems to suggest agreement but actually introduces disagreement?

c Circle the phrases which help you identify the concerns that Tanya and Dylan agree on.

TIP 04

Always read the question carefully – in this example, you don't just need to find *agreement* between Tanya and Dylan about their concerns, but which are *the two most important* concerns that they share.

06 ▶
47

Work in pairs. Student A should look at the questions in the first box, Student B should look at the questions in the second box. Then listen and answer.

TIP 06

Some candidates prefer to read the questions and all the options before the recording starts. Others prefer to only read the questions and then listen to form their own idea as to the answer before checking the options and seeing which one most closely matches their idea.

Student A

Listen and answer the questions.

1 What surprised Dylan about the keynote speaker?
   Write an answer to this question in your own words.
2 What does Tanya say she plans to do before the first class of her Game Design module?
   A research the subject in detail
   B practise her note-taking skills
   C buy the correct study materials

Student B

Listen and answer the questions.

1 What surprised Dylan about the keynote speaker?
   A She gives most of her talks online.
   B She didn't make her main points clear enough.
   C She appeared more reserved than he had expected.
2 What does Tanya say she plans to do before the first class of her Game Design module?
   Write an answer to this question in your own words.

07 ▶ Compare your answers with your partner. For the questions where you wrote an answer, decide which of your partner's three options best matches your idea.

08 ▶ Discuss with a partner. Which do you prefer as a technique: reading the question and the options or reading only the question?

09 ▶ Listen to the next part of the recording and answer
48   questions 3 and 4.

3 What does Dylan say about the other students in his tutorials?
   A They tend to dominate conversations.
   B They are nervous when they do experiments.
   C They usually wait for him to start the discussion.

4 What do Tanya and Dylan agree to do immediately after the keynote speech?
   A go out for dinner
   B go to the more interesting of the two talks that come next
   C take a break and choose lectures to see the following day

[FLOW-CHART COMPLETION]

 Flow-chart completion tasks require you to identify the missing words in a series of steps that describe a chronological process. As with other completion tasks, you will either need to complete the gaps from the words you hear in the recording, or choose your answers from a list given. For the former, pay attention to the word limit stated, and avoid making any changes to the words you hear.

10▶ With a partner, decide on the part of speech for the missing words in the flow-chart and predict what answers you may hear for each question.

Complete the flow-chart below.

*Write **NO MORE THAN TWO WORDS** for each answer.*

> **Lecture summary plan**
> Take lecture notes using **1** _____ .

↓

> Come together to discuss **2** _____ .

↓

> Agree what information to **3** _____ of summary.

↓

> Produce **4** _____ of main themes, ideas, points.

↓

> Email summary to tutor for further **5** _____ .

11▶ Listen to five extracts from Dylan and Tanya's conversation and for each one, decide at which point in the flow-chart you are most likely to be. The extracts are not in order.

🎵 49

Extract 1   Question _____
Extract 2   Question _____
Extract 3   Question _____
Extract 4   Question _____
Extract 5   Question _____

TIP 11

If you miss an answer or lose your place in the recording, look at the next two questions after your last answer, and then quickly decide which one most closely paraphrases what you are hearing.

12▶ Listen to the conversation in full and answer questions 1–5 in exercise 10. Use NO MORE THAN TWO WORDS for each answer.

🎵 50

TIP 12

One way higher-ability candidates are identified is through their ability to recognise and differentiate between singular and plural forms of words as they are spoken, especially if the next word after a plural begins with 's'.

13▶ Listen and complete these extracts from the conversation in exercise 12. Then discuss with a partner what was the *cause* and *effect* referred to in each.

51

1 **Dylan** I think it's better if we both opt for bullet points so that it's clear and consistent.

   Tanya OK, let's use those. _____ , when we meet up again after the lecture, we'll be more able to compare notes …

2 **Dylan** Good plan. We agree what the most significant points are from each lecture, maybe even try to establish some of the common themes. _____ , we can then put together an edited version of these on a separate sheet of paper …

3 **Tanya** _____ get some feedback about this, we should probably contact our tutor …

> Aside from the more common conjunctions and discourse markers of cause and effect (*so*, *because*, *as a result*, etc.), candidates aiming for a higher IELTS score should be able to recognise and use a range of less common, more complex examples, particularly where it helps to avoid repetition.

14▶ Decide which option in each group is *not* grammatically correct for the sentence. Then, for the correct options, decide if they are suitable for both speaking and writing, or speaking only.

1 **In order that she could / So as to / In order so to** practise her listening and note-taking skills, Florence went to as many lectures as she could during the Science and Technology festival.

2 Shall I talk you through what we've been studying in science this week? **This way / The way / That way** you can catch up on the work you missed when you were off sick.

3 The pharmaceutical company successfully applied for a grant from the government. **For doing so / By doing so / After doing so**, they were able to continue their research into cancer prevention.

[EXAM SKILLS]

15▶ Listen and answer questions 1–10.

52

Questions 1 and 2

Choose TWO correct answers.

Which TWO elements of the Science and Technology Festival do Dylan and Tanya agree were most beneficial?

   A They were able to meet new people.

   B They improved their study skills.

   C It helped to prepare them for their course.

   D It allowed them to become familiar with the university campus.

   E It introduced them to new areas of study.

Questions 3–6

Choose the correct answer.

3 The professor believes that the main role of the festival is to
    A make the general public more aware of science and technology.
    B have a different focus each year.
    C show how both fields of study are equally important.

4 The university information stands were there to
    A help people who were lost.
    B generate more interest in current research.
    C allow the people who attended the festival to meet the lecturers.

5 What does Tanya say about the festival guidebook?
    A The map was confusing.
    B There were too many advertisements.
    C The schedules for some lectures were wrong.

6 Dylan says that nowadays festivals
    A have to increase the entry charge every year.
    B make a lot of money from the admission fee.
    C are mostly paid for through advertising.

Questions 7–10

Complete the flow-chart below.

*Choose **FOUR** answers from the list below and write the correct letter, **A–H**, next to questions 7–10.*

Advice for posting summary on department website
Choose four main **7** _____ to summarise.

↓

Refer to previous **8** _____ for guidance on how to write them.

↓

Agree on how **9** _____ is to be shared.

↓

Set a **10** _____ and keep to it.

↓

Upload summary and documents onto website.

A deadline	B timetable	C styles	D workload
E information	F theories	G posts	H ideas

GO FURTHER ONLINE

UNIT /06: SCIENCE AND TECHNOLOGY

SPEAKING

IN THIS UNIT YOU WILL LEARN HOW TO

- improve your score for Grammatical Range and Accuracy (GRA)
- correctly use verb patterns in your answers
- develop strategies for buying time to answer more difficult questions.

0 1 ▶ Under each picture write the year in which it was invented. Work with a partner to see who can get the most answers correct.

| 1280 | 2400 BC | 1783 | 1963 | 1866 | 1710 | 1843 | 1798 |

1

parachute
_____

2

typewriter
_____

3

dynamite
_____

4

vaccination
_____

5

computer mouse
_____

6

eyeglasses
_____

7

thermometer
_____

8
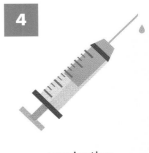

abacus
_____

0 2 ▶ Discuss with a partner which invention you think is the most important and why.

[PART 1]

GRAMMATICAL RANGE AND ACCURACY (GRA)

 Don't think of Part 1 as just a warm-up for the more difficult parts of the exam – this is a real opportunity to show the examiner that you have a wide understanding of Grammatical Range and Accuracy (GRA). Consider in particular how to display your knowledge of:

- a range of structures / tenses / aspects
- subordinate clauses
- hypothetical structures, e.g. 2nd and 3rd conditional
- modal verbs.

03▶ Look at a candidate's answer to the examiner's question. Ignoring the numbers for now, how many different verb tenses does the candidate use in their answer?

Examiner   How often do you use your mobile phone?

Candidate   Not as much as I (**1**) *did in the past*. After I first bought it, I (**2**) *used* it almost constantly, but I (**3**) *think* that maybe I use it too often and I should try to limit how long I spend on it. I don't know if that (**4**) *is* possible, though, as they (**5**) *are* such a big part of everyone's lives these days, but I (**6**) *have to* try. Not completely, though – (**7**) *I need it for my* social life.

TIP 03

One good way to exhibit a wide range of grammar is to consider how you might be able to relate the question you have been asked to:

- present, past, or future situations so that you can show a variety of verb tenses and aspects (simple, continuous, perfect, etc.)
- hypothetical alternatives or results.

04▶ Listen to a recording of the candidate's improved answer and read the script on page 218. Write what the candidate actually says in place of the words and phrases indicated by the numbers 1–7 in exercise 3. How would this help to improve their score for GRA?

1 _____
2 _____
3 _____
4 _____
5 _____
6 _____
7 _____

05▶ Considering how you might be able to demonstrate a wide range of GRA, write an answer to each of the Part 1 questions. Then, ask and answer the questions with a partner. (Don't read out your answers – try to remember them as best you can.)

1 When did you first own a mobile phone?
2 Do you think it is better to send a message or talk to someone on the phone?
3 How often do you watch television?
4 Do you prefer to listen to music through headphones or through speakers?
5 What are you most likely to use a computer for?

PART 2

06▷ Look at the pictures and discuss the questions with a partner.

A

B

C

D

1 Which scientific discovery or invention do the pictures represent?

2 For this Part 2 question, which of the above inventions do you think you would be best able to talk about for two minutes?

   Describe an important scientific discovery or invention.

3 Can you think of any other scientific discoveries or inventions that you would feel more confident in talking about for two minutes?

07▷ Here is the full Part 2 question. Choose one of the discoveries or inventions you discussed in exercise 6 and, in one minute, write brief notes for a two-minute long turn. You will come back to these shortly.

Describe an important scientific discovery or invention that you think is very important.

You should say:

- how you learnt about it
- what it does
- what it is most used for today

and explain why you think it is such an important discovery or invention.

When you learn common verbs, especially those which introduce other verbs, it is important to understand and practise how they can be used in sentences or you may lose GRA marks. Questions you can ask yourself include:

- What form does the verb following this verb take?
- Can it be used to introduce a 'that' clause?
- Does it need an object?

08▷ Read the transcript of a candidate's answer to the Part 2 question in exercise 7. With a partner, decide if the verb patterns in 1–14 are correct. If they are incorrect, what should they be?

(**1**) *I'd like telling* you what I know about one of the most significant inventions in human history: the wheel. Why is it so significant? Well, (**2**) *let me to begin* by saying first of all, it basically (**3**) *enabled us to develop* whole civilisations, as we could for the first time start transporting goods from place to place, and this mobility really (**4**) *made trade grow* at an incredible speed. I (**5**) *remember to be taught* about this at school. Our teacher (**6**) *told us not to see* the wheel itself as the crucial invention, because it was actually the moment someone (**7**) *managed attaching* a non-moving platform to two wheels that was critical. But I (**8**) *can't help think* that you don't have to agree with everything you are told at school, and I would politely (**9**) *refuse to agree* with him, if I was told this today. You see, without a wheel, a platform is just a bit of wood, essentially.

Anyway, wheels in everyday use. Well, can you (**10**) *imagine to live* without them? It's practically impossible. You wouldn't be able to drive anywhere, for one thing. What's more, wheels (**11**) *allow us have* a public transport system, and if wheels didn't exist, aeroplanes wouldn't be able to take off and land, and no one would be able to go on holiday.

How exactly a wheel works, I won't even (**12**) *attempt to explain*, other than the fact they go round. It's something to do with force. I've never been any good at Physics, but maybe I should (**13**) *remember looking it up* on the internet when I get home. But, overall, there's no question about how important the wheel is, and it will (**14**) *continue be* an integral part of our lives forever.

54

Listen to the recording and check your answers.

09▷ Classify the verbs / verb phrases according to the structures they use. Some can appear in more than one column.

would like	let	enable	help	remember	refuse	manage
can't help	tell	imagine	allow	attempt	continue	

Verb + *to* infinitive	Verb + gerund	Verb + object + *to* infinitive	Verb + object + bare infinitive
would like		*would like*	

10▷ Look at the verbs that appear twice. Does the form of the verb phrase affect the meaning?

11▷ Use the notes you made in exercise 7 to write a full answer to the Part 2 question, paying particular attention to verb patterns. Then, in pairs, take turns to deliver your Part 2 answers to each other (*without* reading aloud from what you have written). When it is your turn to listen, check that your partner is using verb patterns correctly.

[PART 3]

12▷ For this Part 3 question, which of the strategies (A–C) in the box below does each candidate (1–8) use to buy themselves some thinking time?

Examiner   How important is it for students to study science at school?

1 Hm. Are science subjects an integral part of study at school? I'm not sure that they are. For one thing …

2 Um, I'm not sure. Are you asking if science should be compulsory for all students, whatever year they are in at school? Or if science is just something we all need some degree of basic knowledge in?

3 Well, I don't think there's one, clear-cut answer to that. It really depends on the individual. By that I mean …

4 I couldn't say for certain one way or another.

5 Do students need to study science at school? Perhaps, yes …

6 As in, science should be studied at the expense of all other subjects?

7 That's a good question. Well, I suppose …

8 By that do you mean, is science one of the main subjects that should be taught at school?

> A Asking the examiner to clarify the question
> B Paraphrasing the question
> C Explaining that the question is not a simple one to answer

13▷ Discuss with a partner which word is incorrect in each of the sentences. Then listen and make the relevant corrections.

55

Examiner   With technology in the home, what sort of dangers do people need to look out for?

1 That's quite a trick question to answer. Let me think …

2 I don't really know how to answer that. It's never crossed over my mind before.

3 I'm not entirely sure what you're running at. Can you rephrase the question, please?

4 Sorry, I don't quite chase your question. Do you mean with appliances, like kettles, or something like internet security?

5 You know, I'd usually be able to answer that question immediately, but my mind has gone clear.

14▷ Which of the three strategies do the sentences in exercise 13 belong to?

> A Asking the examiner to clarify the question
> B Paraphrasing the question
> C Explaining that the question is not a simple one to answer

 In the Speaking test, you will not lose credit if the examiner asks you a question and you don't immediately know *what* to say for an answer (this is more likely to happen in Part 3 than in Part 1). However, you will lose credit if it appears that you are having trouble thinking of *how* to say something, i.e. if you cannot find the right words. It is quite possible to pause for a moment to consider your response, but it is far better to use one of the following strategies/phrases to buy yourself some thinking time.

With a partner, follow these instructions and practise buying yourself some thinking time in Part 3 of the Speaking test.

- Take it in turns to ask and answer the questions below.
- At the same time as you ask a question, you should point to one of the three strategies in exercise 14. Your partner should use this strategy to begin their answer.
- When it is your turn to answer, your partner will point to one of the strategies; you should use this strategy to begin your answer.

1 Are people getting lazier as a result of technology?
2 What will computers be able to do in the future?
3 Why are some scientists world famous while so many others are unknown?
4 Why do some people refuse to own a smartphone?
5 Is it possible that people rely too much on science for their knowledge and understanding of the world?

[EXAM SKILLS]

16▶ **Do this sample test with a partner. Take turns to ask and answer.**

Part 1

1 How often do you use the internet?
2 Do you think it is better to send an email or a text message?
3 What do you use a computer for?
4 What is your favourite item of technology that you own?
5 In your country, do most people study science at school?

Part 2

Describe an invention that has been very important in your life.

You should say:

- where you first used it
- how you use it today
- what you plan to use it for in the future

and explain why it has been so important in your life.

Part 3

1 In the near future, we may see the first driverless cars on the roads. Are there any potential dangers if this happens?
2 As more and more people are becoming victims of online crime, is it time for everyone to stop conducting all their business over the internet?
3 How important is it for governments to invest in space travel?
4 Do you think that people fully appreciate and value the technology that is available to them today?

GO FURTHER ONLINE

UNIT /07: TELEVISION, NEWS AND CURRENT AFFAIRS

READING

IN THIS UNIT YOU WILL LEARN HOW TO

- locate information in a paragraph
- match information to a paragraph
- answer short-answer questions
- match sentence endings
- understand how the passive is formed and used in English.

LEAD-IN

0 1 ▷ Are you a citizen journalist? Which of the following have you done? Tell your partner, giving details.

- liked or rated a news story online
- shared a news story on social media
- commented on a news story online
- sent a photograph/video to a news outlet or website
- written a blog

0 2 ▷ The following pairs of news-related words are either near synonyms or near antonyms (opposites). Write S or A.

1 journalist – reporter
2 research – investigate
3 mainstream – alternative
4 break a story – get a scoop

5 broadcast – publish
6 media outlet – news agency
7 amateur – professional
8 eyewitness – source

0 3 ▷ What are the differences in meaning between the near synonyms in exercise 2?

LOCATING INFORMATION IN A TEXT

0 4 ▷ Skim read the text on pages 140–141 and match the summaries (1–7) to the paragraphs (A–G).

1 Advantages of 'We media'
2 The need for critical thinking
3 The changing definition of a journalist
4 The changing role of the audience and the media
5 A case study
6 What citizen journalists can contribute
7 Media response to participatory journalism

 Most IELTS Reading tasks expect you to find specific information in the text. Skimming the text as a whole first, to understand its structure, will help you predict where in the text the relevant information is likely to be found. Once you think you have located the probable paragraph(s) where the information will be found, scan through it/them quickly to find the information, remembering to look for synonyms or paraphrases of the key words in the question.

THE FUTURE OF JOURNALISM?

A It used to be easy to define what a journalist was. They had a degree in English or journalism, usually owned a camera and were employed full time by a news outlet, TV or radio station or newspaper. Their days were spent conducting interviews, researching the next big story and writing articles. However, in recent years the line between these 'professional' journalists and the public has become blurred. There is a growing trend for amateur journalism that often bypasses the established media sources. The upshot is that virtually anyone can be a journalist. After all, if you are present when a story breaks, or you yourself are part of the news story, why wait for a 'real' journalist to interview you as an eyewitness? You can use the camera on your phone and tell the story yourself and post it on your own blog or on social media.

B It is not only on sites like Facebook and Twitter that amateur journalism is on the rise. There are now open publishing sites, such as the Independent Media Center or 'Indymedia', which aim to bring a 'grassroots dimension' into the news arena. Ohmynews, one of South Korea's most influential online sources for the latest in current affairs, has 2 million readers every day and a nationwide army of 26,000 'citizen' journalists. More and more often these citizen journalists and open sites are getting the scoop on major stories. The first mention of the problems facing the doomed space shuttle Columbia appeared on an online discussion forum 11 minutes before the Associated Press broke the news. What is more, there has been a fundamental change in how we interact with the news. Nowadays, with the growth in online versions of newspapers, the public can easily comment, point out errors, and share alternative viewpoints. These opportunities are particularly vital if you find yourself the subject of a news story – whether for positive or negative reasons. If the story involves you, you can provide vital context and supplementary information which can change readers' views on your story.

C When this trend for participatory media was in its infancy, there was plenty of mistrust of amateur 'journalists' who lacked the credentials of journalists working in established media outlets. If a story didn't come from well-known news organisations like CNN or *The Times*, it wasn't taken seriously. Now that perception is changing. Trust in alternative media sources is growing. In fact, mainstream media now regularly recruit members of their own staff from the ranks of amateur news bloggers. Simultaneously, there has been a general shift away from a 'broadcast model', in which the few broadcast to the many, towards a more inclusive model in which the audience can play an active role. The traditional 'filter then publish' news model has been replaced by 'publish then filter', with millions of keen amateurs involved at all stages of the process.

D So, how have the media establishment reacted to this change? Initially, it was seen as a challenge to their hegemony. They had always been the gatekeepers: those who decided what was news and how that news should be presented. Participatory journalism represents the democratisation of the media: and therefore a threat to this. Media futurists predict that by 2021, 50% of news will be produced by citizen journalists, so traditional media have had little choice but to embrace the trend or be left behind. Many already have, by adding features that invite participation, such as comments sections and links to social media.

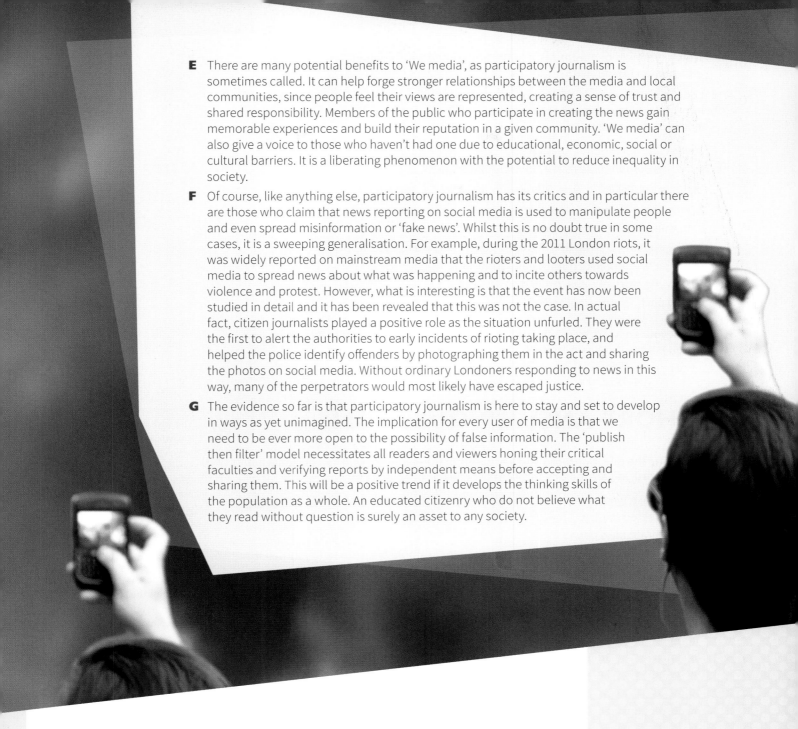

E There are many potential benefits to 'We media', as participatory journalism is sometimes called. It can help forge stronger relationships between the media and local communities, since people feel their views are represented, creating a sense of trust and shared responsibility. Members of the public who participate in creating the news gain memorable experiences and build their reputation in a given community. 'We media' can also give a voice to those who haven't had one due to educational, economic, social or cultural barriers. It is a liberating phenomenon with the potential to reduce inequality in society.

F Of course, like anything else, participatory journalism has its critics and in particular there are those who claim that news reporting on social media is used to manipulate people and even spread misinformation or 'fake news'. Whilst this is no doubt true in some cases, it is a sweeping generalisation. For example, during the 2011 London riots, it was widely reported on mainstream media that the rioters and looters used social media to spread news about what was happening and to incite others towards violence and protest. However, what is interesting is that the event has now been studied in detail and it has been revealed that this was not the case. In actual fact, citizen journalists played a positive role as the situation unfurled. They were the first to alert the authorities to early incidents of rioting taking place, and helped the police identify offenders by photographing them in the act and sharing the photos on social media. Without ordinary Londoners responding to news in this way, many of the perpetrators would most likely have escaped justice.

G The evidence so far is that participatory journalism is here to stay and set to develop in ways as yet unimagined. The implication for every user of media is that we need to be ever more open to the possibility of false information. The 'publish then filter' model necessitates all readers and viewers honing their critical faculties and verifying reports by independent means before accepting and sharing them. This will be a positive trend if it develops the thinking skills of the population as a whole. An educated citizenry who do not believe what they read without question is surely an asset to any society.

MATCHING INFORMATION

◎ This task type asks you to match a piece of information to the paragraph that contains it. The information could be specific details, examples, descriptions, reasons and explanations, or a summary of the ideas. You may not need to use all of the paragraphs and some paragraphs might match more than one piece of information. The information in the paragraphs will be paraphrased differently in the corresponding question.

0 5 ▷ **Scan each paragraph and find the following information.**

Paragraph **A**: something a journalist traditionally <u>possessed</u>

Paragraph **B**: the name of <u>a Korean news site</u>

Paragraph **C**: two well-known <u>media outlets</u>

Paragraph **D**: the year in which <u>half</u> of the news may be produced by amateurs

Paragraph **E**: four types of <u>obstacles</u> to participation in society

Paragraph **F**: two types of <u>criminals</u>

Paragraph **G**: something <u>audiences</u> need to sharpen or improve

0 6 ▷ Which synonym or paraphrase for the underlined words helped you locate the information in exercise 5?

0 7 ▷ Look at the exam task. Without reading the text again, for each numbered piece of information, say where in the text you think it will be found. Write B for beginning, M for middle or E for end.

*The text has seven paragraphs, **A–G**.*

Which paragraph contains the following information?

*Write the correct letter, **A–G**. NB You may use any letter more than once.*

1 Why some journalists fear the new trends
2 Details of civil unrest in a major city
3 Why education is needed in the context of this change in the media
4 Subjects journalists traditionally study at university
5 How the story of a spaceship disaster broke
6 Why participatory journalism is good for disadvantaged groups

0 8 ▷ Check your answers by reading the text. Write the paragraph letter (A–G) next to the questions (1–6) in exercise 7.

SHORT-ANSWER QUESTIONS

This task requires you to answer some direct questions which begin with question words such as *What*, *Which* or *Where*. You will be told the maximum number of words to write. The questions have to be answered with words taken from the text and are in the same order as the information appears in the text. As with similar tasks, it is useful to underline the key words in the questions and predict what kind of information is missing.

0 9 ▷ Underline the question word and key words in these questions. Then decide what kind of word you are looking for. The first one has been done for you.

1 In the <u>past</u>, <u>what</u> <u>role</u> would a <u>member of the public</u> who <u>saw</u> a <u>newsworthy event</u> be expected to <u>play</u>?

role – probably a noun

2 What was the subject of the story given as an example of an amateur journalist scoop before it was reported by a major news agency?
3 From which group of people have the media establishment begun to hire staff?
4 What had mainstream media traditionally seen their role in news reporting as being?

1 0 ▷ Now answer the questions in exercise 9. Choose NO MORE THAN THREE words from the text for each answer.

1 1 ▷ Look at the second part of the task and the possible answers. For each, decide what the correct answer is and say why the other options are incorrect.

7 What has amateur journalism been accused of increasing the risk of?
  A fake news
  B critical thinking
  C untrue stories
8 What did citizen journalists help police to do during the London riots?
  A play a positive role
  B identify offenders
  C alert the authorities
9 According to the text what is the 'new model' of broadcasting?
  A filter then publish
  B publish then filter
  C We media

12 ▷ Answer these short-answer questions. Choose NO MORE THAN THREE WORDS from the text for each answer.

1 Which well-known open publishing site is mentioned in the text?
2 According to the text, what process of change is the media currently undergoing that challenges the establishment's traditional role?
3 What positive effect on society as a whole might citizen journalism produce?

MATCHING SENTENCE ENDINGS ◎

13 ▷ Read the sentence beginning and two possible endings. Read the relevant part of the text (the second half of paragraph B) carefully and choose which one is correct.

The citizen journalist scoop on the Columbia Space Shuttle story is an example of
A how we are interacting more with traditional media.
B how participatory media is growing.

14 ▷ Complete each sentence with the correct ending (A–E) below.

1 Amateur journalists may lack the credentials of professionals
2 Newspaper editors were the gatekeepers of the news
3 Anyone could find themselves the subject of a news story

A which means most of them are afraid of participatory journalism.
B but now they can offer extra information to alter people's perceptions.
C but this is less of a disadvantage than it used to be.
D but formal qualifications are no longer required by media outlets.
E but now they need to accept that this situation is changing.

> This task requires you to match sentence beginnings with a list of possible endings (there will be more sentence endings than you need). Because the beginnings and endings will often all match grammatically and make sense, you can't guess the answers from grammatical or semantic clues. Instead, locate the part of the text mentioned in each sentence beginning and then read it in detail to identify the ending that matches.

GRAMMAR FOCUS: THE PASSIVE

15 ▷ Look at the passive sentence from the text. Identify the parts.

The traditional 'filter then publish' model has been replaced by 'publish then filter'.
1 the subject of the sentence
2 the agent
3 the past participle of the main verb
4 the verb 'to be' in the present perfect tense
5 the preposition introducing the agent

16 ▷ Rewrite the sentence from exercise 15 in the following tenses:

Present simple: *The traditional 'filter then publish' model is replaced by 'publish then filter'.*
Present continuous:
Past perfect:
Future simple with *will*:

17 ▷ Read these statements about the passive and say if they are true or false.

1 Any sentence can be changed from active into passive and vice-versa.
2 The passive helps the writer control the order of information in a sentence.
3 The passive is rarely used in spoken English.
4 Saying who or what did the action (the agent) is optional.
5 Academic English uses the passive voice fairly frequently.

18 ▶ Read the passage and answer questions 1–14.

REALITY TV

A Reality TV accounts for 67% of TV programmes watched by Americans. A huge range of programme types come under the banner 'Reality TV', some of them more edifying than others. There are those which follow the pattern of one of the earliest reality shows, *Big Brother*, where a group of people have to co-exist in a house, their every move being filmed. Then there are the competitive shows where ordinary people compete in skills such as singing, cooking, diving, ice-skating or work-related skills like sales and entrepreneurship. Another sub-genre is the self- or home improvement/makeover type of show, such as *What Not to Wear, The Biggest Loser* or *Hoarders*. Some of the most popular reality TV shows are those of the social experiment sub-genre, such as *The World's Strictest Parents*, where misbehaving teens are sent to live in a less liberal family, usually in a distant country. Perhaps the most educational type which comes under the reality TV heading are the programmes that follow someone with an interesting or useful job doing their ordinary day-to-day work. This is the one type of reality TV show most parents encourage their children to watch, as they can learn about the work of police officers, paramedics, doctors, pilots and teachers.

B So how can we account for the immense popularity of reality TV? One reason it has found favour with viewers is that for most ordinary people it is their best hope of achieving at least a degree of fame or notoriety. A tiny minority might even become really famous and be rewarded with a TV show of their own. A survey of 239 people revealed that, contrary to common belief, most reality TV fans were not less sociable or less intelligent than others. It was thought that the main aim of watching such shows was to be able to discuss them with friends and co-workers. However, that has always been one of the reasons people watch any kind of TV programme. What is different about reality TV aficionados is that they desire a rise in status and strongly value prestige. Reality TV has produced 'stars' with little or no actual talent in conventional terms. Although they can't sing, dance or act, the force of their personality has shot them to stardom through an appearance on a TV show. From there, many have launched careers as 'TV personalities' and achieved the wealth and fame they craved. It is no wonder, then, that so many hope to follow their example.

C One crucial point about reality TV is that the name itself is a misnomer. It is not actually 'real'. While producers don't go as far as having scripts, they edit footage in such a way as to distort what really happened. Events are twisted to create an illusion of conflict or to shape a more interesting storyline. Participants are told to adapt their own personalities to suit the requirements of the show. For example, a lady with a pleasant and gentle personality was told to 'act mean' or be ejected from the show. Similarly, though viewers assume that either judges or the voting public have the power to eliminate contestants, in fact the producers retain the decision-making power. If a candidate in a singing competition has been voted off by the public, he or she may be kept on for amusement value, not for the quality of his or her singing. One producer admitted that a '24-hour bathroom makeover' actually had a crew working on it behind the scenes for at least two weeks.

D Apart from the illusions of reality, what other criticisms are made of reality TV? Author Mark Andrejevic wrote in the *New York Times* in 2012 that reality TV in post 9/11 society represents the 'normalisation of surveillance'. In all our favourite TV shows, the cameras are on the participants 24 hours a day. It therefore doesn't seem so strange when our own activities are caught on CCTV as we move around our cities and workplaces. Another accusation levied at some of these shows is that they glamorise vulgarity and consumerism. An American show called *Toddlers and Tiaras*, for example, shows little girls dressing up in skimpy costumes and make-up to take part in beauty pageants. Their parents spend thousands of dollars to parade their tiny children, some barely old enough to walk, in front of judges, who evaluate their beauty, clothes and modelling skills. The children featured in this and similar shows are growing up to focus only on winning and many are totally unable to accept defeat. Many reality TV shows feature a 'confessional', where contestants are encouraged to back-stab and report on their fellow contestants. Unethical behaviour is valued and rewarded because it boosts viewing figures. The plethora of shows encouraging us to change our weight, wardrobe, job, house and car creates generations of discontented individuals who feel themselves inadequate with who they are and what they have.

E To make matters worse, the experience of being on reality TV is not what it appears. These shows are so popular with the television companies because they are so cheap to produce. The producers' aim is to get as much talent as possible for as low a price as possible. While appearing on a reality show, you can expect your expenses to be paid, but you will probably only receive $20 or $30 a day. What is more, you can expect every aspect of your background and family to be investigated in detail. Anything you would prefer to remain hidden will inevitably come out. And the person who becomes the reality star will not be 'you'. It will be a character created by the producers who happens to have your face. So, if you are longing for your 15 minutes of fame, be aware of the risks of achieving it through reality TV.

Questions 1–6

*The text has five paragraphs, **A–E**. Which paragraph contains the following information?*
*Write the correct letter, **A–E**.*

N.B. You may use any letter more than once.

1 What attracts people to watch reality TV
2 An explanation for the promotion of bad behaviour on reality TV
3 A description of a show the writer disapproves of
4 An example of why the term reality TV is misleading
5 Some examples of shows that might benefit young people
6 A piece of research that reveals information about fans of reality TV

Questions 7–10

*Answer the questions below. Choose **NO MORE THAN TWO WORDS** from the passage for each answer.*

7 How does the writer describe programmes that show people doing their job?
8 What does the writer say can help people achieve fame if they have no special talent?
9 Who has the ultimate decision about the elimination of competitors?
10 What feature of reality TV invites participants to criticise their peers?

Questions 11–14

*Complete each sentence with the correct ending, **A–G**, below.*

11 People who like watching reality TV
12 The effects of reality TV on society
13 Producers of reality TV
14 People who take part in reality TV shows

A include the development of competitiveness and materialistic attitudes.
B will pay lots of money for the right people.
C may not realise how intrusive and financially unrewarding it will be.
D are willing to distort reality to attract more viewers.
E tend to aspire to raising their status in society.
F are usually grateful to be given a chance of becoming famous.
G are particularly damaging for young girls.

GO FURTHER ONLINE

UNIT /07: TELEVISION, NEWS AND CURRENT AFFAIRS

WRITING

IN THIS UNIT YOU WILL LEARN HOW TO

- describe percentages and fractions
- describe a pie chart
- improve your grammatical range and accuracy
- use the passive voice.

LEAD-IN

01 ▷ The pie chart represents the main way of finding out the news by adults in the UK in 2015. Predict which section of the chart represents TV, radio, print, online and 'not specified'. Explain your predictions to your partner.

02 ▷ Match the descriptions (a–e) with the sections of the pie chart (1–5).

- **a** Just over a third of people access the news online.
- **b** The largest proportion of people, about 40%, watch the news on TV.
- **c** Only a tiny minority did not specify how they find out about the news.
- **d** Radio is the least popular way to get news, at just 7%.
- **e** Approximately 15% of people read the news in print.

03 ▷ Where do you get your news from? Talk about:

- the types of news that interest you
- the different sources you use
- why you use them.

Ways of finding out the news

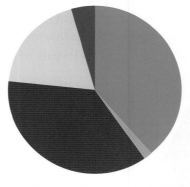

■ 1　■ 2　■ 3　■ 4　■ 5

DESCRIBING PERCENTAGES AND FRACTIONS

04 ▷ Match the percentages (1–6) with the descriptions (a–f).

1	20%	**a**	a little under half
2	77%	**b**	a fifth
3	92%	**c**	just less than a third
4	31%	**d**	about three quarters
5	24%	**e**	approximately 9 out of 10
6	48%	**f**	almost a quarter

TIP 04

When describing the data in pie charts, use a variety of ways to describe the numbers, for example, use a mixture of percentages and fractions, to show the range of your language. Use modifiers, such as *almost*, *just over* and *approximately* if the figures are not exact fractions.

0 5 ▷ Write these fractions as a percentage.

1 four fifths   3 a tenth   5 a quarter

2 two thirds   4 two fifths

0 6 ▷ The pie chart shows the frequency with which adults in the US find out the news through social media. Describe each section without using the numbers. Use the modifiers in the box where appropriate.

almost	about	approximately	roughly
over/under	a little	slightly over/under	just over/under

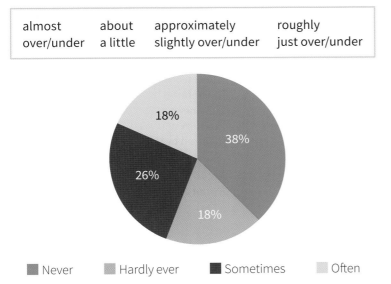

■ Never   ■ Hardly ever   ■ Sometimes   ■ Often

DESCRIBING A PIE CHART

0 7 ▷ The pie charts compare ways of accessing the news in the UK and Brazil. In pairs, discuss what the key features of the data are.

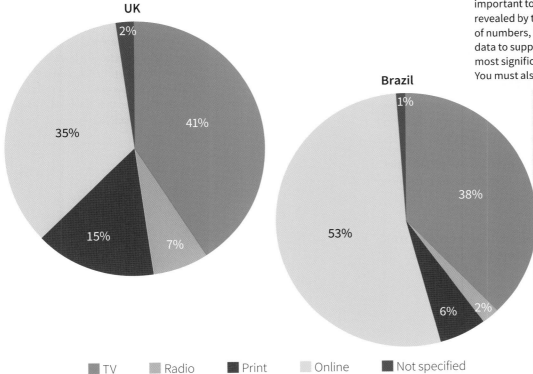

■ TV   ■ Radio   ■ Print   ■ Online   ■ Not specified

◎ You may have to describe a pie chart in Task 1. Sometimes a single pie chart will not provide enough data for 150 words, so you may get two or even three. Alternatively, you may get a pie chart along with a bar chart or other type of graph. As with any graphs and bar charts, it is important to describe the *key information* revealed by the data rather than just giving a list of numbers, but you must also include some data to support your description. Select the most significant data and make comparisons. You must also begin with an overview.

08▷ Read the sample answer and find examples of these features.

1 the overview
2 percentages
3 use of fractions
4 language of comparison
5 introductory and concluding sentences
6 higher level synonyms for these words and phrases:
  • main
  • generally
  • key
  • it is clear
  • preferring
  • each one / in that order

SAMPLE ANSWER

The pie charts show the principle ways of finding out the news in two different countries, the UK and Brazil. The two nations show broadly similar patterns, though there are some differences, both significant and minor.

One of the most prominent features of this data is that, while in the UK over a third of people access the news online, in Brazil the figure is more than half, at 53%. It is apparent that viewing the TV news is popular in both countries, with about two fifths of the UK population favouring this mode of delivery and only 3% fewer in Brazil. One major difference between the UK and Brazil is that over twice as many people read the news in print in the former, compared with the latter. The figures are 15% and 6% respectively. Similarly, listening to the news on the radio is preferred by three times more people in the UK than in Brazil.

Overall, it can be said that the high levels of internet use in Brazil mean that other methods such as radio and print are used less in comparison with the UK.

IMPROVING YOUR GRAMMATICAL RANGE AND ACCURACY

09▷ Find and correct the errors in this description of the pie chart in exercise 6.

The pie chart show frequency with which adults in the us uses social medias to obtain news. Overall, it is clear that less than half are using it in regular basis.

One of the most significant points in the data is that just under two fifths of people report that the news was never accessed by them via social media. To be precise, 38% of respondents gave this response, which is highest from all category. The second highest category is those who sometimes finds out the news from social media sites. Around a quarter (26%) of those surveyed were selected this response, which is 12% less than the 'never' group. Finally, there was a tie for the less common response, equal numbers of respondents 'hardly ever' and 'often' use social media to find out what is going on in the world.

To conclude, social media is use to get news often or sometimes by just 44%. It is evident by the data that majority of citizen does not read news in these sites.

TIP 09

Become aware of the areas in which you make mistakes and focus hard on trying to avoid them. Many students can use more complex structures accurately but still make careless mistakes with subject/verb agreement or articles, for example. Always leave a few minutes when you finish to check for basic errors. It is amazing how often you will discover simple mistakes that you have made which will reduce your grammar score.

10▷ Put the errors in the description in exercise 9 into the following categories. Some categories have more than one error.

1 tenses
2 singular/plural/countable/ uncountable
3 articles
4 active/passive
5 subject–verb agreement
6 punctuation/capital letters
7 prepositions
8 comparatives/superlatives

11▶ Read the following pairs of sentences and decide which one, A or B, would score higher in the IELTS test. Give reasons.

1 A The pie chart data indicate that the primary news source for under 25s in Brazil is social media.

   B Social media is indicated by the pie chart data to be the primary news source for under 25s in Brazil.

2 A One thing we can see from the data is that some media sources are less popular than 20 years ago.

   B One thing that can be seen from the data is that some media sources are less popular than 20 years ago.

3 A The number of online newspaper subscriptions has increased by 20% since 2005.

   B The number of online newspaper subscriptions has been increased by 20% since 2005.

4 A The data reveal that the most popular news stories are sports stories, followed in second place by political news.

   B It is revealed by the data that the most popular news stories are sports stories, followed in second place by political news.

5 A Between 2005 and 2015 the proportion of over 40s using online news sites was almost doubled.

   B Between 2005 and 2015 the proportion of over 40s using online news sites almost doubled.

TIP 11

Showcase your knowledge of grammatical structures, but make sure you use them appropriately. For example, the passive voice is very useful in formal writing for depersonalising what is being said or for foregrounding certain information. However, be careful not to overuse it or use it in ways that are unnatural in English.

EXAM SKILLS

12▶ Answer the Writing Task 1 below.

You should spend about 20 minutes on this task.

The pie charts show the first place Germans and Nigerians go to in order to access the news in a typical week.

Summarise the information by selecting and reporting the main features, and make comparisons where relevant.

Write at least 150 words.

GO FURTHER ONLINE

First place Germans go to for their news

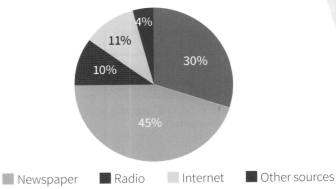

■ TV   ■ Newspaper   ■ Radio   ■ Internet   ■ Other sources

First place Nigerians (urban areas only) go to for their news

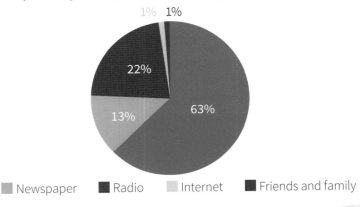

■ TV   ■ Newspaper   ■ Radio   ■ Internet   ■ Friends and family

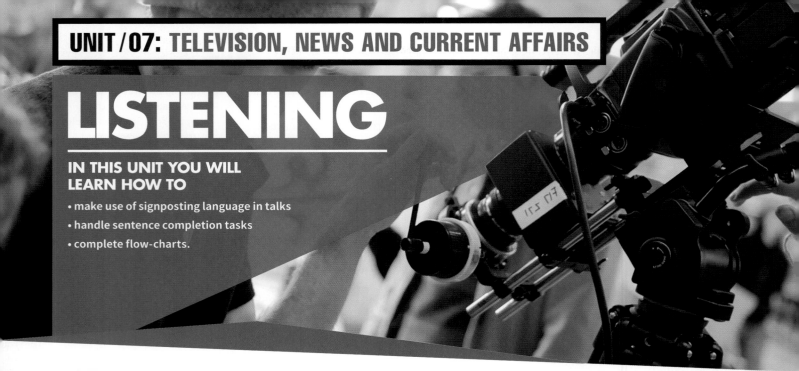

UNIT/07: TELEVISION, NEWS AND CURRENT AFFAIRS

LISTENING

IN THIS UNIT YOU WILL LEARN HOW TO

- make use of signposting language in talks
- handle sentence completion tasks
- complete flow-charts.

LEAD-IN

01▶ Discuss the questions with your group.

1 What kind of news are you interested in?
2 Which current news stories interest you most?
3 What is your favourite news channel or programme?
4 Would you like to be involved in making a news report? Why? / Why not?

USING SIGNPOSTING LANGUAGE TO FOLLOW A TALK

 In Section 4 of the Listening test you will hear a speaker giving a talk. You will probably hear signposting language that helps you follow the structure of the talk. Knowing this language is useful whatever the task type, as it helps you determine which parts of the recording relate to which questions.

02▶ Listen to an academic talk about making a news report. Tick the phrases off as you hear them.

56

a I'd like to start by … ☐
b The reason I've been asked to speak to you is … ☐
c Let's begin our talk with … ☐
d The first one is … ☐
e The next general point I want to make is … ☐
f The last of my general points is … ☐
g Right, so I'll just repeat those general points … ☐
h OK, so let's take a simplified look at … ☐
i The key advice here is … ☐
j After that, it's time to … ☐
k The next stage … ☐
l OK, moving on to … ☐
m I've already mentioned … ☐
n So, that's about it. ☐

03▷ Put the examples of signposting languages (a–n) from exercise 2 into the correct category. The first one has been done for you.

beginning or ending	a,
sequencing / moving on	
referring back	
summing up	
emphasising	
giving reasons	

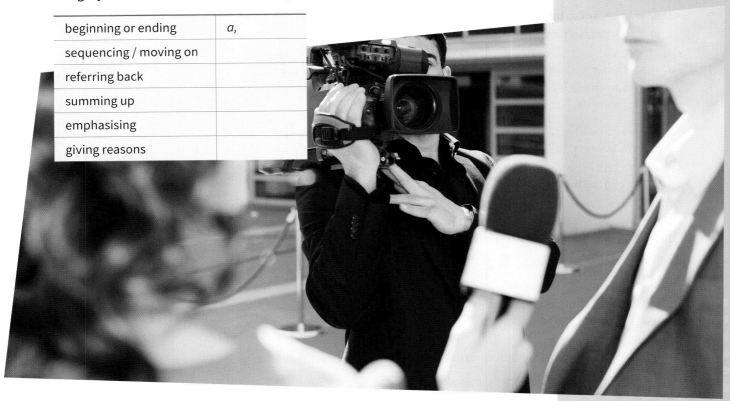

SENTENCE COMPLETION]

◉ This task type asks you to complete sentences and specifies the maximum number of words or numbers you can use. The gaps will often be at the end of the sentence but may be in the middle. There is only one gap per sentence, and the sentences follow the order of the text. The words you need will be heard on the recording in the same form.

04▷ These gapped sentences are based on the first part of the recording from exercise 2. For each gap, make a list of possible answers, using the correct number of words. Think about what the subject of the talk is and what parts of speech are missing.

1 The speaker is a _____ news reporter. (one word)
2 He is employed by _____ . (two words)

05▷ Listen and complete the sentences in exercise 4. Use NO MORE THAN TWO WORDS for each answer. Were you correct about what kind of words they were?

57

06▷ Look at these answers that some candidates wrote in the gaps. Which ones will be marked correct? Why are the others wrong?

1 A freelance
  B freelence
  C freelance news reporter
  D freelancer

2 A news agency
  B news agencies
  C several news agencies
  D agencies

TIP 04

Use your preparation time to look at the task and think about the topic. Try to decide what part of speech the missing word(s) are and make predictions as to what the words might be, so that you know what kind of information to listen for.

TIP 06

The word(s)/number(s) required to complete the sentences must fit grammatically and use the correct spelling. Make sure you don't repeat words in the question or write too many words, or your answer will be marked wrong.

07 ► Match the sentences (1–4) to the extracts from the recording that they paraphrase (a–d).

1 It is important to be aware of the age and attitude of _____ .

2 In-depth research on the viewers matters so that the news stories _____ .

3 Viewers might decide to watch a different _____ in the future.

4 With man-made disasters, are viewers more worried about the effects on the planet or the financial _____ ?

a The reason we try to find out as much as possible about the audience is that we want to interest them.

b If they can't engage with or relate to the stories we choose or how we present them, they'll choose another news channel.

c … if there's an oil spill into the sea, will our audience be more concerned about the environmental or the economic consequences?

d The first one is know your audience. By that I mean, are they older or younger viewers, where are they from, what are their values, ideas or beliefs, what level of education do they have?

TIP 07

Although the missing words you need come directly from the recording, the sentences will usually paraphrase what is said in the recording. In other words, the key ideas in the sentence will be expressed differently in the recording.

08 ► Now listen and complete the sentences in exercise 7. Use NO MORE THAN TWO WORDS for each answer.

58

09 ► Listen and complete the sentences. Write ONE WORD ONLY for each answer.

59

1 The speaker's second general point is about the importance of _____ .

2 Not giving a balance of views in a news story can harm the news station's _____ .

[COMPLETING A FLOW-CHART]

Flow-chart tasks require you to complete visual representations of a process or procedure, usually based on stages or sequences. Sometimes you choose from a list of words to complete them (in which case there will be more options than you need). If there is no list, the maximum number of words required will be specified. You use similar skills to complete a flow-chart as you used in sentence completion, note completion and table completion tasks.

10 ► Look at the flow-chart task in exercise 11. For questions 1 to 3, choose which answers are possible / not possible. Write P or NP next to the options. Explain your answers to your partner.

1 A a plan
  B planning
  C prepare everything
  D preparation

2 A agenda
  B plan
  C script
  D letter

3 A informations
  B information
  C details
  D detail

11▶ Listen and complete gaps 1 to 3 in the flow-chart. Write NO MORE THAN TWO WORDS for each answer.

60

```
┌──────────────────────────────────────────────────────┐
│                Making a TV news report                 │
│   You must start by 1 _____ . Think about the │
│        five Ws: Who, What, When, Where, Why.           │
└──────────────────────────────────────────────────────┘
                           ↓
┌──────────────────────────────────────────────────────┐
│  Write a 2 _____ . Keep it easy to understand. │
└──────────────────────────────────────────────────────┘
                           ↓
┌──────────────────────────────────────────────────────┐
│  Filming: Give an introduction to the story, avoiding needless │
│                  3 _____ .                   │
└──────────────────────────────────────────────────────┘
                           ↓
┌──────────────────────────────────────────────────────┐
│       Interviews: First interviewee should have direct  │
│  involvement in the story, such as a 4 _____ . │
└──────────────────────────────────────────────────────┘
                           ↓
┌──────────────────────────────────────────────────────┐
│  Second interview: Choose someone whose opinions 5 _____ with │
│  those of the previous interviewee so the report gives both sides of the story. │
└──────────────────────────────────────────────────────┘
                           ↓
┌──────────────────────────────────────────────────────┐
│       End of report: Summarise the main points          │
│      of story at this stage and mention potential        │
│      6 _____ in the on-going story.          │
└──────────────────────────────────────────────────────┘
```

12▶ Look at gaps 4 to 6 in the flow-chart above. Write down at least two possible answers that could go in each gap. Compare your words with your partner's. Do all the suggestions make sense grammatically and logically?

13▶ Listen and complete gaps 4 to 6. How close were your predictions?

61

[EXAM SKILLS]

14▶ Listen and answer questions 1–10.

62

Questions 1–5

*Complete the sentences. Write **NO MORE THAN TWO WORDS** for each answer.*

1 A basic definition of the news story is _____ .

2 A key difference between TV and print news stories is that TV editors must be

_____ .

3 Nowadays news stories engage the reader if they have _____ .

4 What an editor chooses to report is highly dependent on their _____ .

5 A good news editor also needs to pay attention to the stories being published by

_____ .

Questions 6–10
Complete the flow-chart below.
Choose **SIX** answers from the list below and write the correct letter, **A–H**, next to Questions 6–10.

A plate	**C** edition	**E** gathering	**G** process
B colour	**D** size	**F** prototype	**H** printing press

How a newspaper is put together

News 6 _____: Researching and writing news items, arranging advertisements.

Editing: Each type of editor marks their changes using a different 7 _____ .

Pre-press: Designing the pages. A 8 _____ of each page is produced.

Press/lithographic stage: When the design process is complete, each page is transferred to a metal 9 _____ .

Impression stage: These are inserted on the 10 _____ and the newspapers are printed.

Circulation: newspapers sent out nationwide.

GO FURTHER ONLINE

SPEAKING

UNIT /07: TELEVISION, NEWS AND CURRENT AFFAIRS

IN THIS UNIT YOU WILL LEARN HOW TO

- talk about TV programmes
- correct yourself and clarify while speaking
- stress words correctly when correcting yourself
- use the passive when speaking.

01▷ Write down an example of each kind of TV programme.

drama	comedy	sports	crime drama	chat show	news/current affairs
reality TV	quiz show	kids	documentary	travel/holiday	science fiction/fantasy

02▷ Check the meaning of these words and expressions for talking about TV programmes. Then write them in three columns: positive, negative, neutral.

gripping
inspirational
intriguing
pointless
absolutely hilarious
a complete waste of time
a definite 5-star rating
compulsive viewing

utter garbage
I can take it or leave it.
I watched it in one sitting.
It gave me food for thought.
It was nothing to write home about.
It has/had me on the edge on my seat.
It's not my cup of tea.
I was glued to the screen.

Positive	Negative	Neutral

03▷ Tell your partner your opinion about the programmes you wrote down in exercise 1. Use some of the expressions from exercise 2 if possible.

In the Speaking test it is OK to correct yourself if you make a mistake. It is better to do so if you realise that your grammar, word choice or pronunciation was wrong. In addition, if you feel you have not explained your ideas clearly – or if the examiner looks confused – you can give more information or explain in different words to clarify what you are saying. There are expressions you can learn to help you in these situations.

04 ▷ **Read and listen to a student called Rashid doing the task below. How many times does he correct or clarify himself? Underline the words and phrases he uses.**

Describe a TV programme you often watch.

You should say

- what type of programme it is
- why you enjoy it
- who you watch it with

and explain how you feel about this programme.

Rashid One of my favourite programmes is *Fear Factor*. Actually, I would say it's a programme that I love to hate! What I mean by that is – I *love* it, but at times the things on there are awesome, sorry, I meant to say they are *awful*. So the type – or rather the *genre* – of show is reality but also it's a competition. What happens is that there are four people – well, you know, four competitors – and they has to do, they have to do a series of tasks. Sometimes they have to dive into – or actually they dive *under* water and open a box – I mean *unlock* a box, or they have to climb up a high building. In the second task, there are nasty animals – not animals as such, but things like cockroaches or snakes which they must to, they must lie in a box with or something. So, I don't like it, but it's compulsory. I'll rephrase that. I watch it even though I don't want to. It's compulsive. It's on Thursday nights on a channel called Reality. I usually watch with my brother – *both* my brothers, actually. Sometimes we play our own version of it and make each other do silly tasks – but not as bad as the ones on the TV.

05 ▶ Identify the grammar or vocabulary mistakes in the sentences below and then correct them using an appropriate expression from the box. Try to use a different expression each time.

I mean …	What I meant to say was …
Let me start again.	Sorry, what I intended to say was …
I'll rephrase that.	Did I say …? I meant to say …
or rather …	Let me put that another way.

Example: My best TV show is *Match of the Day*.
I mean my <u>favourite</u> TV show is *Match of the Day*.

1 Wildlife programmes are not very interested.
2 The presentator of the programme is very good.
3 It is a show they make people beauty.
4 This programme shows you the inside house of a celebrity.
5 Most of people in my country watching this show.
6 I like shows with games and prizes.

PRONUNCIATION

06 ▶ Read these examples of candidates correcting themselves. Underline the words you think should be stressed.

 TIP 06

When we are correcting a mistake, we usually give extra stress to the word, phrase or idea that we have corrected.

Example: I absolutely hate watching the new. Sorry, I meant to say <u>news</u>.

1 Watching TV is a time of waste. Sorry, I'll rephrase that – a waste of time.
2 Comedic shows, or rather comedy shows, are not very popular in my country.
3 I can't understand why realism TV is so popular. Let me start again. I can't understand why reality TV is so popular.
4 The popularity of sports programmes, especially football series, I mean football highlights shows, makes no sense to me.
5 One thing that I dislike about TV is the amount of publicities. Oh, did I say publicities? I meant to say commercials.

Listen and check. Then listen again and repeat.

64

07 ▶ Look at the statements made by candidates in the Speaking test. The statements are very general. Use one of the expressions in the box below to explain or clarify them for the examiner.

Example: I would say that TV is in part to blame for violence in society.

> *Let me elaborate on that. There is a tendency for TV to glamorise violence and make it seem cool, and I think that especially younger viewers are strongly influenced by what they see …*

1 I think TV is a very positive thing.
2 Children should be allowed to watch TV online unsupervised.
3 Watching TV online is far superior to watching conventional TV.
4 The standard of TV programmes is so much better these days.

Let me explain.	Let me clarify that.
What I mean by this is …	To put that another way, …
Let me elaborate on that.	

08 ▶ Work with a partner. Do the Part 2 task in exercise 4. If you make a mistake or are being unclear, use some of the expressions from exercises 5 and 7 to correct or clarify yourself.

GRAMMAR FOCUS: PASSIVE EXPRESSIONS WITH IMPERSONAL *IT*

In Part 3 in particular you are expected to talk about less familiar situations. Rather than speak about your own experiences, you should say what people in general or particular groups of people feel about a situation or what is known about it. There are some useful passive expressions with impersonal 'it' which will help you do this. It also helps you to sound more objective.

09 ▶ Complete the sentences related to TV, news and current affairs with your own ideas.

Example: It could be argued that … *continuing to print newspapers is a waste of money*.

1 It has been said / reported that …
2 It is believed / thought / widely accepted that …
3 It has been proved that …
4 It has been estimated that …

10 ▶ Work with a partner. Read your sentences from exercise 9. React to your partner's sentences to develop short conversations.

Example: **A** It could be argued that continuing to print newspapers is a waste of money.
　　　　　B Well, possibly, but many people still prefer reading the old-fashioned way.

[EXAM SKILLS]

1 1 ▶ Do this sample test with a partner. Take turns to ask and answer.

Part 1

1 How much time do you spend watching TV?
2 What kind of programmes do you enjoy? Why?
3 Are there any kinds of programmes you don't like? Why?
4 Do you prefer watching TV alone or with others? Why?

Part 2

Describe a TV programme you have watched which you did not enjoy.

You should say

- what the programme was
- when and where you watched it
- what others thought of it

and explain why you didn't enjoy it.

Part 3

1 How do you think the range and type of programmes on TV has changed in recent years?
2 What factors need to be considered by those who plan TV programming?
3 How has new technology changed the way people watch TV?
4 What potential problems are raised by online and 'on demand' TV?
5 How do you think TV viewing might change in the future?

GO FURTHER ONLINE

UNIT / 08: CULTURE

READING

IN THIS UNIT YOU WILL LEARN HOW TO

- review reading skills
- review reading task types
- use relative clauses.

LEAD-IN

01 ▷ **Are these statements about the Reading test true (T) or false (F)?**

1 The test takes 60 minutes plus 10 minutes to transfer your answers to the answer sheet.
2 There are three texts and 40 questions.
3 The texts are from academic sources.
4 Some questions are worth two marks.
5 There are more than 12 different task types.

02 ▷ **The following is a list of the task types you might meet in the IELTS Reading test. For each one, briefly describe what you have to do.**

1 Multiple choice
2 True / False / Not Given
3 Yes / No / Not Given
4 Matching information
5 Matching headings
6 Matching features
7 Matching sentence endings
8 Sentence completion
9 Note/table/flow-chart completion
10 Diagram label completion
11 Short-answer questions
12 Summary completion

REVIEWING READING SKILLS

03 ▷ **Skim read the passage *The rise and fall of youth subcultures* on pages 161–162 in 1 to 2 minutes. Tick all the statements that are true about the passage.**

1 The passage gives several examples of youth subcultures.
2 The writer does not share any personal opinions.
3 The text compares young people in the 20th and 21st centuries.
4 The role of the internet is mentioned more than once.
5 The writer appears to be a young person.

 Most Reading sections in the exam will contain a balance of tasks designed to test a variety of reading skills but the main skills you need for virtually all reading tasks are skimming, scanning and reading for detail.

TIP 03

Remember that skim reading the text first will help you gain a global understanding of the text that will benefit you when you come to do the actual tasks.

04 ▷ Scan the text to find the following information. Write the paragraph letter(s) next to each one and find the paraphrase in the text. The key words are underlined for you.

1 a subculture that has <u>passed the test of time</u>
2 an <u>explanation</u> for <u>the rise of youth subcultures</u>
3 an <u>example</u> of the <u>internet</u> being <u>used to raise money and inform people</u>
4 <u>descriptions</u> of <u>various youth groups' fashion and music preferences</u>
5 the <u>influence</u> of the <u>US</u> on <u>youth culture</u> in Britain
6 a discussion of <u>the identity of today's young people</u>
7 the <u>decade</u> in which the older generation began to think <u>youth subcultures were declining</u>
8 the <u>causes</u> of a <u>broader outlook</u> in today's young people

TIP 04

When scanning and reading in detail, you are normally looking for paraphrases of the questions or options in the tasks.

THE RISE AND FALL OF YOUTH SUBCULTURES

A Ask anyone British in their 50s, 60s and 70s to look back at their youth and they will doubtless name a plethora of different subcultures. There were the Mods (Modernists) with their tailor-made suits, motor scooters and R & B music, and their great rivals, the Rockers, a biker subculture, who wore leather jackets and listened to Rock and Roll. Hippies, who emerged in America and spread across the world, represented a more peaceful group. With their long hair and garish clothes, they opposed all forms of violence and the 'establishment', as they called mainstream society. Jumping forward to the 1970s, we see the rise of Punk. Instantly recognisable with their drainpipe jeans, kilts, safety pins and Mohicans, they perhaps more than any of their predecessors embodied youth rebellion, sometimes literally spitting in the face of the world in which they had grown up.

B These days, the average 15-year-old has probably never seen a Mod or Rocker in the flesh. These youth subcultures from that era have all but disappeared, existing only in films and television for today's young people. Sadly, today's youth, at first glance at least, look more homogenous, seemingly having lost their tribalism. So what happened? Where have all the colourful youth subcultures gone? It was in the 1990s that many older commentators started to point out that the youth movements had lost their fire and had become conventional. The colourful 'tribes' of the previous years were disappearing and the young appeared to have stopped rebelling.

C To explain this phenomenon we need to look at the reasons why conditions were ripe for the emergence of youth cultures in the mid-twentieth century. It was the post-war period that saw the rise of distinctive subcultures. Elvis Presley and the advent of Rock and Roll generated the Teddy Boys in the UK, who in turn influenced both Mods and Rockers. It was a time when conventional social values were being questioned and after the austerity of the war, young people found themselves with more freedom. Fuelled by American culture, Britain's youth suddenly had something to say and a desire to express themselves.

D These days American culture is still a dominant force, but in many ways the world is so different. Rises in levels of prosperity have robbed many young people of something to rebel against, and the development of the internet and its widespread availability from the 1990s onwards has fundamentally changed how young people interact with the world. Things change so quickly that young people no longer commit to one look and style of music in order to find their identity. Influences from all over the world – not just America – mean that young people have a vast array of choices in terms of fashion, music and even attitudes and beliefs. Although the younger generation of today has been called 'identity-less', that is not actually the case. The identities they create are more individual and subtle, with a wider range of influences. Teenagers today spend a lot of their time developing their own sense of self through social media. They are free to slip in and out of identities and scenes, which is more liberating than being tied to a specific tribe.

E Common to all those subcultures of the mid- to late twentieth century was a desire to rebel: against parents, government policies and established society. Marking yourself out as different and separate through your clothes and hairstyle is something that does not chime so resonantly with the globalised generation born in the nineties and noughties. Today's young people are more tolerant and international thanks to globalisation, but that does not mean they are apathetic. In fact, it can be argued that they are more likely to contribute towards actual change, which again has been made possible by the internet. They set up and sign online petitions and share information about demonstrations on social media. They take part in charity events such as sponsored runs or shave their heads to raise awareness as well as money. The global phenomenon which was the Ice Bucket Challenge*, for example, raised over $100 million for motor neurone disease and raised awareness of that terrible condition which affects, among others, world renowned physicist, Stephen Hawking.

F There is one subculture that seems to have endured better than the others: the bikers. Characterised by their long hair, scruffy denim jeans, leather jackets and Harley Davidson motorbikes, the most marked feature of the group nowadays is that they are no longer young. At biker rallies in the 2010s, the average age is probably around 50. What sets them apart is that they never grew out of the identity of their youth. Seeing them gathered together invokes a strong sense of nostalgia in those of us who remember the days of youth subcultures.

G While it is sad in many ways to see the vibrant cultures of our youth consigned to the history books, it is, when examined closely, a development which is as positive as it is inevitable. Young people today are free to adopt aspects from a huge range of cultures and continually reinvent themselves. The symbolic rebellions of dress and hairstyle have been replaced by meaningful action which impacts on political and social decision-making at the highest levels. Rather than being without identity as a generation, today's youth are typically broad-minded and well informed, each individual having created their own unique style and set of beliefs, which they are free to change at any moment. But those of us who recall the heady days of the Mods and Rockers, the Punks and Teddy Boys, will always feel a slight regret at their passing.

* Ice Bucket Challenge – a charity action that involved filming yourself pouring ice cold water over your head in order to raise money for charities related to Motor Neurone Disease

REVIEWING READING TASK TYPES

0 5 ▶ The reading passage has seven paragraphs, A–G. Choose the correct heading for each paragraph from the list of headings. Write the correct number, i–x. There are three headings you won't need.

List of headings

  i   Out with the old and in with the new and improved

 ii   The decline of youth subcultures

iii   Regret for a lost era

 iv   Youth subcultures in the second half of the 20th century

  v   The ice bucket challenge raises millions

 vi   Why young people formed their own social groups

vii   Identity-less youth of today

viii A different type of identity

 ix   Survivors of a lost age

  x   Fighting for change in new ways

1 Paragraph A _____
2 Paragraph B _____
3 Paragraph C _____
4 Paragraph D _____
5 Paragraph E _____
6 Paragraph F _____
7 Paragraph G _____

0 6 ▶ Do the following statements agree with the claims of the writer in the text?

Write

YES   *if the statement agrees with the claims of the writer*
NO   *if the statement contradicts the claims of the writer*
NOT GIVEN   *if it is impossible to say what the writer thinks about this*

1 20th-century youth movements had their own distinct way of dressing.
2 Today's youth are less effective at changing society than their predecessors.
3 Young people waste too much time on social media.
4 It is unfortunate that many of the sub-cultures are disappearing.

GRAMMAR FOCUS: RELATIVE CLAUSES

Relative clauses provide extra information about a noun or noun phrase. There are two types: defining and non-defining. **Defining relative clauses** give information that is essential to the meaning of the sentence. **Non-defining relative clauses** give extra but non-essential information, meaning that the clause can be removed, and the sentence will still make sense. Relative clauses usually begin with relative pronouns (*that, who, which, whose, where, when, why*), though these can be omitted in some defining relative clauses.

0 7 ▶ Look at the sentences from the text with underlined relative clauses. Which is defining and which non-defining? How do you know?

1 *There is one subculture <u>that seems to have endured better than the others: the bikers</u>.*
2 *Elvis Presley and the advent of Rock and Roll generated the Teddy Boys in the UK, <u>who in turn influenced both Mods and Rockers</u>.*

0 8 ▶ Find another example each of defining and non-defining relative clauses in the text.

09 ▶ **Look at this sentence with a relative clause and answer the questions.**

The identities <u>they create are more individual and subtle, with a wider range of influences</u>.

1 Why doesn't it use a relative pronoun?
2 Where and which relative pronouns could be added to this sentence?
3 Can the relative pronoun be omitted from the example sentences in exercise 7? Why? / Why not?

10 ▶ **Rewrite these pairs of sentences as one sentence with a relative clause, using the relative pronoun given.**

1 American culture had a major influence on Britain's youth. They copied the style and music but made their own version of it. (who)
2 One of the more memorable groups of the 1970s was the Punks. Their drainpipe jeans, kilts, safety pins and extraordinary hairstyles made them instantly recognisable. (whose)
3 The younger generation of today has been called 'identity-less'. This is not actually the case. (which)

[EXAM SKILLS]

11 ▶ **Read the passage and answer questions 1–6.**

NOMADIC CULTURES

Out of a world population of 7.5 billion, around 30 million people currently lead a migratory lifestyle. Every continent has nomadic groups, leading a life very different from the sedentary communities they come into contact with. Almost all migratory communities are in steady decline for a wide range of reasons: climate change, political unrest, forced resettlement and armed conflict have all impacted on these traditional communities, diminishing their numbers year on year. However, the lure of the travelling lifestyle is as strong as ever. The 'gypsy lifestyle' continues to inspire people – especially the young – who crave the freedom of unstructured movement. Backpacking has become almost a rite of passage for the young. 'Gap years' between school and university often stretch to two years, or even more, as young people become addicted to the culture of travelling light and moving on.

Traditional nomads may be seen as 'wanderers', but their movement is not as unstructured as it may appear. Most nomadic communities are, or were, herdsmen, leading their animals across fixed routes based on pastures and water sources. Their societies were based on strong bonds of kinship. According to 14th-century social historian Ibn Khaldun, the Bedouin community owed their success in battle to *asabiyya* or 'group feeling', which enhanced their ability to protect the group from outsiders. This, along with excellent horsemanship and the rigours of a harsh lifestyle, based around constant alertness needed to protect livestock, made them formidable adversaries in war when compared to their more settled counterparts.

Far from the desert-dwelling Bedouin live a different kind of nomad: the Moken, or sea gypsies, of the Mergui Archipelago between Myanmar and the islands of Thailand's North Andaman coast. During the dry season, they live on traditional houseboats, and during the monsoon season they build temporary villages on sheltered stretches of beach. Theirs is a culture of sharing and giving, to the extent that their language contains no words for individual possessions. This indigenous people has a great understanding of and respect for their environment, making use of over 80 plant species for food and more than 100 for shelter, handicrafts and other purposes. However, the Moken's lifestyle has more recently been affected by government restrictions on their hunter-gathering activities, and legal disputes over ownership of their traditional lands. Somewhat inevitably, they have become a focus for tourism in the area, which they have embraced to some extent as they try to adapt to the modern world.

Nomadic communities exist in Europe too. In the tundras and taigas of northern Scandinavia live a reindeer-herding community, the Sami. Originally travelling freely across the areas which now belong to Norway, Sweden, Finland and Russia, this subculture has had its traditional lifestyle curtailed by the creation of national borders. In contrast to the Bedouin, the Sami's culture stresses the importance of knowledge and acceptance of the Sami language and traditions over bloodlines. It is an open and egalitarian society that welcomes outsiders. Marked by its rich storytelling and musical traditions, Sami culture has enjoyed something of a renaissance in recent years. Like many traditional cultures, it has both suffered and benefitted from a growing tourist industry as well as from government regulations. Norway now has a specific, protected reindeer-herding region, but the activity is prohibited elsewhere in the country.

Perhaps a better known travelling culture in Europe is the Roma, or Romany, of Central, Eastern and South-eastern Europe. The group is now spread across Western Europe too due to permanent migration. While their defining characteristic is the nomadic lifestyle, there have always been settled Roma, and the proportion has continued to grow, largely due to state intervention. However, there are some communities that have managed to retain a semi-nomadic way of life, such as the Thracian Kalajdžii (tinsmiths) in Bulgaria and Kortorari in Romania. The Roma tend to function as 'carriers of tradition' in the countries where they live. Cultural change does not happen as fast as it does in mainstream society, so traditions that have all but died out elsewhere are preserved and adapted by the Roma community. An example of this is the Dodola, a 'ritual for rain' in the Balkans, which used to be widespread, but is now limited to the Roma.

In the UK, the term 'gypsy' covers both Roma and Irish travellers, two diverse groups united by a common nomadic heritage. Irish travellers traditionally move in groups of two to four families, which would typically include married sons and their wives and children. Like many other migratory communities, Irish travellers have strong kinship ties due to the practice of arranged marriages as well as their isolation from settled society. In common with other nomads, their traditional way of life has faced many threats. In particular, the crafts, trades and services they practise, once in high demand, have been made redundant by declining rural populations, the mechanisation of farming, improved rural transport systems and the mass production of cheap plastic goods. Life expectancy for Irish travellers is often well below the national average.

In spite of the many obstacles faced by travelling communities all over the world, the world's fascination with the mobile lifestyle has not diminished. Mainstream culture seems to have a confused and contradictory relationship with travellers. On the one hand, the settled majority have a tendency to look down on those who refuse to adopt the sedentary lifestyle. On the other hand, they hold a romantic view of the horse-drawn caravans and campfires of the gypsy or the camel trains and tents of the Bedouin. What is clear is that travelling communities around the world, though reduced in number, are still alive and well and their contribution to world culture is indisputable.

Questions 1–5

Look at the following statements and the list of traveller communities below.

*Match each statement with the correct community, **A–E**. You may use any letter more than once.*

1 They tend to protect a version of traditions inherited from wider society.
2 Where they live is very dependent on weather conditions and the time of the year.
3 They do not focus heavily on kinship ties.
4 They fully exploit the natural resources available to them.
5 Their success in combat was partly due to the demands of their lifestyle.

List of traveller communities
A The Bedouin   **B** The Moken   **C** The Sami   **D** The Roma   **E** Irish travellers

Question 6

*Choose the correct letter, **A, B, C** or **D**.*

What is the writer's purpose in the Reading Passage?

GO FURTHER ONLINE

A to compare how successful different nomadic groups are in the modern world
B to explain the origins of backpacking culture
C to criticise the lack of tolerance for travelling communities
D to highlight the current state of traditional travelling cultures in the modern world

UNIT /08: CULTURE

WRITING

IN THIS UNIT YOU WILL LEARN HOW TO

• describe a process in Task 1

• give opposing views and your own opinion in Task 2

• write a complete essay.

LEAD-IN

01 ▷ **Read these definitions of culture. Which one do you like best? Why?**

1 The sum of attitudes, customs, and beliefs that distinguishes one group of people from another. Culture is transmitted, through language, material objects, ritual, institutions and art, from one generation to the next. (*www.dictionary.com/browse/culture*)

2 Culture is a fuzzy set of basic assumptions and values, orientations to life, beliefs, policies, procedures and behavioural conventions that are shared by a group of people, and that influence (but do not determine) each member's behaviour and his/her interpretations of the 'meaning' of other people's behaviour. (*Spencer-Oatey 2001*)

3 Culture is the collective programming of the mind which distinguishes the members of one group or category of people from another. (*Hofstede 1994*)

4 Culture means the way we do things around here. (*Unknown*)

02 ▷ **Imagine you are explaining your culture to someone from a completely different one. Make a list of its most significant or interesting features. Use the points below to help you. Compare with a partner.**

Food and cuisine

National dress

Social etiquette

Language

Traditions / festivals

Our national dishes include fish and chips and roast beef but we are not famous for our cuisine. We are famous for drinking a lot of tea …

We are very polite and often apologise for things which are not our fault.

TASK 1 – DESCRIBING A PROCESS

◎ For Task 1 you might be asked describe a process, such as how something is made or something that happens in nature. You are given a diagram. (There may be one or two unfamiliar words but a definition may be given below the diagram.) Study each stage of the process to work out what is happening. Keep the tone quite formal as you would do in other Part 1 tasks.

0 3 ▷ The diagram shows the process of making Wesak lanterns, which Sri Lankans do to celebrate the festival of Wesak in May each year. With a partner, make a list of verbs, nouns and adjectives you could use in describing this process.

Verbs	Nouns	Adjectives
cut	*scissors*	*coloured*

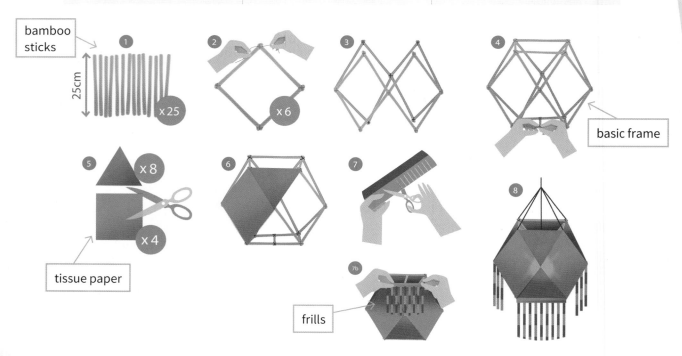

04 ▶ Look at these sentences and the stages in the process they correspond to on the diagram. Rewrite them using the passive.

1 You have to tie the corners of four of these squares together. (Stage 3)
Four of these squares have to be tied together.

2 Next, you can stick the square and triangular tissue paper shapes onto the frame. (Stage 6)

3 The lantern is then ready to hang on a lightbulb. (Stage 8)

TIP 04

The passive is a very useful structure for describing processes. There may be opportunities to use more complex passives, such as modal passives and passive infinitives, which could improve your GRA score:

- You have to glue the paper to the frame. (active) ➔ The paper has to be glued to the frame. (passive)
- The lantern is ready to decorate. (active) ➔ The lantern is ready to be decorated. (passive)

05 ▶ Complete the sample answer using the words in the box.

| after that | this | then | this stage | next | finally | to begin with | followed by | once |

SAMPLE ANSWER

The diagram shows the process of making Wesak lanterns. There are eight main stages, which consist of tying bamboo sticks together to form the frame of the lantern, **1** _____ the cutting and pasting of coloured paper which is used to decorate it.

2 _____ , you need to cut 24 bamboo sticks to a length of 25cm each. Four of the sticks are **3** _____ tied together to make a square. **4** _____ of the process has to be repeated until you have made six squares. **5** _____ , you have to tie the corners of four of the squares together. The remaining two squares are then tied in place at the top and bottom of the ring, which will give you the basic frame of the lantern.

6 _____ your frame is completed, take brightly coloured tissue paper and cut out eight triangles and four squares to sizes which correspond to the squares and triangles on the frame. **7** _____ the tissue paper shapes should be attached onto the frame. The squares at the top and bottom of the frame should be left empty. **8** _____ , fold and cut paper for the frills, and decorate the base of the lantern with them, so that they hang down below it. The lantern is then ready to be hung on a lightbulb.

TIP 05

Learn a variety of sequencing linkers, such as *firstly, secondly, after that, next* for this task.

06 ▶ Look again at the sample answer in exercise 5 and answer the questions.

1 Has the writer included an overview?
2 Find examples of the following grammar structures the candidate has used:
   a relative clauses
   b passive
   c imperatives

TIP 06

Make sure you include an overview of the whole process in the opening paragraph. It should give general information about the process (type of process, how many stages, what is produced) in one or two sentences.

TASK 2 - ESSAY

GIVING OPPOSING VIEWS AND YOUR OWN OPINION

 For this kind of essay, you need to discuss two positions on a question and then give your own. Your own opinion can be to take one side or the other, to partly agree with one or both, or even to disagree with both positions and offer an alternative view. The key is to make sure that your opinion is clear and, as with all Task 2 essays, support your arguments with examples, reasons, explanations, etc.

07 ▷ **Look at the Task 2 essay question. Then read the extracts (1–6) from candidates' answers. Label them A (opinion A) or B (opinion B).**

Some people believe that a person's culture is defined by their country of origin (opinion A), *while others believe that has only a minor influence* (opinion B). *Discuss both these views and give your opinion.*

Give reasons for your answer and include any relevant examples from your own knowledge or experience.

1 In my experience, it depends on which cultural background someone is from. Some people are able to discard their national identities more readily than others.

2 Although many people believe a person's country no longer has a great influence on their culture, what I believe is that, under the surface, the impact of where a person is from is enormous.

3 It is evident to me that we can never truly escape our origins. They are with us from birth and are present during our formative years.

4 Some people are of the opinion that, for example, because the same fast-food chains exist in every country, everyone likes the same food. However, the reality is that in most parts of the world people eat the same food, typical of their own country or region, almost every day.

5 While it may be true that certain aspects of culture are shared by people from all over the world, we cannot deny that our beliefs and behaviours are shaped by the national environment in which we grow up.

6 While I admit that the country of origin is a major factor in determining one's culture, I strongly believe that anyone who moves overseas for work or study can be equally influenced by the culture of this host country.

08 ▷ **Look again at the extracts in exercise 7. Identify the expressions which are used to introduce an opinion.**

09 ▷ **Complete the sentences with your own ideas.**

1 Some people believe that you can learn a language without knowing the culture. My own view is …

2 There is a widespread belief that the world is a global village. However, it seems to me that …

3 On the one hand, it is possible to argue that our country of origin defines us. On the other hand, …

WRITING A COMPLETE ESSAY

10 ▶ Complete the checklist on writing a Task 2 essay using the words in the box.

conclusion	cohesive	examples	plan	topic sentence
paragraphs	highlight	opposing	outline	proof-read

1 Read the question carefully and _____ any key words. Circle any instruction words.

2 Make a brief _____ of the structure of your essay. Decide how many _____ you will need. Note down some key vocabulary.

3 In your introduction and overview, paraphrase the question, include your opinion, if appropriate, and an _____ of what you intend to argue.

4 When writing your body paragraphs, ensure each one contains a clear _____ (usually the first sentence). Remember to give specific _____ or explanations to support each main point.

5 If you are arguing in favour of one opinion, make sure you discuss at least one or two points representing the _____ view.

6 As you write, keep in mind the need for a variety of grammatical structures and a wide range of _____ devices.

7 Include a _____ as a separate paragraph.

8 Finally, _____ your essay for errors, such as spelling mistakes.

11 ▶ Read this essay for the task in exercise 7. Then answer the questions on the next page.

For each essay type you can encounter in the IELTS test, make sure you are clear on how best to plan and organise your writing. It is a good idea to make checklists for each type to use when you are practising and to help you in the exam itself.

SAMPLE ANSWER

If we define culture as shared beliefs, values, attitudes and behaviours, it stands to reason then that a person's country of origin impacts their culture. The question is to what degree. Is nationality the defining influence or is it just one of many factors in play? Personally speaking, I would say both arguments have validity, but I would lean towards the latter.

It is easy to understand the 'defining influence' argument. If someone is born and raised in a place, they will be heavily influenced by it. Psychologists refer to this as the 'nurture argument' – you are a product of your environment. For example, if your country's cuisine uses certain ingredients, your palate gets accustomed to those ingredients, but may struggle with other less familiar flavours. If your country has a traditional style of music, say, reggae or rock, all citizens will be exposed to it and, as a result, are more likely to enjoy it.

On the other side of the argument we need to consider the effects of globalisation. Most people have daily access and exposure to other cultures. The evidence is all around us – restaurants, films and foreign businesses are ubiquitous. One of the benefits of globalisation is that it offers us a selection of cultural possibilities to choose from. It is unlikely that you will find any citizen of a certain country who does not have likes or preferences that come from outside of their country of origin. In addition, more and more people work, study or travel extensively away from their home country. Inevitably, these people will be subject to new influences.

My own view is that while we are influenced by our nationality, in this globalised world, one's country of origin is only one aspect of our collective culture. We all adopt elements from other cultures on a daily basis, unconsciously or according to our preferences and experiences. To my mind, this is what makes the world such an interesting place.

1 Does paragraph 1 (introduction) clearly explain what the essay will be about?
2 Where does the candidate make their position/opinion clear in this essay?
3 Which opinion from the question does the candidate discuss in paragraph 2? Underline the topic sentence that expresses it. How many reasons/examples are given to support it?
4 Which opinion does paragraph 3 discuss? Underline the topic sentence that expresses it. Why do you think the candidate chose to discuss this here?
5 Make a list of opinion phrases used in this essay.

EXAM SKILLS

1 2 ▶ Answer the Writing tasks below.

Task 1

You should spend about 20 minutes on this task.

The diagram illustrates the process of making traditional wooden shoes called clogs.

Summarise the information by selecting and reporting the main features and make comparisons where relevant.

Write at least 150 words.

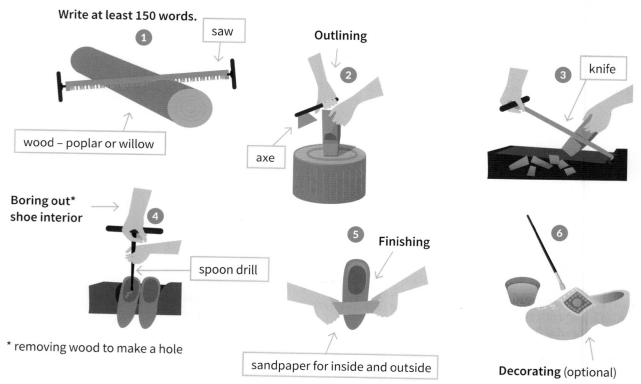

saw

Outlining

knife

wood – poplar or willow

axe

Boring out*
shoe interior

spoon drill

5 **Finishing**

Decorating (optional)

* removing wood to make a hole

sandpaper for inside and outside

Task 2

You should spend about 40 minutes on this task.

Some believe that people today have no interest in maintaining the traditional culture of their country or region. Others believe that it is still important to people that we preserve a traditional way of life. Discuss both these views and give your own opinion.

Give reasons for your answer and include any relevant examples from your own knowledge or experience.

Write at least 250 words.

GO FURTHER ONLINE

UNIT /08: CULTURE

LISTENING

IN THIS UNIT YOU WILL LEARN HOW TO

• use notes to follow a talk

• do note completion and sentence completion tasks

• check your answers

• use prepositions in relative clauses.

LEAD-IN

01▶ Complete the sentences with the correct form of the word *globe*.

1 To change the world, we should think _____ and act locally.

2 Some people believe that the world is now a _____ village.

3 We live in a world where almost everything has been _____ .

4 The internet allows us to interact with people from all around the

_____ .

5 Some people feel that _____ is a threat to traditional cultures.

02▶ Discuss these questions with your group.

1 Which aspects of life do you think have been affected by globalisation?

2 Are there any aspects of culture that have not been affected?

3 Do you agree that traditional cultures are under threat from globalisation?

4 Do you think governments have a duty to protect minority cultures that are at risk?

For any note, table or sentence completion task, it is vital that you look through the information on the page *before* the recording begins to get a feel for what the speaker(s) will talk about. This is particularly the case for Section 4, which is based on an academic talk, as the tasks and recording are more complex, and there is no long pause during the recording, so doing this will help you to navigate where you are in the recording with respect to the questions.

03▶ **Look at a note completion task based on a talk about the globalisation of culture. Start with the headings. What is the structure of the talk?**

*Complete the notes below. Write **ONE WORD AND/OR A NUMBER** for each answer.*

Globalisation of culture

Definitions

- Not everyone agrees on how to define culture.

- **1** _____ aspects: music, clothes, food, architecture
  Unseen features: values, beliefs

- Need to look deeper to comprehend the **2** _____ attached to cultural phenomena
  Example
  Titanic's popularity in China not because of the popularity of US culture, but due to
  3 _____ factors

Negative view

- Increasing globalisation of culture due to global **4** _____

- Global business does not distinguish between cultures and so does not take into account **5** _____ cultural requirements.

- 1999 survey in France: **6** _____ of people felt globalisation a danger to the French way of life

Positive view

- People seen as global **7** _____ , able to choose the food, music and clothes they like

- Profound characteristics of culture, such as views on **8** _____ are not as likely to alter

Effect of the internet

- Has helped save local traditions and **9** _____

Conclusion

- Important to stress the role of **10** _____ in the debate on cultural globalisation

04▶ **Listen to the talk and follow the notes. Don't try to fill in the gaps at this stage. Tick each bullet point as you hear it. Your teacher will stop the recording at different stages and ask you to point to where you are in the notes.**

NOTE COMPLETION]

⊚ This is common for Section 4 academic talks and, in fact, it is possible that this section will have a single note completion task with up to 10 gaps to cover the whole recording. You may have to listen to the whole talk with only one very short pause in the middle.

05▶ Look at gaps 1 to 3 in exercise 3. Which word or phrase is NOT possible in each gap? Why?

1 **A** obvious   **B** defined   **C** definition
2 **A** interesting   **B** ideas   **C** beliefs
3 **A** political and economic **B** political   **C** social

TIP 05

Although the words you need come from the recording, remember that the notes will most likely be phrased differently from the recording and remember also that your answers need to fit grammatically.

06▶ Look at gaps 4 to 6. What type of word goes in each gap?

4 **A** a noun   **B** an adjective   **C** a verb
5 **A** a noun   **B** an adjective   **C** an adverb
6 **A** a number **B** a date   **C** a fraction or percentage

07▶ For gaps 7 to 10 write one or two words that could go in each gap.

08▶ Listen to the recording again and complete the notes with NO MORE THAN ONE WORD AND/OR A NUMBER.

65

SENTENCE COMPLETION]

⊚ Completing sentences is very similar to completing notes. The main difference is that the gaps will be in complete, grammatical sentences. There also might be less of a connection from one sentence to the next than in a set of notes.

09▶ You are going to hear an extract about language and culture. Read the sentences and try to predict the kind of words that could go in the gaps.

1 Language can help us understand societies, much the same as _____ help us understand the history of a place.

2 Political, social and economic reasons can cause some languages to _____ to the disadvantage of others.

3 Swahili is seen as the language used in _____ in East Africa and this has had a negative impact on other languages.

4 Immigrants may be motivated to neglect their native tongues as part of their _____ into their new culture.

5 Joshua Hinson was worried that the fluent speakers of Chikasaw were

_____ .

6 Young Chikasaw speakers are working with professionals in the field to develop a

_____ .

10▶ Now listen and complete the sentences in exercise 9. Write NO MORE THAN TWO WORDS for each answer.

66

In the actual test, after the recording finishes, you have some time to transfer your answers to an answer sheet. Under exam conditions it is easy to make a mistake when you do this, so make sure you check spellings, grammatical fit, and that your answers are legible. If you have missed an answer, make a guess by using clues in the question.

11▶ Transfer your answers to exercise 9 to the exam answer sheet opposite using this checklist.

1 Have I completed every gap, including making a sensible guess for any answers I missed?

2 Do all my answers comply with the word limit?

3 Is every word clearly written and correctly spelt?

4 Does every answer make sense grammatically?

5 Are singular/plural forms used correctly?

6 Do the completed sentences make sense?

7 Have I repeated any words that are already in the sentences?

GRAMMAR FOCUS: PREPOSITIONS IN RELATIVE CLAUSES

12▶ Look at this sentence and focus on the underlined relative clause. Answer the questions.

Globalisation has fundamentally changed the world <u>in which we live</u>.

1 What are the subject and object of the relative clause?

2 Which word or phrase from the first part of the sentence does the relative pronoun replace?

3 Where is the preposition in relation to the relative pronoun?

4 Where could you move the preposition to in order to make the sentence less formal?

 A preposition is sometimes needed if the relative pronoun is the object of a relative clause. In formal English, the preposition comes immediately before the relative pronoun, and in everyday spoken English it comes at the end of the relative clause. Note that for very formal English, the relative pronoun *who* is replaced by *whom* after a preposition, but this is quite rare nowadays.

13▶ Move the preposition in these sentences to make them more or less formal. Make any other changes that are needed.

1 The man to whom you need to speak is Mr Brodie.

2 Chapman Brothers, the company for which I worked for 20 years, is closing down.

3 Camilla Stark, who I went to school with, is now a well-known actor.

4 Yasmin demanded the goods which she had paid for.

5 Christmas is the holiday for which children wait all year.

6 The man on whose life the film is based died a long time ago.

[EXAM SKILLS]

1|4▶ Listen and answer questions 1–10.

🔊 67

🖱 **GO FURTHER ONLINE**

Questions 1–4

Complete the sentences below.

*Write **NO MORE THAN TWO WORDS** for each answer.*

1 The Eastern side of the island of New Guinea, Papua New Guinea, became an _____ in 1975.

2 Only 18% of the inhabitants of Papua New Guinea reside in _____ .

3 Papua New Guinea tribes should be seen as separate _____ .

4 There are a small number of tribes who have had no _____ with neighbouring groups and the world beyond.

Questions 5–10

Complete the notes below.

*Write **NO MORE THAN TWO WORDS AND/OR A NUMBER** for each answer.*

Tribes of Papua New Guinea

Huli-Wigmen
- 40,000 members
- decorate their faces with **5** _____
- have belts of pigtails, apron of leaves, wigs made of own hair
- do dances which imitate local birds

Asaro mud men
- cover their bodies in mud to resemble **6** _____ in order to frighten off other tribes
- have very long fingernails
- put on **7** _____ to make themselves look fiercer

Chimbu skeleton dancers
- Men and women used to live in separate houses.
- Now families live together.
- Now perform dances for the benefit of **8** _____ .

Mount Hagan Sing-Sing
- Over 50 tribes take part.
- Begun by **9** _____ in 1961 to bring together tribes in peace.
- Tribespeople wear headdresses made of flowers, shells and feathers.
- Some loss of authenticity, such as the replacement of **10** _____ dyes on their wonderful costumes with artificial ones.

UNIT / 08: CULTURE

SPEAKING

IN THIS UNIT YOU WILL LEARN HOW TO

- review speaking skills
- review all parts of the Speaking test
- use relative clauses with indefinite pronouns, *some-*, *every-*, *any-*, *no-*

LEAD-IN

01▸ This advice was given to candidates before their Speaking test. Decide if you think it is good advice (G) or bad advice (B). Give reasons for your answers.

1 Stay up late watching English movies the night before the test so that your mind is full of English.

2 Try to memorise some Part 2 talks and just change the details when you get your topic.

3 Record yourself answering practice questions to help you identify your strengths and weaknesses when you speak.

4 Try to smile and maintain eye contact with the examiner during the exam.

5 Allow yourself plenty of time to get to the Speaking test on time. If necessary, get there early.

6 Speak as quickly as you can so that the examiner thinks you are fluent.

02▸ Work in pairs or groups. Make a list of more good and bad advice for the Speaking test. Exchange your list with another pair or group.

03▷ These speaking skills have been introduced in this book. Match the skills (1–6) with the phrases (a–f).

1 Using discourse markers to extend answers
2 Expressing and justifying opinions
3 Agreeing and disagreeing
4 Buying time to answer questions
5 Asking for clarification
6 Correcting and clarifying yourself

a That's a good question. / Let me see …
b In addition / For example / However, ….
c To put it another way / What I mean by that is / In other words …
d If you ask me / Obviously / It is absolutely vital that …
e Definitely not! / Absolutely! / It's hard to say.
f What do you mean by …? / Are you asking me if …?

04▷ Can you add a few more phrases to each skill category in exercise 3?

05▷ Take turns to ask and answer the questions with your partner. Try to use expressions from exercises 3 and 4. Record your conversation if possible.

1 How do you think people from your country would describe themselves?
2 Which aspects of your country's culture are most important to you?
3 Are there any aspects of your country's culture you don't like or don't identify with?
4 Are there any other countries' cultures or traditions that interest you?

06▷ Listen to your recording. Give each other feedback, based on these questions.

1 Did your partner use any of the language reviewed in exercises 3 and 4?
2 Were the answers well developed and explained?
3 Is there any other advice you would give your partner, based on their performance?

07 ▶ **You will hear a recording of Part 1 of the test with a candidate called Luis from Spain. Listen and complete the summary of this part of the test. Use ONE or TWO WORDS in each gap.**

68

The examiner greets Luis and asks him what she should **1** _____ .
She also asks where he is from and asks to see **2** _____ .
The first set of questions are about Luis's **3** _____ . After that there are some questions about **4** _____ . Luis says his taste in music is **5** _____ .
The final set of questions in Part 1 is about **6** _____ . Luis says he likes
7 _____ .

08 ▶ **Listen to Part 1 again and read the listening script. Find examples of the following.**

68

1 future perfect
2 passive voice
3 first conditional
4 relative clauses
5 second conditional

TIP 08

Remember that to score high in Grammatical Range and Accuracy, you need to use a variety of different language structures correctly.

09 ▶ **Read the task card for Luis's Part 2 task. Listen and make notes on what Luis says for each point on the card. Do you think he does Part 2 well?**

69

Describe a country that interests you.

You should say

- why it interests you
- how you learnt about it
- what you know about it

and say whether you have any plans to visit this country.

10 ▶ Listen to Part 2 again and read the listening script. Find words or phrases which mean the same as the phrases below.

69

1 nations next to mine
2 it's very different to
3 close to visit by boat
4 ever since I was a child
5 I have strong memories of
6 made me feel hungry
7 style of food
8 visit somewhere a little more distant

TIP 10

Remember that to increase your Lexical Resource score, you need to correctly use a variety of vocabulary, including collocations and less common words and phrases.

11 ▶ Listen to and read Part 3 of Luis's Speaking test in the Listening script on pages 222–3 and answer the questions.

70

1 How many sub-topics does the examiner ask Luis about?
2 What follow-up questions does the examiner ask in response to what Luis says?

TIP 11

The examiner has a list of questions to ask the candidate but may also add in follow-up questions which respond directly to what the candidate has said in order to clarify or better understand the candidate's answers.

12 ▶ Listen and read again. Then categorise the expressions in the box by their function.

70

Given this fact	Personally speaking	Let me think.	I mean
in my view	Take Spanish, for example.	to some extent	Obviously
The thing is	That's a good question.	it depends	such as
I wouldn't say so.			

Showing agreement / disagreement	Giving examples	Buying time	Giving opinions	Explaining / Clarifying
				Given this fact

13 ▶ Work with a partner. Using the questions from all three parts of Luis's test, take turns to practise the test as candidate and examiner. Examiners should give feedback on the candidates' Fluency and Cohesion, Grammatical Range and Accuracy, Lexical Resource, and Pronunciation.

CLAUSES WITH INDEFINITE PRONOUNS *SOME, EVERY, NO, ANY*

Indefinite pronouns (*somebody/someone*, *everybody/everyone*, etc.) allow you to talk about people or things in general, without being specific, and are often used with defining relative clauses in English, e.g. *Anyone who travels a lot learns a lot about different cultures.* This is a useful structure, particularly in Part 3, in order to make generalisations in answer to the questions.

14 ▶ **Complete the sentences with an indefinite pronoun from the box. There may be more than one possible answer.**

anything	something	everybody	nowhere
anyone	everywhere	nothing	someone

1 I remember _____ we went together.
2 Do you know _____ who can help with this?
3 _____ told me you were in town.
4 There is _____ I can do.
5 We got gifts from _____ who came to the wedding.
6 I have _____ very interesting to tell you.
7 Is there _____ you need from the shops?
8 There is _____ I'd rather be.

15 ▶ **Complete these sentences so that they are true for you.**

1 Everyone who visits my country …
2 I am someone who …
3 Cultural difference is something that …
4 Somewhere that I'd really love to visit is …
5 I don't know anybody who …

16 ▶ **Read your sentences to your partner. After each one add a sentence or two to explain your ideas.**

Example: *Everyone who visits my country loves the food. They usually say that the seafood is really fresh and delicious. Some say it's a bit too spicy though.*

EXAM SKILLS

 17 ▶ **Do this sample test with a partner. Take turns to ask and answer.**

Part 1

1. Do you live in a house or a flat?
2. Is it big or small?
3. What do you like most about your house/flat?
4. Is there anything you would like to change about the place you live?
5. What kind of clothes do you like wearing?
6. What colours do you prefer to wear?
7. How much time do you spend shopping for clothes?
8. How important is fashion to people in your country?
9. Do you enjoy dancing?
10. On which occasions do people dance in your culture?
11. How do you feel about watching professional dancers performing?
12. Do traditional dances have an important place in your culture?

Part 2

Describe a wedding you have been to or heard about.

You should say

- whose wedding it was
- what the ceremony was like
- what clothes people wore

and say how you felt about the wedding.

GO FURTHER ONLINE

Follow-up question: Do you often go to weddings?

Part 3

1. Is getting married important in your culture?
2. Have wedding ceremonies changed much in recent years?
3. What do you think is the ideal age to get married? Why?
4. Is it common for married couples to live with their parents or other family members?
5. What are the advantages and disadvantages of living in an extended family?
6. Do you think extended families will become more or less common in the future?

ANSWER KEY

Unit 1 URBAN AND RURAL LIFE

READING

1 No article used for:

individual islands: e.g. *Mallorca*

names of most countries: e.g. *Spain, France, Germany, China*

names of beaches: *Alcudia Beach*

names of cities/towns/regions: *Palma de Mallorca, Algaida, Binissalem*

names of mountains: *Mount Everest, Mont Blanc*

Use 'the' for:

groups of islands: *the Balearic Islands*

coastal areas: *the Valencian Coast*

oceans and seas: *the Mediterranean Sea, the Persian Gulf*

nationalities: *the Spanish, the Omanis, the Chinese*

countries which are Republics, Kingdoms or Unions: *the Republic of China, the United Kingdom (the UK), the United States of America (the USA)*

mountain ranges: *the Tramuntanas, the Himalayas*

geographical areas: *the northeast, the southwest*

Other geographical features:

lakes: no article, usually begins with the word Lake (*Lake Windermere*)

rivers: definite article before name of river. Capitalise the word 'river' or it can be omitted (*the Thames, the River Thames*).

3 *Students' own answers*

4 Heading B seems to fit best, as it contains paraphrases of the sentence: designed = planned and built

an imperfect world = today's world of conflict, greed and constant struggles for power

an urban ideal = the ultimate model of unity, peace and harmony

Heading A: There is nothing in the sentence that matches 'always fail'.

Heading C: The sentence talks about 'peace and harmony', which contradicts the idea of 'conflict' in the heading.

5 Heading B is correct.

6 At this point, the best heading appears to be B: A city at the top of the world

7 The best heading is C: An unusual approach to regulation, because the paragraph talks about other examples of rules and laws that could be seen as unusual. It is not A – An unwelcoming place to die – because the text tells us that it is forbidden to die there.

8 But what really sets it apart is that it can also lay claim to some of the world's strangest rules.

9 A *regulation* = not allowed to build fences around their houses

B *dangers of the wild* = the constant threat of visits from wild animals

C *humans and animals* = lions and hippopotamuses [and] anxious residents; *co-exist* = residents are not allowed to … keep out their neighbours

10 A An <u>unusual</u> approach to regulation – still possible as a correct answer, and you would need to read more of the paragraph to be sure.

B Dealing with the *occasional* dangers of the wild – no longer possible as it contradicts 'the constant threat'.

C Where humans and animals *cautiously* co-exist – most likely to be correct as it paraphrases the sentence.

11 Heading C is correct.

12 Everywhere in Marloth Park, a wary understanding exists between man and beast.

13 *Students' own notes*

14 Heading A – A conflict between reality and imitation – is correct.

15 *un-* = not/opposite; *im-* = not; *co-* = together

16 *post-* = after, behind – postgraduate, post-mortem, postpone

for-/fore- = before – forecast, forward, forehead

sub- = under, below – submarine, subway, subtitle

multi- = many, much – multinational, multiply, multicultural

anti- = against, opposite – antivirus, antiseptic, antiperspirant

mis- = wrong, bad, badly – misunderstand, misjudge, misspell

non- = not – non-profit, non-fiction, nonsense

pre- = before – preview, prepay, prejudge

over- = above, too much – overload, overtake, oversleep

under- = below, not enough – underwater, underwear, underage

17 A forewarned / pre-warned B overpopulated C misinformed D anti-government(al)

18 1 ii 2 vi 3 iii 4 v 5 viii 6 vii

WRITING

1 2 Between 1980 and 1990 sales *grew rapidly* to 90,000.

3 From 2020 to 2030 *sales will / are predicted to / are expected to grow rapidly* to 90,000.

4 By the year 2000, *sales had grown rapidly* to 90,000

5 By the year 2025, *sales will have grown rapidly* to 90,000.

3 *Suggested answers*

All three reasons have risen over the period. Overall, the number of people moving away from the capital city is on the up.

Traffic saw the steepest rise, particularly from 2000 to 2010.

Rising cost of living rose the least over the whole period and this reason was the only one to show any fall (2000–2010). However, in terms of numbers it was the main reason for moving to the countryside across the whole period by a significant margin.

The increase in people leaving for lifestyle reasons was steady across the whole period but relatively low.

4 *Suggested answers*

Some of the data and categories are incorrectly reported. (Incorrect: *The main reason was traffic; 70,000 left in 2010*)

The third paragraph does not include any data to support its arguments.

There is no concluding paragraph.

The answer is considerably less than 150 words.

The level of language is OK, but unlikely to impress the examiner.

Note: it is also recommended that when you write your introduction, you put it in your own words as this demonstrates the ability to paraphrase (Lexical Resource). This introduction borrows heavily from the question.

5 1 B 2 A 3 D 4 C

6 A This is not a good conclusion: (a) to say 'people left the city for three main reasons' is not necessarily true: the graph did supply three reasons – however, there may have been others that were not included in the graph; (b) there is incorrect reporting of data, which should be 'between 1990 and 2010', not '1990 and 2000'. Also, life style did not change the least, since, given the fall between 2000 and 2010, rising cost of living changed the least for the whole period.

B This is the best conclusion. It is less mechanical than A, mentions the main features and expresses what had started to happen by the end of the period.

C The worst conclusion of all three. Not only has the candidate included data in their concluding paragraph, but it also repeats what has already been stated in the main body. The candidate does not 'step back' and present a summary of the main trends or features.

7 1 highest 2 overall 3 notable 4 consistent 5 stable
6 lowest 7 joint-lowest

8 Inappropriate adverbs for a Task 1 essay: *amazingly, shockingly, predictably, surprisingly*.
The adverbs *significantly* and *noticeably* are arguably subjective, but used in the correct way are not necessarily so:
The increase in people moving for a better quality of life is significantly higher than in the other categories.
The rise in people moving for a better quality of life is noticeably higher than in the other categories.

9 *inconsistently*: the line changes in a way that doesn't demonstrate an obvious pattern
significantly: the change showed by the line is marked or major, perhaps in comparison to another line on the graph
progressively: the change is slow and consistent
noticeably: the change showed by the line is clearly visible, especially in comparison to another line on the graph
gradually: the tendency to change on the graph is slow
sharply: the change indicated by the line is fast and dramatic
markedly: the change showed by the line is clearly visible, especially in comparison to another line on the graph
abruptly: the change indicated by the line is fast and dramatic

10 *Sample answers*
2 Traffic experienced a steady rise as a reason for moving to the countryside between 1990 and 2000 …
3 but then increased markedly between 2000 and 2010.
4 The number of people moving to the countryside for lifestyle reasons saw a consistent growth across the whole period shown in the graph.

11 *Sample answer*
The line graph sets out the key motivations for people relocating to the capital of a specific country between 2000 and 2015.
Moving for the purpose of study saw the greatest rise overall, with a jump of approximately 62,000. It rose considerably in two periods – from 2000 to 2005 (by 22,000), and then again from 2010 to 2015 (by 33,000), with a more gentle growth of around 7,000 in between.
Elsewhere, the figure of people relocating for work began at 61,000 in 2000, then peaked at 92,000 in 2010 – the highest of any reason, in any year – before finishing as the joint-highest in 2015 (87,000 – on a level with those relocating in order to study). Notably, this category was the only one of the four that underwent a downturn.
Turning to 'adventure', this category rose the most stably and steadily of all four categories, from 11,000 to 15,000 over the fifteen-year period. Meanwhile, the number of people relocating for 'family and friends' reasons climbed gently in the first five years (12,000 to 14,000), followed by an upswing to 22,000, before eventually levelling off at around 23,000 in 2015.
All in all, the graph tells us that, 'employment' aside, there was an increase in each of the four reasons for moving over the period in question, with the greatest rise occurring in those citing study as the main motivating factor. (*212 words*)

LISTENING

2 1 *book* and *reserve* are synonyms; *select* means to choose or decide.
2 *discount* and *reduction* are synonyms; *bargain* means that you get something for a very favourable price.
3 There are no synonyms here; a *curator* is someone who organises the exhibits in a gallery or museum; a *presenter* is someone who introduces a television or radio show; a *guide* is someone whose job is to show a place to visitors or tourists.
4 *visitors* and *guests* are synonyms; *explorers* travel to new and unknown places. You can explore a museum, but you cannot be a museum explorer.
5 the *front desk* and *main entrance* are synonyms here; the *guard room* is more likely to be in a prison and not a place where you show your tickets.

6 *explore* and *wander around* are synonyms here; *navigate* means to direct the course of a vehicle, such as a ship.
7 *pick us up* and *collect us* are synonyms; *let us on* means allow us to board the bus.

3 *Suggested answers*
1 adjective (the earliest, ancient, prehistoric)
2 adjective (ancient, prehistoric, early)
3 plural or collective noun (treasure, objects, items, scenes, displays)
4 adjective or noun (present day, contemporary, current day)
5 ordinal number or adjective (22nd, twenty-second, next, forthcoming)

4 1 ancient 2 prehistoric 3 objects 4 Contemporary
5 22nd / twenty-second

5 1 *exciting visit, which … traces the history of this vast and ever-changing city*
2 *life from the point of view of prehistoric men, women and children*
3 *when all this around us was fields*
4 *take in the fascinating pieces of history*
5 *we'll move away from our present, here in the 21st century, and head off into the 22nd*

7 1 James Graeme 2 16 Mount Hill 3 E15 2TP 4 770 464
5 15/fifteen 6 15/fifteen 7 4/four 8 (£)4.25 9 Underground
10 12/12th/twelfth

8 1 B 2 A,C 3 A 4 C 5 B 6 C 7 A,B 8 B

9 *Suggested answers*
1 *show to collect his ticket* – produce in order to be able to enter, have as proof of identity to get his ticket
passport – identification document, ID
debit card – bank card, payment card
smartphone – no obvious synonym except telephone/phone
2 *most appreciates* – likes the most/best, thinks is the most important, is most impressed by, thinks is key
designed – structured, put together, connected, linked, built
talks about the city's inhabitants – shows/paints a picture of the life of city dwellers / citizens / the local people
is involved in fundraising for the local community – does local charity work, raises money for local causes, donates money to worthwhile community organisations

10 1 B 2 B

11 *Question 1*
1 The options are mentioned in the order A C B.
2 Option A: *So, I should bring my passport, then, for proof of ID?*
Option B: *But you'll get your tickets fine as long as you can produce the payment card you bought the tickets with. That's the only ID we need to see.*
Option C: *People usually have a copy of their booking on their email, and they just show this on their smartphones and go straight through.*

Question 2
1 The options are mentioned in the following order: C B A
2 Option A: *because of the way the exhibition designers have connected each section to the next with a real sense of development and design. It just flows so well from one room to the next. Better than any other museum I've been into, certainly.*
Option B: *But what's so good for visitors – and is absolutely key for me – is that, as you walk through from one room to another, you always, always get a real sense of who has lived here over the years, and what sort of people they are, or have been.*
Option C: *One important thing is that the museum here has formed some extremely worthwhile partnerships with a wide range of local charities. In London, like any capital city, there are a lot of social problems, and the museum's help in reaching out to the world outside is greatly appreciated by so many.*

12 Condition in blue, result in red

1 I'll book tickets for that as well today, provided there is something special that I'm particularly interested in.
2 You'll get your tickets fine, as long as you can produce the payment card you bought the tickets with.
3 Once we leave the part of the exhibition called 'Contemporary London', we will move into the 22nd century.
4 Unless something dramatic happens, I should be working here for a long time.

13 1 provided   2 as long as   3 Once   4 Unless

We can replace *provided* and as *long as* with if. *Once* could be replaced with *when*. *Unless* means 'if not', so we can change it if we change the whole cause clause: *If something dramatic doesn't happen, …*

14 Future time conditionals follow the same structure as the *first* conditional:

If + present simple … / … *will* + bare infinitive.

Note that all present tenses are possible in the *If* clause, although the present simple is the most commonly used. In the result clause, instead of *will* we can use *be going to* and other modal verbs such as *can, should* and *must*. We can also use an imperative in the result clause.

15 *Sample answers*

1 You can get a discounted ticket as long as you show your student card.
2 Once everybody has bought their ticket, we will go to the first exhibit room.
3 You won't get lost provided you use the map you were given.
4 Now everybody is free to explore the museum. You can go wherever you like as long as you return to the main entrance for 4 pm.
5 Your bus back to the hotel will depart as soon as everybody is on board.
6 Do not touch or take photos of the exhibits unless there is a sign saying that it is allowed.

16 1 David Cottenham   2 DV12 8HA   3 7.30 pm / 19.30 /half past seven   4 £60,000   5 244 510   6 we-move-u   7 B   8 C   9 C

SPEAKING

1 1 B   2 C   3 C   4 B   5 C   6 C   7 A   8 A
2 *Students' own answers*
3 The following questions would not be asked: 2, 3, 5, 7
4 These answers are not likely to impress the examiner.

Question 1: The candidate repeats the word 'apartment' several times. She could improve this by using reference words like 'it' and 'one', and the flow of her answer would improve (along with her score for Fluency and Coherence).

Question 2: The language used is very good, but it doesn't answer the question. It is highly likely to be a memorised answer, which should be avoided completely – the vocabulary is not relevant to the topic at all. This limits the score for both Fluency and Coherence and Lexical Resource.

Question 3: There are several problems with the grammar used; these would limit the score the candidate might get for Grammatical Range and Accuracy.

5 Task card A
6 This candidate talked about all four points, exploring three of them in some detail. He used a good range of vocabulary and grammar; the organisation of the answer was also very good indeed, and the long turn flowed naturally from one idea to the next. It is not important that he spoke about the third prompt only very briefly, as he clearly had decided to spend more time on the points he felt he could expand on more easily, and in more detail.

7 1 D   2 E   3 A   4 C   5 B
8 A iii   B v   C ii   D iv   E i
9 1 P   2 GRA   3 FC   4 GRA   5 LR   6 FC   7 P   8 LR   9 FC

11 The grammar is incorrect: *As soon as we will finish class, we will go.* This is the grammatical structure often known as the first conditional (*If* + present tense, *will* + bare infinitive) but with *As soon as* instead of *If*.

12 A As long as   B By the time   C Providing that   D As soon as   E Unless

13 1 *Unless* suggests that the speaker sees the changes as completely necessary, but they doubt whether the changes will ever happen. On the other hand, *Once* suggests that the speaker sees the changes as certain to happen, with a natural result (which they give). Using *Once* in this sentence is still grammatically correct and logical. However it wouldn't work in the answer given by the candidate.

2 *When* suggests the speaker believes that people will definitely, at some point, be happy to use buses and bikes instead of their cars (A), and that she will definitely, at some point, make enough money to buy a top-floor flat (C). *As long as* and *Provided that* both suggest that the speaker is not convinced that the result given in each case is definite – people may not be happy about using buses and bikes; she may not ever earn enough money to buy the top-floor flat.

3 Sentence D is different. The speaker is not thinking about the future in particular, but is stating something as a constant fact (in their opinion). The structure is a *zero conditional* (present simple / present simple), whereas the other sentences use the *first conditional* (present simple / *will* + bare infinitive).

14 B By the time I'm a grandparent, I think it will be even more different.
C Providing that I make enough money, I'll definitely be on a top floor myself one day.
D As soon as you get older and have a family, you start thinking it's time to move.
E Unless this changes, we are going to need more and more homes for everyone.

Unit 2   HEALTH

READING

1 **Noun:** -ism -tion -ian -er -ment

Adjective: -ic -ful -less -al -ious -ative -ary -able

2 1 They are essentially antonyms. *-ful* derives from the word *full* meaning 'a lot of' and *-less* means 'without'. For example, *harmful* means 'causing harm' and *harmless* means 'not causing harm'.
2 It is possible or it can be done. For example, *treatable* means it can be treated.
3 Normally to a verb. For example, *treat* (v) + *-able*, *prevent* (v) + *-able*
4 They normally refer to people, for example, *doctor, technician, manager*.
5 They are common verb suffixes.

3 The second sentence mimics the technique you should aim to use while skim reading. Aim to 'blank out' the *grammar* words (conjunctions, prepositions, auxiliaries, determiners) and concentrate on noticing the *content* words (nouns, verbs, adjectives).

4 1 paragraph C   4 paragraph D
2 paragraph F   5 paragraph B
3 paragraph A   6 paragraph E

5 1 *Research suggests that there is an evolutionary reason as to why people compulsively overeat*
2 *it is difficult to see how … can ever be halted*
3 *have taken over the world […] levels of growth that show no signs of slowing down […] increasing body of evidence*
4 *causes the heart to pump faster while transporting blood through the veins […] immediately start […] Thereafter the body starts to digest the food […] the same process lasts at least three days.*
5 *While local authorities … have taken measures to combat the rise in this trend … critics argue that people have every right to make their own decisions*
6 *young people […] a child […] their parents […] a child […] children*

6 All of these suggestions for scanning are useful apart from the first – moving your eyes from left to right along each line. By doing this, you are so closely copying the acts of reading for understanding or skimming that it becomes difficult for your brain to scan the text. Reading for understanding, skimming and scanning are all completely different skills.

7 1 *dopamine* – paragraphs C and E; *sodium* – paragraphs C and D
  2 *rose by 45 per cent* – paragraph A
  3 *calorie* (as in *600-calorie burger*) – paragraph C
  4 *brain* – paragraphs C and E; *blood* – paragraphs C–D; *kidneys* – paragraph D; *veins* – paragraph D; *heart* – paragraph D

8 Paragraphs C–E talk about the effects of fast food on the body.

9 1 processed food   2 (the) brain   3 surge   4 (The) kidneys
  5 the elderly   6 hunger   7 three days / 3 days

10 Paragraph E focuses on the different effects on adults and children.

11 8 maturity   9 urge   10 restraint

12 1 chasing   2 much of this expansion
  3 explosion in the takeaway trade   4 increasing body of evidence

13 1 growth   2 less developed   3 dietary disaster

14 1 the world doesn't want to listen
  2 taken measures to combat the rise in this trend
  3 part of our innate behaviour
  4 changing widespread dietary habits
  5 stylish

15 1 processed food   2 outlets   3 (compulsively) overeat
  4 aspirational/stylish

16 1 B   2 C   3 A

17 1 the gut   2 medical assistance   3 Local community
  4 treatment   5 slaughter   6 (the / infected) meat / flesh
  7 systems / bodies
  8 course   9 online   10 laboratory capacity   11 new tools
  12 health benefits   13 (worldwide) overuse   14 crisis

WRITING

1

Advantages	Disadvantages
benefits	on the downside
pros	issues
positives	negatives
on the plus side	cons
on the upside	problems
	drawbacks

2 *Sample answers*
  1 **Advantages:** more likely to have better access to better facilities (sports clubs, gyms, sports centres, hospitals)
  Disadvantages: stress of city life can affect mental health; pollution can cause health problems such as asthma and eczema; office jobs tend to be sedentary (= involving little physical activity)
  2 **Advantages:** everybody wants to live longer; older people can lead satisfying lives after retirement – more time to pursue their dreams; can provide more support and guidance to other family members
  Disadvantages: more strain and costs on health services due to increased numbers of patients; older people often require more frequent and longer term health care; caring for older family members may be a burden on the family; people are retiring later, which means fewer jobs available

3 *Sample answers*
  2 The main advantage of doing contact sports is that you can learn to defend yourself.
  3 The principle issue with living in a city is the effect of pollution on health.
  4 One obvious negative effect of living in a city is the risk of being a victim of violent crime.
  5 Another disadvantage of contact sports is that you are at risk of getting hurt or seriously injured.

6 Overall, the benefits of living in a city outweigh the drawbacks because there are many more facilities available than in small towns or in the countryside.

4 Idea 3 is illogical because it immediately argues the opposite to the topic sentence, leaving the original idea stated in the topic sentence undeveloped.

Idea 5 is not effective because it does not logically develop the original idea in the topic sentence, which introduces the idea of personal fitness. It does not make sense to expand this into a discussion about the problems caused by a busy doctor's surgery.

Ideas 1, 2, 4 and 6 follow on logically from the topic sentence.

5 a idea 2   b idea 1   c idea 4   d idea 6

6 *Sample answer*
(1) There is evidence that some sports, such as boxing, can cause long-term brain damage.
(2) What is more, broken bones and muscle problems are common even in non-violent contact sports like football or cricket.

7 *Suggested answers*
There are two obvious ways to order these notes:
  1 In cities – many gyms
  2 250 gyms in my capital city
  3 Gyms part of larger chains, people can use any in city
  4 Traditional idea – rural life is healthier; not true
  OR
  1 Traditional idea – rural life is healthier; not true
  2 In cities – many gyms
  3 250 gyms in my capital city
  4 Gyms part of larger chains, people can use any in city

8 1 (example) By way of example, For instance, For example
  2 (addition of information / an idea) What is more, In addition to this, Moreover
  3 (cause and effect) Because of this, As a result, Consequently

9 1 Yes. *One of the advantages of living in a city is that there are many gym facilities.*
  2 Yes. The writer is clearly arguing the case that the number of gyms in cities is good for the health of citizens.
  3 Example: *For example*
  Cause and effect: *What this means is that*; *This is because*; *because*
  Addition: *Furthermore*
  Contrast: *Despite this*; *However*
  4 *because*. The obvious alternative here is *so* (*because* gives the cause and *so* gives the effect). If we start a new sentence after 'chains', we could also use *Therefore, Thus, As a result* to begin the next sentence.
  5 The following discourse markers could be cut without impeding the flow of ideas: *Furthermore, This is because*. *However* could also be cut as the contrast is implied in the final sentence.

10 Introduction A: This is a good introduction. It paraphrases the question well and leaves the reader in no doubt about what the essay is going to discuss, without revealing the ideas it will cover. However, it does not state the candidate's position and it is a good idea to do so, because candidates can run out of time before writing their conclusion and therefore not manage to state their position.
Introduction B: This is the best of the three introductions. It paraphrases the question well and uses the very useful introduction phrase *In this essay I will discuss …* which clearly tells us what the essay will be about. It also states the candidate's position, as requested in the question.
Introduction C: It is clear what the candidate will talk about in their essay but basically it restates the question without paraphrase. It also doesn't clarify what the candidate's opinion is.

11 *Suggested answers*
  1 Conclusions B and C are both good as they clearly state the writer's opinion without going into detail. They both paraphrase the original question clearly and briefly state the position of the writer. Conclusion A, on the other hand, simply restates the question and does not give the writer's position on the question in any way.
  2 In conclusion; Overall; the advantages of … outweigh the disadvantages; In summary; weighing up both sides of the argument, I would say …

12 *Sample essay*

Medical care over the past century has improved dramatically. As a consequence, the world's population is increasingly living long into old age. Is this having a harmful effect on societies across the globe, or are there more benefits than drawbacks?

One obvious issue with an ageing population is that it can create enormous demands on a nation's health service. As people live longer into their old age, the chances of them suffering from serious illnesses increases. As a result, the likelihood of them requiring medical treatment becomes higher, and it becomes more difficult to provide care for everyone. A further downside is that living longer does not necessarily bring happiness. By this I mean, an older person is unable to do many of the activities that they want to do, leading to the likelihood of depression and a deterioration in their physical health.

Having said that, one obvious benefit to people living longer is that young people can benefit for a longer time from the wisdom handed down to them by older members of their families. In today's fast-paced world, it is often comforting to seek advice from older generations. Consequently, the physical health of a grandparent is almost irrelevant, as the children and grandchildren will benefit from the experience of an older mind. What is more, retired people today are generally much healthier than they have ever been, and often enjoy their lives more than they did when they were young. They have the best of both worlds – a family that can care for and look up to them, and better health than at any time in human history.

Weighing up both sides of the argument again, although there are a number of problems that old age brings – predominantly health-related – the benefits that it brings to the family unit and to society as a whole are impossible to ignore. (*310 words*)

LISTENING

1 1 everyday, social – 2 speakers
   2 everyday, social – 1 speaker (Although it is possible you may hear a second voice at the start, the majority of the audio will be a monologue.)
   3 educational or training – 2 or more speakers
   4 educational or training – 1 speaker

2 You might hear any of the following: 2, 3, 5, 6

3 2 Section 4 3 Section 2 5 Section 1 6 Section 3

4 A Olympic Records Exhibition
   B Medical Discoveries in History
   C Sports Centre Classes

5 2 Womens 10K (a) 3 penicillin (g) 4 Swiss (c) 5 gene therapy (e)
   6 6.30 pm (h) 7 Marco and Victor (b) 8 table tennis (f)

6 Table A: Section 2   Table B: Section 4   Table C: Section 1

7 1 the name of a society or club, e.g. a game or hobby which could take place in a room indoors
   2 the name of a room or place in the university
   3 the name of a room or place in the university
   4 the name of a society or club, e.g. a game or sport that could take place in the gym
   5 a person's name or people's names

8 1 Vegetarian 2 A14 3 C16 4 Hot Air 5 Siobhan

9 1 a number of 2 Both of them / Both 3 either of those
   4 All of the / All 5 None of those 6 The whole / The whole of the

10 1 Some people 2 all 3 any 4 no 5 all of us
   6 Some of the / Some 7 Many 8 either (correct)
   9 both 10 all

11 1 d 2 b 3 c 4 f 5 e 6 a

12 1 The President of a Society is likely to be named in full, forename and surname. 'Claire' is a forename, and it would be a little too informal.
   2 It is unlikely that a society of keen runners would only complete a distance of 20km in a whole year.
   3 Although some 100km races exist, a team of amateur students would not run this far. And as this society is focused on distance running, not sprinting, 100m is also unlikely.

   4 They would also be unlikely to run in a sports centre, given that the society is called to Road Running (also, 'a sports centre' is over the TWO WORD limit).
   5 In this case, the answer 'blue dark' will not be correct, but this is for a grammatical reason, i.e. the shade (light, dark, vivid, etc.) goes before the colour.
   6 Given the financial situation of the majority of students, a membership fee of £5000 per year would be excessive.

13 1 Claire Enwark 2 fortnight 3 10K/10km 4 Manchester
   5 pale blue 6 50

14 1 vegetarian 2 Wednesford 3 7/seven o'clock / 7.00 / 7 pm
   4 covered market 5 Coffee Club 6 free / nothing / £0
   7 2/two hours 8 10% 9 (an) email 10 celebrity chefs

SPEAKING

1 1 *going round in circles* = continuing to talk about – or going back to – the same idea without moving the discussion on
   2 *losing your thread* = forgetting what you were talking about; bringing irrelevant ideas into the discussion
   3 *stumbling over your words* = making mistakes while speaking, often caused by a lack of vocabulary, which can cause hesitation, repetition or mispronunciation
   4 *labouring the point* = explaining or discussing something at excessive length
   5 *beating about the bush* = trying to avoid talking about the central issue or problem, possibly because you don't know enough about the subject, or because you think it would be impolite to do so
   6 *talking at a mile a minute* = speaking so quickly that you cannot be understood

2 1 stumbling over my words / losing my thread / talking at a mile a minute 2 talking at a mile a minute 3 beat around the bush
   4 going round in circles 5 labouring the point 6 lost her thread

3 Although it may sound as if the first candidate lacks control of FC, he is speaking in a completely natural way. Saying 'um' or 'er', or pausing slightly, or beginning a sentence and then starting again, are all features of natural speech that are acceptable in the IELTS test. You will only lose credit if you do any or all of these things too often, and it becomes noticeable to the examiner that you are stumbling over your words.

The second candidate is speaking in an unnatural way, talking at a mile a minute, possibly in a misguided attempt to sound 'fluent'. Ultimately, she ends up going round in circles, repeating both vocabulary and ideas, and her turn lacks both fluency and coherence.

4 Although Candidate 1 personalises her response, she has actually failed to answer the question asked of her. She talks about eating, but not in the context she was given. In fact, this is more like an answer to a Part 1 question such as 'What do you like to eat when you go out for dinner?'

Candidate 2 considers the question in a more abstract way, relating it to other people and to the society in which we live, and goes on to question the concept of the word 'healthy'. As such, this answer is far more appropriate to a Part 3 question, not a Part 1 question. Again, it doesn't answer the question that was asked.

Candidate 3 provides the best answer. He personalises his response, sticks to what the question is asking, and extends his answer to the appropriate length for Part 1.

5 Adding detail to the previous point: *and, also*
Introducing a contrasting idea: *but, even if, however*
Giving a reason/explanation: *so, because*
Giving an example or clarification: *For example, it depends*
Introducing an opinion: *To be honest, Personally*

6 1 *The thing is* – A Giving a reason for the previous point
   2 *On top of that* – C Adding detail to the previous point
   3 *In particular* – B Giving an example related to the previous point
   4 *That said* – D Introducing an idea that contrasts with the previous point.

7 *Sample answers*
  a The thing is, I'm actually really into sports and fitness, but I'm so busy with study that I can barely find time to turn on a microwave, let alone prepare healthy balanced meals on a daily basis.
  b For instance, I need to find a way to eat more green vegetables. I'm perfectly happy with tomatoes and carrots, say, but I know that I should force myself to have more greens.
  c I would add that I think doing regular exercise is just as important as a healthy diet. In fact, I would say that you have to do both if you want to look after your body.
  d Having said that, I don't believe we should be pressurised into eating five portions of fruit or vegetables a day, so maybe the stubborn part of me thinks: no, I'm not going to eat this lettuce because the government recommends that I do.

8 1 The candidate 'widens' his answer very well indeed. The only reference to his own views comes in the last sentence. The rest of his turn explores the question in terms of how other people might feel. In other words, this is a very good example of *speculation*.
  2 After the rhetorical question at the start, he makes the following four points:
    – It is a moral issue for some people.
    – Others become vegan, as avoiding meat alone does not satisfy their objections.
    – Some people believe eating meat is unhealthy.
    – Many people follow the medical evidence that supports this view.
    Overall, this answer is very well balanced. The candidate addresses the question from two main angles, providing a number of possible reasons for becoming vegetarian. He also rounds off his turn with a summarising statement which refers back to what he has said – rather like a conclusion in a Task 2 essay.
  3 i – b ii – a iii – d iv – c

9 1 Both *so that* and *on the grounds that* fit grammatically, but the latter would score higher. *Essentially* does not fit grammatically or in terms of meaning; it also tends to appear at the start of a sentence when it is used to introduce a reason.
  2 Both *In particular this is true of my country,* and *Take my country by way of example* are grammatically correct and display a good control of less common discourse markers, but the latter would probably score higher. *Such as* cannot be used to begin a sentence.
  3 All fit grammatically in spoken English. In terms of what might score more highly, *On the other hand* and *That said* would score more highly than *But*.
  4 None would score particularly high but *as well* and *too* are the best because they are used in the correct position; *also* is acceptable here, as we are dealing with spoken English, but is not entirely natural in terms of its position in the sentence.
  5 *Ultimately* and *At the end of the day* work best here. *Overall* does not work in this context, because the candidate is not summarising her argument but is concluding her argument with one final point.

10 3 Adding detail to the previous point: *Moreover, Furthermore, What's more*
  Introducing a contrasting idea: *Whereas, Conversely*
  Giving a reason/explanation: *For this reason, This is why, As a consequence*
  Giving an example or clarification: *such as, like, say*
  Introducing an opinion: *If you ask me, In my opinion, To my mind*
  Concluding with a final point or summarising an argument: *To sum up, In the end, In a nutshell, What it all comes down to is*

Unit 3 ART AND ARCHITECTURE

READING

2 installations – exhibitions
  materials – media
  concepts – ideas
  groundbreaking – innovative
  abstract – conceptual
  sculpture – figure
  experiment – innovate
  techniques – methods
  cast – mould

3 B
4 1 C 2 F 3 A 4 B 5 D 6 E
5 1 NG 2 T 3 F
6 1 We are told Warhol was 'a sickly child' but nothing is said about Rauschenberg's health as a child.
  2 *His* [Rauschenberg's] *mother supported her son as much as she could … Like Rauschenberg, Warhol was close to his mother.*
  3 *Though he was missing a lot of school, he was developing his artistic skills and tastes. … He eventually enrolled in the Carnegie Institute in Pittsburgh.*
  The words 'sickly child' might have led some students to choose True for question 1, but this refers to Warhol, not to Rauschenberg.
7 1 b 2 c 3 a
8 1 T 2 NG 3 F 4 T 5 NG
9 *Sample answer*: They were both innovators.
10 A 3 B 4 C 2 D 1
11 A Wrong – The text says *Like Rauschenberg, Warhol was close to his mother* but it does not say that the mothers were the most important influence on them.
  B Correct
  C Wrong – The text implies they didn't have family support to go to Art School.
  D Wrong – The artists themselves, not their families, were pulled (gravitated) towards New York.
12 1 Correct answer D – the whole paragraph goes through Warhol's work in the 60s and uses phrases like *one of the most definitive images of the Pop Art movement* and *which confounded critics and helped cement his credentials as an artist challenging the status quo.*
    A Wrong – This is a topic in paragraph F.
    B Wrong – The only mention of Rauschenberg is very brief and refers to a similarity between them (*Like Rauschenberg, he didn't limit himself …*)
    C Wrong – The text says their work was *equally innovative*, but it makes no comparison about quality.
  2 Correct answer A – *Not content with subverting the conventional art forms of painting and sculpture, both Rauschenberg and Warhol experimented beyond them.*
    B Wrong – Warhol *dabbled in* (= experimented with) … *rock music* but did not influence it and this is just one example of working outside of traditional genres.
    C Wrong – Warhol *engaged in Performance Art*, and it is suggested that Rauschenberg did too, but this is not the **main idea** of paragraph E.
    D Wrong – This is true, but it is not the main idea of paragraph E.
13 1 past simple 2 past perfect continuous 3 past continuous
  4 past perfect simple 5 present perfect simple (passive)
  6 present perfect continuous
14 a past simple   b past continuous
  c present perfect continuous   d past perfect simple
  e present perfect simple   f past perfect continuous
15 1 have been 2 married; lasted 3 have now been developing
  4 has had 5 had been living and working
16 1 F 2 T 3 NG 4 T 5 T 6 F
  7 D (*began with Rodin's technique of repeatedly casting the same figure and using multiple casts to create a new piece*)
  8 D (the paragraph is essentially a list of innovative forms and the final sentence uses the paraphrase *pioneering forms of sculpture*)
  9 C (*Touch, physical participation and social interaction are now common features of the experience of going to see art.*) A is contradicted by *often though not necessarily in mixed media;* B is contradicted by *usually exhibited in an indoor gallery space in an arrangement specified by the artist.* D is not mentioned, although the word 'time' does appear (*Installations are multi-sensory experiences built for a specific time and space*).

WRITING

1

Build	Change	Remove
put up	extend	*demolish*
develop	enlarge	knock down
erect	alter	tear down
construct	modernise	flatten
	replace	
	relocate	
	expand	
	renovate	
	convert	

2

put up (v)	putting up (n)
develop (v)	development (n)
erect (v)	erection (n)
construct (v)	construction (n)
enlarge (v)	enlargement (n)
alter (v)	alteration(s) (n)
modernise (v)	modernisation (n)
replace (v)	replacement (n)
relocate (v)	relocation (n)
expand (v)	expansion (n)
renovate (v)	renovation (n)
convert (v)	conversion (n)
knock down (v)	knocking down (n)
tear down (v)	tearing down (n)
flatten (v)	flattening (n)

4 1 D   2 A   3 B   4 C

5 children's play area – recreational
Bayley Mansions – residential
café – commercial (recreational)
terraced houses – residential
railway line – industrial
laundry – commercial
Bayley Street Park – recreational
shops – commercial
wasteland – industrial

6 *Sample answer*
- residentially: replacement of terraced housing with flats
- industrially: removal of railway and wasteland
- commercially: relocation and expansion of shops and other facilities
- recreationally: construction of a park and children's play area

7 1 Overall   2 Whereas   3 Furthermore   4 Another major change to the area   5 On the commercial side   6 To sum up

8 a To sum up   b Furthermore   c Whereas
d Another major change to the area / On the commercial side
e Overall

9 *Suggested answers*
Whereas – but, i.e. *In 1990 a railway line ran through the neighbourhood*, but *by 1935* … (However, this repeats the structure of the previous sentence, so it would not be a good alternative in this case.)
Furthermore – In addition
Another major change to the area – One other key way in which the area changed
On the commercial side – Turning to the commercial facilities
To sum up – In summary, In conclusion, Overall

10 1 b   2 e   3 d   4 c   5 a

11 4 and 6 were not included. The other features are key to the structure of this writing task, which should focus on presenting the facts. Feature 4 is speculation (offering possible reasons for something) and 6 is giving an opinion. Candidates should not offer opinions, speculation or commentaries.

12 *Suggested answer*
accommodation: more rooms, and a second storey for the hotel
facilities: have been relocated
recreation: swimming pool moved and enlarged and made more attractive, access to the beach has been improved by removing fence; water sports facilities have been added

13 1 The most striking alteration is to the hotel's capacity / Recreation had more prominence by 2013.
2 Generally speaking, Another significant change, On top of this, To summarise
3 show – illustrate   facilities – amenities   change –alteration
relocation – moved   during the ten year period – in the ten years between 2003 and 2013 – ten years previously   extend – expand – extension – expansion – increase – enlarged
4 second sentence: *its*   final sentence in paragraph 2: *its*
paragraph 3: *This can be seen*; *On top of this*   paragraph 4: *its*

14 Past simple and past perfect would be the main two tenses.
Used to is also possible and good to use as a variation on the past simple to demonstrate a good knowledge of grammar.

15 *Sample answer* 1
Past simple: In 1900, this area had a combination of residential and industrial features; a railway line ran through the neighbourhood; made room for a spacious park; some new shops were built; the café and laundry were relocated and expanded
Past perfect: by 1935 the industrial features <u>had</u> largely <u>disappeared</u>; [terraced houses] <u>had been replaced</u>; the areas of wasteland <u>had gone</u>
Used to: the terraced houses which <u>used to</u> dominate the 1900 map
Sample answer 2
Past simple: Recreation <u>had</u> more prominence; the fence which <u>divided</u> the hotel; the hotel <u>underwent</u> an expansion
Past perfect: By 2013, the swimming pool and restaurant <u>had been relocated</u> and its seating area <u>had been enlarged</u>; a water sports centre <u>had been built</u>; [the fence] <u>had been removed</u> by 2013

16 *Sample answer*
The two maps show the outskirts of the town of Fosbury in 1980 and 2015. The 35-year period saw changes to the road layout, and to the residential, recreational and commercial facilities.
In terms of the road layout, the main change was the addition of a roundabout in the centre of this area, which necessitated the demolition of a block of flats and a grocer's shop. The residential accommodation underwent further changes with the removal of a street of terraced houses on the right side of the map and the construction of additional housing on the left side. New houses replaced the park, which was relocated to the other side of the road and decreased in size. By 2015 a supermarket with a car park had been erected on the site of the terraced houses.
The area industrialised further during the 35-year period, with warehouses being put up where fields had been earlier. The area's sporting facilities had also been developed, with a new sports centre taking the place of the old tennis courts.
In summary, the area of Fosbury shown on the maps modernised and developed between 1980 and 2015. (*191 words*)

LISTENING

1 1 into/through/across; on   2 in; of   3 between; from/via; from/via
4 to   5 opposite/across from/close to
6 at; opposite; on   7 up   8 at; behind
You cannot use *above* and *below*.

2 2 *the lobby*: an entrance room similar to reception
3 *the drawing room*: a room where guests are entertained (originally called the 'withdrawing room' where guests used to withdraw to from the dining room after a meal)
4 *the cloakroom*: a room where coats, hats and other belongings can be left; it sometimes has a toilet
5 *the pantry*: a storeroom for food, crockery and other kitchen items
6 *the cellar*: an underground area, usually used for storage
7 *the attic*: a room or area at the top of the house, under the roof, often used for storing things

8 *the ballroom*: a room where balls (dances) and special events would be held

9 *the servants' quarters*: small rooms where the servants lived/slept

10 *the conservatory*: a room with direct sunlight, like an indoor greenhouse, often full of plants

3 1 C 2 B 3 A

4 *Sample answer*
Go in the main entrance and turn right. It is right in front of you, next to the library.

5 B

6 Portrait gallery

7 Spiral staircase and Exhibition Room are already labelled. Anteroom is not correct because you 'cross this little anteroom to enter the next turret' and room B is in the turret.

8 C sewing room D dining room

9 1 b 2 c 3 a

10 B (*It was not until the 12th century that living quarters were added.*)

11 drawbridge: The castle needed to be easy to defend and have a secure entry gate and *would have had a drawbridge at the main point of entry*
turrets: *the round towers at the corners*
moat: *vital defence, around the building, is now a dry ditch* (implies it once had water)

12 C (*The drawbridge is no longer standing; the moat is now a dry ditch.*)

13 storerooms, tunnels, dungeons

14 A

15 1 E 2 G 3 A 4 C 5 B 6 I 7 A 8 B 9 B 10 A

SPEAKING

1 1 NS 2 Y 3 Y 4 NS 5 Y 6 N 7 NS 8 Y 9 N 10 N

3 *Suggested answer*
The notes are incomplete (no mention of how his/her work makes her feel) perhaps because she has wasted time on unnecessary words and writing words out in full. Notes should be key words only.

4 *Suggested answer*
Sal. Dali
Born 1904? Catalunya, Spain
Died – 1980s?
Type: Surrealist, used symbolism e.g. Persistence of Memory – about time
Why like?
– interested in Maths, Sci like me
– unconventional, eccentric – interesting character
– later in life – sculpture / film sets – innovative
– colours
Feel? – proud

9 *Advantages of mind maps*: easy to add to, easy to access at a glance, can show relationships between ideas.
Possible disadvantages: notes like these don't put the points in order, so you need to make sure your talk follows a logical order; you also need to be sure you don't omit any of the points on the card.

11 Yes, she talked about the four points in order.
what you know about the life of this person
The creative person I have chosen is Salvador Dalí. I visited the Dalí Foundation in Figueres last year, and it made a great impression on me. He was born in Catalunya in Spain. I'm not sure of the exact year but I think maybe around 1904 and he died in about the late 1980s, when he was in his 80s.
what kind of creative work this person does/did
He was a surrealist painter, so he used symbolism a lot. What that means is in his paintings things don't look like what they are. One of his most famous paintings is called *The Persistence of Memory* and it shows watches or clocks that are very soft, which is supposed to show that time is not as most people understand it.

why you like his/her work
He was fascinated by Maths and Science, and so am I, so that is one reason why I like him. Another reason is that he was quite unconventional – and even eccentric in his behaviour, so that makes him an interesting character, who was not like other people. The same is true of his art. And what's more, he didn't just stick with painting. Later in his life he did sculpture and worked on film sets. So, to put it in a nutshell, I like the fact that he was innovative and totally different from others. Oh, and one more thing, the colours in his work are amazing, so they're good to hang on your walls – not the originals of course!
describe the way his/her work makes you feel
His work makes me feel proud because he's from my country – from my region, actually, and he brought fame to Catalunya.

12 1 d 2 b 3 h 4 g 5 f 6 c 7 i 8 e 9 a

13 I'll start by   possibly   I'm not 100% sure about that.   OK, so moving on   As well as   so   for some reason
So why do I like him?   Primarily   because of   yet   Finally, I suppose   So, that's about it.

14 1 I'll start by 2 so, moving on 3 As well as 4 Primarily
5 yet 6 Finally 7 that's about it

Unit 4 BUSINESS AND FINANCE

READING

1 2 A *loan* is an amount of money borrowed for any purpose. A *mortgage* is an amount of money borrowed specifically to buy a property.

3 *Regulations* are the procedures or rules set by any authority or person in charge in order for an organisation/business to function properly. *Laws* are instructions that are put in place by the government and apply to everyone in the country, and regulations can be part of them.

4 There is little effective difference in meaning. *Go bust* is more informal and used in spoken communication rather than written.

5 A *lender* provides a *borrower* with the money that they have asked for. In other words, a *borrower* receives a loan and a *lender* gives a loan.

6 *Savings* are money that is put into a safe place so that it cannot easily be spent, and may even make some profit in interest. *Investments* are money that is put into a less safe place, such as shares in a company, in the hope that it will make a profit.

2 The answers are in the reading passage.

3 1 Their full name is given.
2 Usually just a surname is given.
3 It is in italics. Sometimes titles may appear in 'quotation marks'.
4 The exact words written appear in 'quotation marks'.

5 1 A (Alicia Pillory) paragraph 2: *The grand, misguided theory was that any repayments would have to be made to the companies or people who now owned the mortgages, and everyone would get rich.*

2 C (Charles Vane) paragraph 3: *The main purpose of these organisations is to evaluate in a neutral way the amount of risk an individual or company might face in a potential investment. […] these credit rating agencies were actually paid by the investment banks themselves, […] which is actually very far from being neutral.*

3 C (Charles Vane) paragraph 3: *We have to take that into consideration before isolating and criticising the investment banks too harshly.*

6 4 A (Alicia Pillory) paragraph 4: 'So many people were taken advantage of (= exploited),' writes Pillory, and 'this *irresponsible lending behaviour* (= careless way of working) was never made to stop, with no ultimate consequences for the bankers, who simply *became very, very rich* (= got more wealthy)'.

5 B (Dr Alfred Moran) paragraph 5: 'The AAA ratings gave everyone a *dishonest guarantee* (= false assurance) that the system could not collapse. Unfortunately for the *world's economy* (= global economy), the insurance companies *followed those ratings blindly* (= accepted [those ratings] without question).'

6 A (Alicia Pillory) paragraph 4: She maintains that the *authorities* (= government) could, and should, have *put a stop to it* (= brought [the problem] to an end) earlier. Instead, 'at this point, *another industry saw the potential for profit* (= a new profit-driven industry) and greedily *stepped in* (= became involved)'.

7 It is the view of Charles Vane, who is mentioned several lines earlier in the paragraph. Although it may appear that the opinion belongs to the writer of the passage, it is actually the case that the writer is reporting, rather than quoting, Vane's words. The phrase 'By extension' also helps you to understand that this is not the view of the writer, but that it follows logically from what Charles Vane said.

8 C – The global financial crisis was created by a number of groups and has had only negative effects.
  1 A – *incorrect*. The writer only mentions debtors' prisons in the first and final paragraphs to show how attitudes to debt have changed. However, there is no mention of them in the rest of the text, so this is not the main idea.
  B – *incorrect*. In paragraph 6, Charles Vane compares the 'unwise' way in which people in the West save, compared to Chinese people. This is the opinion of *Charles Vane*, not the writer, and it only appears in this section, not the whole passage.
  C – *correct*. Three (= 'a number of') main groups are focused on – commercial banks, investment banks, insurance companies (and, arguably, 'investors'). There are no positive effects mentioned throughout the passage.
  D – *incorrect*. It is true that widespread attitudes to financial responsibility are heavily criticised throughout the passage. However, the word 'worldwide' makes this the incorrect option because the writer does not suggest that everyone has the wrong attitudes.

9 A – *incorrect*. There is no comparison made between the two eras. The 19th century is mentioned but not how they approached saving their money.
  B – *correct*. Three differing views from three writers are brought together in a summary of the topic.
  C – *incorrect*. The writer's tone is critical, but not just of investment banks. Also the writer is specifically evaluating the causes of the financial crash, rather than the more abstract 'unhealthy concept of debt'.
  D – *incorrect*. The writer does list some of the failing processes, such as the mishandling of the AAA credit rating. However, the writer has chosen to include various interpretations of what brought about the crisis and in the final paragraph says 'Whatever the root causes of this highly devastating period in our history', which tells us that the writer is not committing to one interpretation or another.

10 The best title is D.
  A – *incorrect*. The passage is not a historical account of debt, as it focuses on a short period of time from 2008 until the present. This is not enough time to be considered 'the modern era'. Furthermore, although there is reference to another point in history (the 19th century), there is no description of what happened between then and now.
  B – *incorrect*. The passage suggests that, although the banks were very much responsible for creating the recession, they were not alone.
  C – *incorrect*. The text focuses on a specific disaster, not many disasters, and one which resulted from the actions of specific groups of people working in specific industries. Finance and investment' is too broad a term to fit.
  D – *correct*. The writer may not state conclusively who they think is to blame, but the text presents different perspectives about where the responsibility for the crash lies.

11 1 present 2 past 3 past 4 present 5 present 6 present

12 1 have to 2 should not have / shouldn't have 3 must be 4 ought to have got 5 are supposed to sign in

13 1 C (paragraph 5: *Furthermore, although younger people are traditionally thought to be more willing to try any number of routes into work before deciding on an industry in which they want to develop, such an approach to employment no longer excludes workers of a more advanced age.*)
  2 B (paragraph 3: '*Older people are taking opportunities away from their grandchildren. Post-education, those new to the world of work are not able to earn any sort of living wage, nor are they getting the opportunity to develop the 'soft skills', e.g. social intelligence, that will enable them to flourish in the job market.*')
  3 B (paragraph 4: *The 'zero-hours' worker ... can be instantly dismissed without any hope of recourse. Employment laws [...] do not protect the new breed of worker from being unfairly dismissed at a moment's notice by their manager.*)
  4 A (paragraph 2: *This has a number of debilitating long-term effects, not least because this assurance of a growing economy is based more in myth than fact. Thomas explains, 'Without tax income, the economy cannot grow; if the economy stays weak, new jobs will not be created.'*)
  5 A (paragraph 3: *... created a problem for a huge number of retired workers, who are starting to find that the sum of money they have saved for their retirement does not stretch far enough to provide the financial security that they had expected.[...] there has been a widespread return of these workers to the job market*)
  6 A (paragraph 5: *Thomas agrees: 'Most of today's self-starters believe that the job market offers a vast array of potential opportunities from which they can learn and gain experience. Whether they have a wide range of existing experience, or none at all, is irrelevant to them.'*)
  7 C (paragraph 5: *A 2015 study by William Haroldson,* **How the Market Adjusts to Opportunity**, *advocated a definition of a new type of multi-skilled worker: the model employee who not only refuses to age, but also does not want to work in the same office every day, or even to be an employee in the first place. In such a progressive, forward-looking environment ...*)
  8 C *The Changing Face of Working Life*
  A is incorrect because the conflict between younger and older people looking for the same work is used as an example to support Lawrence's point that younger people are becoming worse off because of older people's return to the workplace. Furthermore, in paragraph 5 the writer quotes Haroldson, who actively encourages cooperation between young and old.
  B is incorrect because, although modern workers' adaptability is praised, it is also suggested that exploitation in the workplace is widespread, and even the most adaptable could suffer.
  D is incorrect because, if anything, the passage discusses the type of qualities that today's workforce *needs*, rather than wants.

WRITING

1 *Sample answer*
There is no clear definition of this term. Some would argue that meeting your minimum credit card repayment every month is being financially responsible, while others would disagree, saying that being in any kind of debt, however small, is irresponsible.
Broadly speaking, being financially responsible might include:
  • not spending more than you earn
  • knowing the difference between luxuries and essentials, and adjusting your spending on each according to your earnings
  • saving for old age
  • paying for things upfront, rather than on a credit card.

2 *Sample answers – these issues and arguments will form the basis of essay questions in later exercises*
  1 Today's world places a high value on consumer spending and having the most up-to-date versions of technology.
  Human nature is competitive, and people want to possess more and have better products.
  Technological developments, such as social media and new electronic devices, mean that people spend less time communicating face to face and more time online.

However, it can be argued that social media make it easier for people to communicate with friends and family wherever they are in the world.

It is a generalisation to say that everybody puts possessions before relationships.

2 The consumer nature of society encourages people to spend money on things that they cannot necessarily afford, and young adults are less experienced when it comes to making financial decisions.

Most teenagers leave school without a basic understanding of personal finance, such as how credit cards work or what is involved when getting a mortgage, so they don't necessarily realise how to make sure they avoid getting into serious debt.

Banks and moneylenders encourage debt because this is how they make their money.

On the other hand, people are free to choose what they want to buy and everybody has to take responsibility for how they manage their own personal finances.

3 1 The A statement asks you to evaluate if, how much, and why people in today's society value their possessions over their friendships.

The B statement is more confrontational, with a more pessimistic slant; it asks you to consider if people value their possessions so much that they are willing to sacrifice their relationships with family and friends. While the first question asks you to weigh up this statement, the second requires you to discuss whether the issue is *black-and-white*.

2 There is a greater sense of urgency in the B statement – 'increasing *dramatically*' – and a suggestion that we have little choice but to force students all over the world to learn how to be financially responsible – 'a new *compulsory* subject *must* be introduced in *all* secondary schools'. The first statement allows you more room to consider when and how the matter should be addressed. Again, the B statement is less equivocal than the A statement.

4 1 D   2 B   3 A   4 C

5 *Sample answers*

Essay Type 1 is a more conventional, balanced essay. The first paragraph presents arguments that agree, the second – arguments that disagree. In a balanced essay like this, candidates often write an introduction that presents the topic, but do not state their opinion until the conclusion. However, it is also good practice to state your opinion in the introduction in case you run out of time in the exam.

Essay Type 2 is a plan for an essay that agrees more than it disagrees. Over the first two paragraphs, the writer intends to make three main points to express this agreement. The third paragraph discusses two opposing arguments. It is likely that the conclusion – and the introduction – will both express the fact that the writer is broadly in agreement with the statement given.

In **Essay Type 3** the writer intends to show their strong disagreement with the statement. In the first paragraph, they plan to provide two strong main points to support their disagreement. In the second paragraph, they plan to discuss two possible arguments that do agree with the statement but with the explicit intention of *arguing that they are incorrect*, rather than simply *presenting* them and expressing disagreement in the conclusion.

6 1 ✓   2 ✓   3 ✗   4 ✗   5 ✓

7 1 Three agree: 1, 2, and 5; two disagree: 3 and 4.

2 They are in a logical order.

3 *Suggested answer*: Arguments 1 and 2 could form one paragraph and arguments 3–5 another.

4 This is a type 3 essay.

5 *Suggested answer*: The candidate seems to agree strongly – see how the strength of their opinion is presented when they disagree with the counterarguments: 'in my experience, neither of these points are particularly valid' – so the likeliest option is **a**.

8 1 *First* and *To begin with* announce the writer's first argument of a series. *Primarily* is incorrect, as this is an adverb which highlights or emphasises a point in comparison with (an)other(s).

2 *Secondly* introduces the second point, *Next* introduces a subsequent point. *Following* is lexically/grammatically incorrect. *Following* (on from) *this* would work in its place.

3 *That said* and *On the other hand* both introduce a contrasting or opposing argument. *Alternatively* is incorrect, as this is an adverb which offers the reader another option or possibility.

5 *Despite of this* is grammatically incorrect; the other two options are correct.

9 **Paragraph A:** The topic sentence has established the main idea of the paragraph: that the considerable financial rewards are not worth the problems that are caused in these professionals' lives as a result. The candidate then introduces a contrasting idea with the discourse marker *That said*, but their counter-argument does not follow on clearly or logically from the previous two sentences. The examiner would struggle to establish what argument the candidate is making.

Paragraph B: There is no real consideration or evaluation of the opposing idea, just a statement of belief from the writer that their opinion is correct.

10 *Sample answer*

That said, there is an argument that those at the very top of their profession were aware of these potential outcomes when they began their careers, and so any sympathy for their problems should be limited.

11 a sentence 2   b sentence 4   c sentence 1

Sentence 3 does not fit, as it introduces a new idea that the candidate didn't previously discuss in their essay.

Conclusion

In conclusion, I can see no reason why people in high profile positions should not be paid as well as they usually are. Granted, others in society often earn too little for the important work they do, but it shouldn't mean that these talented individuals are paid less. These high-earners create happiness and act as role models for younger people, often while their own privacy and well-being suffers.

12 **Appropriate:** To conclude; To sum up; On the whole; In summary,

Inappropriate: CONCLUSION (Headings cannot be included in IELTS essays); Summarising (lexically/grammatically incorrect); The point is / Basically (acceptable in the Speaking test, but too informal for a written essay)

13 *Sample conclusion*

In conclusion, financial responsibility should absolutely be taught as a genuine subject at school. Granted, there are concerns over some students' level of maturity or mathematical ability, but young people should not be denied the chance to become financially independent. It would help to ensure that current levels of debt are managed better in the future.

14 *Sample answer*

It is widely accepted that, for most people, their daily working lives will not be spent in their dream jobs. Despite this, I do not feel that people should instead prioritise becoming a high earner above all other concerns.

To begin with, I strongly believe that people need stimulation in their daily working lives in order to feel a sense of reward. Very few of us can go through an entire career staying in a position or an industry that we find boring purely for the financial incentive. Secondly, there are so many people who see their working life as a search for fulfilment and contentment in helping others, rather than a search for wealth. It seems unlikely that the priority for, say, every nurse or teacher in the world is to become well-off, and jobs such as these are rarely extremely well-paid.

Despite this, some would argue that those people who have families to support should always prioritise earning a high income; after all, it means securing their children's future. Others point out that, as the job market becomes increasingly unstable across the globe, it is vital to earn more and therefore save more. However, I do not agree that a good salary should necessarily be the number one concern for everyone. Too many people become preoccupied with the next pay rise or career move, and eventually become unhappy or even depressed, neither of which helps them to save or to provide for their family.

In summary, earning as much money as is humanly possible should not be anyone's main concern. Granted, it arguably brings financial stability, for individuals and for their families, but it is simply not worth tolerating a lifetime of unhappiness at work purely for the money. (*291 words*)

LISTENING

2 *Suggested answer*
The questions suggest that the talk will feature some detailed discussion of early coins and how they are made, and have been made, in different parts of the world. Around the middle of the talk, there appears to be a section in which the lecturer will focus in more detail on Chinese coins.

3 1 You will need to listen out for a plural rather than a singular noun for your answer. It is likely that this will either be a plural noun, an adjective + plural noun, or a compound plural noun.
2 The word *natural* suggests that the lecturer will say that these coins are made of a material that is found in the physical world rather than one that is artificially created.
3 You will need to listen for a single material or substance of some sort.
4 As is often the case in IELTS questions, the adverb that is used in the question is very important. This one tells you that you will probably need to listen out for a paraphrase of *most*, and also that you may hear a distractor – in this case, another quantifier.

4 *Students' own answers*: Sample answers
2 different metals, e.g. gold and copper, iron and silver
3 material: wood, stone, clay, metal
4 some kind of shape that looks like a well-known thing: a star, a key, a sword, a heart, an arrow head, an egg

5 *Sample answers*
2 Ancient Greeks mixed together gold and bronze to create their earliest examples of currency.
3 More than 2700 years ago, Chinese coins were manufactured from wood.
4 The majority of ancient Chinese coins were star-shaped.

6 1 sea shells 2 gold and silver 3 bronze 4 knife blades

7 *Sample answers*
5 *distinguished*: differed, differentiate, set apart, made distinctive
round: circle-shaped, circular, disc-shaped
6 *based on*: derived from, inspired by
7 *aspect*: feature, thing, characteristic, attribute, quality
kept: preserved, maintained, retained, held onto, saved
8 *primitive*: simple, basic, rudimentary, early
example: version, form, instance, case, specimen

8 5 square hole 6 (royal) gifts 7 elaborate design
8 mass production

9 1 a number or a quantifier such as *much* 2 a noun (phrase)
3 a noun (phrase) 4 a noun (phrase)
5 an adjective to describe light

10 1 15 percent 2 (see-through) window 3 silver patch
4 rainbow effect 5 UV/ultra-violet

11 1 Incomplete answer: without *percent* 15 does not make sense.
2 Word limit: written in this way, the answer is three words long, not two.
3 Spelling mistake: silver
4 Incomplete answer: we don't know what kind of effect.
5 Word limit: UV and ultra-violet are the same thing and repetition of *light* exceeds word limit.

12 1 thieves 2 locking device 3 4,000 BC 4 steel springs
5 precise construction 6 brass 7 strong / steel / curved bar
8 pushed down 9 pins 10 (combination) dial(s)

SPEAKING

1 *Students' own answers. Answers checked in exercise 2.*
2 1 market research 2 product development
3 launch a new product 4 business opportunity
5 make a profit 6 target market 7 customer satisfaction
8 time management 9 sales figures 10 close the deal
11 apply for a loan 12 file for bankruptcy

3 *Suggested answers*
2 the stages or steps in the process of creating a product, including design, testing, marketing
3 to release or present a new product to the public/markets
4 a situation with the potential to be beneficial for a business
5 to make more money than you spend / have spent
6 the intended customers of a product
7 how well a product meets the expectations of the people it is intended for
8 the effective and productive use of your time, particularly at work
9 figures which show how much money you make, or how many products you sell
10 to finalise a business agreement with a customer or client
11 to complete the paperwork requesting a bank to lend you money
12 When a business is no longer able to pay its costs or debts, it must do this legal process.

4 1 e 2 g 3 b 4 d 5 h 6 c 7 f 8 a

5 *Students' own answers*

6 I suspect it might be because it has become so easy to get credit from banks: credit cards, overdrafts, **whatever it is you might need**. Of course, there are a number of real plus points to this – you can buy whatever you want more quickly, and you don't have to pay the loan off until later, so I do see why **it holds so much appeal**. And online banking has actually made it easier to do this **without having to deal with the hassle of going into the branch** and standing in a queue for ever. **There's very little you can't do** through your online account. For example, you can apply for a loan **wherever you might be**, and most of the time you'll be given the money. But, for me, there's no substitute for speaking face-to-face, where a bank advisor can **point you in the right direction**, as far as savings or debt is concerned. **Above all else,** they won't allow you to get into debt that you can't pay back.

7 1 N 2 N 3 I 4 N 5 I 6 N 7 I

8 *Sample answers*
1 For me, it's a must. Too many people spend more than they can afford and go into debt as a result. They spend their lives paying even more money on interest payments and can become trapped in debt their whole lives.
For an increasing number of people these days, it's not a matter of life or death. After all, most people can't afford to buy a house and so they take on a mortgage and buy their house gradually. Most people use credit cards to buy essential things they don't have the money for at that moment, but knowing they can pay the money back.
2 I'm not sure. It's pretty inconsequential to my life, but I know I'm in the minority. Society is obsessed with having the latest versions of smartphones or tablets and it can be argued that buying new products is good for the economy.
Perhaps they just think that it's an absolute necessity, and that if they don't have the most up-to-date products, they'll be left behind. So many people depend on technology for their everyday lives and feel that having it will improve their quality of life.
3 It's hard to say. Personally, I don't really think it matters, but the world we live in seems to be built on the idea of accumulating wealth. Perhaps it's just human nature to want to have more than the next person.
For some people, it's absolutely essential because they or perhaps their society lacks the resources that other societies have and, as a result, they prioritise money and wealth in order to look after themselves and their families.

9 1 apparently, supposedly 2 clearly, undoubtedly
3 arguably, conceivably, feasibly 4 for the most part, by and large
5 as far as I'm concerned, from where I stand

10 *Sample answers*

2 I can understand why some people might think this. *Supposedly* young people are highly irresponsible with money, and so having the ability to spend money they don't have is risky.

3 *Arguably* this is the case for many people, but *from where I stand*, people need to take responsibility for their own debt and not blame technology.

4 *By and large*, having a degree in Business Studies would benefit a businessperson, but *clearly* it is not absolutely necessary. Many of the most successful business people in my country don't have higher qualifications in this subject.

5 *Clearly* this is a ridiculous idea. Businesses are about profits, not about human beings. Politicians may not be perfect, but they have a far better understanding of the importance of society and community than business people.

6 *Conceivably* people would manage their finances better if they saved more and didn't get into debt. But *as far as I'm concerned*, I don't think it really matters. It's an individual choice.

11 1 **had to:** the grammar is incorrect, as the speaker is referring to how they see the general situation in the present, not referring to a particular time in the past.

have to / have got to: both correct and acceptable in the Speaking test. However, *have got to* is a little too informal for the Writing part of the IELTS test.

2 **mustn't:** incorrect. The speaker is saying that there was no obligation to be 'ultra-qualified' at that time; *mustn't* is used when a speaker wants to suggest that there IS an obligation NOT to do something. Also, *mustn't* refers to the present, not the past.

don't have to / didn't have to: both correct, but *don't have to* suggests that the speaker is again generalising, while *didn't have to* is referring to the situation at the time when his/her father left school.

3 **had to / would have to / needed to:** all correct. *Had to* again refers to the particular time at which his/her father started in business, and what the father felt he knew. *Would have to* has essentially the same meaning, but the grammar is slightly different, i.e. the father said at the time, 'I will have to use my natural business acumen to get ahead'; this then changes into reported speech as the father is quoted in the present time.

4 **must:** incorrect (see explanation for question 2)

should have: incorrect, as the grammar here – *should* + *have* + past participle – is used to express regret or blame (i.e. he should have worked long hours, but he didn't). When referring to a present time, *should* can be used to suggest 'I think there is an obligation to …', e.g. 'You should work long hours every day, if you want to become successful.'

had to: correct, again this refers to a past obligation.

5 **didn't have to** + *made* is incorrect grammatically.

shouldn't have / needn't have: suggest slightly different meanings. Consider: 'He shouldn't have made such a risky investment!' = It's his fault we have no money. Whereas 'He needn't have made such a risky investment!' = Although it worked out OK in the end, there was no need to take such a big risk. Therefore, in this context, *shouldn't have* seems to fit better.

6 **didn't have to:** correct; there was no obligation, need or requirement to wait long before the money returned.

mustn't have to / hadn't to: both grammatically incorrect.

12 1 strong 2 strong 3 weak 4 weak 5 weak

Unit 5 HISTORY

READING

1 *Sample answers*
Bahrain – King Hamad bin Isa; Belgium – King Philippe; Denmark – Queen Margrethe; Morocco – King Mohammed VI; Norway – King Harald V; Saudi Arabia – King Salman bin Abdulaziz al-Saud; Spain – King Felipe; Sweden – King Carl XVI Gustaf; UK – Queen Elizabeth II

2 rule, era, heir, dynasty, leader

3 *Suggested answers*

1 *dynasty*: it is a period of time, or a series of rulers from the same family; the others are synonyms for the lands ruled by a king or emperor

2 *regent*: a person acting for a monarch – the others are actual monarchs or rulers

3 *abdicate*: it means to give up the role of monarch; the others mean to lead as the monarch

4 *crown*: it is an object; the others are events

4 1 A   2 C (Someone who is pro-royalty would be unlikely to write a text that focuses on the eccentricity of royalty and someone who is anti-royalty is unlikely to defend rulers and royalty, which this text does at times.)

5 1 claim   2 claim   3 claim   4 view

6 1 C   2 D   3 A   4 B

7 **c** (= It is claimed he talked to celestial bodies.)

8 He forgot that he had a wife and children / that he was king.
He believed that he was made of glass.
His son-in-law had to take over as regent.
He ran around the palace grounds, howling like a wolf.
Statement 1 in exercise 6 relates to Charles VI.

9 Fyodor I – statement 2; George III – statement 4

10 1 b   2 d   3 a   4 c

11 1 *Happily for him, his subjects saw his childlike simplicity as being divinely inspired.*

2 *On the other hand, by many accounts she was a gifted and intelligent woman with a talent for diplomacy.*

3 *However, it should be pointed out that many of these 'reports' about Caligula were written more than 80 years after his death, so their accuracy is open to question.*

12 We might expect this to be true, given the title and subject of the text, but the writer never claims that the majority are eccentric. The closest it comes to this is when the text says 'there have also been a number of bizarre, frankly eccentric, rulers', which is not a confirmation, and the text also carries the message that we should not believe everything we read about eccentric monarchs.

13 1 No (… *for one thing we should celebrate royal eccentricity. It certainly makes reading history much more interesting.*)

2 Not Given (the text only mentions this in the case of Charles VI, Fyodor and Joanna)

3 Yes (*Had he left an heir, Russian history might well have gone in a different direction.*)

14 1 D   2 A   3 C   4 B

15 1 second   2 third   3 third   4 mixed 1

16 1 Yes (*the pharaoh's chief responsibility was to maintain Ma'at or Universal Harmony, and warfare was an essential part of this*)

2 Yes (*many women held considerable power as the 'great wife', the first wife of the reigning pharaoh*)

3 Yes (*Hatshepsut, the first female pharaoh, … made her mark on history. … history remembers her as a great leader*)

4 No (*In ancient Egypt kingship usually passed from father to son. … Some, like Hatshepsut, seized power illegally*)

5 Not Given

6 No (*the team from Pennsylvania managed to piece together most of King Senebkay's skeleton*)

7 B   8 D   9 C   10 A

WRITING

2 1 c   2 a   3 d   4 b

3 1 The general trend is a decline in the number of mines.

2 1913–1943 – the number of mines almost halved
1963–1983 – about 80% of mines closed
2003–2015 – very few mines left

4 *Suggested answers*

Strengths of the essay
TA: The description is accurate and there is data to support the description.
CC: Overall structure makes sense, with logical paragraphing
LR: A fairly good range of vocabulary is used to avoid repetition: *decline, disappeared, decrease, fell sharply, dropped, only 5 left.*
GRA: Past tenses are generally used correctly

Weaknesses
CC: Some of the cohesion is faulty: *obviously, nevertheless, surprisingly* and *at last* are used incorrectly.
CC: A wider range of linkers / cohesive language could be used. For example, when referring to time periods, the writer almost always uses *In* + year to introduce the information.

5 1 The clear trend in the figures is that 2 For example
3 It is striking that 4 By the end of the period shown, in 2015,

6 2 The overall trend is clearly
3 However,
4 in the 100-year period between 1913 and 2015; by the end of the given time frame; In the early decades of the twentieth century; By the middle of the century; by the turn of the twenty-first century

7 *Sample answers*
1 China/Europe have the highest proportion of car manufacture. Between them, countries in South East Asia (China, Japan/Korea, South Asia) produce more cars than the rest of the world put together (approximately 51%)
Few cars are made in the Middle East/Africa.
2 Greater China manufactures slightly more cars than Europe. North America produces nearly five times as many cars as South America.

8 1 For the purposes of this data set 2 What stands out is
3 in terms of 4 respectively 5 By contrast 6 Turning next to 7 Whereas 8 moving on to 9 although

9 1 Showing contrast: *whereas, although, by contrast*
2 Introducing a new point/idea/section: *in terms of, moving on to, turning next to*
3 To emphasise or exemplify an idea or point that you are making: *What stands out is*
4 To introduce a statement which clarifies the data: *For the purposes of this data set*
5 To indicate that some information is in the same order as connected information mentioned in a previous statement: *respectively*

10 2 *the given time frame* is a paraphrase of *the 100-year period between 1913 and 2015* to avoid repetition
3 *of them* replaces *coal mines* to avoid repetition
4 *the number* is short for *the number of coal mines* to avoid repetition
5 *this type of vehicle* is a paraphrase of *passenger car* to avoid repetition

11 *Sample answer*
The bar charts divide the UK workforce into five categories based on the type of industry they work in for the years 1841 and 2011.
The overall trend shown in the data is a steep rise in the proportion of employees engaged in the service industry, coupled with a decline in manufacturing. The most salient feature is that in 2011 81% of the workforce were involved in providing services, which contrasts sharply with the figure of 33% in 1841. In contrast, we observe a huge drop in the manufacturing industry from over a third in the mid nineteenth century to just 9% by the early twenty-first century.
Furthermore, the 170-year period saw a marked fall in the agriculture and fishing sectors, leaving food production with a tiny 1% of UK workers. Similarly, workers in energy and water companies decreased by two thirds. On the other hand, the construction industry experienced significant growth from 5% to 8% over the period.
In conclusion, the job profile of the UK workforce changed radically between 1841 and 2011, with the increases coming in the construction and service industry but all other areas seeing a decline.

LISTENING

1 a on b end c season d from e in f between, in g on h era i recent

2 1 g – since the ninth century AD
2 b – in the mid-twentieth century
3 d – between 1642 and 1649
4 i – in the last 200 years
5 a – during the 1070s
6 f – from 1914 to 1918
7 e – after the restoration of the monarchy
8 c – during the Victorian era
9 h – in the first decade of the twenty-first century

3 A home – residence; king or queen – royalty
B arms – weapons
C place of worship – church
D destination – attraction; sightseers – tourists
E currency – money; manufactured – made

4 C

5 *Suggested answers*
B controlled – ran, managed
C enemies – opponents; lost their lives – died, were killed
D zoo – wild animals; six centuries – six hundred years
E got back – regained, recovered, recaptured

6 C, D

7 A, E

8 1 sub-standard 2 dazzling 3 phenomenal
4 My favourite part was 5 frightening 6 apprehensive
7 famous 8 challenging

9 1 B 2 C 3 A 4 B 5 A

10 C, D

11 *Possible paraphrases*
A display – exhibition; clothes – costumes, outfits
B artists – painters; buried – in tombs
C updates – renews, changes; exhibits – displays, objects; from time to time – occasionally, regularly
D lived up to its reputation – was as good as you hoped/expected it would be
E queues – lines, standing in line
F flower displays – floral exhibits
G hosted royal weddings – been the venue for royal weddings, royal weddings took place there, royalty was married there

12 1 C 2 A 3 G 4 E 5 D

13 1 C 2 E 3 B 4 D 5 G 6/7 B, D

SPEAKING

1 *Sample answers*
2 between the 5th and the 15th century
3 after the Middle Ages, from the 14th to the 17th century, at the rebirth of classical learning
4 in 1999–2000
5 between 1900 and 1920
6 in 2000
7 before recorded history
8 three thousand one hundred years before the birth of Jesus Christ

2 a 7 b 5 c 2 d 1 e 8 f 4, 6 (Y2K = the Year 2000) g 3

3 *Students' own answers*

4 1 He mentions all the points.
2 He mentions them in order.
3 Yes. He covers all the points, uses correct grammar and vocabulary, he speaks for the correct amount of time and has excellent pronunciation.

5 1 j 2 h 3 a 4 i 5 e 6 g 7 f 8 b 9 d 10 c

6 1 past perfect tense needed – I had never been to Beijing before.
2 present participle needed – … costumes flying across the stage.
3 third conditional error – If one had made a mistake, the whole show would have been ruined.

4 unnecessary article – ~~the~~ Beijing
5 article missing x2 – <u>the</u> Opening Ceremony, <u>the</u> Olympics
6 subject/verb agreement in passive – small children <u>were</u> dressed …
7 future simple needed – I <u>will</u> never forget …
8 superlative error – It was the <u>most</u> exciting day of my life.
9 verb pattern error – My father explained <u>to</u> me that it was OR My father explained ~~to me~~ that it was
10 past continuous not needed – A small girl <u>sang</u> beautifully.

7 Answer 3 is the best. This answer is the optimal length and does not introduce new ideas. Answer 1 is impressive but too long and introduces new ideas. Answer 2 is clearly too short.

8 1 c 2 a 3 d 4 b

9 *Sample answers*
Do you think it's important for children to learn history at school?
primary school – should learn about own community/country – help them understand own identity
You said children should learn the history of their own country. What about world history?
national history should come first, world history later, possibly at secondary school
Do you think most children are interested in learning history these days?
more interested in technology – could use it to learn about history
Can technology help us learn about history?
examples of how technology can be used in learning history – going to place where the event took place is best way to learn

10 *Agree*: Certainly.   Of course.   Sure.   Without a doubt
Neither agree nor disagree: Well, there are two ways to look at this.   Possibly.   To some extent   It's hard to say.
Disagree: Not really.   Definitely not!   No, not at all.   To be frank, it's not very …

11 1 I remember learning, I think learning
2 without knowing
3 should be taught, how history is taught, needs to be made
4 the best way
5 should, could
6 where the event took place

12 1 d 2 b 3 a 4 c, b

13 *Students' own answers*

14 *Students' own answers*

Unit 6   SCIENCE AND TECHNOLOGY

READING

1 Technology has greatly improved the <u>life</u> of many people around the world, according to a considerable amount of <u>researches</u> that has been conducted over the past century. The use of the internet in <u>particularly</u> has become so widespread in so many countries that our daily existence would now be <u>imaginable</u> without it. This is not necessarily a positive <u>developed</u>. As the work of Guillerme Vínculos concludes, when social media first started to become <u>popularly</u>, it was an <u>innocence</u> extension of the standard types of interaction between friends and new acquaintances. These days, however, there are two <u>noticeably</u> extremes; both negative. One, where the platform is used as a <u>substituted</u> for human-to-human contact. The second is where it is <u>employment</u> as a way to bully or aggressively intimidate other people.

2
Incorrect	Correct
2 *researches* (noun, countable)	*research* (noun, uncountable)
3 (in) *particularly* (adverb)	(in) *particular* (adjective)
4 *imaginable* (noun, positive)	*unimaginable* (noun, negative)
5 *developed* (verb, past or adjective)	*development* (noun)
6 *popularly* (adverb)	*popular* (adjective)
7 *innocence* (noun)	*innocent* (adjective)
8 *noticeably* (adverb)	*noticeable* (adjective)
9 *substituted* (verb, past or adjective)	*substitute* (noun)
10 *employment* (noun)	(is) *employed* (verb, past participle to form the passive)

3 1 All the words are adjectives. There are more options than gaps, so there are distractors.
2 a It is about the future of VR.
 b The acronyms 'HMDs', 'CDs' and 'PDAs', plus the date '2030', are all useful when scanning the passage to locate the correct places in the text where the answers will be found. Although the acronym 'VR' is mentioned twice, it is the topic of the whole passage and is included in this form throughout and so is not very helpful for locating the right paragraphs to scan.
 c paragraph A (*To what exent VR establishes itself as an integral part of our lives …*)
 d paragraph H

4 1 A 2 I 3 E 4 G 5 D

5 1 mainstream = P (*integral part of our lives; move from niche technology to common usage*)   2 conceivable = P (*many experts are of the opinion that VR <u>may well</u> have become sufficiently developed for it to form an essential part of life by 2030*)   3 outmoded = P (*consigned to history*)   4 incapable = P (*the vast majority of computers and consoles available for the home market lack the required processing power*)   5 reluctant = P (*unwilling*)

6 1 paragraphs D–G   2 Not necessarily. The rubric says *no more than two words* so it is likely that some answers are more than one word.

7 1 The gap requires an adjective (phrase), not an adverb (phrase).
2 The gap requires a singular noun, not a plural.

8 3 noun (phrase)   4 adjective (phrase)
5 noun (phrase) beginning with a vowel   6 noun (phrase)
7 adjective (phrase)   8 noun (phrase), probably plural nouns for a group of people

9 1 far-reaching   2 field / industry   3 creativity   4 secondary
5 immersive world   6 composition   7 interconnected
8 (avid) travellers

10 Paragraphs B and C

11 1 computer   2 (natural) differences   3 tailored picture
4 aircraft flight

12 *Suggested answers*
1 A The suggestion is that the development of this new form of non-physical communication will begin and end in 2030.
 B The verb form changes the meaning completely, so the writer is suggesting that this new form will already be in use by 2030. The completion date of the development is unclear, but we know it takes place at some point between now and 2030. More often, with this grammatical form, *in* + year/month/etc. is replaced with *by* + year/month/etc.
 C The active, rather than passive, verb form suggests something different again, and something rather strange. In this case, the writer is stating their belief that this new form communication will inevitably begin in 2030, but as a natural process, apparently without human involvement. As such, it does not really make logical sense.
2 A This sentence suggests that the inventor has a fully tested and functional product ready to launch – or recently launched – into the marketplace. They are entirely confident in its potential to sell from the moment it is available to buy. They are expressing their confidence as a given fact, rather than a prediction.
 B This example is similar to A in terms of the inventor's confidence in the product. However, this time, the verb form reflects a prediction. The prediction is that the product will work once the inventor has finished developing it.
 C In this example, the inventor still feels positive about the outcome – i.e. that he/she is going to be rich – but the use of the word *could* throws a little more doubt onto the product. Maybe it is still in development; maybe the market research they have conducted suggests that its success is far from guaranteed. In fact, to make more sense, the sentence should read, 'I *might* be rich soon because I know this *could* work.'
3 A The writer is making a 'soft' prediction. The popularity or importance of Coding as a subject is not guaranteed, neither does the writer offer any timescale as to when it can be expected to become 'the most important and popular subject'.

B The writer is more confident in their prediction, and they are suggesting that its future importance and popularity is much more likely to happen than not. This effect is achieved by the addition of the word *well* after the modal verb. A similar meaning is expressed by *might/may/could* + *well* + bare infinitive.

C Here, the writer is suggesting that Coding is, in the eyes of educators, very soon to become the most important and popular subject in schools, etc. This is not a prediction based on any form of subjectivity or guesswork; perhaps educators all over the world have produced overwhelming evidence to support their claim. Using 'about to' allows the writer to produce a more objective statement than with options A and B, which are more speculative/hypothetical.

13 1 G 2 D 3 F 4 J 5 A
6 lighting rig 7 beam 8 mirrored surface 9 transparent (foil)

WRITING

2 1 all correct 2 all correct 3 advise 4 suggested
5 recommended

3 *Suggested answers*
to advise
(i) *advise* + *(that)** + clause
*I (would**) advise that you record yourself practising a Part 2 Speaking task.*
(ii) *advise* + someone + *to* infinitive
I advised him to record a Part 2 test and listen back to it.
(iii) *advise* + *-ing*
*I don't/wouldn't** advise turning up to the IELTS test without ID – they won't let you sit the test.*
(iv) advise + *against* + *-ing*
My teacher advises against learning answers off by heart.

to suggest
(i) *suggest* + *(that)** + clause
I suggest (that) you spend more time working on your pronunciation.
(ii) *suggest* + *-ing*
I suggest spending more time working on your pronunciation.
(iii) *suggest* + *to* + someone + *that* + clause
I suggested to him that he watch an online video of the Speaking test to help him improve.
* optional
** *would* is more polite/formal

4 1 In part. The candidate makes it clear they believe social media to have had a positive effect. However, they do not answer the question that has been given. As a result, the position they state relates to their argument, but not to the one that they should be writing about.
2 No. The candidate begins well, by describing how it has become easier for people to communicate at any time of the day. They go on to state what they see as a second reason for the usefulness/ benefits of social media, but it does not relate to the question, which focuses on relationships between family and friends, not performers and their fans.
3 No. The example that the candidate gives does not actually relate to the question. Rather than explaining how useful social media is in strengthening relationships, they have actually written about how useful it is to own a mobile phone.
4 No. The candidate mentions that there are negative sides in both the introduction and conclusion, but the main body of the essay only discusses the positives. In any essay of this length, but particularly one that has two questions to answer, it is difficult to go into a great amount of detail. However, if you are going to state that there are negatives, you should aim at least to suggest what they are. Additionally, the candidate recommends a course of action for everyone to take, but this is not asked for in the question.

5 'In the past, people were able to talk to each other on the phone, but they had to make sure that they were both at home to make or answer the call at an agreed time.'
'Despite the fact that people need to communicate regularly with their loved ones in order to be happy, it appears that physical contact is not as vital as once thought.'

6 1 and 3. *Despite* can be used with the following structures: *Despite the fact that …*; *Despite* + *-ing* verb; *Despite* + noun phrase (no verb)

7 2 *Although* is usually followed by a normal sentence structure (subject + verb). Note that it can also be followed by a past participle or an adjective if the subject of both clauses is the same.

8 1 Incorrect. Corrected version: *In the past, although people were able to talk to each other on the phone, they had to make sure …*
Grammar point: Do not use *although* and *but* in adjacent clauses. They have the same function, so you don't need both.
2 Incorrect. Corrected version: *In the past, although the ability to talk to each other on the phone **was available**, people had to make sure …* OR *In the past, although **they had** the ability to talk to each other on the phone, people had to make sure …* OR *In the past, although **people had the ability** to talk to each other on the phone, they had to make sure …*
Grammar point: *Although* is usually followed by a normal sentence structure (subject + verb). The only exception to this can be seen in sentence 4.
3 Incorrect. Corrected version: *In the past, **despite being** able to talk to each other on the phone, people had to make sure …*
Grammar point: *Despite* can be used with the following structures: *Despite the fact that …*; *Despite* + *-ing* verb; *Despite* + noun phrase (no verb)
4 Correct. Grammar point: If both clauses have the same subject (in this case 'people') **and** the word *although* is followed by an adjective or past participle, it is not essential to have the subject in both clauses. For example: *Although (they are) concerned about how much time their children spend online, parents tend not to impose a time limit on them.*

9 *Sample answers*
1 Despite wi-fi technology being cheaper than ever, certain parts of the world still have no internet access. OR Despite the fact that wi-fi technology is cheaper than ever, certain parts of the world still have no internet access. OR Although wi-fi technology is cheaper than ever, certain parts of the world still have no internet access.
2 Despite the fact that Virtual Reality headsets are now available to buy, most home computers lack the processing power to make them worthwhile. OR Despite Virtual Reality headsets being now available to buy, most home computers lack the processing power to make them worthwhile. OR Although Virtual Reality headsets are now available to buy, most home computers lack the processing power to make them worthwhile.
3 Although it is extremely important to learn science at school, some students are better suited to studying arts subjects. OR Despite the fact that it is extremely important to learn science at school, some students are better suited to studying arts subjects. OR Despite it being extremely important to learn science at school, some students are better suited to studying arts subjects.
4 Despite its limited amount of government funding worldwide, space exploration has uncovered a huge amount of information about the way the universe works. OR Despite the fact that space exploration receives a limited amount of government funding worldwide, it has uncovered a huge amount of information about the way the universe works. OR Despite receiving a limited amount of government funding worldwide, space exploration has uncovered a huge amount of information about the way the universe works. OR Although space exploration receives a limited amount of government funding worldwide, it has uncovered a huge amount of information about the way the universe works.

10 1 The subject of both original sentences is the same (*social media*, *It*) and the verb in the first sentence is passive. Therefore, the writer has used a past participle clause to connect the two sentences. The words *Social media was first introduced* have been edited to form *First introduced*, while the subject *Social media* has been moved to replace *It* (the subject of the second clause). If the subject had been left as *it* (i.e. *First introduced to the internet around twenty years ago, it has since gone from strength to strength*) the reader would not know what was being discussed. It is therefore

important to make sure that the subject is stated clearly, not referred to by a pronoun; this needs to happen after the comma that ends the participle clause.

2 Again, the subject is the same for both original sentences and the second original sentence suggests the reason for the first. In the second sentence, the verb is active, so the writer is joining the sentences together with a comma and a present participle clause, replacing the words *They argue* with *arguing*. Again, the presence of the comma is all-important. It would not be correct to write: *Many critics have suggested that it is affecting the closeness of family relationships arguing that people spend too much time staring at screens rather than actually talking to each other*. In this case, it is also possible to invert the order of these two clauses so we could begin this participle clause sentence with the second clause: *Arguing that …*

11 1 Greatly excited by social media, young people believe that it is a necessary way to keep in contact with their friends. OR Young people are greatly excited by social media, believing that it is a necessary way to keep in contact with their friends.

2 Some people argue that social media is the perfect tool for modern communication, drawing attention to the fact that family members and friends often find it impossible to spend time with each other. OR Drawing attention to the fact that family members and friends often find it impossible to spend time with each other, some people argue that social media is the perfect tool for modern communication.

12 A: Although it is possible to argue that it has created a society in which people spend less face-to-face time with friends and family, social media has revolutionised the way in which we relate to one another.

B: Most people would not welcome a return to an old-fashioned style of communication, being more accustomed now to this convenient new form of interaction.

13 Conclusion A is the best. It clearly restates the answers to both questions in the essay.

Conclusion B only answers the second question in the essay. It does not sum up the reasons for social media's success.

Conclusion C also only focuses on the second question and in fact contradicts the points made in Paragraph 3 about social media being on the whole a positive development.

14 *Sample answer*
It would be difficult to imagine life without computers. Over recent years in particular, their use and potential have grown at an incredible rate and I strongly believe that this growth will continue as more innovative ways to use them are developed. Although there are definitely some downsides to their use, I do believe the positives outweigh the negatives.

Computers enable us to do a wealth of tasks that would have been unthinkable for previous generations. We can bank online, book holidays, do our weekly shopping – the list of labour-saving activities is almost endless. Given the speed at which they have evolved and altered the way we do things, I am convinced that this evolutionary trend will continue. Take, for example, the rise of virtual reality. We can already do amazing things with it, and, as a computer-based technology, it is only in its infancy. It has so many practical applications, from improving gaming to providing training for doctors or pilots to handle real-life situations. As computer processing power increases, so will its potential to enhance everything we do.

Despite this, there are dangers in relying quite so heavily on computers. So much of our daily lives is controlled by them, that without them, modern-day life as we know it would be impossible. Furthermore, computers store all our important data and the risk of hacking exposes us to crimes such as fraud. However, I would argue that the technological advances made possible by computers have improved our world in so many ways. I believe that most people would argue that any negative aspects of computers are outweighed by all the benefits they have brought.

In conclusion, I believe we will probably become more dependent on computers but that our lives will improve as the technology improves. While there is a negative side to such a dependency, there are many more positives that we can focus on. (*317 words*)

LISTENING

3 A 3,6   B 4,8   C 1,7   D 5,10   E 2,9

4 C and B

5 1 My biggest worry is   2 You've got a point
   3 The real issue we've got   4 I quite agree
   5 I'm not exactly confident   6 That's absolutely true
   a concerns: 1, 3, 5; agreement/disagreement: 2, 4, 6
   b You've got a point
   c phrases 3–4 (option C); phrases 5–6 (option B)

6/7 Student A: 1 *own answer*   2 A
    Student B: 1 C   2 *own answer*

9 3 C   4 C

10 1 noun (phrase)   2 noun (phrase)
   3 verb (phrase) that collocates with *of*   4 noun (phrase)
   5 noun (phrase)

11 Extract 1 – Question 3   Extract 2 – Question 5   Extract 3 – Question 2   Extract 4 – Question 1   Extract 5 – Question 4

12 1 bullet points   2 initial impressions   3 leave out
   4 edited version   5 feedback

13 1 That way *Cause*: use bullet points *Effect*: easier to compare notes
   2 By doing so *Cause*: agree some significant points / establish common themes from lectures *Effect*: put together an edited version
   3 In order for us to *Cause*: contact tutor *Effect*: get some feedback

14 1 Incorrect: *In order so to*
     Correct: *In order that she could, so as to* – suited to writing but can be used in speaking as well
   2 Incorrect: *The way*
     Correct: *This way, That way* – both better suited to speaking
   3 Incorrect: *For doing so*
     Correct: *By doing so, After doing so* – suited to writing but can be used in speaking as well

15 1/2 B,D   3 A   4 B   5 C   6 C   7 F   8 G   9 D   10 A

SPEAKING

1 1 1783 = parachute
  2 1843 = typewriter
  3 1866 = dynamite
  4 1798 = vaccination
  5 1963 = computer mouse
  6 1280 = eyeglasses
  7 1710 = thermometer
  8 2400 BC = abacus

3 2 – past and present simple

4 1 used to   2 'd be using   3 've been thinking   4 will be
  5 have become   6 'm going to   7 if I didn't have one, I wouldn't have a
  The candidate has used a wide range of grammatical forms and structures correctly here in a very short space of time. If they continued in this way, they could expect a very high score for GRA.

6 1 A (the) radio; B electricity / bringing electricity to people's homes; C the aeroplane; D the compass   2 / 3 *students' own answers*

8 1 I'd like to tell   2 let me begin   3 correct   4 correct
  5 remember being taught   6 correct   7 managed to attach
  8 can't help thinking   9 correct   10 imagine living
  11 allow us to have   12 correct   13 remember to look it up
  14 continue to be / continue being

9

Verb + 'to' infinitive	Verb + gerund	Verb + object + 'to' infinitive	Verb + object + bare infinitive (i.e. without 'to')
would like remember continue manage refuse attempt	remember continue can't help imagine	*would like* enable help tell allow	let

10 *would like*
would like + *to* infinitive expresses a personal plan, hope, expectation, etc., e.g. *I would like to tell you about …*
would like + object + *to* infinitive expresses a plan, hope expectation, etc. of someone or something else, e.g. *I would like you to tell me about …*

continue
There is no difference in meaning between *continue* + infinitive and *continue* + gerund, e.g. *They will continue being / to be an integral part of our lives forever.*

remember
remember + gerund = the action expressed by the gerund happens first, e.g. *I remember* (second action, now) *being taught* (first action, past) *about this at school. Do you remember learning your first words in English?*
remember + *to* infinitive = the action expressed by the *to* infinitive happens second, e.g. *I should remember* (first action) *to look it up* (second action) *on the internet when I get home. Did you remember to finish your homework?*

12 1 B   2 A   3 C   4 C   5 B   6 A   7 C   8 A
13 1 That's quite a tricky question.
   2 It's never crossed my mind before.
   3 I'm not entirely sure what you're driving at.
   4 Sorry, I don't quite follow your question.
   5 my mind has gone blank
14 1 C   2 C   3 A   4 A   5 C

Unit 7   TELEVISION, NEWS AND CURRENT AFFAIRS

READING

2 1 S   2 S   3 A   4 S   5 S   6 S   7 A   8 S
3 1 *Journalist* is a more generic word for anyone who works in media; a *reporter* is someone who writes or presents the news only.
   2 This is dependent on context: for the news, *research* means looking at different sources to be clear on the facts of a story. *Investigate* implies a more active role of finding out information that was not previously known, or solving something.
   4 same meaning – be the first to publish a news story
   5 *Broadcast* is used for TV/radio and *publish* for printed stories.
   6 A *media outlet* is a more generic organisation, for example a newspaper, magazine, or TV channel that offers a variety of information, whereas a *news agency* is just news focused.
   8 An *eyewitness* is a person who was present and saw the events of the news story first hand. A *source* is a person or organisation that provides information for a news story.
4 1 E   2 G   3 A   4 C   5 F   6 B   7 D
5 A a camera / a degree   B Ohmynews!   C CNN, The Times   D 2021
   E educational, economic, social, cultural   F rioters, looters
   G their critical faculties
6 A possessed – owned   B a Korean news site – one of South Korea's most influential online sources   C media outlets – news organisations
   D half – 50%   E obstacles – barriers   F criminals – offenders
   G audiences – readers and viewers

7 *Students' own answers*
8 1 D   2 F   3 G   4 A   5 B   6 E
9 2 What was the subject of the story given as an example of an amateur journalist scoop before it was reported by a major news agency?
   subject – probably a noun
   3 From which group of people have the media establishment begun to hire staff?
   group of people – a plural or collective noun
   4 What had mainstream media traditionally seen their role in news reporting as being?
   role – a noun
10 1 eyewitness   2 space shuttle Columbia
   3 (amateur) (news) bloggers   4 gatekeepers
11 7 A correct   B incorrect – the text says critical thinking is desirable, not a 'risk'   C incorrect – the words are not in the text
   8 A incorrect – too many words   B correct   C incorrect – the authorities *are* the police
   9 A incorrect – this is the old model   B correct   C incorrect – We media is not a 'model' of broadcasting
12 1 Independent Media Center / Indymedia   2 democratisation
   3 reduce inequality
13 B
14 1 C   2 E   3 B
15 1 The traditional 'filter then publish' model   2 'publish then filter'
   3 replaced   4 has been   5 by
16 Present continuous: The traditional 'filter then publish' model is being replaced by 'publish then filter'.
   Past perfect: The traditional 'filter then publish' model had been replaced by 'publish then filter'.
   Future simple with *will*: The traditional 'filter then publish' model will be replaced by 'publish then filter'.
17 1 F. Some sentences would not make sense or would sound very wrong. For example, the active sentence *I passed the IELTS test* would sound wrong in the passive (*The IELTS test was passed by me*).
   2 T. The passive allows us to shift focus from the person or thing doing an action to the person or thing affected by the action.
   3 F. It is used a lot. However certain forms of the passive, such as those that use *It* as a subject (*It is believed …, It has been estimated …*) sound very formal when spoken.
   4 T. Sometimes it is not important or relevant to say who or what does the action. For example, *My bicycle was stolen* – we don't need to say *by a thief* because this is understood.
   5 T. For example, the passive is commonly used in scientific texts and language as it expresses the objectivity for a situation.
18 1 B   2 D   3 D   4 C   5 A   6 B
   7 educational (type)   8 (their) personality   9 (the) producer(s)
   10 (the) confessional   11 E   12 A   13 D   14 C

WRITING

2 a 3 (online)   b 1 (TV)   c 2 (not specified)   d 5 (radio)   e 4 (print)
4 1 b   2 d   3 e   4 c   5 f   6 a
5 1 80%   2 66% / 67%   3 10%   4 40%   5 25%
6 *Sample answers*
   Almost two fifths of adults in the US never read news on social media.
   Just under a fifth often access news on social media.
   About / Approximately / Roughly a quarter of people sometimes get their news from social media.
   A little under a fifth hardly ever access news on social media.
7 *Sample answers*
   More than half of Brazilians access news online.
   TV is a popular way to get the news in both countries.
   Print and radio are both much more popular in the UK.
   Very few listen to the news on the radio in Brazil.

8 1 The two nations show broadly similar patterns, though there are some differences, both significant and minor.
   2 53%, 3%, 15% and 6%
   3 over a third of people, more than half, two fifths of the UK population
   4 broadly similar patterns   while in the UK … , in Brazil   more than half   3% fewer   one major difference   over twice as many people   compared with   Similarly   three times more   are used less   in comparison with
   5 *Introductory sentence*: The pie charts show the principle ways of finding out the news in two different countries, the UK and Brazil.
      Concluding sentence: Overall, it can be said that the high levels of internet use in Brazil mean that other methods such as radio and print are used less in comparison with the UK.
   6 main (ways) – principle   it is clear – it is apparent
      generally (similar) – broadly   preferring – favouring
      key (features) – most   each one / in that order –
      prominent   respectively

9 *Corrections are underlined*
   The pie chart <u>shows the</u> frequency with which adults in the <u>US</u> <u>use</u> social media to obtain news. Overall, it is clear that less than half <u>use</u> it <u>on a</u> regular basis.
   One of the most significant points in the data is that just under two fifths of people report that <u>they never access the news</u> via social media. To be precise, 38% of respondents gave this response, which is <u>the highest of all categories</u>. The second highest category is those who sometimes <u>find</u> out the news from social media sites. Around a quarter (26%) of those surveyed <u>selected</u> this response, which is 12% <u>fewer</u> than the 'never' group. Finally, there was a tie for the <u>least</u> common response. <u>Equal</u> numbers of respondents 'hardly ever' and 'often' use social media to find out what is going on in the world.
   To conclude, social media is <u>used</u> to get news often or sometimes by just 44%. It is evident <u>from</u> the data that <u>the</u> majority of <u>citizens</u> <u>do</u> not read news <u>on</u> these sites.

10 1 are using, was never accessed
   2 social medias, category, citizen
   3 frequency, regular basis, highest, majority
   4 news was never accessed by them, were selected, is use
   5 the pie chart show, adults in the US uses, those who sometimes finds, majority of citizen(s) does not
   6 US, response, equal
   7 in regular basis, highest from, by the data, in these sites
   8 highest, 12% less, less common response

11 1 Sentence A is more natural. Sentence B, whilst grammatically possible, feels unnatural. Verbs for describing visual data such as *indicate, show, reveal, demonstrate, suggest* are intransitive in this context and rarely used in the passive in this way.
   2 Sentence B. Using *we* in *One thing we can see* has a more informal feel. Using the passive here gives a more objective tone and demonstrates the use of modal passive forms.
   3 Sentence A is more natural. Sentence B gives the impression that somebody made the number of subscriptions increase. We don't usually use verbs of increase or decrease (*rise, fall, go up/down, reduce*, etc.) in the passive in this kind of report.
   4 Sentence A is more natural. (see answer 1)
   5 Sentence B. Sentence A gives the impression that somebody doubled the number of over 40s rather than it simply increased. See answer 3 for other verbs that we probably wouldn't use in the passive in this kind of essay.

12 *Sample essay*
   The pie charts represent which sources the citizens of two countries, Germany and Nigeria, turn to first in order to access the news. It should be noted that the figures for Nigeria do not include figures for rural areas of the country. Overall, it is clear from the data that the two countries have vastly different tendencies when it comes to news sources.

For Germans, the primary news source is newspapers, with just under half of the population using them, followed in second place by television with 30 percent. In Nigeria, however, television is the dominant first news provider, more than doubling the German figure with 63 percent, and whilst newspapers are a relatively popular source of first news in Nigeria, only 13 percent use them in this way. The second most popular first news provider in Nigeria is actually radio, with numbers approaching a quarter of the population. In Germany, however, the figure is less than half that, only reaching 10 percent. In fact, the internet is more commonly used by Germans than radio, with 11 percent of the population turning to it first. This contrasts sharply with Nigerians, of whom only 1 percent say that they use it for initial news access.

In summary, it can be said that whilst television is one of the favoured first news providers for both countries, the two countries otherwise exhibit very different first news consumption habits. (*232 words*)

LISTENING

3 beginning or ending   a, c, n
   sequencing / moving on   d, e, f, h, j k, l,
   referring back   m
   summing up   g, n
   emphasising   i
   giving reasons   b

4 *Sample answers*
   1 professional, freelance, sports – adjective
   2 national/local/international newspapers, television channels, news agencies, media outlets, news websites – plural noun phrase

5 1 freelance   2 news agencies

6 1 A correct   B wrong spelling   C words from question repeated (which also means the answer exceeds the word limit)   D the word is spelt correctly but should be the adjective form
   2 A singular form   B correct   C too many words – the candidate has added a word which fits grammatically but is not in the audio   D 'agencies' alone is not sufficient, two words are permitted and both words are needed

7 1 d   2 a   3 b   4 c

8 1 your/the audience   2 interest them   3 news channel
   4 consequences

9 1 pictures   2 reputation

10 1 A NP – wrong grammar   B P   C NP – wrong grammar   D NP – doesn't go with the preposition by
   2 A NP – *a* not *an* before gap   B P (but is a repetition of the previous stage)   C P   D NP – not logical here
   3 A NP – *information* is uncountable   B P   C P   D P

11 1 planning   2 script   3 detail

12 *Possible answers*
   4 singular noun for a person: *victim, police officer, witness, politician*
   5 verb: *disagree, differ, conflict, contrast*
   6 plural noun phrase: (*future*) *developments, participants*

13 4 witness   5 contrast   6 next steps

14 1 anything new   2 more selective   3 personal relevance
   4 audience   5 the competition
   6 E   7 B   8 F   9 A   10 H

SPEAKING

2 **Positive**   **Negative**
   gripping   pointless
   inspirational   utter garbage
   intriguing   a complete waste of time
   absolutely hilarious   It's not my cup of tea.
   a definite 5 star rating   **Neutral**
   compulsive viewing   I can take it or leave it.
   I watched it in one sitting.   It gave me food for thought.
   It has/had me on the edge on   It was nothing to write home
   my seat.   about.
   I was glued to the screen.

4 He corrects himself or clarifies 12 times:
One of my favourite programmes is *Fear Factor*. (1) <u>Actually</u>, I would say it's a programme that I love to hate! (2) <u>What I mean by that is</u> – I love it, but at times the things on there are awesome, (3) <u>sorry, I meant to say</u> they are *awful*. So the type – (4) <u>or rather</u> the *genre* – of show is reality but also it's a competition. What happens is that there are four people – (5) <u>well, you know</u>, four competitors – and they has to do, (6) they have to do a series of tasks. Sometimes they have to dive into – (7) <u>or actually</u> they dive *under* water and open a box – (8) <u>I mean</u> *unlock* a box, or they have to climb up a high building. In the second task, there are nasty animals – (9) <u>not animals as such</u>, but things like cockroaches or snakes which they must to, (10) they must lie in a box with or something. So, I don't like it, but it's compulsory. (11) <u>I'll rephrase that</u>. I watch it even though I don't want to. It's compulsive. It's on Thursday nights on a channel called Reality. I usually watch with my brother – *both* my brothers, (12) <u>actually</u>. Sometimes we play our own version of it and make each other do silly tasks, but not as bad as the ones on the TV.

5 *Sample answers*
1 I mean, they're not very *interesting*.
2 What I meant to say was the *presenter* is very good.
3 Let me start again. It's a show which gives people makeovers.
4 I'll rephrase that. It's a programme where you get to see inside celebrities' homes.
5 Sorry, what I intended to say was most people in my country watch this show.
6 Let me put that another way. I like game shows, especially when there are big prizes.

6 1 Watching TV is a time of waste. Sorry, I'll rephrase that – a <u>waste of time</u>.
2 Comedic shows, or rather <u>comedy</u> shows, are not very popular in my country.
3 I can't understand why realism TV is so popular. Let me start again. I can't understand why <u>reality TV</u> is so popular.
4 The popularity of sports programmes, especially football series, I mean football <u>highlights shows</u>, makes no sense to me.
5 One thing that I dislike about TV is the amount of publicities. Oh, did I say publicities? I meant to say <u>commercials</u>.

7 *Sample answers*
2 I think TV is a very positive thing. Let me explain. Children can improve their imaginations and learn a lot from watching TV.
3 Children should be allowed to watch TV online unsupervised. To put that another way, I don't think it's very practical to expect parents to supervise their children all the time they are online.
4 Watching TV online is far superior to watching conventional TV. What I mean by this is you can choose when you're going to watch and watch anywhere you like.
5 The standard of TV programmes is so much better these days. Let me clarify that. In the past, there wasn't much to see at the weekends but nowadays we have so many channels, we can always find something to watch.

9 *Sample answers*
1 It has been said/reported that children who watch a lot of TV are less sociable.
2 It is believed / thought / widely accepted that most newspapers are biased.
3 It has been proved that TV can damage your eyesight.
4 It has been estimated that by 2025, 80% of TV viewing will be done online.

Unit 8 CULTURE

READING

1 1 F (60 minutes only – no transfer time is given)
2 T
3 F (the texts are from a variety of sources but all written for a non-specialist audience)
4 F (each question is worth one mark)
5 T

2 1 Choose from four options A–D or choose two or more options from a larger list.
2 Decide if statements about factual information in the text is confirmed by the text (True), contradicted by the text (False) or not included (Not Given).
3 Decide if statements about views or claims in the text are mentioned (Yes), contradicted by the text (No) or not included (Not Given).
4 Match information from the text with the paragraphs that contain it.
5 Match main ideas with paragraphs or sections.
6 Match statements with people, places or things mentioned in the text.
7 Complete sentences about the text, choosing from a list of options with distractors.
8 Complete sentences about the text, using words from the text, keeping to a word limit.
9 Complete information in note, table, or flow-chart (process) formats, using words from the text, keeping to a word limit.
10 Complete missing information in a diagram, either choosing from a list or using words from the text, keeping to a word limit.
11 Answer *What/Where/Why/When/How* questions, keeping to a word limit.
12 Complete a summary of part of the text, either choosing from a list or using words from the text, keeping to a word limit.

3 1, 3, 4 (2 and 5 are false because in the last paragraph the writer expresses regret at the passing of some youth cultures, and says. 'those of us who recall', which tells us he/she remembers them personally.)

4 1 F *There is one subculture that seems to have endured better than the others: the bikers.*
2 C *It was a time when conventional social values were being questioned and […] young people found themselves with more freedom. Fuelled by American culture, Britain's youth suddenly had something to say and a desire to express themselves.*
3 E *made possible by the internet. They […] share information about demonstrations on social media. They take part in charity events […] to raise awareness as well as money.*
4 A (the whole paragraph)
5 C *… Elvis Presley and the advent of Rock and Roll generated the Teddy Boys in the UK, who in turn influenced both Mods and Rockers.*
6 D, G *The second half of paragraph D, beginning Although the younger generation of today has been called 'identity-less', that is not actually the case …*
and in paragraph G: *Rather than being without identity as a generation, today's youth are typically broad-minded and well informed, each individual having created their own unique style and set of beliefs*
7 B *It was in the 1990s that many older commentators started to point out that the youth movements had lost their fire and had become conventional.*
8 D, E *the development of the internet and its widespread availability from the 1990s onwards has fundamentally changed how young people interact with the world* (paragraph D); *Today's young people are more tolerant and international thanks to globalisation* (paragraph E)

5 1 iv 2 ii 3 vi 4 viii 5 x 6 ix 7 i

6 1 Y 2 N 3 NG 4 Y

7 1 defining – no commas, relative clause can't be omitted
2 non-defining – commas, relative clause can be omitted

8 *Sample answers*

Defining: *… we need to look at the reasons why conditions were ripe for the emergence of youth cultures in the mid-twentieth century*

Non-defining: *Hippies, who emerged in America and spread across the world, represented a more peaceful group.*

9 1 *The identities* is the object of the defining relative clause and so the relative pronoun can be omitted.

2 *that* and *which* could be added between *identities* and *they*.

3 No. In both cases the relative pronoun is the subject of the relative clauses.

10 1 American culture had a major influence on Britain's youth, who copied the style and music but made their own version of it.

2 One of the more memorable groups of the 1970s was the Punks, whose drainpipe jeans, kilts, safety pins and extraordinary hairstyles made them instantly recognisable.

3 The younger generation of today has been called 'identity-less', which is not actually the case.

11 1 D   2 B   3 C   4 B   5 A

6 D (A is wrong as there is no comparison of success. B is wrong as backpacking culture is only mentioned in the first paragraph as a modern example of the desire to travel. C is wrong as the text does mention that society has 'a confused and contradictory relationship with travellers' but the writer does not criticise any particular attitude.)

WRITING

3 *Sample answers*

Verbs	Nouns	Adjectives
cut	*scissors*	*coloured*
make	lantern	colourful
tie	glue	main
paste / glue / stick / attach	bamboo sticks	
insert	square	
need	triangle	
repeat	frills	
decorate	tissue paper	
hang	frame	
	top	
	bottom/base	

4 2 Next, the square and triangular tissue paper shapes can be stuck onto the frame.

3 The lantern is then ready to be hung on a lightbulb.

5 1 followed by   2 To begin with   3 then   4 This stage

5 Then / Next / After that   6 Once   7 Then / Next / After that

8 Finally

6 1 Yes. The second sentence in the first paragraph.

2a relative clauses: *which consist of tying bamboo sticks together / which is used to decorate it / which will give you the basic frame of the lantern / which correspond to the squares and triangles on the frame*

2b passives: *This stage of the process has to be repeated / is used to decorate it / Four of the sticks are then tied together / The remaining two squares are then tied in place / Once your frame is completed / the tissue paper shapes should be attached onto the frame / The squares at the top and bottom of the frame should be left empty / The lantern is then ready to be hung on a lightbulb.*

2c imperatives: *take brightly coloured tissue paper / cut out eight triangles / fold and cut paper / decorate the base of the lantern*

7 1 B   2 A   3 A   4 A   5 A   6 B

8 1 In my experience

2 what I believe is that

3 It is evident to me that

4 The reality is that (used to present an opposing opinion)

5 We cannot deny that

6 I strongly believe that

9 *Sample answers*

1 My own view is that any language is a reflection of culture and contains words and phrases that are specific to that culture. For example, in English there is an expression 'It's not my cup of tea', meaning 'It is not to my taste', which I think reflects the fact that the British are predominantly a nation of tea drinkers.

2 However, it seems to me that what affects our lives most are issues on a local or national level rather than on a world level.

3 On the other hand, our lives are so inundated with aspects of other cultures – restaurants, music, fashion, to name but a few examples – that it is sometimes impossible to separate the culture of one nation from another.

10 1 highlight   2 plan; paragraphs   3 outline

4 topic sentence; examples   5 opposing   6 cohesive

7 conclusion   8 proof-read

11 *Sample answers*

1 Yes. The candidate gives a definition of culture, mentions both views but clearly states their own opinion on the question.

2 At the end of the introduction (*I would lean towards the latter*) and again in the conclusion (*My own view is that while we are influenced by our nationality, in this globalised world, one's country of origin is only one aspect of our collective culture.*)

3 Opinion A. The topic sentence is: *If someone is born and raised in a place, they will be heavily influenced by it.* There are three reasons/ examples: the psychologist argument, the cuisine of a country and the music of a country.

4 Opinion B. The topic sentence is the first one. The candidate has probably decided to include this argument here because it supports his/her opinion given in the introduction, and having it at the end makes her conclusion stronger.

5 *Personally speaking, my own view is* and *To my mind.*

12 *Sample answers*

Task 1

The diagram shows the traditional techniques used for carving wooden shoes known as clogs. The process consists of six main stages, which are done by hand rather than using automated processes.

The first stage is to obtain wood from either poplar or willow trees. The wood is cut into pieces of the correct size using a saw. Next, each clog is roughly outlined using an axe. After this, the clog maker takes a long knife to cut the shoe to the exact shape it should be. Once the exterior is finished, the next stage in the process is to bore out the interior of the clogs using a spoon drill to make space for the foot.

Once this is done, the shoes are nearly finished. Sandpaper is used to smooth down the wood on both the interior and the exterior of the clog. The final task for the clog maker is to decorate the completed wooden shoe using various different colours, although this is an optional stage. The clog is then ready to be worn.

This completes the process of making traditional wooden footwear, or clogs, by hand. (*188 words*)

Task 2

Today we live in a globalised world and the development of global culture is often at the expense of local traditions. There are certainly many people who show indifference to local customs in favour of embracing global ideas, but there are still many who see the value in maintaining them, myself included.

It is easy to argue that people are strongly influenced by the effects of globalisation. Technology in particular seems to dominate the leisure time of young people, whether it be gadgets or the internet. As a result, there are trends which can be described as global in all aspects of culture. For instance, many people now prefer listening to music by Ed Sheeran or Beyoncé rather than the traditional music of their country, which is often seen as outdated by comparison. Similarly, many would rather try exotic 'foreign' foods than use traditional recipes, which they might see as dull or old-fashioned.

However, it would be a mistake to think that everyone thinks this way. Older people especially feel nostalgia for how things used to be done. For example, in the UK, the Royal Family are as popular as ever, and thousands of people turn out to see them wherever they go. It should also be remembered that many of today's global pop stars were themselves inspired by more traditional genres of music. Ed Sheeran, for example, embodies many musical traditions, such as folk music and busking. In the same way, it is still common to see performances of more traditional forms of music, such as classical and jazz.

My own opinion is that there is truth in both views. There are certainly people so focused on global trends that there is no space in their lives for, or interest in, preserving the past. On the other hand, there are many who prefer to live their lives more nostalgically and value the traditions that have been handed down. I would say that I belong more to this second group of people, although I admit I would struggle without the internet. (*343 words*)

LISTENING

1 1 globally 2 global 3 globalised 4 globe 5 globalisation

3 The headings in bold tell you what the structure is: Definitions of culture – Negative view – Positive view – Effect of the internet – Conclusion

5 1 C – the gap needs a noun
   2 A – the gap needs an adjective
   3 A – exceeds word limit

6 4 A 5 B 6 C

7 *Sample answers*
   7 the comma suggests it will be a noun, someone who is able to choose
   8 noun: e.g. *politics, economics, religion*
   9 noun: e.g. *knowledge, appreciation*
   10 noun: e.g. *the internet, conflict, nationalism*

8 1 visible 2 meanings 3 historical 4 capitalism 5 individual
   6 60% / 60 percent 7 citizens 8 society 9 languages
   10 education

9 1 plural noun or noun phrase (the verb *help* suggests it will be plural)
   2 verb (related to the effect one language can have on another)
   3 noun or noun phrase, related to a particular context or aspect of life
   4 noun or noun phrase, one that collocates with the preposition *into*
   5 adjective or adjective phrase OR verb phrase in gerund form
   6 singular countable noun or noun phrase, beginning with a consonant

10 *NB do not reveal these answers until students have completed exercise 11.*
   1 ancient monuments 2 dominate 3 business 4 integration
   5 getting older 6 complete course

12 1 subject: *we*; object: *which* 2 (the) world 3 before it
   4 to the end of the relative clause: *the world (which) we live in*

13 1 The man (who) you need to speak to is Mr Brodie.
   2 Chapman Brothers, the company (which) I worked for for 20 years, is closing down.
   3 Camilla Stark, with whom I went to school, is now a well-known actor.
   4 Yasmin demanded the goods for which she had paid.
   5 Christmas is the holiday which children wait for all year.
   6 The man whose life the film is based on died a long time ago.

14 1 independent country 2 urban areas / cities 3 social groups
   4 contact 5 yellow paint 6 (river) spirits 7 (terrifying) masks
   8 tourists 9 (the) government 10 natural

SPEAKING

1 1 B Students who have rested before an exam tend to do better. In addition, the language you need for the exam is very different from what you would hear in movies. What's more, by doing this you are practising listening, not speaking.
   2 B There is a big risk in memorising answers for the exam. It is highly unlikely you will be asked a question that corresponds exactly to what you memorised and the examiner will most likely realise what you are doing and this could lower your score.

3 G Many students are not aware of mistakes they make when they speak, but recording yourself gives you the chance to notice consistent errors and correct them.
   4 G Smiling makes you seem more confident and friendlier, and eye contact helps you focus on what the examiner is asking you, as you can see their body language. It also stops you mumbling (speaking unclearly).
   5 G You are already stressed on the day of the test, so don't add to this by risking being late.
   6 B Fluency is not just about speed, but also clarity. It is more important to speak clearly and accurately, so try not to rush your answers. Use phrases for buying time to allow you to think of good answers rather than saying the first thing that comes into your head.

2 *Sample answers*
   Good advice: Practise functions like comparing and contrasting, speaking hypothetically, speculating, and learn different language structures for these functions.
   The best way to improve your speaking is to speak more often, especially by doing practice tasks under test conditions.
   Don't panic if you make a mistake. One mistake will not ruin your overall score, and, if you realise, why not correct yourself so the examiner sees you realise the mistake?
   Bad advice: Ask other students who did the test recently what questions they answered, and learn your own answers by heart.
   Keep your answers short and your grammar simple so that you avoid mistakes?
   Don't ask the examiner any, questions, even if you are unsure what to do.
   Keep talking, even if you are not answering the question, because you want the examiner to hear your English.

3 1 b 2 d 3 e 4 a 5 f 6 c

4 *Sample answers*
   1 Furthermore, Nevertheless, Despite this, On the other hand, What's more, …
   2 In my view, To my mind, Clearly, The reason for this is …
   3 That's right. Not really.
   4 That's not an easy question to answer. Let me think …
   5 Could you explain what you mean? So what you're saying is …
   6 Sorry, I'll start again. I mean, …

7 1 call him 2 his identification 3 work/job 4 music 5 eclectic
   6 food 7 sweet food(s) / desserts / cheesecake, pancakes

8 1 future perfect: *I will have been at my company for three years in March*
   2 passive voice: *The problem is that my sleeping patterns are affected.*
   3 first conditional: *As soon as I get a Master's, I can become a manager and I think my work will be more varied and interesting*
   4 relative clauses: *and also I have music on my phone, which I listen to when I'm walking*
   5 second conditional: *I really wouldn't have time for such a big meal with my parents if I visited them during the week!*

9 *Sample answers*
   why it interests you: Neighbouring country but different, his city has a cathedral that used to be a mosque
   how you learnt about it: At school and he has been there
   what you know about it: Food is tasty, spicy and healthy, couscous and flat bread, stews cooked in tagine
   plans to visit this country: Casablanca in spring with friends
   Luis gives a very good performance. He covers all the points on the card and speaks for the correct amount of time. He also gives an appropriate answer to the examiner's follow-up question.

10 1 our neighbouring countries 2 it's worlds apart from
   3 a short boat ride away 4 dating back to my childhood
   5 I remember very vividly 6 made my mouth water
   7 cuisine 8 travel a little further afield

11 1 Two sub-topics: language and culture; culture and change
   2 So, do you think when we learn a language we need to learn the culture as well?
     But isn't there a culture associated with the language itself?
     Can you give me an example of that?
     Do you think globalisation has changed Spanish culture at all?

12

Showing agreement / disagreement	Giving examples	Buying time	Giving opinions	Explaining / clarifying
I wouldn't say so. to some extent it depends	Take Spanish, for example. such as	That's a good question. Let me think.	in my view Personally speaking Obviously	*Given this fact* The thing is I mean

14 1 everywhere 2 anyone 3 Someone 4 nothing 5 everybody
   6 something 7 anything 8 nowhere

15 *Sample answers*
   1 Everyone who visits my country loves the food.
   2 I am someone who is very dedicated to their career.
   3 Cultural difference is something that we all need to respect.
   4 Somewhere that I'd really love to visit is Argentina.
   5 I don't know anybody who doesn't use social media.

16 *Sample answers*
   2 I am someone who is very dedicated to their studies. This is because I understand the amount of money it cost my parents to get me to university. In addition, in today's world the job market is very competitive, so it is important to get the best grades possible in order to succeed in a future career.
   3 Cultural difference is something that we all need to respect. It can teach us different ways to look at the world we live in and understanding someone's culture can help you understand their opinions and beliefs.
   4 Somewhere that I'd love to visit is Argentina. It is a vast and fascinating country with amazing scenery and is very culturally diverse. In particular, I love the tango, a style of music and dance very specific to Argentina, and would love to see it in person.
   5 I don't know anybody who doesn't use social media. Even my grandparents use it to communicate with me.

LISTENING SCRIPTS

Unit 1 URBAN AND RURAL LIFE

LISTENING

4 & 5 ▐▌ 02

Guide: Ladies and gentlemen, welcome to the Museum of London Life. My name's Peter, and I'll be your guide, taking you through your exciting visit, which lasts for approximately ninety minutes, and traces the history of this vast and ever-changing city. But before we eventually arrive back here in the present, we begin our walk in ancient London, where we're going to take a look at life from the point of view of prehistoric men, women and children, looking at how they lived thousands of years ago, when all this around us was fields. At this point, London was little more than a few settlements dotted about here and there. Certainly nothing like the metropolis you see surrounding you today. So, from there, the walk allows you to see the city grow as you progress through the exhibits and take in the fascinating pieces of history that have been found and donated to the museum over the years – including maps, photos, images and thousands of other objects here. And finally, when we leave the part of the exhibition called 'Contemporary London', we'll move away from our present, here in the 21st century, and head off into the 22nd.

7 ▐▌ 03

Museum employee: Hello, the Museum of London Life. How can I help?

James: Oh, hi. I was wondering if you could send me some information. I've been looking on your website and can't seem to find what I need to know.

Museum employee: Certainly, sir. Can I take your name first of all?

James: Yes, it's James Graeme.

Museum employee: Ah, OK … so that's G-R-A-H-A-M, correct?

James: No, it's G-R-A-E-M-E.

Museum employee: OK, great. Got there in the end. So, how can I help?

James: Well, it says that I can print off some vouchers for reduced entry, but I haven't got a printer. Could you send me some through the post?

Museum employee: Sure. What's your address?

James: 16, Mount Hill Road, – that's M-O-U-N-T Hill Road, London, E15 2TP.

Museum employee: OK. Can I take a contact number for you for our records?

James: Yes, it's double 7-0, 3-6-4. Sorry, I mean double 7-0, 4-6-4.

Museum employee: OK, great. I'll get some vouchers sent out to you.

James: Thanks. Could you just clarify what the discount structure is?

Museum employee: Of course. So, for groups of four or more there's a ten percent discount applied. If you manage to get together a larger gang of people – ten or more, to be precise – then that figure goes up to 15 percent.

James: And what about students like me? Anything extra?

Museum employee: Yes, all students get that same 15 percent discount automatically, but in groups of four or more that goes up by another 5 percent to 20 percent. Would you be coming with friends?

James: No, I think the likelihood is that I'll be on my own. So how much exactly would that cost me for entry?

Museum employee: That's four twenty-five.

James: So with the discount that makes … three pounds sixty-one, doesn't it?

Museum employee: No, sorry, that price was with the discount already applied.

James: Oh, OK. And are there any special exhibitions at the moment? I'll book tickets for that as well today, provided there's something special that I'm particularly interested in.

Museum employee: There is, actually. You've just missed a really popular one that took in the Viking period, and coming up we've got the period known as 'The Industrial Revolution', but the one we're currently running is called 'Underground London', which looks at the tunnels, sewers and catacombs beneath the streets of the city.

James: Great! Ideally, I'd like to visit on my birthday, the 13th July.

Museum employee: Let me check … No, that's a Monday. We're closed on Mondays.

James: Ah, that's a shame. Never mind, I'll come the day before. Can I book over the phone now?

Museum employee: Certainly, so that's one student ticket for the 12th. Let me take your payment details.

10 & 11 ▐▌ 04

Museum employee: Your pre-printed ticket will be available to collect as soon as you arrive at the front desk.

James: So, I should bring my passport, then, for proof of ID?

Museum employee: People usually have a copy of their booking on their email, and they just show this on their smartphones and go straight through. But if, for some reason, you can't get any internet connection here, you obviously can't pull up your ticket details to show the museum assistant. But you'll get your tickets fine, as long as you can produce the payment card you bought the tickets with. That's the only ID we need to see.

James: Great. Well, thanks for all your help today. Anything you'd recommend personally? What do you like most about the museum?

Museum employee: One important thing is that the museum here has formed some extremely worthwhile partnerships with a wide range of local charities. In London, like any capital city, there are a lot of social problems, and the museum's help in reaching out to the world outside is greatly appreciated by so many. But what's so good for visitors – and is absolutely key for me – is that, as you walk through from one room to another, you always, always get a real sense of who has lived here over the years, and what sort of people they are, or have been. And that's really easy to do, because of the way the exhibition designers have connected each section to the next, with a real sense of development and design. It just flows so well from one room to the next. Better than any other museum I've been into, certainly.

James: Wow. You really like it there, don't you?

Museum employee: Absolutely. Unless something dramatic happens, I should be working here for a long time.

16 ▐▌ 05

You will hear a conversation between an employee at a removals company and a man who is planning to move to London.
First you have some time to look at questions 1 to 6.
[pause]
Now listen carefully and answer questions 1 to 6.

Woman: Good afternoon, We-Move-U, how can I help you?

Man: Hello, there. I'd like some help with my move to London. I'm currently living a long way away in the southwest of the UK. Is that an area you cover?

Woman: Yes, we cover all of the UK, so that's no problem. Can I take your name first, please?

Man: Yes, it's Mr David Cottenham.

Woman: C-O-T-N-A-M?

Man: No, it's C-O-T-T-E-N-H-A-M.

Woman: OK, Mr Cottenham, you said that you live in the southwest …

Man: Yes, at 4 West Cottages in Humblington. It's a small town near Exton. Well, it's more of a village really.

Woman: Mm-hm, and the postcode there, please, so I can look up exactly where you are?

Man: DV12 8HA.

Woman: OK, I've found your home on the system here. My goodness, that's very much in the countryside, isn't it?

Man: Yes, it is. London's going to be a bit of a shock for me. It's so crowded.

Woman: Well, it can be, but it depends where you live. What address are you moving to?

Man: 8b Greenend Road, E19 4RR. 'Greenend' is one word.

Woman: Well, that area's one of the quieter parts of London, at least. Not as busy as other places, certainly. When are you looking to move?

Man: 30th August.

Woman: That's good for us. People are on their summer holidays, children aren't at school … so there's less traffic on the roads. What sort of time are you thinking of leaving?

Man: Around half seven would be good.

Woman: That may be difficult, because our staff need a lot of time to pack your things into the lorry. They'll need to start in the middle of the night if you want to leave that early.

Man: No, no, I mean half seven in the evening.

Woman: Oh, I see. We can do that. And do you want to take out insurance, in case there's any damage to your property?

Man: Yes, I think so. I've looked at everything I own, and I think that it's all worth about £40,000 in total.

Woman: Shall we say a little bit more, just in case? I know you probably think it'll be much more expensive to take a higher amount, but the difference in what you pay for 40,000 or 50,000 in insurance is actually just a few pounds. It's £10 higher for 50,000, and £15 higher for 60,000.

Man: Yes, OK. Make it 50,000. No, on second thoughts 60,000. So, how much do you think the relocation will cost in total?

Woman: Let me check … I think we can do everything for approximately £2,000. That figure may change, of course – it's just an estimate for now – but it gives you a good idea of the price you'll have to pay.

Man: That's pretty good, actually. I was expecting a lot more.

Woman: Would you like to book now? Or shall I take your mobile number? I can call you back tomorrow, after you've had some time to think about it, maybe?

Man: Sure. It's 0-7-2-3-8-2 double 4-5-1-0.

Woman: Great. I'll speak to you tomorrow. And if you have any other questions, either call us back on the number you first dialled, or have a look at our website.

Man: What's the website address, please?

Woman: www-dot, we-hyphen-move-hyphen-u, (that's the *letter* u, not the *word* 'you') dot-co-dot-uk.

Man: OK, thanks for your help. I'll speak to you tomorrow.

Before you hear the rest of the conversation you have some time to look at questions 7 to 9.

[pause]

Now listen and answer questions 7 to 9.

Woman: Hello, Mr Cottenham, it's Maria here from We-Move-U. How are you?

Man: Oh, hi there. Yes, I'm very well. I've actually been thinking about our conversation yesterday. You said that the total cost of the package with insurance would be around £2,000. Does that insurance cover everything?

Woman: It depends what you mean by 'everything'. That's how much our 'Silver' package would cost, and as well as insurance for anything that gets broken or damaged, it also covers your costs if our delivery drivers are late getting to London.

Man: Are there any other packages?

Woman: Yes, our 'Economy' cover is the same as 'Silver', but without the cover for late arrival, and that would cost you around £1,800. Our 'Premium' package has the same insurance as 'Silver', but on top of that our removals team men come and pack all your things, put everything into boxes for you.

Man: And that's the 'Premium'? Hm, I guess that's quite a benefit. How much is that?

Woman: It would be £2,500 for this job. … So shall we agree on the 'Premium'?

Man: Hm … no, let's stick with 'Silver'. I'll have plenty of time to do the packing. Actually, I've been looking at some reviews of your company online. Generally very good – the thing that seems to impress most people is the cost.

Woman: Well, yes, I think most people are surprised by our low prices. Others believe that our level of customer care is the best thing about us, and I've also seen some reviews where people are most impressed by how quickly we complete the job. I agree with everything they say, of course, but *I'm* probably most proud of our reputation for customer care and satisfaction.

Man: Great. Well, I think that's everything. Oh, one final question – once I make the booking, will I have to pay more if I need to make any changes?

Woman: In most cases, there's nothing extra that you'll need to pay once your initial payment is completed. Unless, that is, you decide to cancel the booking completely – in that case, there will be a charge of 10 percent of the total fee if you cancel less than 15 days before the date of the move. And if you need to *move* the date, for any reason, we'll usually do that for a very low cost.

Man: Fantastic. Great. Well, I think I'm ready to book.

SPEAKING

4 06

Examiner: In this first part of the exam, I'd like to ask you some questions about yourself. Let's talk about where you live. Do you live in a house or an apartment?

Candidate 1: Apartment. It's a small apartment in the centre of my home town, but it's still bigger than the apartment I live in now. My apartment now is just one room, really. I used to live in a huge apartment, but it was my parents' apartment and it was time for me to go to university. I left, found a place. And that's the apartment where I live now.

Examiner: What do you like about the area where you live?

Candidate 2: I used to live in Guangzhou, the capital city of Guangdong Province in south-eastern China. Once an important stop-off point on the Maritime Silk Road, Guangzhou maintains to this day its importance as a major port and transportation hub.

Examiner: Do you often visit parks in your city?

Candidate 3: Actually, I have gone to my local park last week. I've really enjoyed it. I have a friend, he never been to my town, so yesterday we have decided to go together next week. We will go on next Tuesday, I think. As soon as we will finish class, we will go.

6 07

Candidate: So, I'm going to tell you about a town in the Lake District, which is a beautiful region in the northwest of England, pretty close to the border of Scotland. There are dozens of fantastic little villages and towns there, but the one that tops the rest is called Windermere. It sits on a huge lake and is surrounded by hills, trees and rocks. I've been lots of times already, and I can't wait to go back – as soon as I finish the second semester at university, I'm going to head up there again.

Being far up in the north, as you can imagine, it can get pretty cold in Windermere, particularly in winter. Too cold for some. Having said that, there's a real stark beauty to the town at that time, when your breath comes out like mist, and the streets get white with the snow that falls. Summer is the opposite extreme – it can actually get pretty warm, comfortable enough to wear just a t-shirt and shorts – but if you wanted to visit at that time, you'd have to get yourself prepared for all the tourists. Other times? Autumn is pretty, I've been told, but I tend to visit in spring.

I go every year, just me; I have to say that I generally prefer not to go with anyone else. For one thing, you can make friends really easily if you stay in a hostel. There are young people from all over the world who make it their mission to spend a few days or a week there. As I say, it's an ideal place to go hiking or hill-walking, so that's the priority for me and for hundreds of others. There's also a really interesting variety of independent local shops, selling everything from cheap souvenirs to galleries full of extremely expensive art. When I go back, I'm going to do what I always do – browse through the shops after a long day walking in the countryside.

7 & 10 08

Candidate: *(Answer 1)* For a number of reasons. Often, I think, because they are exhausted; capital cities in particular can be very demanding places to live – the noise, the traffic, the cost of living – and people often grow tired of all that. It's just too over the top for some. They start to feel drawn to the peace and quiet that rural life might be able to give them. Generally speaking, though, I do think that it's the case that younger people – people like me – are more drawn to that vibrant, city lifestyle. As soon as you get older and have a family, you start thinking it's time to move.

(Answer 2) Well, one possibility that I can foresee is that buildings will keep getting taller and taller. This has been going on for some time, all over the world, and so many people now are moving to the city. Unless this changes, we're going to need more and more homes for everyone. We might even see a 500-storey skyscraper one day. That might sound ridiculous now, but cities are likely to keep expanding at the rate they are currently, so there will be no other option that I can think of.

(Answer 3) Oh, I think that would be a bit of a disaster, to be honest. Insisting that everyone uses public transport could create more problems than currently exist. Fine, if you were just visiting the city, it probably wouldn't bother you too much, but if you were a resident there … then again, the streets would be safer for pedestrians. And it might do something about the levels of pollution. I do think it is bound to happen, to be honest. So, as long as people are happy to use buses and bikes instead of their cars, life will continue as normal.

(Answer 4) I can understand why people want a huge, old-fashioned house. In a similar way to living in the middle of the bright lights of the big city, there's something quite romantic about it. Having said that, I do think it depends on your age. Most people of my age, for example, prefer the idea of coming home to a smart, modern apartment every day, high up in the sky, overlooking the city, well – it just sounds amazing. Providing I make enough money, I'll definitely be on a top floor myself one day.

(Answer 5) Well, in the old days, your whole life was in one place. You married someone from the same town, you had a job in the same village, and your family stayed around you. In some places, life is still like that – people only need to go next door or downstairs to see their parents, for example – but after people were given the opportunity to move around from one town to another, on trains or even aeroplanes, the traditional family unit started to change, I think, and people are now much more spread out. Not just nationally, but internationally. By the time I'm a grandparent, I think it will be even more different.

12, 14 & 15 09

A As long as people are happy to use buses and bikes instead of their cars, life will continue as normal.

B By the time I'm a grandparent, I think it will be even more different.

C Providing I make enough money, I'll definitely be on a top floor myself one day.

D As soon as you get older and have a family, you start thinking it's time to move.

E Unless this changes, we're going to need more and more homes for everyone.

Unit 2   HEALTH

LISTENING

6 10

Recording 1

Well, good afternoon, ladies and gentlemen, and welcome to the tour today. It's great to see that so many people out there are as fascinated as I am by the astonishing achievements of our great Olympic athletes. My name is Tom, and I'll be taking you through the exhibition and pointing out particular areas of interest. We'll begin with a bang, with many people's favourite event, the Men's 100m sprint …

Recording 2

Good morning, everyone. Welcome to your introductory science lecture. We'll begin the course by looking at some of the most vital discoveries in medical history. Why would I do this? Why, when so much of science is about looking into the future? Well, if it wasn't for the discovery in 1928 of penicillin …

Recording 3

Man: Good evening, Camgate Sports Centre. How can I help?

Woman: Oh, hello. I'm ringing to enquire about some of the classes you run. I've just moved into the area and I'd like to find out more.

Man: Of course. Is there a particular day or class you're interested in?

Woman: Yes, I was wondering if you have any aerobics classes …

8 11

Claude: Hi, I was wondering if you could help me. This is my first week here and I'd like to find out about any societies that could be good for me.

Woman: Of course. Well, we have literally hundreds of socs here – 'soc' is often what we call societies. What sort of thing are you interested in joining?

Claude: I'm really into health and fitness.

Woman: Oh, there are a number of socs that might suit you. Let's start with the ones closest to where we're standing now. A12, that's where you'll find the Vegetarian Soc, which is run by Paul, and two rooms along you'll be able to find Peter, who's in charge of the Vegan Soc, so that's in A14. Peter and Paul are actually brothers. Both of them are really nice.

Claude: I don't think either of those socs are for me – I like meat too much, I'm afraid.

Woman: Maybe the Healthy Eating Soc then? If you go down the corridor and past the library, then you'll come to room <u>C16</u>, where you'll find Catherine, who can fill you in about their events and activities.

Claude: Thanks, I may well do that. But you mentioned fitness – that's more like the kind of thing I'm looking for. What about societies for doing some sort of cardiovascular exercise?

Woman: All of the main types of exercise are covered here. What exactly are you looking for? Cycling, rowing, swimming?

Claude: Mm, none of those are really my kind of thing – I'm more of a runner.

Woman: In that case, definitely head for the gym. Go through the main building, and on your way you'll probably see the Push and Pull Soc, but if I were you, I'd steer clear of that. The people in it are all a bit weird. So carry on past them and you'll find Sarah, who runs the <u>Hot Air</u> Soc.

Claude: Sounds intriguing. What do they do – organise races and running events?

Woman: They do, yes, and other sports as well, like rowing in the inter-university boat races. That's a lot of fun. The whole university turns out to support them. But if it's only running that you want to do, go and see the Road Running Soc out in the car park. The person running their stall today is Siobhan. I'll spell that for you – it's an old Irish name – S-I-O-B-H-A-N.

Claude: Never heard that one before. Great. Well that should keep me busy, lots of interesting stands to visit.

Woman: Yes, there's so much to choose from.

13 ▦ 12

Claude: Hi, are you … Siobhan? My name's Claude. I was told to come and talk to you about the Road Running Soc? So you must be the president, I suppose.

Siobhan: Actually no, I'm standing in for her today. I can probably answer any questions you have, but if you need to contact the president you can look her up in the Contacts section of your college email account. Her first name is Claire – <u>C-L-A-I-R-E</u>.

Claude: And her surname?

Siobhan: Her surname's Enwark. <u>E-N-W-A-R-K</u>.

Claude: OK, thanks. … So, first of all, what sort of distance do people usually run each week?

Siobhan: Well, on average, if you take into consideration all of our members, probably 10 kilometres – or, as we say it, 10K – a week, and 20 over a <u>fortnight</u>. That said, it's not unusual for a road runner to cover 20K each week.

Claude: Great. I like to push myself, so hopefully I can keep up with them all. Do you take part in any organised races?

Siobhan: Yes, we do. We've done 10Ks in London, 5Ks in Cambridge, a marathon in Newcastle. <u>The most recent was a 10K</u> in <u>Manchester</u>. The race before that was in Oxford. Both went really well, we got some amazing times.

Claude: And do you have a team kit?

Siobhan: We do, actually. It's white with a dark blue stripe. Well, it *has* been, but we're changing it for this year. Someone recently pointed out that the university colours are white and pale blue, so this year we're going to keep the same design but have <u>a pale blue stripe</u> instead.

Claude: Well, they're my favourite colours, so I've got to join now. How much does it cost to become a member?

Siobhan: To cover the cost of your vest, there's a one-off signing-on fee of £15. You can begin your annual membership at any point after that, and once you start, you can either pay monthly or <u>you can pay for the</u> <u>full year in a single payment. That's £50</u>, but if you find that too expensive the monthly fee is £5, which is taken directly out of your bank account.

14 ▦ 13

You will hear a student, Claude, asking for information about the Healthy Eating Society. First you have some time to look at questions 1 to 5.

[pause]

Now listen carefully and answer questions 1 to 5.

Claude: Hello, is that the Healthy Eating Soc?

Catherine: Yes, it is, Catherine speaking. How can I help?

Claude: I was given one of your leaflets and am interested in joining. I know you go out for dinner twice a week, but what else do you do?

Catherine: Well, we don't do anything on Sundays, Mondays or Tuesdays, but every Wednesday is our first restaurant visit of each week. It's not always the same place – sometimes we'll go to *The Red Tomato*, other times we go to *Herbs and Flowers* – but <u>it's always</u> <u>somewhere that serves vegetarian food</u>. We meet at half past seven on the High Street.

Claude: Sounds good. What about Thursdays?

Catherine: Well, on Thursdays, we usually go off to my aunt's house. She lends us her kitchen and we all prepare a meal together – a big curry, or something. There's a limit of twelve people, so you need to put your name down. We get there for eight o'clock. She lives in <u>Wednesford</u>, so you'll need money for the bus fare.

Claude: Wednesford? That's funny, it's like, 'When's the food?'

Catherine: Ha! No, it's spelt W-E-D-N-E-S-F-O-R-D. It's a village a few miles out of town. Anyway, Friday is our other restaurant evening, not vegetarian this time. We usually meet around 6 o'clock in a juice bar, and once everyone has arrived, we'll head off to a fantastic restaurant in town that serves European food. <u>We always sit down to</u> <u>eat at 7.00</u>.

Claude: And that's in town, is it?

Catherine: It's right in the centre, so you get the bus to Central Square, which is where the juice bar is. It's right next to the little theatre. <u>The</u> <u>restaurant we go to is round the corner in the covered market</u>. It's opposite the cinema.

Claude: OK, I think I've got that. And do you do anything over the weekend?

Catherine: Not a lot. It gets busy in town on a Saturday night, so the only thing we do is <u>meet at midday for what we call Coffee Club</u>, just in the canteen in the Students' Union. They do good pastries.

Before you hear the rest of the conversation you have some time to look at questions 6 to 10.

[pause]

Now listen and answer questions 6 to 10.

Claude: Well, it all sounds lots of fun. How much does it cost to join?

Catherine: It depends. If you go to all of the activities every week – believe me, I know – it can cost you around £40 or more. I originally thought about charging people something like £5 per week as a membership fee, but it takes so much time to collect that it's not worth it. So <u>it's actually free to be a member</u>.

Claude: Mm, £40 is a bit above my budget.

Catherine: Oh, don't worry. You don't have to come to everything, and you don't have to come every week. It's entirely up to you.

Claude: How long do you usually take to have dinner?

Catherine: <u>We're usually in a restaurant for two hours having dinner</u>, so the whole evening lasts about three hours, if you include the drink in the juice bar beforehand.

Claude: And what about the service charge at the end of a meal? Do people in this country usually give something extra for the waiters?

Catherine: In general, people often leave a tip of about 12–15% of the total bill. On the other hand, if the service or the food has been bad, they may leave nothing. <u>We always try to make sure we give our</u> <u>waiters 10%</u>. We'd like to give them 15 or 20%, but we're not very rich. We're only students, after all.

Claude: So how do I book a place on these trips? Shall I give you a call?

Catherine: No, I don't always answer my phone. Some of our members send me a text message, which is fine, but I get so many that I might forget yours. The most reliable way to contact me is to send an email.

Claude: Great. So is there anything else I need to know?

Catherine: No, I don't think so. Oh, there is one more thing. It's really important.

Claude: What's that?

Catherine: Well, a lot of the people have very strong opinions about which is the best restaurant in town, which is the best national dish, which country has the best cooks. All of those things are fine, but if you want to fit in with the group, try to avoid talking about celebrity chefs. That's when the arguments really start!

SPEAKING

3 ▥ 14

Examiner: How can people be encouraged to do more exercise?

Candidate 1: Well, it's not an easy thing to do. Um, I tend to think that, you know, if people don't want to exercise of their own volition, they're certainly not going to, not really, make a concerted effort simply because the, er, the government or whoever has issued some sort of advertising campaign to get people going. What's more, there's a general, kind of, lack of facilities that makes this possible. It's, it's … Having said that, it's not really an option to simply do nothing. People are getting bigger on average, all over the world, and the health implications for that are, well, extremely serious. So, really, I'm not sure exactly how we could do it … um, but it's something that is getting quite pressing these days.

Examiner: How can people be encouraged to do more exercise?

Candidate 2: It's not an easy thing to do, it's not an easy thing to do, it's genuinely difficult and I tend to think that if people don't want to exercise of their own volition, they're certainly not going to make a concerted effort simply because it's difficult, or if the government or an authority of the government has issued some sort of advertising campaign to get people going. It's not an easy thing to do if you just have the government there insisting, it's really quite difficult and what's more, I have to add something here, furthermore, there's a general lack of facilities that make this possible. So, of course it's not an easy thing to do but having said that, there's not really an option to simply do nothing just because it's a difficult thing to do. People are getting bigger on average all over the world and the health implications for that are extremely serious. Maybe it's too difficult to do, maybe it's not for the government at all, I'm not sure exactly how we could do it, but it's something that's getting quite pressing these days.

4 ▥ 15

Examiner: How often do you eat healthy meals?

Candidate 1: I'm very much a sociable type of person, so whether I'm eating at a restaurant or at home, as long as there's company around me – could be with friends, could be with family, could be both – personally, I tend not to notice too much where I am and I'll eat pretty much anything.

Candidate 2: Well, there's a lot of pressure these days on people to eat the right sort of things. However, it seems like every day there are new pieces of conflicting advice from the government, or from doctors, about what we should and shouldn't be eating, so who actually knows? For example, one week there's a study telling us chocolate is bad for us and then the next week, there's another which says it's good for us. I try to eat healthy food when I can, but I think it depends on what you mean by 'healthy'.

Candidate 3: It depends what you mean by 'healthy', but I try to keep my intake of junk food down to a minimum. And most days I make sure that I have at least some fruit and vegetables, even if it isn't as much as I should. Also, because I'm young and in relatively good shape, I don't worry about my diet too much at the moment, to be honest.

6 ▥ 16

Examiner: How do you like to relax?

Candidate 1: If I had to choose, I'd say that I most like to sink into the sofa, put my feet up and lose myself in a good movie. The thing is, I've got a lot of pressure on at the moment, as I'm in my final year of study, so I really need time to switch off. Watching a film helps me to forget that pressure for a while.

Examiner: How do you like to relax?

Candidate 2: If I had to choose, I'd say that I most like to sink into the sofa, put my feet up and lose myself in a good movie. On top of that, in an ideal world, if I wanted to relax completely, I'd switch my phone off, settle down and have something delicious to eat, say a pizza or popcorn. That way I can really start to unwind.

Examiner: How do you like to relax?

Candidate 3: If I had to choose, I'd say that I most like to sink into the sofa, put my feet up and lose myself in a good movie. In particular, films directed by Ang Lee, whose work I've always admired. So if I could relax in any way I could choose, it would be watching something of his, I'd say.

Examiner: How do you like to relax?

Candidate 4: If I had to choose, I'd say that I most like to sink into the sofa, put my feet up and lose myself in a good movie. That said, I can only do that at weekends currently. I've got far too much study to do during the week, so I tend to leave the films for the weekend as a reward for finishing everything on time.

8 ▥ 17

Examiner: What reasons do people have for becoming vegetarian?

Candidate: What motivates people to stop eating meat? Usually, on the grounds that they object in some way to animals being kept simply as food, often in really unhealthy surroundings. I think it's a moral decision that people take. They just decide to avoid meat completely. And some people, to build on my point a little more, go even further and become vegan. They don't agree with the idea of animals being killed for food, or for making people's clothes, or even for dairy products. Looking at it from another point of view, other people give up meat purely for the sake of their health. Take red meat as an example. There's a great deal of evidence to suggest that it causes all sorts of health issues, and people in general are increasingly trying to limit how much they eat. Ultimately, I suppose, it's a question of health – either of the animal or of yourself.

Unit 3   ART AND ARCHITECTURE

LISTENING

5 ▥ 18

Welcome to Westchester Castle, everyone. I know some of you have come a long way today, so I hope you will enjoy your time with us. Westchester Castle dates back to the 11th century and was home to the Westchester family until the 19th century, when it was donated to the National Trust. We are now standing at the main entrance. As you will have seen, the castle is rectangular-shaped, with four turrets, or towers, one at each corner. So, as we enter, you'll see on your left the Grand Hall, where balls were held when the family lived here. If you walk through the Grand Hall, you can see one of the four turrets in the corner. You'll see that it's now a gift shop, though it used to be Lord Westchester's bedroom. It has a magnificent view of the aviary, where the birds are kept. You will have plenty of time to purchase your souvenirs there after the tour.

6 & 7 📊 19

Now as we move out of the Grand Hall, notice this wonderful spiral staircase in front of you. It's not in use any more due to health and safety reasons, but at one time that was the only way to get to the upper level. Now we have a lift, situated just down the hallway. If you would like to follow me, we will move straight ahead into the Exhibition Room. At the moment, as you can see, there's a fascinating exhibition of clothes from the 15th and 16th centuries, which you can spend some time looking at later. Now please turn to your left and cross this little anteroom to enter <u>the next turret, which is the portrait gallery</u>. Here you can see portraits of all the Westchester lords and ladies through the ages.

8 📊 20

Right, I hope you've had enough time to look at those fantastic portraits. Please follow me back into the Exhibition space. We're going to cross this room and you'll see that this corner of the castle is almost a mirror image of the Portrait gallery, so again we're going to go through a little anteroom into the turret. You can see that this room has been designed to look like a room from the 14th century. All the furniture and even the drapes and tapestries are authentic. Can you guess what this room was used for? A sitting room? No. Well, people did sit in here, but only the ladies. <u>This was the sewing room!</u> It has the best light in the castle. That's why it was used for this purpose.

Next to us is the library, but we can't access it through here. We need to go back through the Exhibition Room and out into the hallway. The library has some ancient manuscripts which are really valuable; that's why you can only look through the door and not enter. But if you keep going, back towards the main entrance, there's a room you *can* enter on your left. This was <u>the dining room, situated next to the kitchens,</u> which I suppose makes sense.

9 & 10 📊 21

OK, so now you've had a look around inside, I'd like to tell you a little about the architecture of the castle building. Westchester Castle has its origins in the 11th century but it was unrecognisable as the castle we see before us. <u>It was not until the 12th century that living quarters were added</u>. The castle was owned by the Westchester family from the 13th to the 19th centuries.

11 & 12 📊 22

As you probably know, the aim of a castle was to provide a secure base against attack. It needed to be easy to defend, while preventing exposure to the attackers. It had to have thick, high walls and a secure entry gate. Westchester, like other medieval castles, would have had a drawbridge at the main point of entry, but sadly, it is no longer standing. <u>The four turrets – the round towers at the corners – remain in a remarkably well-preserved state</u> for such an ancient castle. You can see that there used to be a moat – another vital defence against invaders – but now all you see around the building is a dry ditch.

13 📊 23

The castle would have had <u>storerooms</u> in the basement to store enough food for many months in case of a siege. Unfortunately, we are no longer able to enter the basement area as it's not safe, but we know that there are underground <u>tunnels</u> used for escape and for making sorties, or attacking raids, against the enemy. This castle is unusual in that there has been no evidence found of <u>dungeons</u> – underground prison cells. Perhaps they never took any prisoners!

15 📊 24

You will hear a tour guide giving information about a historic house and the organisation that owns it. First you have some time to look at questions 1 to 6.

[pause]

Now listen carefully and answer questions 1 to 6.

As you know, Holloway Estate is one of the few surviving estates in this area that still retains many of the farming features of the past. Let me quickly explain where you can find some of the key attractions.

If you take a look on your map, we are now standing at the foot of the steps to the Manor House. Can everyone see it, marked with an arrow? Don't forget – this is our meeting point for when we leave. So, directly behind us is the fountain. From here, heading left, the path takes you to a gate which leads into the famous Holloway orchards, where for hundreds of years the estate has been growing its highly prized apples, cherries and plums. Incidentally, if you fancy trying them, a range of delicious Holloway jams and preserves are available in the gift shop. <u>Speaking of which, the gift shop is to the right of the main house.</u> <u>If you go through the gate, the left-hand path takes you to the apiary, that's to say, the bee hives,</u> where Holloway honey has been collected for more than 250 years. And yes, before anyone asks, you can also buy Holloway honey.

If you take the right-hand path, you will come to some old farmer's cottages which have been renovated and <u>are rented out as holiday cottages</u>. Please feel free to admire them from the outside, but as there may be guests staying in them right now, please respect their privacy.

From the back of the main house, crossing the car park and just before you get to the cattle fields, you will find a row of three buildings. <u>The middle one is the old dairy</u>. The dairy is actually working, producing butter and cheeses using traditional methods. Next to that, on the left are the former cattle sheds, where the livestock was kept. <u>Nowadays it's used as a museum</u>, so those of you who are keen to explore Holloway's farming past should pay it a visit. The building furthest from the manor house is the old ice house, which is no longer in use and is due to be restored, hopefully next year.

Last but not least, you may have noticed on the way in that on either side of the main gates are two small houses. This is a traditional feature of country houses of the period. <u>On the right-hand side as you enter the estate is what was known as the gatekeeper's lodge. This has now become the estate office.</u> This has now become the estate office, and the estate manager runs the estate from there. OK, I think that just about covers everything …

Before you hear the rest of the talk you have some time to look at questions 7 to 10.

[pause]

Now listen and answer questions 7 to 10.

OK, everyone, before we begin the tour of the Manor House, I'd like to take a few minutes to tell you about the organisation that now owns the estate, and for which I work – the National Trust. The National Trust is the largest membership organisation in the UK with 4.24 million members. Our annual revenue is £494 million. At the present time, we have 5,899 paid members of staff <u>and an additional 62,000 volunteers</u>. That's an approximate number because new volunteers are joining us all the time.

The Trust owns about 350 heritage properties. Many of these are large country houses that the owners donated to us because they could no longer afford to maintain them. The Trust also owns gardens and industrial monuments. The Trust's sources of income include membership subscriptions, entrance fees, donations and revenue from the gift shops and restaurants within our properties, with much of the money raised being invested back in the preservation of the properties themselves. And of course, <u>this is the principal purpose of the National Trust: the conservation and protection of historical places and spaces,</u> with a view to making them available to the public.

As well as owning stately homes and houses associated with famous people, the National Trust has gradually extended its collection of art, and it also owns valuable books, clothing, furniture, ceramics and all kinds of unusual objects.

Now if you would like to join the National Trust, I have the forms here, or you can visit our website, and join online. You will get unlimited access to hundreds of wonderful days out across the country. Lifetime membership costs £1,555, but most members join for a year at a time. Individual membership is currently £64 annually but it's cheaper to join with your partner or another family member as it'll be £108 for two people living at the same address. For a family of four (two adults and two children) a year's membership costs £114. It's a great gift for a birthday or other special event. There are lots of benefits to being a member. As well as free parking at all our locations, you receive a National Trust handbook full of information to help you plan your visits, and if you pay by direct debit, you'll receive a free pair of binoculars. Oh, I almost forgot, all members receive a free copy of the National Trust magazine sent to you by post three times a year.

SPEAKING

4 25

The creative person I have chosen is Salvador Dalí. I visited the Dalí Foundation in Figueres last year, and it made a great impression on me. He was born in Catalunya in Spain, I'm not sure of the exact year but I think maybe around 1904 and he died in about the late 1980s, when he was in his 80s. He was a surrealist painter, so he used symbolism a lot. What that means is in his paintings things don't look like what they are. One of his most famous paintings is called *The Persistence of Memory* and it shows watches or clocks that are very soft, which is supposed to show that time is not as most people understand it. He was fascinated by Maths and Science, and so am I, so that is one reason why I like him. Another reason is that he was quite unconventional – and even eccentric in his behaviour, so that makes him an interesting character, who was not like other people. The same is true of his art. And what's more, he didn't just stick with painting. Later in his life he did sculpture and worked on film sets. So, to put it in a nutshell, I like the fact that he was innovative and totally different from others. Oh, and one more thing, the colours in his work are amazing, so they're good to hang on your walls – not the originals of course! His work makes me feel proud because he's from my country – from my region, actually, and he brought fame to Catalunya.

13 & 14 26

For my creative person, I'm going to talk about the British artist David Hockney. So, I'll start by saying that he was born somewhere in the North of England, possibly Yorkshire, but I'm not 100% sure about that. I'd say he was born in about the 1930s as he's still alive today but he's getting on a bit. OK, so moving on to talk about his art. He's a modern artist and he was part of the Pop Art movement. As well as a painter, he's a photographer and printmaker, so he's pretty versatile. He paints country scenes and for some reason he used to love painting swimming pools. So why do I like him? Primarily, it's because of the colours he uses. His paintings are so bright and cheerful. They show real things you can recognise; yet they have a modern feel. Lots of modern art is so abstract, you have no idea what it's supposed to be, but Hockney is different. Finally, when I see Hockney's paintings, I feel happy and relaxed. I feel as if it's warm and sunny. I suppose it's that feel-good factor that makes me like him so much. So, that's about it.

Unit 4   FINANCE AND BUSINESS

LISTENING

6 27

Good afternoon, everyone. Today, the next in our series of lectures on the development of currency, we are going to focus on how and why there was such growth in ancient trade and commerce: the arrival of a physical, portable means of payment. I'm going to give you a brief overview of what type of currency was first used, and describe how it developed later in the form of coins.

Now, going back thousands of years, you might imagine that precious stones were the first form of currency, but these were not found in sufficient numbers at that time. We do though have firm evidence of sea shells being used as a primitive form of money. They were very much valued items at the time, and were perfect for trade. They were taken in vast quantities along the great trade routes, and I'm sure you can imagine how significantly they enabled these civilisations to grow as a result.

For now, let's move on to a time when we first find precious metals and minerals being used in the form of coins. Now, there's some debate as to when and where this happened, but it seems to have taken place at some point around the 7th century BC in and around Greece and the Middle East. In the past, archaeologists believed that the first coins were made from pure gold, or artificial mixtures or alloys, but we can now be sure that they were actually produced from a substance known as electrum, an alloy that occurs naturally, and is a blend of gold and silver. Meanwhile, thousands of miles away to the east, the Chinese appear to have had the same idea at the same time. While those in Greece and the Middle East were busy forging coins from electrum, their contemporaries in China had the same idea of creating coins to use as currency, but with a completely different manufacturing process. For years prior to this, the Chinese had used paper money made from white deerskin, but now they turned to casts and moulds, into which they poured liquid bronze and left it to set, eventually forming coins. If we were to look at examples of these coins, we would see that there was some variety in their shape – some looked like little spades, but the vast majority resembled knife blades. There is intricate decoration on each surface, demonstrating magnificent workmanship.

8 28

Moving forward from the 7th century, and 400 years later, we meet Shi Huangdi, one of the first emperors of China. Sometime around the year 220 BC he took these early forms of currency and simplified them into more basic coins of a circular shape with a distinctive square hole in the middle. Its design reflected a number of Chinese beliefs. For example, the round shape symbolised heavenly commandment, while the square symbolised the authority of the emperor. Some historians suggest that these types of coin had been invented hundreds of years before and that Shi Huangdi's coins were derived from ring-shaped jade discs from the Zhou dynasty, which are believed to have been used as royal gifts for dignitaries. Whatever the case, we know that Shi Huangdi decreed his new coins as the only legal currency in his empire and perhaps this is the secret of their longevity; they survived for over two thousand years. The coins themselves were fashioned of gold and bronze and weighed around 8 grams, though this varied as time went by. Sadly, one thing these coins did not retain was the elaborate design of earlier coins. Instead Shi Huangdi's coin was more functional and could be made in a short space of time. In fact, it can be argued that in order to do this, Shi Huangdi created an early model of what eventually became mass production, though of course a cruder and less efficient version of what we see today. But an interesting thought nonetheless.

10 29

In your previous talks, you have looked at coins and then the rise of bank notes as the form of currency. Now today I'd like to briefly cover the idea of bank note security. I thought that the 2017 introduction of a new £5 note in the UK would provide a great example of how banks are fighting against fake or counterfeit money.

Now you may already know that the newer note is not as large as the previous one, 15 % less to be exact, and is made of a durable polymer, sometimes referred to as 'plastic', which will give the note a longer life and make the note harder to copy. On the left-hand part of the note there are three security elements of particular interest: a small portrait of the Queen, … the Elizabeth Tower, with Big Ben, … and lastly a pound sign which changes from purple to green depending on the angle you look at it. All these are incorporated on a see-through window.

In addition, the image of the Elizabeth Tower shows as gold coloured on the front of the note, but on the back of the note it is silver.

Directly below this is a kind of hologram. It's a silver patch which shows either the word 'five' or the word 'pounds' depending on how you look at it.

And above the Elizabeth Tower is a similar feature, but this one shows the coronation crown in three dimensions, and produces a rainbow effect when viewed at certain angles.

Interestingly, on the back of the note this patch shows the word 'Blenheim', but the metal foil here, that's to say, the metal that forms the patch, is green.

Last but not least, is something you cannot see, well, at least not under normal conditions. In the top-middle section of the note, the number 5 will appear in the white triangular shape underneath the words 'Bank of England', but only when viewed under UV or ultra-violet light.

Most bank notes these days have similar features and …

12 🎚 30

You will hear part of a lecture about the history of locks. First you have some time to look at questions 1 to 10.

[pause]

Now listen carefully and answer questions 1 to 10.

Good afternoon, ladies and gentlemen, and welcome back, as we continue our lecture series on currency, from ancient times to the modern day. For today's talk, we're going to discuss a need that emerged from an age-old, negative side to human nature. When wealth is portable – particularly when it can be easily compressed into thousands of individual items of coinage – it inevitably becomes more attractive to a certain group of people. Even in ancient times, the wealthy, people of status, traders and so on, realised that, to discourage thieves, their money would need to be either hidden or protected. And to do that, they had a choice. They could either keep their riches safe by keeping them in temples which were guarded twenty-four hours a day, or they could find a way to store their assets somewhere closer to home, where access was more convenient. And so the ancient Egyptians came up with a locking device. This was a mechanism similar to what is known today as a dead bolt that required the insertion of a key. The key operated a series of pins, and allowed a long metal bolt to be withdrawn from its locking position, which in turn gave the owner access to their valuables. How long ago did this happen? We're a little vague on this, but definitely at some point later than 4,000 BC . Since the Egyptians wanted their locks to be very strong, these locks suffered from one notable problem – their size. Some of the bigger examples we have found are over half a metre long, and weigh around 30 kilos.

The Romans later adapted these Egyptian locks to make them more functional and available for use in regular homes. They took the Egyptians' designs, made them smaller, and added their own inspired invention, one that enabled them to create a more sophisticated locking system: steel springs. One negative side-effect they did suffer from was that, by using a spring instead of a bolt, it was relatively easy for a particularly dedicated and powerful thief to damage or remove the lock using brute force. However, the Roman locking mechanisms made it difficult to actually *force the lock open*, thanks to their precise construction. For their time, it's hard not to be impressed by such technology.

[short pause]

The examples we have talked about so far are key-based locks, but next I'd like to look at a variation on this – the combination lock. The combination lock is the basis of many modern safes. As we will see, the combination lock shares many features of those used by the Egyptians and Romans.

For the purposes of this explanation I'll begin by looking at a combination padlock, which is easy to grasp.

One of the most important aspects of any locking system is protecting the lock itself. In the case of the padlock, there's a secure outer casing to protect the delicate lock mechanism inside. This casing is usually constructed from a hard metal, such as brass. Having this strong outer casing prevents a potential thief from simply breaking the padlock with a tool, such as a hammer.

The main moveable part of the lock, the part which opens and closes, is a strong bar, often made of reinforced or galvanised steel. As you can see, the bar is curved, almost u-shaped, but much longer on one side. At the end of this longer side is a metal spring, which is pushed down when the padlock is locked.

So how is a combination lock unlocked? The metal bar has four pins on it, which prevent it from being opened. However, each of the pins can be released by moving a combination dial. These are circular and numbered from 0 – 9. Move all the dials into the correct position, and the spring is released, forcing the lock to open.

Now that is a very simple combination lock. The lock of a safe, on the other hand …

SPEAKING

2 & 3 🎚 31

Examiner: What qualities would you say are needed to become a successful businessperson?

Candidate: I'm not sure there's an easy answer to that one. There's so much to being successful. For example, you can't just come up with an idea for a new product and then sell it. You have to be sure that people will actually want it, so it's vital to do a good deal of market research and spend time on product development, so you can correct all the potential problems first. Then you can devise a plan to launch the product into the market place. But I suppose, yes, some people are just naturally gifted in seeing new business opportunities, and will always make a profit because they understand their target market – you know, the people who the product is aimed at – because, after all, customer satisfaction is key in anything like that. Having said that, it's not just the creative qualities that are enough; the other stuff is also necessary, like having good time management skills, keeping a close eye on sales figures, being able to close the deal, knowing when to apply for a loan or even, if things go badly, how to avoid having to file for bankruptcy because you owe too much money to too many other companies.

4 🎚 32

Examiner: Why has online shopping become so popular with so many people?

Candidate: To be honest, I understand why people like it, but I'm not sure why it holds so much appeal. I suppose the main reason must be that it's so easy and convenient. You can just relax at home, at work, wherever you are, and do your shopping. Plus, there's very little you can't buy on the internet – and, above all else, once you've paid, it quickly gets delivered to your door without having to deal with the hassle of going to a busy high street. So there are plenty of real plus points to online shopping. But, for me, there's no substitute for heading to the store itself and having a look at whatever it is you're thinking of buying. Also, you have the sales assistants to talk to, and they can point you in the right direction.

6 🎚 33

Examiner: Why do some people have problems managing their personal finances?

Candidate: I suspect it might be because it has become so easy to get credit from banks: credit cards, overdrafts, whatever it is you might need. Of course, there are a number of real plus points to this – you can buy whatever you want more quickly, and you don't have to pay the loan off until later, so I do see why it holds so much appeal. And online banking has actually made it easier to do this without having to deal with the hassle of going into the branch and standing in a queue for ever. There's very little you can't do through your online account. For example, you can apply for a loan wherever you might be, and most of the time you'll be given the money. But, for me, there's no substitute for speaking face-to-face, where a bank advisor can point you in the right direction, as far as savings or debt is concerned. Above all else, they won't allow you to get into debt that you can't pay back.

12 📶 34

Examiner: Should school children have /hæv/ lessons on financial responsibility?

Candidate: Yes, for me, it is absolutely essential. I didn't have /hæv/ lessons like these at school but I think they would have /əv/ benefitted me a great deal. For example, when I got my first credit card, I now know I should have /əv/ paid more attention to the implications of using it. I found I was spending too much, and often forgot to make the repayments, so I got into debt very quickly. Perhaps if I'd understood them better, I might have /əv/ avoided this.

Unit 5 HISTORY

LISTENING

2 📶 35

1 The monarchy has existed in England since the ninth century AD.
2 Elizabeth II became Queen of England in the mid-twentieth century.
3 There was a Civil War in England between 1642 and 1649.
4 The Tower of London has had many functions in the last 200 years.
5 The Tower of London was built by William the Conqueror during the 1070s.
6 The First World War lasted from 1914 to 1918.
7 King Charles II gained control of the Tower of London after the restoration of the monarchy.
8 The Tower of London became a tourist destination during the Victorian era.
9 The number of visitors to the Tower of London rose to 2 million per year in the first decade of the twenty-first century.

4 📶 36

Welcome to the Tower of London. Before the tour starts, I would like to give you some background information about the Tower.

The Tower of London is one of the UK's most popular tourist attractions with over 2 million visitors per year. It was during the Victorian era – that is when Queen Victoria was on the throne – that it became a tourist attraction. Before that, the Tower had many other functions. It was a royal residence, a menagerie – that's a kind of zoo – it even had lions. And it used to house the Royal Mint – that's where money is printed and coins made. It also served as a storehouse for weapons, a fortress and most famously of all, a prison!

6 📶 37

The Tower of London was built in the 1070s by William the Conqueror, who had invaded England and defeated the English king, Harold. He wanted a strong fortress to consolidate his rule over the English people. The Tower was then extended by later kings, including William II, Henry VIII and Edward I, the last two being chiefly responsible for creating the form in which the Tower exists today.

It has a long and interesting past which places it at the heart of many key events in British history. During the reign of Henry VIII, the Tower housed a large number of political and religious prisoners. Many of them were executed. When Henry VIII broke away from the Church of Rome, many of those who opposed this move ended up in the Tower, including the second of his six wives, Anne Boleyn, who was also executed here.

The Tower also played a key part during the English Civil War from 1642 to 1649, when it was fought over by the armies of the King, Charles I, and his opponents, the Parliamentarians. The enemies of the King gained control of the Tower and the Crown Jewels – the ceremonial jewellery of the royal family – were destroyed and melted down so the gold and jewels could be sold and the money used for the good of the people. However, after the restoration of the monarchy in 1660, the new king, Charles II, regained control of the Tower and it became the home of the new Crown Jewels which he had specially made.

And here's another fact which may surprise you – it was once home to lions and tigers! As long ago as the 1200s, King John founded the Royal Menagerie for the entertainment of the court. The first creatures were lions, an elephant and even a polar bear, a gift from the King of Norway. Attached on a lead, the polar bear was allowed to swim and catch fish in the River Thames! The Menagerie survived for 600 years, until the mid 1800s, when it was closed and the animals moved to Regent's Park and became the basis of London Zoo, which you can visit today.

7 📶 38

Most visitors to the Tower ask about the ravens – the big, black birds who live within the walls of the Tower. They are known as the Guardians of the Tower and there are always at least six of them. They are fed on raw meat by a Raven Master and visitors are asked not to feed them as they can attack. Legend has it that if the ravens ever leave the Tower of London, the kingdom will fall.

Another famous sight at the Tower is the Beefeaters, or as they are correctly called, the Yeoman Warders. They were first appointed in 1485 by Henry VIII as the ceremonial guards of the Tower and the Crown Jewels. Nowadays they entertain visitors from all over the world with their colourful stories of the Tower's history. However, it's not a position many of us can aspire to. To become a Beefeater, you need 22 years' military service with a medal of good conduct.

10 📶 39

Student 1: So, what are we going to focus on for our Tower of London presentation?

Student 2: There are lots of aspects we could talk about, but we've only got eight minutes, remember. Our topic needs to be simple and attention-grabbing. What about a time line? I mean a brief history of the Tower, you know, covering all the major events.

Student 1: Do you think we can really cover nearly a thousand years of history in eight minutes? I don't.

Student 2: No, I suppose not. You're right.

Student 1: We need to be specific and focus on one aspect of the Tower only. We could, say, talk about the history of the Beefeaters and the ravens. For example, I don't think many people realise that it's actually the ravens who are the ones that eat the beef, not the guards.

Student 2: That's worth considering, though I'm not sure there's enough for an eight-minute talk. Surely there isn't that much to say about them?

Student 1: OK, I take your point. … I'm also interested in military history, so the Fusilier Museum fascinated me. We could actually do a whole presentation on the weapons in there.

Student 2: Not *everyone's* interested in weapons and war. We need to think of a topic with broader appeal.

Student 1: All right … um … Well, don't they conduct special ceremonies in the Tower, like the Ceremony of the Keys, every evening, when they close up the Tower for the night? It's a bit like the Changing of the Guard at Buckingham Palace, only better. That should have more general appeal.

Student 2: But it doesn't have that wow factor, does it? Oh wait. Speaking of wow factor, we haven't mentioned the Crown Jewels.

Student 1: Yes! There's so much history associated with them and they still get used for state occasions like coronations and royal weddings. I can't see anyone being bored by that topic.

Student 2: Hey! We could ask the other students to guess the value of some of the jewels as part of the presentation? We could give a prize for the closest guess!

Student 1: But the jewels are priceless really, so it would be impossible to put an accurate value on them. Not one of your best ideas!

Student 2: OK, so summing up based on what we've talked about then, it should be either the Beefeaters, the Ceremony of the Keys or the Crown Jewels. I would go for the last one myself.

Student 1: I'd still like to do the Fusilier Museum personally speaking, but OK, let's settle on the Crown Jewels. It would probably have the most universal appeal. Shall we meet after lunch and start planning the presentation?

12 ▯▯▯ 40

Harry: So Olga, how did your visit to London go? Did you get to see everything on your list?

Olga: Well, on the whole pretty well, though I didn't get to do everything I wanted. I'd love to go back and do it again.

Harry: Did you manage to get into Madame Tussauds this time? I know you didn't last time you were in London.

Olga: Oh, yes. No problems with long queues or exhibits being closed this time around. I loved seeing the waxworks of the Royal Family again. Did you know that they change the waxwork of the Queen every few years, as she gets older? And it's the same with Prince William and Kate, and Prince Harry. It's scary how life-like they look. They even recreate their clothes.

Harry: Well, you've always been fascinated by the British Royal Family so you were bound to enjoy that. Speaking of which, did you get on that tour of Buckingham Palace? I know it was top of your list of places to see.

Olga: Oh, yes, I did, and I wasn't disappointed. My favourite part was the State Rooms. They were so impressive. I loved the interior design. There are so many masterpieces there from some of the world's most famous painters: Rubens, Van Dyck …

Harry: When I went, they had an exhibition to celebrate the Queen's 90th birthday. It was called 'Fashioning a Reign' and it showed outfits the Queen has worn from the 1930s right up to the present. And after Buckingham Palace, where was next?

Olga: Westminster Abbey. I had to see that. So many famous people are buried there. Kings, queens, prime ministers, the list is endless. And let's not forget Prince William and Kate got married there, like many royals before them.

Harry: I can tell from your voice that you loved it there. How about the Tower of London? Now there's a place full of royal history. Think of all the executions that took place there. They say it's a terrifying place.

Olga: I wouldn't know. On the day we went there, there was some kind of event going on to do with poppies – red flowers – and we couldn't even get close to the entrance. It felt like the whole of London was there, standing in line.

Harry: Oh yes, I read about that. Hundreds of thousands of ceramic poppies decorating the building. I saw photos online – it looked very impressive.

Olga: It was. The flowers looked amazing from the outside, but I didn't have the patience to wait for hours and hours. Instead we went to a newer attraction called the London Bridge Experience. It's supposed to be 'The UK's scariest year-round attraction', so I thought it would be fun. It didn't disappoint. I can't remember how many times I screamed.

Harry: Doesn't sound very historical to me.

Olga: Maybe not, but certainly worth a visit.

13 ▯▯▯ 41

You will hear a student discussing his dissertation with his tutor. First you have some time to look at questions 1 to 5.

[pause]

Now listen carefully and answer questions 1 to 5.

Adrian: So, I'd like to talk to you about my dissertation. I have to do something about the city of Petra, you know, in Jordan. But I'm not sure which aspect to look at.

Jayne: Oh, OK, yes, there's plenty to write about there. What topics have you thought about?

Adrian: Well, there's the historical angle. Petra dates back to prehistoric times, but there's a lot of information available from about 2,000 years ago.

Jayne: OK, so you'd have to concentrate on sometime in the last 2,000 years. But that's still a long time with a huge number of changes happening. That's really too wide a focus. You need to narrow it down. Why did Petra become well known at that time, do you think?

Adrian: Well, because of the trading routes mainly. Its location made it an ideal place for traders to stop when they were travelling between East and West.

Jayne: True, and the trade route is interesting. But … you wouldn't really be talking just about Petra itself, as it was only one of many places on the trade route. I would rule that one out because your topic needs to concentrate on one place.

Adrian: OK. I'm also interested in the various *conflicts* that took place as people started to travel and mix with very different cultures.

Jayne: Right, but to be honest, that's going to be a lot of research. For such a small sub-topic, there's a surprisingly large amount of material to read on this. I think it might take too long.

Adrian: Yes, I had noticed that. So, I guess that leaves Petra's architecture, though it might be seen as rather an obvious choice.

Jayne: Well, there's a lot of potential there. You could talk about the unique style of half building and half carving into the rocks.

Adrian: That is really fascinating, but I'm worried that it might require some specialist knowledge of building techniques and so on. I'm *interested* in architecture, but my background is more history and social studies.

Jayne: Understood. So any other thoughts?

Adrian: Actually I'm very interested in the buildings in the context of the present day community of Petra. Apparently, people go and sleep in the cave dwellings, even though they've been given modern houses to live in. Living in caves is very much part of their culture.

Jayne: Well, I agree it's interesting, but I think you would get drawn into talking about tourism and that's not really suitable for your degree. I think some kind of focus on the past would be more relevant for a dissertation.

Before you hear the rest of the discussion you have some time to look at questions 6 and 7.

[pause]

Now listen and answer questions 6 and 7.

Jayne: OK, Adrian, so you've finally decided to focus on one aspect of Petra, which is the water management systems. What have you found out so far?

Adrian: Well, mainly that the people of Petra had a really good understanding of how to make use of every bit of groundwater and rainwater they had access to.

Jayne: Can you give me some examples of that?

Adrian: Well, agriculture was one of the most important uses of water. Petra is located in the middle of the desert, so keeping their plants well irrigated was essential and they developed systems to do that.

Jayne: You mentioned that you haven't studied much science. Do you think this area is going to be too technical for you?

Adrian: Well, actually the water supply process is fairly simple to grasp. They used clay pipes and thought about the height of different areas so they could make use of gravity. You don't need a degree in engineering to understand it.

Jayne: OK, that's good. And what about the storage of water?

Adrian: They built huge reservoirs – as simple as that.

Jayne: And is there anything else that's particularly noteworthy?

Adrian: There's an aqueduct in Petra which is around 2,000 years old. That's a bridge which carries water. It was unbelievably ahead of its time. Other similar regions were uninhabitable at that time because of the lack of water management.

Jayne: OK, and what other aspects do you want to focus on?

Adrian: Well … the social history angle – apart from the benefits of irrigation, initially it was the elite – that is the rich – who gained from all this technology. Ordinary people didn't have the luxury of baths and running water, for example.

Jayne: Hmm, and that's still the case with any new technology, isn't it?

4 & 5 📊 42

See exercise 5 for Listening script.

7 📊 43

Answer 1

Daniel: Yes, this is something children all over the world learn about because it represents the end of the 'Cold War'. The Cold War is the name given to the relationship between the USSR and the USA after World War 2 and Germany was caught up in the middle and became a divided country. The wall was erected in 1961 and separated East and West Germany for the next 28 years, probably the key period of the Cold War. So yes, it is something that is taught in schools.

Answer 2

Daniel: Yes, they do.

Answer 3

Daniel: Yes, I think this is a significant event in history that children all over the world learn about. Certainly, back home in Germany, it's considered extremely important, especially since the reunification of Germany.

8 & 9 📊 44

Examiner: So, Minji, we've been talking about a historical event and I'd like to discuss with you one or two more general questions related to this. Do you think it is important for children to learn history at school?

Minji: Yes, definitely. At primary school they <u>should be taught</u> the history of their own country and community. It's a way of helping them understand who they are, and their place in the world, and also the relationships between different countries.

Examiner: You said children should learn the history of their own country. What about world history?

Minji: I'm not so sure about that. I think the history of their own country <u>should</u> definitely come first. <u>I remember learning</u> about Romans and Egyptians when I was quite a young child, <u>without knowing</u> *anything* about my own country or even my own continent – I mean Asian history. <u>I think learning</u> about world history should come later, say at high school or secondary school.

Examiner: Yes, that's a good point. Do you think most children are interested in learning history these days?

Minji: To be honest, I'd say probably not, which is quite sad, as it's a really important subject. Even though kids are obsessed by their smart phones and computers nowadays, they <u>could</u> still use the technology to learn about history. I think the problem is <u>how history is taught</u>. It <u>needs to be made</u> more fun and attractive to children.

Examiner: Right. You mentioned technology. I was going to ask you about that. Can technology help us learn about history?

Minji: Absolutely! We have the technology to really bring history alive. Lots of museums now have interactive exhibits with holograms and so on. Websites are also becoming more exciting, with videos of re-enactments of historical events, interactive quizzes, and things like that. But, for me personally, <u>the best way</u> to learn about history will always be to go to the place <u>where the event took place</u>. For example, I'll never forget the trip we made to Berlin when I did a tour of Europe with my family. Seeing where the Berlin Wall used to stand and visiting the museums. That really brought history alive for me.

Unit 6   SCIENCE AND TECHNOLOGY

LISTENING

4 📊 45

Dylan: Hi, Tanya.

Tanya: Oh, hi, Dylan. How's your course going?

Dylan: Really well. I'm enjoying most of the lectures, and I'm looking forward to the Science and Technology Festival next week. Are you?

Tanya: Definitely. Although I haven't checked how much each talk costs to get in – I really hope it's not too much. If we do have to pay a lot on the door, I'll only be able to see one or two. My biggest worry is that there won't be anything related to my studies.

Dylan: You've got a point, but it's not so much that I'm worried about it being a waste of time for our course, and with a student discount we definitely shouldn't have any concerns about ticket prices. <u>The real issue we've got is how to pick which ones to go to.</u>

Tanya: <u>I quite agree</u> – there are so many interesting speakers, it's almost impossible to decide who to see. Plus, <u>the lecture rooms around campus are pretty spread out, so I'm not exactly confident we'll be able to make it to each venue in time.</u>

Dylan: <u>That's absolutely true, neither am I.</u> We'll have to look at the timings in the programme, but hopefully the organisers will have thought of that and won't be expecting everyone to run from one talk to another.

Tanya: I'm not sure about that. The schedule must be really tricky to plan; there are bound to be problems.

5 📊 46

Tanya: If we do have to pay a lot on the door, I'll only be able to see one or two. My biggest worry is that there won't be anything related to my studies.

Dylan: You've got a point, but it's not so much that I'm worried about it being a waste of time for our course, and with a student discount we definitely shouldn't have any concerns about ticket prices. The real issue we've got is how to pick which ones to go to.

Tanya: I quite agree – there are so many interesting speakers, it's almost impossible to decide who to see. Plus, the lecture rooms around campus are pretty spread out, so I'm not exactly confident we'll be able to make it to each venue in time.

Dylan: That's absolutely true, neither am I.

6 📊 47

Tanya: Anyway, which talks are you planning on seeing?

Dylan: Definitely the keynote speaker. I saw her present once before, at a conference in Los Angeles, which was interesting because we had previously thought she only uploaded her talks onto the internet. <u>When she presented to us, I couldn't believe how normal she seemed in real life, even a little shy</u>, because she seemed to have such a *big* personality on those videos, and sometimes the content of the lecture got lost a little bit as a result.

Tanya: Sounds impressive. So she'll be opening the festival on Tuesday. What's her talk about?

Dylan: It'll be something about new technologies in Computer Game Design.

Tanya: Oh, perfect timing. I've got the first class of a Game Design module beginning next Thursday, so it would be good to get prepared for that. For example, I know my study skills aren't as good as they could be. I really should work on those, because I'll probably have forgotten everything by the time I go into class. The problem is finding the time for that and I'm too busy right now to work on them. I've bought the course books for the module already, and <u>I'm definitely going to do some in-depth background reading beforehand. That has to be my priority.</u>

9 📊 48

Dylan: Good idea. And *my* note-taking skills need work as well, but science and technology students don't seem to get much help. In laboratory tutorials, it sometimes seems like everyone's a little nervous about coming up with ideas for particular experiments, so I just start talking, even if I don't know what I'm talking about. I always feel like I'm dominating the conversation and speaking too much, but after I've made my point everyone else suddenly discovers what they want to say and we can relax.

Tanya: Mm, I know how you feel. Anyway, let's think about what to do after the keynote speech on Tuesday. There are two talks which immediately follow it, but neither of them look that interesting, so it would probably be a better idea if we used that time to decide which of tomorrow's lectures we should attend. Shall we grab a coffee while we're doing that?

Dylan: That's a great idea. Then we can go to that final lecture on virtual reality applications a bit more refreshed. Once that one has finished, let's head over to that cheap Italian restaurant for something to eat. We'll be starving by then.

Tanya: You're on. And it's your turn to pay.

11 📊 49

1 We should try to review what we see as the main ideas, the most important technical features, that sort of thing. We'll then be able to decide together what …

2 Also, when we post it on the department web page, we'll need to show how it all relates to our courses. In order for us to get some feedback about this, we should probably contact our tutor …

3 That way, when we meet up again after the lecture, we'll be more able to compare notes, and to go over …

4 I've tried using those before. Diagrams are often a great way to learn or explain things in science, but they *can* make your notes a little difficult to follow.

5 Good plan. We agree what the most significant points are from each lecture, maybe even try to establish some of the common themes.

12 📊 50

Tanya: We also need to consider what to include in our summary for the department web page.

Dylan: As neither of us are brilliant at taking notes, let's try to find a system that will work for us both.

Tanya: Well, so how about mind maps?

Dylan: I've tried using those before. Diagrams are often a great way to learn or explain things in science, but they *can* make your notes a little difficult to follow. I think it's better if we both opt for bullet points so that it's clear and consistent.

Tanya: OK, let's use those. That way, when we meet up again after the lecture, we'll be more able to compare notes, and to go over our initial impressions, stating what was particularly relevant. We should try to review what we see as the main ideas, the most important technical features, that sort of thing. We'll then be able to decide together what to include – and what to leave out – when we come to the summary.

Dylan: Good plan. We agree what the most significant points are from each lecture, maybe even try to establish some of the common themes. By doing so, we can then put together an edited version of these on a separate sheet of paper, and when we eventually come to write the summary, the main points will be even clearer.

Tanya: Also, when we post it on the department web page, we'll need to show how it all relates to our courses. In order for us to get some feedback about this, we should probably contact our tutor and send her a summary of the main points.

Dylan: OK, let's make sure we email her tonight, then.

13 📊 51

1 **Dylan:** I think it's better if we both opt for bullet points so that it's clear and consistent.

   Tanya: OK, let's use those. That way, when we meet up again after the lecture, we'll be more able to compare notes …

2 **Dylan:** Good plan. We agree what the most significant points are from each lecture, maybe even try to establish some of the common themes. By doing so, we can then put together an edited version of these on a separate sheet of paper …

3 **Tanya:** In order for us to get some feedback about this, we should probably contact our tutor …

15 📊 52

You will hear two students talking to their professor about the Science and Technology Festival they attended.

First you have some time to look at questions 1 to 6.

[pause]

Now listen carefully and answer questions 1 to 6.

Prof Dickens: Hi Dylan, hi Tanya, thanks for coming to see me. I'm very interested to hear what you thought about the Science and Technology Festival.

Dylan: Well, we're both very pleased we went.

Prof Dickens: Glad to hear it. Was there anything you both found especially useful?

Tanya: Yes, definitely. I saw at least two lectures that directly relate to the subjects I'm studying in this first semester. I already feel a little more prepared than I did last week.

Dylan: There wasn't anything that had the same effect on me, but that wasn't my only focus. I saw the festival as a chance to explore new ideas and other subject areas, so I also tried to attend some lectures that looked *interesting*, rather than just the ones I thought would only be relevant to my course.

Tanya: I'm glad I didn't do that – I get too stressed when I don't concentrate on one thing. But wasn't it great to be able to wander around the university and get a better idea of where everything is?

Dylan: Well, I certainly I feel more confident now I've explored the area a bit more. And I also found it very easy to meet people who share the same interests as me. When I was waiting for some of the lectures to start, I just got talking to whoever was sitting next to me.

Tanya: I was too busy going through my notes to do that. I have to say, going to so many lectures in a short space of time has really helped me to improve one area of study – my note-taking technique.

Dylan: I wasn't so sure about that originally. But looking at my notes again this morning, I could see how they got better as the week went on.

Prof Dickens: I'm glad the week was of use to you. It seems to change focus annually; sometimes the emphasis is more on science, sometimes on technology, but there was an excellent balance this time. It really brings these areas of study and research to the attention of the wider world and, for me, that's the primary reason the festival exists. You may have noticed when you were there that there were a number of university information stands set up around the campus. Did you see the free reference booklets that they were giving out?

Dylan: No, I assumed the stands were there to provide people with directions to each talk.

Prof Dickens: Well, their aim was to encourage everyone to read some of the latest studies coming out of our labs and classrooms. Many of the lecturers at the festival actually wrote the studies that were listed, so the talk and the booklets together are a great introduction to their work for anyone who attended. But the staff were certainly happy to point people in the right direction if it was needed.

Tanya: I have to admit, it was quite confusing, trying to follow some of the signs around the campus telling us where to go, so we used the map in the festival guidebook to find our way around. It was great for that. And, although one or two of the talks actually started at different times to what was printed on the page, one other thing I did like about the guidebook was that it wasn't full of adverts.

Dylan: Oh, I agree, but that's always the case with festivals now. I don't mind that, if it means that the festival is free to enter, as more and more of them are these days. And even if there is a fee for admission, the festival organisers hardly make any money from that, though they do tend to put the price of entry up each year. They have to make money to run the festival somehow, so it makes sense to get the majority of that through ads.

Tanya: That's a fair point.

Before you hear the rest of the conversation you have some time to look at questions 7 to 10.

[pause]

Now listen and answer questions 7 to 10.

Prof Dickens: So, what next? Do you still want to write something for the department website?

Dylan: Oh, definitely. Can you give us some advice on how we do that?

Prof Dickens: Well, it's a simple process, but it can mean a lot of work. First, you need to make sure that you have fully discussed and compiled the notes you made during the festival. For the next step I would recommend selecting a set number of principal theories that generate the most ideas and summarise those – four is probably the ideal number. Then you'll need to go to the website and go through what people have written before. These posts will help you to understand which style seems most appropriate – how academic in tone you need to be, or how informal, and so on. And as this is going to be a joint project, it's really important to make sure that you both come to a joint decision about the best way to divide up the workload. Believe me, arguments can happen. Further to that, you should also agree on exactly when you're aiming to publish it, so establish a deadline. Make sure you don't go past the agreed date, as it will become more difficult to finish if you do. Then, after all this is completed, you're ready to upload your summary and any other documents and post them onto the department website.

Tanya: Wonderful, thanks so much, Professor Dickens. Hopefully we can come back to you if we need any more help …

SPEAKING

4 🎵 53

Examiner: How often do you use your mobile phone?

Candidate: Not as much as I used to. After I first bought it, I'd be using it almost constantly, but I've been thinking that maybe I use it too often and should try to limit how long I spend on it. I don't know if that will be possible, though – they've become such a big part of everyone's lives these days, but I'm going to have to try. Not completely, though – if I didn't have one, I wouldn't have a social life.

8 🎵 54

I'd like to tell you what I know about one of the most significant inventions in human history: the wheel. Why is it so significant? Well, let me begin by saying, first of all, it basically enabled us to develop whole civilisations, as we could for the first time start transporting goods from place to place, and this mobility really made trade grow at an incredible speed. I remember being taught about this at school. Our teacher told us not to see the wheel itself as the crucial invention, because it was actually the moment someone managed to attach a non-moving platform to two wheels that was critical. But I can't help thinking that you don't have to agree with everything you are told at school, and I would politely refuse to agree with him, if I was told this today. You see, without a wheel, a platform is just a bit of wood, essentially.

Anyway, wheels in everyday use. Well, can you imagine living without them? It's practically impossible. You wouldn't be able to drive anywhere, for one thing. What's more, wheels allow us to have a public transport system, and if wheels didn't exist, aeroplanes wouldn't be able to take off and land, and no one would be able to go on holiday. How exactly a wheel works, I won't even attempt to explain, other than the fact they go round. It's something to do with force. I've never been any good at physics, but maybe I should remember to look it up on the internet when I get home. But, overall, there's no question about how important the wheel is, and it will continue to be an integral part of our lives forever.

13 🎵 55

1 That's quite a tricky question to answer. Let me think.
2 I don't really know how to answer that. It's never crossed my mind before.
3 I'm not entirely sure what you're driving at. Can you rephrase the question, please?
4 Sorry, I don't quite follow your question. Do you mean with appliances, like kettles, or something like internet security?
5 You know, I'd usually be able to answer that question immediately, but my mind has gone blank.

Unit 7   TELEVISION, NEWS AND CURRENT AFFAIRS

LISTENING

2 🎵 56

OK, everyone, I'd like to start by introducing myself. My name is Warren Short and I'm a freelance news reporter. So, what that means is that news agencies hire me to go to different parts of the world and report on on-going stories as they develop. The reason I've been asked to speak to you is to give you some tips on making your own news reports, which I know is something you have to do for your media course.

Let's begin our talk with a few general points. The first one is know your audience. By that I mean, are they older or younger viewers, where are they from, what are their values, ideas or beliefs, what level of education do they have? The reason we try to find out as much as possible about the audience is that we want to interest them. If they can't engage with or relate to the stories we choose or how we present them, they'll choose another news channel. The same story can be presented in different ways for different audiences. So, for example, if there's an oil spill into the sea, will our audience be more concerned about the environmental or the economic consequences?

The next general point I want to make is that pictures are as important as words. You need to choose very carefully what you're going to show, in what order and for how long. The first and last shots the audience sees are the ones that make the most impact. The last of my general points is that you must be fair and balanced. The reputation of the TV station is at stake here, so it's crucial not to give the impression that the station is trying to push its own agenda. If you interview someone from one side of a debate, you should then interview someone from the other side. Without this balance, you will definitely get complaints from viewers.

Right, so I'll just repeat those general points for you before we move on. Get to know your audience, choose your pictures wisely and avoid bias.

[pause]

OK, so let's take a simplified look at the process of making a news report. As with any project, the first stage is planning. What you have to remember is the five Ws: Who, What, When, Where and Why. These are the five questions you need to have answers to. Once you've gathered the information about the story, you need to put together a script. The key advice here is – keep it simple or you may lose your audience. As part of writing the initial script, try to visualise the report in your mind.

Make sure you're clear on who you're going to interview, where this interview will take place, the questions you want to ask, and what shots you're going to include.

After that it's time to get the camera rolling. A news report begins with the reporter talking to the camera and giving a brief introduction to the story. Keep it snappy. Don't go into unnecessary detail or say things that will be covered by the interviewees. Just outline the story that your report will tell in a straightforward and appealing way.

The next stage of the report is the interview or interviews. Choose someone directly affected by the story who can put their ideas across in a clear and concise way. This could be, say, a witness who observed the events of the story directly. The ideal place to interview them is somewhere that reveals something about the person or the events of the story. For example, if he or she works in a factory affected by the story, interview him or her inside the factory with machinery and workers in the background. On the other hand, there shouldn't be too much going on in the background as that would detract from the story.

OK, moving on to the second interview. This person's views should contrast with those of the first speaker. I've already mentioned the need to avoid being accused of bias, and that's why his or her position on the story must be different. So, if the first person was a worker in the factory explaining why jobs must be saved, the second interviewee could be one of the factory managers giving their perspective on why job cuts are necessary.

Now, depending on the length of your report, you might or might not have time for other views and shots. But the piece should finish with the reporter on camera again, rounding up the story, and if possible saying something about the possible next steps in this story. For example, if the story is about a court case, when the verdict is expected.

So, that's about it. To sum up, be fair, be balanced and be interesting. Now, are there any questions?

5 57

OK, everyone, I'd like to start by introducing myself. My name is Warren Short and I'm a freelance news reporter, So, what that means is that news agencies hire me to go to different parts of the world and report on on-going stories as they develop. The reason I've been asked to speak to you is to give you some tips on making your own news reports, which I know is something you have to do for your media course.

8 58

Let's begin our talk with a few general points. The first one is know your audience. By that I mean, are they older or younger viewers, where are they from, what are their values, ideas or beliefs, what level of education do they have? The reason we try to find out as much as possible about the audience is that we want to interest them. If they can't engage with or relate to the stories we choose or how we present them, they'll choose another news channel. The same story can be presented in different ways for different audiences. So, for example, if there's an oil spill into the sea, will our audience be more concerned about the environmental or the economic consequences?

9 59

The next general point I want to make is that pictures are as important as words. You need to choose very carefully what you're going to show, in what order and for how long. The first and last shots the audience sees are the ones that make the most impact. The last of my general points is that you must be fair and balanced. The reputation of the TV station is at stake here, so it's crucial not to give the impression that the station is trying to push its own agenda. If you interview someone from one side of a debate, you should then interview someone from the other side. Without this balance, you will definitely get complaints from viewers.

Right, so I'll just repeat those general points for you before we move on. Get to know your audience, choose your pictures wisely and avoid bias.

11 60

OK, so let's take a simplified look at the process of making a news report. As with any project, the first stage is planning. What you have to remember is the five Ws: Who, What, When, Where and Why. These are the five questions you need to have answers to. Once you've gathered the information about the story, you need to put together a script. The key advice here is keep it simple or you may lose your audience. As part of writing the initial script, try to visualise the report in your mind. Make sure you're clear on who you're going to interview, where this interview will take place, the questions you want to ask and what shots you're going to include.

After that it's time to get the camera rolling. A news report begins with the reporter talking to the camera and giving a brief introduction to the story. Keep it snappy. Don't go into unnecessary detail or say things that will be covered by the interviewees. Just outline the story that your report will tell in a straightforward and appealing way.

13 61

The next stage of the report is the interview or interviews. Choose someone directly affected by the story who can put their ideas across in a clear and concise way. This could be, say, a witness who observed the events of the story directly. The ideal place to interview them is somewhere that reveals something about the person or the events of the story. For example, if he or she works in a factory affected by the story, interview him or her inside the factory with machinery and workers in the background. On the other hand, there shouldn't be too much going on in the background as that would detract from the story.

OK, moving on to the second interview. This person's views should contrast with those of the first speaker. I've already mentioned the need to avoid being accused of bias, and that's why his or her position on the story must be different. So, if the first person was a worker in the factory explaining why jobs must be saved, the second interviewee could be one of the factory managers giving their perspective on why job cuts are necessary.

Now, depending on the length of your report, you might or might not have time for other views and shots. But the piece should finish with the reporter on camera again, rounding up the story, and if possible saying something about the possible next steps in this story. For example, if the story is about a court case, when the verdict is expected.

So, that's about it. To sum up, be fair, be balanced and be interesting. Now, are there any questions?

14 62

You will hear someone giving a talk about writing for a newspaper and the printing process. First you have some time to look at questions 1 to 10.
[pause]
Now listen carefully and answer questions 1 to 10.

Good afternoon, everyone. So today's talk is divided into two parts. In the first part I'm going to try to explain the decision-making process behind choosing what stories to publish in a newspaper. Later, in the second part of my talk, I will explain the process of producing a print newspaper.

So, first of all, I'd like to consider the question 'What is news?' It's a question I get asked all the time. Well, to put it in very simple terms, it is 'anything new'. However, that definition is extremely vague and open to interpretation. In other words, it doesn't really help a newspaper editor decide what stories to include. So a better question would be 'What factors help newspaper editors decide which stories make it into their newspaper?' Well, of course, it's a slightly different process for TV news programmes because TV editors have to be more selective about what to include. TV news shows are restricted by length and can be as short as five minutes. Newspapers don't have these restrictions but even with print or online newspapers, there are many more stories vying for attention than those that actually appear in the final edition. Returning to the question then, what makes a news story newsworthy?

What is it that grabs the attention and makes you want to interact with the story? Basically, it is anything with personal relevance for the reader. This presents us with two more questions: How do we as newspaper editors decide what is relevant and what is not? And what is it that makes a story personal? The answer is that it very much depends on your audience, and a good newspaper editor chooses stories based on their relevance and personal interest to their audience. He or she needs to know what sells their newspaper because at the end of the day, if our newspapers don't sell, we don't have a job.

A successful editor doesn't just think about their audience, they also need to keep an eye on the competition, and this is the final factor I want to address in this part of my talk. To clarify, the competition is other newspapers or news channels. If a story is getting a lot of attention and coverage elsewhere, then, as an editor, you need to find a way to include it in your newspaper.

[short pause]

So, now to move on to the second part of my talk, which is the process of putting together an edition of a printed newspaper. The first stage is a continuous process in which journalists are collecting and writing up stories and the marketing people are positioning the advertisements, and this is known as the news gathering stage. As soon as an article is finished, it's passed on to the second stage of the process – editing. Both content and language have to be edited. Facts may need to be checked and changes made to the language to ensure the tone of the piece fits the style of the newspaper and the message the editor wants to convey. There may be a number of different editors, depending on the size of the newspaper, and each editor needs to use a contrasting colour to edit so that it's easy to see who has made the changes. For example, sub-editors use red, the chief sub-editor uses blue and the editor uses green.

Once all the editing is finished, we move on to the next stage, which is called pre-press. This stage is concerned with layout. Each page of the newspaper is laid out and designed with stories, pictures and adverts. A prototype – or first version – of each page is made. Nowadays, these are then transformed into digital form by graphic designers.

The pre-press stage is followed by the press or lithographic stage. Traditionally, and in places where digital printing isn't used, the stories and adverts are registered on a plate – an iron sheet in the size and shape of the newspaper.

Next comes the impression stage. The plates are hung on the printing press and the final copies are printed out. For some of the national newspapers this can run to thousands of copies that need to be collected and put in order before the final stage – circulation, when the newspapers are sent out to be distributed across the country.

Although digital technology now plays a part in this whole process, it's actually remarkably similar to the way it has always been done. The process from beginning to end typically takes about 12 hours as it's a very fast moving business.

SPEAKING

4 📁 63

One of my favourite programmes is *Fear Factor*. Actually, I would say it's a programme that I love to hate! What I mean by that is – I *love* it, but at times the things on there are awesome, sorry, I meant to say they are *awful*. So the type – or rather the *genre* – of show is reality but also it's a competition. What happens is that there are four people – well, you know, four competitors – and they has to do, they have to do a series of tasks. Sometimes they have to dive into – or actually they dive *under* water and open a box – I mean *unlock* a box, or they have to climb up a high building. In the second task, there are nasty animals – not *animals* as such, but things like cockroaches or snakes, which they must to, they must lie in a box with or something. So, I don't like it, but it's compulsory. I'll rephrase that. I watch it even though I don't want to. It's compulsive. It's on Thursday nights on a channel called Reality. I usually watch with my brother – *both* my brothers, actually. Sometimes we play our own version of it and make each other do silly tasks – but not as bad as the ones on the TV.

6 📁 64

Example I absolutely hate watching the new. Sorry, I meant to say news.

1 Watching TV is a time of waste. Sorry, I'll rephrase that – a waste of time.
2 Comedic shows, or rather comedy shows, are not very popular in my country.
3 I can't understand why realism TV is so popular. Let me start again. I can't understand why reality TV is so popular.
4 The popularity of sports programmes, especially football series, I mean football highlights shows, makes no sense to me.
5 One thing that I dislike about TV is the amount of publicities. Oh, did I say publicities? I meant to say commercials.

Unit 8   CULTURE

LISTENING

4 & 8 📁 65

Good afternoon, everyone. Today we continue our series of talks about globalisation, and today's talk is on the globalisation of culture. This is quite a complex topic as there are lots of different ways in which we can look at culture. To begin with, there is no agreed consensus on how best to define culture. Culture can cover both visible aspects, such as music, clothes, food and architecture, as well as less visible ones such as value and belief systems. An important point I want to stress from the beginning is one that anyone who studies culture needs to understand. It's not enough to just look and see what's happening on the surface. You need to look beneath the surface to understand the meanings that people assign to cultural phenomena. Let me give you an example. The American film *Titanic* proved hugely popular in China when it was released in 1998. When this was studied in detail by sociologists, it was found that it had nothing to do with the popularity of American culture. The film was understood by the Chinese purely in terms of their own historical circumstances. So, the whole idea of cultural globalisation needs to be looked at beyond the superficial level.

(*Stop to check if students are following notes.*)

OK, let's move on to discuss some different views on the globalisation of culture. For some it's seen to be a very negative thing indeed. Many critics see it as an extension of global capitalism. They see capitalism attempting to extend its influence to all corners of the globe through advertising and marketing, creating needs people didn't know they had in order to sell their products and services. One of the main criticisms of this economic approach is that it has led to corporations trying to find uniform answers to the needs of everybody, a kind of one-size-fits-all approach to products and services they produce. In other words, this approach does not consider or cater to the different personalities that different cultures have, and therefore either ignores or is detrimental to their individual needs. Some even see this process as a form of corporate imperialism, comparable perhaps to the colonisation of the 'new world' by European powers in the 15th to 19th centuries. This can lead to a form of cultural extinction; long-held customs and traditions slowly disappear or die out. This is a fear that many nations have expressed. In 1999, for example, a survey in France found that 60% of people in that country felt that globalisation was the greatest threat to the French cultural way of life.

Many people, however, view globalisation in a much more positive light. Some see it as giving people more options to choose from and improving life for everyone. For example, we can get the benefits of Japanese technology, Italian food, British music, American films and Swedish interior design wherever we live in the world.

(*Stop to check if students are following notes.*)

The fact that a Chinese family eats out at an American burger restaurant once a month doesn't alter the fact that on the other 30 days, they make and eat their traditional food at home. Although Japanese businessmen dress in British suits, they still do business in a very different way from their Western counterparts. In this view of cultural globalisation, <u>people are viewed as world citizens</u> who knowingly choose from a menu of options when it comes to music, food, clothes and so on. In other words, we have much more variety to suit our individual needs, thanks to such influences. It should also be remembered, though, that when it comes to the more deeply rooted aspects of culture, these are less susceptible to change. We can change the music we listen to, but <u>our deeper profound beliefs about society cannot be altered so readily.</u>

(*Stop to check if students are following notes.*)

To add another point to the discussion, I believe that the internet and other media that have led to a so-called 'global culture' can actually work to the advantage of national and regional cultural groups. The internet helps spread information about these cultures and <u>contributes towards preserving not only their customs, but also their languages</u>. For example, many Native American tribes have used social media to re-engage younger tribe members with the skills to learn and use their mother tongues.

In concluding my talk this afternoon, I would like to <u>emphasise the part that education can play</u> in this discussion of the globalisation of culture. If we can all learn to respect other cultures and *appreciate* their differences rather than fearing them, it is perfectly possible for them to flourish alongside a shared global culture. Now, does anyone have any questions?

10 〓 66

Language is more than a collection of words and sounds. It is an essential part of a culture that helps not only with communication, but is a reminder of a culture's heritage. It can give us a valuable insight into the beliefs and the way a group of people think, <u>in the same way ancient monuments give us insight into the past</u>. Currently, the UNESCO Atlas of World Languages believes that there are 575 languages that are in danger. This includes languages that have just a handful of speakers such as Yagán in Chile and Ainu in Japan, but also some languages where there are still thousands of speakers. For example, it is estimated that there are around 170,000 speakers of Navajo, but the language is still in danger as younger generations are not learning it.

So why are so many languages dying out? Why are fewer people learning the languages of their ancestors? One explanation is globalisation. When a language becomes socially, politically and economically stronger than a native language, we often see displacement – <u>the stronger language will dominate at the expense of the so-called weaker ones</u>. One example of this can be seen in East Africa, where Swahili is spoken by 100 million people across Tanzania, Mozambique and Kenya. In other words, it has become the lingua franca for this pocket of Africa and in particular <u>the language of business</u> for these nations. This has led to other languages in the region coming close to extinction. By extension it will probably become the language of art and culture as technology increases in the region.

Another factor of globalisation that affects language is the movement of people. As people move to other countries to find work and education possibilities, immigrant parents tend to be less likely to teach their children the language and customs from the 'old' country. However, it's not clear if this is because these parents are driven by concerns about theirs and their children's <u>integration into the new culture</u> and local language or just that as immigrants they may have to work hard to establish themselves and not have the time to teach their children.

Nevertheless, there are some ways in which languages that may have died out in the past are being saved, and this is thanks to the globablisation and technology that have threatened languages in the past. For example, Joshua Hinson, a member of the Chikasaw tribe in North America, <u>was concerned about the fact that the tribe members who could speak the language well were getting older</u> and the younger members were not interested. He therefore developed an app that taught the Chikasaw alphabet and language. This was a great success with the younger members and they have formed a Youth Speaking Language Club and <u>are partnering with language experts to produce a complete course</u>, which they hope to make available in the near future.

14 〓 67

You will hear a talk about the island of New Guinea and some of the people of Papua New Guinea. First you have some time to look at questions 1 to 10.

[pause]

Now listen carefully and answer questions 1 to 10.

Today's talk is about the fascinating culture of New Guinea, an island divided in two politically but with huge diversity in both parts. For those of you who don't know, New Guinea is located in Oceania, in the south western Pacific Ocean, north of Australia. <u>Since 1975 the eastern side has been the independent country of Papua New Guinea</u>, while the western side consists of the Indonesian administered provinces of Papua and West Papua. Papua New Guinea has 7 million inhabitants and is an incredibly rural country with <u>only 18% of the population living in urban areas</u>. It has 852 known languages and is one of the least explored terrains on the planet.

Now, one of the reasons that Papua New Guinea, and indeed the whole of New Guinea, is such an interesting place is that it's home to hundreds of traditional tribes – perhaps better <u>described as distinct social groups</u>, each one numbering hundreds or even thousands of members. In the Indonesian part of New Guinea, that is the provinces of Papua and West Papua, there are 312 different tribes, including around 44 uncontacted ones. <u>These are tribes who up until now hadn't had any contact with the outside world</u>, even with other neighbouring tribes. Of course, everyone is most curious to know about these tribes, but, by definition, we have little or no information on them.

[short pause]

I am now going to talk about the tribes of the Papua New Guinea highlands. These people only rarely had contact with the outside world until the 1960s, so they are still relatively isolated. When we start to examine the tribes, we see a common theme, which is the use of various methods to intimidate other groups so as to protect their own tribe. Let's look first at the Huli-Wigmen, a tribe of about 40,000 from the Tari Highlands of Papua New Guinea. <u>They have given their faces a very distinctive look by using yellow paint</u>, and they wear belts made of pigtails, aprons made of leaves, and wigs, which are a sort of hat, made from their own hair. This look is designed to scare off outsiders, which they also do with their bird dances which mimic the birds of paradise that inhabit their land.

Another highland tribe, the Asaro mud men, have the same intention as the Huli-Wigmen – to ward off outsiders. <u>By smearing themselves in clay and mud they adopt the form of the river spirits</u>, which are known to terrify their enemies. Their elaborate appearance is further supplemented with extended fingernails and <u>they wear terrifying masks which serve to accentuate their ferocious look</u>. The Asaro mud men were discovered by the outside world less than 80 years ago, but have now become a symbol of Papua New Guinea and make an important contribution to the tourist trade.

A third tribe that has become well known is the Chimbu, who live high in the mountains. The Chimbu skeleton dancers used to dance to intimidate their enemies. This tribe traditionally lived in male/female segregated houses, though they're now increasingly living in family groups. This group too <u>now display their traditional dances not to scare off other tribes, but more to entertain tourists</u>.

An interesting event, the Mount Hagan Sing-Sing, takes place every year, involving over 50 tribes. This came about due to the constant fighting between tribes, which became a serious problem for the Papua New Guinea <u>government, so in 1961 it came up with the idea of a cultural show which would bring together as many tribes as possible in peace</u> and pride in their cultural heritage.

The Mount Hagan Sing-Sing is a wonderful opportunity for Papua New Guinea to showcase its fascinating cultural heritage. At this event, tourists and locals alike can witness the spectacular costumes, including six feet high headdresses made of flowers, shells and feathers. Inevitably, there is some loss of authenticity associated with this kind of event. For example, <u>chemical dyes are now used instead of the natural ones</u> the tribes used earlier. However, a poor, developing country has to exploit whatever resources it has, and the wealth of this region is its tribal peoples.

SPEAKING

7 & 8 🔊 68

Examiner: Good morning. My name is Paula Brady. Can you tell me your full name, please?

Luis: Yes, it's Luis Moreno Gonzalez.

Examiner: Thank you. And what shall I call you?

Luis: You can call me Luis.

Examiner: Thank you. And can you tell me where you're from?

Luis: I'm from Cordoba in the south of Spain.

Examiner: Can I see your identification, please?

Luis: Yes, here it is.

Examiner: Thank you. … Now, Luis, in this first part, I'm going to ask you some questions about yourself. Let's talk about what you do. Do you work or are you a student?

Luis: At the moment, I'm working, but I'm hoping to go to the UK to do my Master's next September.

Examiner: What do you like most about your job?

Luis: Well, I work in IT and, in fact, <u>I will have been at my company for three years in March</u>, so I know my job really well. The part I like best is helping people with their computer problems. Sometimes they're quite stressed, but when they call me and I tell them how to solve the problem, they calm down. It can be quite rewarding.

Examiner: And is there anything you don't like about your job?

Luis: Yes! The hours! As I said, my job involves helping people having computer problems and obviously these can happen at all times of the day and night, so sometimes I have to work on evening and night shifts. <u>The problem is that my sleeping patterns are affected.</u>

Examiner: Would you like to change jobs in the future?

Luis: Yes, but I want to stay in IT. <u>As soon as I get a Master's, I can become a manager and I think my work will be more varied and interesting</u>. And less disruptive for my sleep.

Examiner: OK, Luis, now let's move on to talk about music. How much time do you spend listening to music?

Luis: Oh, lots of time. Probably about three or four hours a day on working days, and a lot more on my days off.

Examiner: And what type of music do you listen to?

Luis: I would say my taste in music is … eclectic. I like all types, really, although I'm not so keen on classical music, but all types of modern music – pop, rock, R and B, hip hop, dance music. I always keep up to date with new releases and follow the charts.

Examiner: Where do you usually listen to music?

Luis: Everywhere! I have a stereo in my car <u>and also I have music on my phone, which I listen to when I'm walking</u> or travelling by bus or train. I listen at home and even at work sometimes.

Examiner: Is music important in your culture?

Luis: Yes, definitely. Spanish music, especially guitar music, is known all over the world. It's very … haunting music about love and tragedy. The words are very poetic and of course people dance our traditional dances to it. We really like to express our culture through music and it's important in all our festivals.

Examiner: OK, now we're going to talk a little about food. What are your favourite types of food?

Luis: Er, well, I'm quite adventurous when it comes to food. I'll try anything. But I have a really sweet tooth, so I suppose my favourite food has to be desserts … like cheesecake or pancakes.

Examiner: Do you prefer eating out or eating at home?

Luis: Without a doubt, I prefer eating out! In our culture it's very normal to eat out several times a week. I like it because I can go with my friends and try new dishes. I'm not a very good cook, so eating at home is hard for me.

Examiner: How often do you eat with your family?

Luis: I try to have lunch with my parents every weekend. We usually have a huge feast, prepared by my mother, all the family are there, and we spend hours sharing our news and catching up on the gossip. But I can only do this at weekends. <u>I really wouldn't have time for such a big meal with my parents if I visited them during the week!</u>

9 & 10 🔊 69

Examiner: Right, Luis, now I'm going to give you a topic and I'd like you to talk about it for one to two minutes. Before you talk, you'll have one minute to think about what you're going to say and you can make some notes if you wish. Do you understand?

Luis: Yes.

Examiner: Here's a pencil and some paper for making notes and here's your topic. I'd like you to describe a country that interests you.

[The examiner times one minute.]

Examiner: OK, remember you have one to two minutes for this, so don't worry if I stop you. I'll tell you when the time is up. Can you start speaking now, please?

Luis: OK, so the country that interests me is Morocco. It's <u>one of our neighbouring countries</u>, and yet in many ways, <u>it's worlds apart from</u> Spain. I learnt about it in many different ways. At school, first of all, but also I've been over to Tangier a few times as <u>it's only a short boat ride away</u>. In my city, Córdoba, we have a cathedral called La Mezquita because it used to be a mosque. So, <u>dating back to my childhood</u> I've been exposed to aspects of the culture of the Arab world.

I guess I learnt most by visiting. <u>I remember very vividly</u> my first trip to Tangier. I walked around a Moroccan market. The sights and sounds were so different, and the smell of those ingredients <u>made my mouth water</u>. I only spent the day there the first time, but when I went back a few years later, I spent several days there.

One thing that fascinates me is Moroccan food. It's spicier than the food we eat at home, and they use different ingredients – couscous rather than rice, for example, and their bread is flatter than ours. Their <u>cuisine</u> is healthy and delicious, with lots of vegetables and pulses. They cook stews in a tagine, a kind of clay cooking pot, which makes the food come out smelling and tasting amazing.

As for my travel plans, well, next time I go to Morocco, I want to <u>travel a little further afield</u>, maybe Casablanca, which I think must be a really romantic and fascinating city. I'll probably go with some of my friends and stay at least a week. I don't have any definite plans yet, but I was thinking of going next spring, as the summer may be too hot.

Examiner: Thank you. And are you interested in other countries in the same region?

Luis: Yes, I would be interested in visiting Algeria and Tunisia as well, as they are culturally quite similar to Morocco. Oh, and Egypt – I've always wanted to see Giza and the Valley of the Kings.

11 & 12 🔊 70

Examiner: We've been talking about a country you would like to visit and I'd like to discuss with you one or two more general questions related to that. First, let's talk about the importance of languages in culture. How do you think language helps us to understand a culture?

Luis: <u>Personally speaking</u>, I would say it helps a lot. I feel quite bad that I don't know any Arabic at all. I think that's the reason we find countries like Morocco so strange and exotic. I'd feel more at home there if I knew at least the basics of their language. And also, <u>in my view</u>, it's kind of a mark of respect to be able to greet someone and say thank you, that kind of thing.

Examiner: So, do you think when we learn a language we need to learn the culture as well?

Luis: Well, <u>it depends</u>. <u>The thing is</u> that languages like Spanish, English and even French are not associated with just one country. <u>Take Spanish, for example</u>. In a class, different students might be planning to use their Spanish in Spain, in Argentina, Venezuela, Colombia, so many places with different cultures. With English, the countries that use it are even more diverse, as it's spoken not only in the UK, the US, Australia and countries like that, but also places further afield <u>such as</u> India, Singapore, Hong Kong and African countries. <u>Given this fact</u>, English is quite separate from any culture.

Examiner: But isn't there a culture associated with the language itself?

Luis: Well, I suppose there is <u>to some extent</u>. So, in Spanish, we have different forms of address for different people. <u>I mean</u>, there's a more respectful form if you are speaking to older people or a stranger. In English, it seems to be part of the language to be very polite all the time, you know, say 'please', 'thank you' and 'excuse me' a lot, but I don't know if that's true everywhere that English is spoken.

Examiner: OK, let's talk about how cultures change. What aspects of culture do you think are most resistant to change?

Luis: <u>That's a good question</u>. <u>Obviously</u>, anything embedded in the language is not going to change quickly and also anything connected to religion. I would say the most deeply rooted aspects of culture are those we cannot see.

Examiner: Can you give me an example of that?

Luis: Well, I suppose things like the fact that the Spanish are eternally optimistic. It's a kind of belief that good will triumph over evil or everything will be alright in the end. What you see is people always smiling, singing and dancing, but underneath the belief is that life is basically good.

Examiner: That's interesting. Do you think globalisation has changed Spanish culture at all?

Luis: Er, <u>let me think</u>. <u>No, I wouldn't say so</u>. Not the culture at least, which is something we Spanish are very proud of. It has changed things superficially, and these days you'll notice the presence of more international businesses and chains. There are more international films and TV programmes available, and younger people probably listen to more international music than, for example, when my parents were children. But deep down, we are the same. We still do things our own way.

Examiner: Thank you very much, Luis. That's the end of the Speaking test.

Cambridge University Press
www.cambridge.org/elt

Cambridge Assessment English
www.cambridgeenglish.org

Information on this title: www.cambridge.org/9781316649268

© Cambridge University Press and UCLES 2018

First published 2018

20 19 18 17 16 15 14 13 12 11 10 9 8 7 6

Printed in Malaysia by Vivar Printing

A catalogue record for this publication is available from the British Library

ISBN 978-1-316-64926-8

Additional resources for this publication at **www.cambridge.org/mindset**

The authors and publishers would like to thank the following people for their work on this level of the Student's Book.

Alyson Maskell for her editing and proof reading and Bill Inge for his proof reading.

Design and typeset by emc design.

Audio produced by Leon Chambers at The Soundhouse Studios, London.

The publishers would like to thank the following people for their input and work on the digital materials that accompany this level.

Jonathan Birkin; Anthony Cosgrove; Peter Crosthwaite; Deborah Hobbs; Kate O'Toole; Bryan Stephens; Emina Tuzovic.

Cover and text design concept: Juice Creative Ltd.

Typesetting: emc design Ltd.

Cover illustration: MaryliaDesign/iStock/Getty Images Plus.

The authors and publishers acknowledge the following sources of copyright material and are grateful for the permissions granted. While every effort has been made, it has not always been possible to identify the sources of all the material used, or to trace all copyright holders. If any omissions are brought to our notice, we will be happy to include the appropriate acknowledgements on reprinting and in the next update to the digital edition, as applicable.

Key: B = Below, BG = Background, BL = Below Left, BR = Below Right, BC = Below Centre, C = Centre, CL = Centre Left, CR = Centre Right, L = Left, R = Right, T = Top, TR = Top Right, TL = Top Left.

Text

Graph on p. 110 adapted from 'World passenger car production'. Copyright © IHS Markit . Reproduced with kind permission; Text on p. 173 adapted from www.moken-island.com. Reproduced with kind permission; Text on p. 219 adapted from www.nationaltrust.org.uk. Reproduced with kind permission.

Photo

p. 8 (header), p. 14 (header) & p. 73 (header): Monty Rakusen/Cultura/ GettyImages; p. 8 (B): cinoby/E+/GettyImages; p. 9 (T): Amith Nag Photography/Moment/GettyImages; p. 10: Paul Souders/Corbis Documentary/GettyImages; p. 11 (T): kasto80/iStock/Getty Images Plus/ GettyImages; p. 11 (B): bluejayphoto/iStock/Getty Images Plus/GettyImages; pp. 12–13: National Geographic Creative/Alamy Stock Photo/Almay; pp. 12–13 (B): Bettmann/GettyImages; p. 15 (R): Cultura RM Exclusive/ Sofie Delauw/Cultura Exclusive/GettyImages; p. 18 (B): Juergen Sack/ iStock/Getty Images Plus/GettyImages; p. 19 (header): Image Source/ DigitalVision/GettyImages; p. 20 (TL): ilbusca/iStock/Getty Images Plus/ GettyImages; p. 20 (R): duncan1890/iStock/Getty Images Plus/GettyImages; p. 20 (BL): fotoVoyager/Vetta/GettyImages; p. 24: Chris Ryan/Caiaimage/ GettyImages; p. 25 (header): SolStock/E+/GettyImages; p. 25 (CR): David Gould/The Image Bank/GettyImages; p. 26 (L): Paola Cravino Photography/Moment/GettyImages; p. 28: Corey Ford/Stocktrek Images/ GettyImages; p. 29 (B): sandsun/E+/GettyImages; p. 30 (header): Peter Dazeley/Photographer's Choice/GettyImages; p. 32: Christopher Robbins/ DigitalVision/GettyImages; p. 36: Rafe Swan/Cultura/GettyImages; p. 38 (header): gruizza/E+/GettyImages; p. 38 (B): Brendan Moran/Sportsfile/ GettyImages; p. 39 (T): Billy Hustace/Photographer's Choice/GettyImages; p. 39 (B): Dmytro Aksonov/E+/GettyImages; p. 40: Caiaimage/Robert Daly/ Caiaimage/GettyImages; p. 42 (header): John Davis/Taxi/GettyImages; p. 44: Caiaimage/Agnieszka Olek/Caiaimage/GettyImages; p. 45: Maica/E+/ GettyImages; p. 47 (header): Ralf Hiemisch/GettyImages; p. 48: fstop123/E+/ GettyImages; p. 49: kizilkayaphotos/iStock/Getty Images Plus/GettyImages; p. 50: bhofack2/iStock/Getty Images Plus/GettyImages; p. 51: Ariel Skelley/ Blend Images/GettyImages; p. 52 (header): Stefan Cristian Cioata/Moment/ GettyImages; p. 53: DANIEL LEAL-OLIVAS/AFP/GettyImages; p. 57 (L): Sourced Collection/Alamy Stock Photo/Alamy; p. 57 (R), p. 71 (R): Peter Horree/Alamy Stock Photo/Alamy; p. 58: STAN HONDA/AFP/GettyImages; p. 59 (header): BryanLever/E+/GettyImages; p. 61: Norman Smith/Hulton Archive/GettyImages; p. 65 (header): miroslav_1/iStock Editorial/Getty Images Plus/GettyImages; p. 67 (L): Sami Sarkis/Photographer's Choice RF/GettyImages; p. 67 (C): Cultura/Cultura Exclusive/GettyImages; p. 67 (R): tamara_kulikova/iStock/Getty Images Plus/GettyImages; p. 68: Loop Images/Universal Images Group/GettyImages; p. 69 (header): Anadolu Agency/GettyImages; p. 69 (L): GeorgePeters/DigitalVision Vectors/ GettyImages; p. 69 (R): johnwoodcock/DigitalVision Vectors/GettyImages; p. 69 (C): Kypros/GettyImages; p. 71 (L): Michael Bowles/Getty Images Entertainment/GettyImages; p. 72: JTB Photo/Universal Images Group/ GettyImages; p. 75: erhui1979/DigitalVision Vectors/GettyImages; p. 78: Caiaimage/Robert Daly/OJO+/GettyImages; p. 79 (header): Jupiterimages/ Stockbyte/GettyImages; p. 82: Image Source/Vetta/GettyImages; p. 83 (BR): Boris Lyubner/Illustration Works/GettyImages; p. 84 (header): IMAGEMORE Co, Ltd./GettyImages; p. 85: UniversalImagesGroup/ Universal Images Group/GettyImages; p. 86: © Bank of England; p. 88 (header): arabianEye/GettyImages; p. 89: visualspace/E+/GettyImages; p. 91: Ezra Bailey/Taxi/GettyImages; p. 92 & p. 131: Hero Images/GettyImages; p. 93 (header): Lucas de Heere/GettyImages; p. 94 (TL): Photo 12/Universal Images Group/GettyImages; p. 94 (BL): Universal History Archive/ Universal Images Group/GettyImages; p. 94 (TL): UniversalImagesGroup/

GettyImages; p. 101 (CR): DEA/A. DAGLI ORTI/De Agostini/GettyImages; p. 101 (BR): Imagno/Hulton Archive/GettyImages; p. 98–99 (BG) & p. 109 (TR): Nick Brundle Photography/Moment/GettyImages; p. 99 (BG): Andrew McConnell/robertharding/GettyImages; p. 99 (T): De Agostini/A. Dagli Orti/De Agostini Picture Library/GettyImages; p. 100 (header): Past Pix/SSPL/GettyImages; p. 100 (B): icarmen13/iStock/Getty Images Plus/ GettyImages; p. 101: Topical Press Agency/GettyImages; p. 104: Topic Images Inc./Topic Images/GettyImages; p. 105 (header): Bjorn Holland/The Image Bank/GettyImages; p. 106: Julian Love/AWL Images/GettyImages; p. 108:Katie Garrod/AWL Images/GettyImages; p. 109 (BL): LatitudeStock/ ArcaidImages/GettyImages; p. 109 (BR): Patrice Hauser/Photographer's Choice RF/GettyImages; p. 110 (header): geoffsp/iStock/Getty Images Plus/ GettyImages; p. 110 (CR): Universal History Archive/Universal Images Group/GettyImages; p. 110 (BR): Steven Weinberg/NonStock/GettyImages; p. 111: GERARD MALIE/AFP/GettyImages; p. 112: sampics/Corbis Sport/ GettyImages; p. 113: Salvator Barki/Gallo Images/GettyImages; p. 114 (header): ANDRZEJ WOJCICKI/SCIENCE PHOTO LIBRARY/Science Photo Library/GettyImages; p. 116: Dong Wenjie/Moment/GettyImages; p. 117: Wavebreakmedia/iStock/Getty Images Plus/GettyImages; p. 120–121: Jason Merritt/Getty Images Entertainment/GettyImages; p. 122 (header): pixelfit/E+/GettyImages; p. 124: Mike McKelvie/arabianEye/GettyImages; p. 126: T.T./Iconica/GettyImages; p. 127 (header): John Lund/Blend Images/ GettyImages; p. 129: kali9/E+/GettyImages; p. 133 (header): Westend61/ GettyImages; p. 135 (photo A): hundreddays/E+/GettyImages; p. 135 (photo B): Iain Masterton/Photographer's Choice/GettyImages; p. 135 (photo C): Bloomberg/GettyImages; p. 135 (photo D): Pingebat/iStock/ Getty Images Plus/GettyImages; p. 136: Andreas_Zerndl/iStock/Getty Images Plus/GettyImages; p. 138: Stockbyte/GettyImages; p. 139 (header) & p. 146 (header): PeopleImages/DigitalVision/GettyImages; p. 140–141: Jen Grantham/iStock Editorial/Getty Images Plus/GettyImages; p. 144–145: ZUMA Press, Inc./Alamy Stock Photo/Alamy; p. 150 (header): bjones27/ E+/GettyImages; p. 151: Paul Bradbury/OJO Images/GettyImages; p. 154: Erik Tham/Corbis Documentary/GettyImages; p. 155 (header): Everett Collection Inc/Alamy Stock Photo/Alamy; p. 156: DreamPictures/Shannon Faulk/Blend Images/GettyImages; p. 157 (L): JUNG YEON-JE/AFP/ GettyImages; p. 157 (C): 1001slide/E+/GettyImages; p. 157 (R): SolisImages/ iStock/Getty Images Plus/GettyImages; p. 159: Photo and Co/Photolibrary/ GettyImages; p. 160 (header): Jeremy Rice/Cultura/GettyImages; p. 161 (R): LE TELLIER Philippe/Paris Match Archive/GettyImages; p. 161 (L) & p. 170: ullstein bild/GettyImages; p. 162: Ethan Miller/Getty Images Entertainment/ GettyImages; p. 164: tirc83/E+/GettyImages; p. 165 (TL): Pierre Perrin/ Sygma/GettyImages; p. 165 (CR): Cultura RM Exclusive/Philip Lee Harvey/ Cultura Exclusive/GettyImages; p. 165 (BL): Jean-Philippe Tournut/ Moment/GettyImages; p. 166: Christopher Furlong/Getty Images News/ GettyImages; p. 167 (header): fitopardo.com/Moment/GettyImages; p. 168 (T): Dhammika Heenpella/Images of Sri Lanka/Moment/GettyImages; p. 173 (header): courtneyk/E+/GettyImages; p. 173 (BL): Bartosz Hadyniak/ E+/GettyImages; p. 173 (BR): Yuri_Arcurs/DigitalVision/GettyImages; p. 177 (BL): Reinhard Dirscherl/WaterFrame/GettyImages; p. 177 (BC): Marc Dozier/Corbis Documentary/GettyImages; p. 177 (BR): Timothy Allen/Photonica World/GettyImages; p. 177 (CR): David Kirkland/ Perspectives/GettyImages; p. 178 (header): Thanachai Wachiraworakam/ Moment/GettyImages; p. 179: benkrut/iStock Editorial/Getty Images Plus/ GettyImages; p. 180: Sylvia_Kania/iStock/Getty Images Plus/GettyImages; p. 181: MAISANT Ludovic/hemis.fr/hemis.fr/GettyImages; p. 182: Hemant Mehta/Canopy/GettyImages; p. 183: Bob Thomas/The Image Bank/ GettyImages.

Illustration by Ana Djordjevic (Astound US); Andrew Gibbs (Eye Candy Illustration).

Video still on p. 25 by Mike Dowds at Cambridge Assessment.

IELTS sample answer sheet on page 176 *reproduced with permission of Cambridge Assessment English © copyright UCLES 2017.*